Solutions Manual

Financial Accounting
An Introduction to Concepts, Methods, and Uses

THIRTEENTH EDITION

Clyde P. Stickney
Dartmouth College

Roman L. Weil
University of Chicago

Katherine Schipper
Duke University

Jennifer Francis
Duke University

SOUTH-WESTERN
CENGAGE Learning

© 2010, 2007 South-Western, Cengage Learning

ALL RIGHTS RESERVED. No part of this work covered by the copyright herein may be reproduced, transmitted, stored, or used in any form or by any means graphic, electronic, or mechanical, including but not limited to photocopying, recording, scanning, digitizing, taping, Web distribution, information networks, or information storage and retrieval systems, except as permitted under Section 107 or 108 of the 1976 United States Copyright Act, without the prior written permission of the publisher except as may be permitted by the license terms below.

For product information and technology assistance, contact us at
**Cengage Learning Academic Resource Center,
1-800-423-0563.**

For permission to use material from this text or product, submit all requests online at **www.cengage.com/permissions**.
Further permissions questions can be emailed to **permissionrequest@cengage.com**.

ISBN-13: 978-0-324-78901-0
ISBN-10: 0-324-78901-7

South-Western Cengage Learning
5191 Natorp Boulevard
Mason, OH 45040
USA

Cengage Learning is a leading provider of customized learning solutions with office locations around the globe, including Singapore, the United Kingdom, Australia, Mexico, Brazil, and Japan. Locate your local office at: **international.cengage.com/region**.

Cengage Learning products are represented in Canada by Nelson Education, Ltd.

For your course and learning solutions, visit **www.cengage.com**.

Purchase any of our products at your local college store or at our preferred online store **www.ichapters.com**.

NOTE: UNDER NO CIRCUMSTANCES MAY THIS MATERIAL OR ANY PORTION THEREOF BE SOLD, LICENSED, AUCTIONED, OR OTHERWISE REDISTRIBUTED EXCEPT AS MAY BE PERMITTED BY THE LICENSE TERMS HEREIN.

READ IMPORTANT LICENSE INFORMATION

Dear Professor or Other Supplement Recipient:

Cengage Learning has provided you with this product (the "Supplement") for your review and, to the extent that you adopt the associated textbook for use in connection with your course (the "Course"), you and your students who purchase the textbook may use the Supplement as described below. Cengage Learning has established these use limitations in response to concerns raised by authors, professors, and other users regarding the pedagogical problems stemming from unlimited distribution of Supplements.

Cengage Learning hereby grants you a nontransferable license to use the Supplement in connection with the Course, subject to the following conditions. The Supplement is for your personal, noncommercial use only and may not be reproduced, posted electronically or distributed, except that portions of the Supplement may be provided to your students IN PRINT FORM ONLY in connection with your instruction of the Course, so long as such students are advised that they may not copy or distribute any portion of the Supplement to any third party. Test banks and other testing materials may be made available in the classroom and collected at the end of each class session, or posted electronically as described herein. Any material posted electronically must be through a password-protected site, with all copy and download functionality disabled, and accessible solely by your students who have purchased the associated textbook for the Course. You may not sell, license, auction, or otherwise redistribute the Supplement in any form. We ask that you take reasonable steps to protect the Supplement from unauthorized use, reproduction, or distribution. Your use of the Supplement indicates your acceptance of the conditions set forth in this Agreement. If you do not accept these conditions, you must return the Supplement unused within 30 days of receipt.

All rights (including without limitation, copyrights, patents, and trade secrets) in the Supplement are and will remain the sole and exclusive property of Cengage Learning and/or its licensors. The Supplement is furnished by Cengage Learning on an "as is" basis without any warranties, express or implied. This Agreement will be governed by and construed pursuant to the laws of the State of New York, without regard to such State's conflict of law rules.

Thank you for your assistance in helping to safeguard the integrity of the content contained in this Supplement. We trust you find the Supplement a useful teaching tool.

Printed in the United States of America
1 2 3 4 5 6 7 13 12 11 10 09

PREFACE

This book presents answers and solutions for the questions, exercises, and problems contained in each chapter of the textbook *Financial Accounting: An Introduction to Concepts, Methods and Uses* Thirteenth Edition. We do not attempt to give all possible ways to work a problem, showing the multiple paths to the correct solution. We do not even try to give the most commonly chosen one, even if we know what that is, which is rare. Our students often ask the equivalent of, "Why can't I work the problem this way?" or "Is it OK to work the problem this other way?" In a word, yes. You can work most problems in several different ways. If you get the right final answer, then do not worry if you reached it via a path different from the one we show.

If you have any suggestions as to how this book might be improved in subsequent editions, please feel free to bring them to our attention.

C.P.S.

R.L.W.

K.S.

J.F.

This page is intentionally left blank

CONTENTS

CHAPTER 1: INTRODUCTION TO BUSINESS ACTIVITIES AND OVERVIEW OF FINANCIAL STATEMENTS AND THE REPORTING PROCESS
Questions, Exercises, and Problems: Answers and Solutions .... 1-1 — 1-18

CHAPTER 2: THE BASICS OF RECORD KEEPING AND FINANCIAL STATEMENT PREPARATION
Questions, Exercises, and Problems: Answers and Solutions .... 2-1 — 2-58

CHAPTER 3: BALANCE SHEET: PRESENTING AND ANALYZING RESOURCES AND FINANCING
Questions, Exercises, and Problems: Answers and Solutions .... 3-1 — 3-32

CHAPTER 4: INCOME STATEMENT: REPORTING THE RESULTS OF OPERATING ACTIVITIES
Questions, Exercises, and Problems: Answers and Solutions .... 4-1 — 4-20

CHAPTER 5: STATEMENT OF CASH FLOWS: REPORTING THE EFFECTS OF OPERATING, INVESTING, AND FINANCING ACTIVITIES ON CASH FLOWS
Questions, Exercises, and Problems: Answers and Solutions .... 5-1 — 5-43

CHAPTER 6: INTRODUCTION TO FINANCIAL STATEMENT ANALYSIS
Questions, Exercises, and Problems: Answers and Solutions .... 6-1 — 6-43

CHAPTER 7: REVENUE RECOGNITION, RECEIVABLES, AND ADVANCES FROM CUSTOMERS
Questions, Exercises, and Problems: Answers and Solutions .... 7-1 — 7-60

CHAPTER 8: WORKING CAPITAL
Questions, Exercises, and Problems: Answers and Solutions .... 8-1 — 8-32

CHAPTER 9: LONG-LIVED TANGIBLE AND INTANGIBLE ASSETS
Questions, Exercises, and Problems: Answers and Solutions .... 9-1 — 9-22

CHAPTER 10: NOTES, BONDS, AND LEASES
Questions, Exercises, and Problems: Answers and Solutions .... 10-1 — 10-40

CHAPTER 11: LIABILITIES: OFF-BALANCE-SHEET FINANCING, RETIREMENT BENEFITS, AND INCOME TAXES
Questions, Exercises, and Problems: Answers and Solutions .... 11-1 — 11-31

CHAPTER 12: MARKETABLE SECURITIES AND DERIVATIVES
                Questions, Exercises, and Problems: Answers and Solutions .... 12-1—12-42

CHAPTER 13: INTERCORPORATE INVESTMENTS IN COMMON STOCK
                Questions, Exercises, and Problems: Answers and Solutions .... 13-1—13-30

CHAPTER 14: SHAREHOLDERS' EQUITY: CAPITAL CONTRIBUTIONS, DISTRIBUTIONS, AND EARNINGS
                Questions, Exercises, and Problems: Answers and Solutions .... 14-1—14-33

CHAPTER 15: STATEMENT OF CASH FLOWS: ANOTHER LOOK
                Problems and Cases: Answers and Solutions .... 15-1—15-48

CHAPTER 16: SYNTHESIS OF FINANCIAL REPORTING
                Exercises and Problems: Answers and Solutions .... 16-1—16-22

APPENDIX: TIME VALUE OF CASH FLOWS
                Questions, Exercises, and Problems: Answers and Solutions .... A-1—A-14

CHAPTER 1

INTRODUCTION TO BUSINESS ACTIVITIES AND OVERVIEW OF FINANCIAL STATEMENTS AND THE REPORTING PROCESS

Questions, Exercises, and Problems: Answers and Solutions

1.1 The first question at the end of each chapter asks the student to review the important terms and concepts discussed in the chapter. Students may wish to consult the glossary at the end of the book in addition to the definitions and discussions in the chapter.

1.2 *Setting Goals and Strategies*: Although a charitable organization must obtain sufficient resources to fund its operations, it would not pursue profits or wealth increases as goals. A charitable organization would direct its efforts toward providing services to its constituencies.

Financing: A charitable organization may obtain some or all of its financing from donations (contributions). A charitable organization does not issue common stock or other forms of shareholders' equity, nor does it have retained earnings.

Investing: Similar to business firms, charitable organizations acquire productive capacity (for example, buildings) to carry out their activities.

Operations: A charitable organization might prepare financial statements that compare inflows (for example, contributions) with outflows. While these statements might appear similar to income statements, there would be no calculation of net income because the purpose of the charitable organization is to provide services to its constituents, not seek profits.

1.3 The balance sheet shows assets, liabilities and shareholders' equity as of a specific date (the balance sheet date), similar to a snapshot. The income statement and statement of cash flows report changes in assets and liabilities over a period of time, similar to a motion picture.

1.4 The auditor evaluates the accounting system, including its ability to record transactions properly and its operational effectiveness, and also determines whether the financial reports prepared by the firm's managers conform to the requirements of the applicable authoritative guidance. The auditor provides an audit opinion that reflects his professional conclusions. For most publicly traded firms in the U.S. the auditor also provides a sepa-

1.4 continued.

rate opinion on the effectiveness of the firm's internal controls over financial reporting.

1.5　Management, under the oversight of the firm's governing board, prepares the financial statements.

1.6　Employees and suppliers of goods such as raw materials or merchandise often provide the services or goods before they are paid. The firm has the benefit of consuming or using the goods or services before it transfers cash to the employees and suppliers. The length of the financing period is the number of days between when the employees and suppliers provide goods and services and when the firm pays cash to those employees and suppliers.

1.7　Accounts receivable represent amounts owed by customers for goods and services they have already received. The customer, therefore, has the benefit of the goods and services before it pays cash. The length of the financing period is the number of days between when the customer receives the goods and services and when the customer pays cash to the seller of those goods and services.

1.8　Both kinds of capacity represent investments in long-lived assets, with useful lives (or service lives) that can extend for several or many years. They differ in that land, buildings, and equipment represent physical capital, while patents and licenses represent intangible or intellectual capital.

1.9　A calendar year ends on December 31. A fiscal year ends on a date that is determined by the firm, perhaps based on its business model (for example, many retailers choose a fiscal year end that is close to the end of January). A firm can choose the calendar year as its fiscal year, and many do. Both calendar years and fiscal years have 12 months.

1.10　Most firms report the amounts in their financial statements using the currency of the country where they are incorporated and conduct most of their business activities. Some firms use a different currency.

1.11　A current item is expected to result in a cash receipt (assets such as accounts receivable) or a cash payment (liabilities such as accounts payable) within approximately one year or less. A noncurrent item is expected to generate cash over periods longer than a year (assets, such as factory buildings that will be used to produce goods for sale over many years) or use cash over periods longer than a year (liabilities such as long term debt). Users of financial statements would likely be interested in this distinction because the distinction provides information about short term cash flows separately from long term cash flows).

1.12	Historical amounts reflect the amounts at which items entered the firm's balance sheet, for example, the acquisition cost of inventory. Historical amounts reflect economic conditions at the time the firm obtained assets or obtained financing. Current amounts reflect values at the balance sheet date, so they reflect current economic conditions. For example, the historical amount for inventory is the amount the firm paid to obtain the inventory and the current amount for inventory is the amount for which the firm could sell the inventory today.

1.13	An income statement connects two successive balance sheets through its effect on retained earnings. Net income that is not paid to shareholders as dividends increases retained earnings. A statement of cash flows connects two successive balance sheets because it explains the change in cash (a balance sheet account) from operating, financing, and investing activities. The statement of cash flows also shows the relation between net income and cash flows from operations, and changes in assets and liabilities that involve cash flows.

1.14	The U.S. Securities and Exchange Commission (SEC) is the government agency that enforces the securities laws of the U.S., including those that apply to financial reporting. The Financial Accounting Standards Board (FASB) is the private-sector financial accounting standard setter in the U.S. The International Accounting Standards Board (IASB) is a private-sector financial accounting standard setter that promulgates accounting standards that are required or permitted to be used in over 100 countries. Neither the FASB nor the IASB has any enforcement powers.

1.15	U.S. GAAP must be used by U.S. SEC registrants and may be used by other firms as well. International Financial Reporting Standards (IFRS) may be used by non-U.S. firms that list and trade their securities in the U.S, and these firms may also use U.S. GAAP.

1.16	The purpose of the conceptual framework developed by the Financial Accounting Standards Board (FASB) is to guide the standard setting decisions of the FASB. For example, the conceptual framework specifies the purpose of financial reporting, and the qualitative characteristics of financial information that would serve that purpose. FASB board members use this conceptual structure as they consider solutions to accounting issues.

1.17	The accrual basis of accounting is based on assets and liabilities, not on cash receipts and disbursements. It provides a better basis for measuring performance because it is based on revenues (inflows of assets from customers) not cash receipts from customers, and on expenses (outflows of assets from generating revenues) not cash payments. It matches revenues with the costs associated with earning those revenues and is not sensitive to the timing of expenditures.

1.18 (Colgate Palmolive Company; understanding the balance sheet.)

a. Property, plant and equipment, net = $3,015.2 million.

b. Noncurrent assets = $6,493.5 (= $3,015.2 + $2,272.0 + $844.8 + $361.5).

c. Long-term debt = $3,221.9 million.

d. Current assets − Current liabilities = $3,618.5 − $3,162.7 = $455.8 million.

e. Yes, Colgate has been profitable since its inception. We know this because its Retained Earnings, of $10,627.5 million, is positive. Colgate may have had a loss in one or more prior years; cumulatively, it has had positive income.

f. Total Liabilities/Total Assets = $7,825.8/$10,112.0 = 77.4%.

g. Total Assets = Total Liabilities + Shareholders' Equity

$10,112.0 = $7,825.8 + $2,286.2

1.19 (Mayr Melnhof Karton; understanding the income statement.)

a. Cost of Goods Sold = €1,331,292.1 thousand.

b. Selling and distribution expenses = €172,033.4 thousand.

c. Gross margin percentage = 23.4% (= €405,667.1/€1,736,959.2).

d. Operating profit = €169,418.2 thousand.

Profit before tax = €170,863.9 thousand.

Difference equals €1,445.7 thousand (= €169,418.2 − €170,863.9). The items comprising this difference are sources of income (expense) of a nonoperating nature for Mayr Melnhof.

e. Effective tax rate = €54,289.9/€170,863.9 = 31.8%.

f. Profit = €116,574.0 thousand.

1.20 (Bed, Bath and Beyond, Inc.; understanding the statement of cash flows.)

a. Cash inflow from operating activities = $614,536 thousand.

b. Cash inflow from investing activities = $101,698 thousand

1.20 continued.

c. Cash inflow used in financing activities = $705,531 thousand.

d. Net cash flow equals $10,703 thousand (= $614,536 + $101,698 − $705,531).

e. Change in cash balance equals $10,703 thousand (= $224,084 − $213,381). The increase was attributable to the net cash inflow during the year of the same amount, $10,703 thousand.

1.21 (Alcatel-Lucent; balance sheet relations.) (Amounts in Millions)

Current Assets	+	Noncurrent Assets	=	Current Liabilities	+	Noncurrent Liabilities	+	Shareholders' Equity
€20,000	+	€29,402	=	€15,849	+	?	+	€17,154

Noncurrent liabilities total €16,399 million.

1.22 (Gold Fields Limited; balance sheet relations.) (Amount in Millions of Rand)

Current Assets	+	Noncurrent Assets	=	Current Liabilities	+	Noncurrent Liabilities	+	Shareholders' Equity
R6,085.1	+	R49,329.8	=	R4,360.1	+	R13,948.4	+	?

Shareholders' Equity totals R37,106.4 million.

1.23 (Rolls Royce Group Plc.; income statement relations.)

Sales	£ 7,435
Less Cost of Sales	(6,003)
Gross Margin	£ 1,432
Less Other Operating Expenses	(918)
Loss on Sale of Business	(2)
Net Financing Income	221
Profit before Taxes	£ 733
Less Tax Expense	(133)
Net Income	£ 600

1.24 (General Motors Corporation; income statement relations.)

Sales	$ 207,349
Cost of Sales	(164,682)
Other Operating Expenses	(50,335)
Net Financing Income	5,690
Net Loss	$ (1,978)

1.25 (Gold Fields; retained earnings relations) (Amounts in Millions of Rand)

Retained Earnings at End of 2006	+	Net Income for 2007	−	Dividends Declared for 2007	=	Retained Earnings at End of 2007
R4,640.9	+	R2,362.5	−	?	=	R5,872.4

Dividends declared during 2007 totaled R1,131.0 million.

1.26 (Sterlite Industries; retained earnings relations.) (Amounts in Millions of Rupees)

Retained Earnings March 31, 2006	+	Net Income for 2006	−	Dividends Declared for 2006	=	Retained Earnings March 31, 2007
Rs26,575	+	?	−	Rs3,544	=	Rs70,463

Net income for the year ended March 31, 2007 (fiscal 2006) was Rs47,432 million.

1.27 (Target Corporation; cash flow relations.) (Amounts in Millions)

Cash at Feb. 3, 2007	+	Cash Flow from Operations	+	Cash Flow from Investing	+	Cash Flow from Financing	=	Cash at Feb. 2, 2008
$813	+	$4,125	+	$(6,195)	+	$3,707	=	?

Cash balance at February 3, 2008 = $2,450 million.

1.28 (Edeneor S.A.; cash flow relations.) (Amounts in Millions)

Cash at End of 2006	+	Cash Flow from Operations	+	Cash Flow from Investing	+	Cash Flow from Financing	=	Cash at End of 2007
Ps32,673	+	Ps427,182	+	?	+	Ps(21,806)	=	Ps101,198

The net cash outflow for investing for 2007 = Ps(336,851) million.

1.29 (Kenton Limited; preparation of simple balance sheet; current and noncurrent classifications.)

January 31, 2008

Assets

Cash	£ 2,000
Inventory	12,000
Prepaid Rent	24,000
Total Current Assets	£ 38,000
Prepaid Rent	£ 24,000
Total Noncurrent Assets	£ 24,000
Total Assets	£ 62,000

Liabilities and Shareholders' Equity

Accounts Payable	£ 12,000
Total Current Liabilities	£ 12,000
Total Noncurrent Liabilities	--
Total Liabilities	£ 12,000
Common Stock	£ 50,000
Total Shareholders' Equity	£ 50,000
Total Liabilities and Shareholders' Equity	£ 62,000

1.30 (Heckle Group; preparation of simple balance sheet; current and noncurrent classifications.)

June 30, 2008

Assets

Cash	€ 720,000
Total Current Assets	€ 720,000
Property, Plant and Equipment	€ 600,000
Patent	120,000
Total Noncurrent Assets	€ 720,000
Total Assets	€ 1,440,000

Liabilities and Shareholders' Equity

Accounts Payable	€ 120,000
Total Current Liabilities	€ 120,000
Note Payable	€ 400,000
Total Noncurrent Liabilities	€ 400,000
Total Liabilities	€ 520,000
Common Stock	€ 920,000
Total Shareholders' Equity	€ 920,000
Total Liabilities and Shareholders' Equity	€ 1,440,000

1.31 Boeing Company; accrual versus cash basis of accounting.)

    a. Net Income = Sales Revenue − Expenses

        = $66,387 million − $62,313 million = $4,074 million.

    Net Cash Flow = Cash Inflows − Cash Outflows

        = $65,995 million − $56,411 million = $9,584 million.

    b. Cash collections may exceed revenues for at least two reasons. First, Boeing may have collected in 2007 on customer credit sales made in 2006. Second, Boeing may have collected cash from customers in advance of providing them with goods and services.

    c. Cash payments may be less than expenses for at least two reasons. First, Boeing may have received goods and services from suppliers, but not yet paid for those items (i.e., the amounts are to be paid in the next year). Second, Boeing may have accrued expenses in 2007 that will be paid in cash in future periods; an example would be the accrual of interest expense on a bond that will be paid the next year.

1.32 (Fonterra Cooperative Group Limited; accrual versus cash basis of accounting.)

Calculation of net income for the year ended May 31, 2007:

	May 31, 2007
Revenue	$ 13,882
Cost of Goods Sold	(11,671)
Interest and Other Expenses	(2,113)
Income before Taxes	$ 98
Tax Expense	$ (67)
Net Income	$ 31

Calculation of net cash flow for the year ended May 31, 2007:

	May 31, 2007
Cash Receipts from Customers	$ 13,882
Miscellaneous Cash Receipts	102
Total Cash Receipts	$ 13,996
Cash Payments to Employees and Creditors	$ (5,947)
Cash Payments to Milk Suppliers	(6,261)
Cash Payments for Interest Costs	(402)
Cash Payments for Taxes	(64)
Total Cash Payments	$ (12,674)
Net Cash Flow	$ 1,322

Solutions

1.33 (Dragon Group International Limited; balance sheet relations.) (Amounts in Millions)

The missing items appear in **boldface** type below.

	2007	2006
Assets		
Current Assets	$ 170,879	$ 170,234
Noncurrent Assets	**28,945**	17,368
Total Assets	$ 199,824	$ **187,602**
Liabilities and Shareholders' Equity		
Current Liabilities	$ 139,941	$ 126,853
Noncurrent Liabilities	7,010	**7,028**
Total Liabilities	$ **146,951**	$ **133,881**
Shareholders' Equity	$ **52,873**	$ 53,721
Total Liabilities and Shareholders' Equity	$ **199,824**	$ **187,602**

1.34 (Lenovo Group, Inc.; balance sheet relations.)

The missing items appear in **boldface** type below.

	2008	2007
Assets		
Current Assets	$ 4,705,366	$ 3,062,449
Noncurrent Assets	2,494,481	**2,388,389**
Total Assets	$ **7,199,847**	$ 5,450,838
Liabilities and Shareholders' Equity		
Current Liabilities	$ 4,488,461	$ 3,527,504
Noncurrent Liabilities	1,098,123	**789,058**
Total Liabilities	$ **5,586,584**	$ **4,316,562**
Shareholders' Equity	$ **1,613,263**	$ 1,134,276
Total Liabilities and Shareholders' Equity	$ **7,199,847**	$ **5,450,838**

1.35 (Colgate Palmolive Company; income statement relations.)

The missing items appear in **boldface** type below.

	2007	2006	2005
Sales	$ 13,790	$ **12,238**	$ 11,397
Cost of Goods Sold	**(6,042)**	(5,536)	(5,192)
Selling and Administrative Expenses	(4,973)	(4,355)	(3,921)
Other (Income) Expense	(121)	(186)	(69)
Interest Expense, Net	(157)	(159)	(136)
Income Tax Expense	(759)	(648)	(728)
Net Income	$ 1,738	$ 1,354	$ 1,351

1.36 (Polo Ralph Lauren; income statement relations.) (Amounts in Millions)

The missing items appear in **boldface** type below.

	2007	2006	2005
Net Revenues	$ 4,295.4	$ 3,746.3	$ 3,305.4
Cost of Goods Sold	(1,959.2)	(1,723.9)	(1,620.9)
Selling and Administrative Expenses	(1,663.4)	(1,476.9)	(1,377.6)
Operating Income	$ 672.8	$ 545.5	$ 306.9
Other Income (Expense)	(34.0)	**(43.8)**	(2.7)
Interest Income (Expense), Net	**4.5**	1.2	(6.4)
Income Tax Expense	(242.4)	(194.9)	(107.4)
Net Income	$ 400.9	$ 308.0	$ **190.4**

1.37 (Ericsson; statement of cash flows relations.)

ERICSSON
Statement of Cash Flows
(Amounts in SEK Millions)

	2007	2006	2005
Operations:			
Revenues, Net of Expenses	SEK 19,210	SEK 18,489	SEK 16,669
Cash Flow from Operations	SEK 19,210	SEK 18,489	SEK 16,669
Investing:			
Acquisition of Property and Equipment	SEK (4,319)	SEK (3,827)	SEK (3,365)
Acquisition of Businesses	(26,292)	(18,078)	(1,210)
Sale Property and Equipment	152	185	362
Sale of Short-Term Investments	3,499	6,180	6,375
Other Investing Activities	(573)	663	(1,131)
Cash Flow from Investing	SEK (27,533)	SEK (14,877)	SEK 1,031
Financing:			
Proceeds from Borrowings	SEK 15,587	SEK 1,290	SEK 657
Repayment of Borrowings	(1,291)	(9,510)	(2,784)
Sale of Common Stock	94	124	174
Dividends Paid	(8,132)	(7,343)	(4,133)
Other Financing Activities	406	58	(288)
Cash Flow from Financing	SEK 6,664	SEK (15,381)	SEK (6,374)
Change in Cash	SEK (1,659)	SEK (11,769)	SEK 11,326
Cash, Beginning of Year	29,969	41,738	30,412
Cash, End of Year	SEK 28,310	SEK 29,969	SEK 41,738

1.38 (Jackson Corporation; statement of cash flows relations.)

JACKSON CORPORATION
Statement of Cash Flows
(Amounts in Millions)

	2008	2007	2006
Operations:			
Revenues Increasing Cash	$ 19,536	$ 19,083	$ 17,233
Expenses Decreasing Cash	(16,394)	(18,541)	(18,344)
Cash Flow from Operations	$ 3,142	$ 542	$ (1,111)
Investing:			
Sale of Property, Plant and Equipment	$ 332	$ 401	$ 220
Acquisition of Property, Plant and Equipment	(3,678)	(3,640)	(1,881)
Other Investing Transactions	71	(1,501)	268
Cash Flow from Investing	$ (3,275)	$ (4,740)	$ (1,393)
Financing:			
Proceeds of Long-Term Borrowing	$ 836	$ 5,096	$ 3,190
Issue of Common Stock	67	37	3
Repayments of Long-Term Debt	(766)	(922)	(687)
Cash Flow from Financing	$ 137	$ 4,211	$ 2,506
Change in Cash	$ 4	$ 13	$ 2
Cash, Beginning of Year	117	104	102
Cash, End of Year	$ 121	$ 117	$ 104

1.39 (JetAway Airlines; preparing a balance sheet and an income statement.)

a.
JETAWAY AIRLINES
Balance Sheet
(Amounts in Thousands)

	Sept. 30, 2008	Sept. 30, 2007
Assets		
Cash	$ 378,511	$ 418,819
Accounts Receivable	88,799	73,448
Inventories	50,035	65,152
Other Current Assets	56,810	73,586
Total Current Assets	$ 574,155	$ 631,005
Property, Plant and Equipment (Net)	4,137,610	5,008,166
Other Noncurrent Assets	4,231	12,942
Total Assets	$ 4,715,996	$ 5,652,113

1.39 a. continued.

Liabilities and Shareholders' Equity

Accounts Payable	$ 157,415	$ 156,755
Current Maturities of Long-Term Debt	11,996	7,873
Other Current Liabilities	681,242	795,838
Total Current Liabilities	$ 850,653	$ 960,466
Long-Term Debt	623,309	871,717
Other Noncurrent Liabilities	844,116	984,142
Total Liabilities	$ 2,318,078	$ 2,816,325
Common Stock	$ 352,943	$ 449,934
Retained Earnings	2,044,975	2,385,854
Total Shareholders' Equity	$ 2,397,918	$ 2,835,788
Total Liabilities and Shareholders' Equity	$ 4,715,996	$ 5,652,113

b. **JETAWAY AIRLINES**
Income Statement
(Amounts in Thousands)

For the Year Ended:	Sept. 30, 2008
Sales	$ 4,735,587
Salaries and Benefits Expense	(1,455,237)
Fuel Expense	(892,415)
Maintenance Expense	(767,606)
Other Operating Expenses	(1,938,753)
Interest Expense	(22,883)
Interest Income	14,918
Net Income	$ (326,389)

c.
Retained Earnings, September 30, 2007	$ 2,385,854
Plus Net Loss for 2008	(326,389)
Less Dividends Declared during 2008 (Plug)	(15,390)
Retained Earnings, September 30, 2008	$ 2,044,075

1.40 (Block's Tax and Bookkeeping Services; cash versus accrual basis accounting.)

a. **Income for July, 2008:**

(1) **Cash Basis Accounting**

Sales Revenues	$ 13,000
Rent (Office)	(6,000)
Rent Equipment	(12,000)
Office Supplies Expense	(370)
Income (Loss)	$ (5,370)

Solutions

1.40 a. continued.

(2) Accrual Basis Accounting

Sales Revenues	$ 44,000
Rent (Office)	(2,000)
Rent (Equipment)	(2,000)
Salaries Expense	(6,000)
Office Supplies Expense	(90)
Interest Expense	(133)
Income (Loss)	$ 33,777

b. Cash on Hand:

Beginning Balance, July 1	$ 0
Financing Sources and (Uses):	
Jack Block Share Purchase	40,000
Bank Loan	20,000
Total Financing Sources	$ 60,000
Operating Sources and (Uses):	
Cash Collected from Customers	$ 13,000
Office Rent	(6,000)
Equipment Rental	(12,000)
Office Supplies Expense	(370)
Net Operating Uses	$ (5,370)
Ending Balance, July 31	$ 54,630

The ending balance in cash contains the effects of both operating activities, which have net cash flow of $(5,370) and financing activities, which have net cash flow of $60,000. The firm is financing its operating activities with a bank loan and with funds invested by its owner; both of these sources of funds represent claims on the firm's assets, not increases in net assets.

1.41 (Stationery Plus; cash basis versus accrual basis accounting.)

a. **Income for November, 2008:**

(1) Cash Basis Accounting

Sales	$ 23,000
Cost of Merchandise	(20,000)
Rent	(9,000)
Salaries	(10,000)
Utilities	(480)
Income (Loss)	$ (16,480)

1.41 a. continued.

(2) Accrual Basis Accounting

Sales	$ 56,000
Cost of Merchandise	(29,000)
Rent	(1,500)
Salaries	(10,000)
Utilities	(480)
Interest	(1,000)
Income (Loss)	$ 14,020

b. **Income for December, 2008:**

(1) Cash Basis Accounting

Sales Made in November, Collected in December	$ 33,000
Sales Made and Collected in December	34,000
Cost of Merchandise Acquired in November and Paid in December	(20,000)
Cost of Merchandise Acquired and Paid in December	(27,500)
Salaries	(10,000)
Utilities	(480)
Interest	(2,000)
Income (Loss)	$ 7,020

(2) Accrual Basis Accounting

Sales	$ 62,000
Cost of Merchandise	(33,600)
Rent	(1,500)
Salaries	(10,000)
Utilities	(480)
Interest	(1,000)
Income (Loss)	$ 15,420

1.42 (ABC Company; relation between net income and cash flows.)

a.

Month	Cash Balance at Beginning of Month	+ Cash Receipts from Customers	− Cash Disbursements for Production Costs	= Cash Balance at End of the Month
January	$ 875	$1,000	$ 750	$ 1,125
February	1,125	1,000	1,500	625
March	625	1,500	1,875	250
April	250	2,000	2,250	0

1.42 continued.

b. The cash flow problem arises because of a lag between cash expenditures incurred in producing goods and cash collections from customers once the firm sells those goods. For example, cash expenditures during February ($1,500) are for goods produced during February and sold during March. Cash is not collected from customers on these sales, however, until April ($2,000). A growing firm must generally produce more units than it sells during a period if it is to have sufficient quantities of inventory on hand for future sales. The cash needed for this higher level of production may well exceed the cash received from the prior period's sales. Thus, a cash shortage develops.

The difference between the selling price of goods sold and the cost of those goods equals net income for the period. As long as selling prices exceed the cost of the goods, a positive net income results. As the number of units sold increases, net income increases. A firm does not necessarily recognize revenues and expenses in the same period as the related cash receipts and expenditures. Thus, cash decreases, even though net income increases.

c. The income statement and statement of cash flows provide information about the profitability and liquidity, respectively, of a firm during a period. The fact that net income and cash flows can move in opposite directions highlights the need for information from both statements. A firm without sufficient cash will not survive, even if it operates profitably. The balance sheet indicates a firm's asset and equity position at a moment in time. The deteriorating cash position is evident from the listing of assets at the beginning of each month. Examining the cash receipts and disbursements during each month, however, identifies the reasons for the deterioration.

d. Strategies for dealing with the cash flow problem center around (a) reducing the lag between cash outflows to produce widgets and cash inflows from their sale, and (b) increasing the margin between selling prices and production costs.

To reduce the lag on collection of accounts receivable, ABC might:

(1) Provide to customers an incentive to pay faster than 30 days, such as offering a discount if customers pay more quickly or charge interest if customers delay payment.

(2) Use the accounts receivable as a basis for external financing, such as borrowing from a bank and using the receivables as collateral or selling (factoring) the receivables for immediate cash.

(3) Sell only for cash, although competition may preclude this alternative.

To delay the payment for widgets, ABC might:

1.42 d. continued.

> (1) Delay paying its suppliers (increases accounts payable) or borrow from a bank using the inventory as collateral (increases bank loan payable).
>
> (2) Reduce the holding period for inventories by instituting a just-in-time inventory system. This alternative requires ordering raw materials only when needed in production and manufacturing widgets only to customer orders. Demand appears to be sufficiently predictable so that opportunities for a just-in-time inventory system seem attractive.

To increase the margin between selling price and manufacturing cost, ABC might:

(1) Negotiate a lower purchase price with suppliers of raw materials.

(2) Substitute more efficient manufacturing equipment for work now done by employees.

(3) Increase selling prices.

The cash flow problem is short-term because it will neutralize itself by June. This neutralization occurs because the growth rate in sales is declining (500 additional units sold on top of an ever-increasing sales base). Thus, the firm needs a short-term solution to the cash flow problem. If the growth rate were steady or increasing, ABC might consider obtaining a more permanent source of cash, such as issuing long-term debt or common stock.

1.43 (Balance sheet and income statement relations.)

a. Bushels of wheat are the most convenient in this case with the given information. This question emphasizes the need for a common measuring unit.

1.43 continued.

b.
IVAN AND IGOR
Comparative Balance Sheets
(Amounts in Bushels of Wheat)

	IVAN		IGOR	
Assets	**Beginning of Period**	**End of Period**	**Beginning of Period**	**End of Period**
Wheat	20	223	10	105
Fertilizer	2	--	1	--
Ox..................................	40	36	40	36
Plow	--	--	--	2
Land	100	100	50	50
Total Assets...........	162	359	101	193
Liabilities and Owner's Equity				
Accounts Payable	--	3	--	--
Owner's Equity...........	162	356	101	193
Total Liabilities and Owner's Equity...................	162	359	101	193

Questions will likely arise as to the accounting entity. One view is that there are two accounting entities (Ivan and Igor) to whom the Red Bearded Baron has entrusted assets and required a periodic reporting on stewardship. The "owner" in owner's equity in this case is the Red Bearded Baron. Another view is that the Red Bearded Baron is the accounting entity, in which case financial statements that combine the financial statements for Ivan and Igor are appropriate. Identifying the accounting entity depends on the intended use of the financial statements. For purposes of evaluating the performance of Ivan and Igor, the accounting entities are separate—Ivan and Igor. To assess the change in wealth of the Red Bearded Baron during the period, the combined financial statements reflect the accounting entity.

1.43 continued.

c.
IVAN AND IGOR
Comparative Income Statement
(Amounts in Bushels of Wheat)

	IVAN	IGOR
Revenues	243	138
Expenses:		
Seed	20	10
Fertilizer	2	1
Depreciation on Ox	4	4
Plow	3	1
Total Expenses	29	16
Net Income	214	122

Chapter 1 does not expose students to the concept of depreciation. Most students, however, grasp the need to record some amount of expense for the ox and the plow.

d.
(Amounts in Bushels of Wheat)	IVAN	IGOR
Owner's Equity, Beginning of Period	162	101
Plus Net Income	214	122
Less Distributions to Owner	(20)	(30)
Owner's Equity, End of Period	356	193

e. We cannot simply compare the amounts of net income for Ivan and Igor because the Red Bearded Baron entrusted them with different amounts of resources. We must relate the net income amounts to some base. Several possibilities include:

	IVAN	IGOR
Net Income/Average Total Assets	82.2%	83.0%
Net Income/Beginning Total Assets	132.1%	120.8%
Net Income/Average Noncurrent Assets	155.1%	137.1%
Net Income/Beginning Noncurrent Assets	152.9%	135.6%
Net Income/Average Owner's Equity	82.6%	83.0%
Net Income/Beginning Owner's Equity	132.1%	120.8%
Net Income (in bushels)/Acre	10.70	12.20

This question has no definitive answer. Its purpose is to get students to think about performance measurement. The instructor may or may not wish to devote class time at this point discussing which base is more appropriate.

CHAPTER 2

THE BASICS OF RECORD KEEPING AND FINANCIAL STATEMENT PREPARATION

Questions, Exercises, and Problems: Answers and Solutions

2.1 See the text or the glossary at the end of the book.

2.2 Accounting is governed by the balance sheet equation, which shows the equality of assets with liabilities plus shareholders' equity:

$$\text{Assets} = \text{Liabilities} + \text{Shareholders' Equity}.$$

To maintain this equality, it is necessary to report every event and transaction in a dual manner. If a transaction results in an increase in the left hand side (Assets), dual transactions recording requires that one of the following must occur, to maintain the balance sheet equation: decrease another asset; increase a liability; increase shareholders equity. Similarly, if a transaction results in an increase in a Liability account, then one of the following must occur, to maintain the balance sheet equation: decrease another liability; decrease shareholders equity; increase an asset.

2.3 A T-account is used to record the effects of events and transactions that affect a specific asset, liability, shareholders' equity, revenue or expense account. It captures both the increases and decreases in that specific account, without reference to the effects on other accounts. It also shows the beginning and ending balances of balance sheet accounts. A journal entry shows all the accounts affected by a single event or transaction; each debit and each credit in a journal entry will affect a specific T-account. Journal entries provide a record of transactions, and T-accounts summarize the effects of transactions on specific accounts.

2.4 Temporary accounts are for recording revenues and expenses. These accounts are temporary in the sense that once they have served their purpose of accumulating specific revenue and expense items for an accounting period, they are closed, so that they begin the following accounting period with a zero balance, ready for the revenue and expense entries of the new period. While it would be possible to record both revenues and expenses directly in the Retained Earnings account, doing so would suppress information about the components of net income. The temporary revenue and expense accounts accumulate the information that is displayed

2.4 continued.

in the line items or rows on the income statement. This display provides information about the sources and amounts of revenues and the nature and amounts of expenses that net to earnings for the period.

2.5 The distinction is based on time. Current assets are expected to be converted to cash within a year, for example, Accounts Receivable. Noncurrent assets are expected to be converted to cash over longer periods.

2.6 The balance sheet and the income statement are linked (that is, they *articulate*) through the shareholders' equity account, Retained Earnings. Retained Earnings measures the cumulative excess of net income over dividends for the life of a firm; all undistributed earnings are aggregated in Retained Earnings. The following equation describes the articulation of the Retained Earnings:

Retained Earnings (beginning) + Net Income – Dividends = Retained Earnings (end).

2.7 The purpose of the income statement is to show the user of the financial statements the components of net income, that is, the causes of net income. A user of financial statements can calculate net income by analyzing the change in retained earnings, but this analysis does not reveal the specific factors that combine to produce the net income number.

2.8 An adjusting entry is used to record the effects of an event or transaction that was not previously recorded. Many adjusting entries result from the effects of the passage of time, for example, interest accrues on amounts owed over time. The accrual of interest at the end of an accounting period is an example of an adjusting entry. A correcting entry is a special case of an adjusting entry. A correcting entry is used to record properly the effects of an event or transaction that was improperly recorded during the accounting period.

2.9 Contra accounts provide disaggregated information concerning the net amount of an asset, liability, or shareholders' equity item. For example, the account, Property, Plant and Equipment net of Accumulated Depreciation, does not indicate separately the acquisition cost of fixed assets and the portion of that acquisition cost written off as depreciation since acquisition. If the firm used a contra account, it would have such information. The alternative to using contra accounts is to debit or credit directly the principal account involved (for example, Property, Plant and Equipment). This alternative procedure, however, does not permit computation of disaggregated information about the net balance in the account. Note that the use of contra accounts does not affect the total of assets, liabilities, shareholders' equity, revenues, or expenses, but only the balances in various accounts that comprise the totals for these items.

2.10 The key difference is in the presentation of Cash from Operations. The direct method displays (lists) cash receipts and disbursements from operating activities. The indirect method begins with net income and adjusts that amount for noncash items. Both methods arrive at the same amount for Cash from Operations. The display of Cash from Investing and Cash from Financing does not differ between the direct method and the indirect method.

2.11 (Fresh Foods Group; dual effects on balance sheet equation.) (Amounts in Millions)

Transaction	Assets	=	Liabilities	+	Shareholders' Equity
(1)	+$ 678		+$ 678		
(2)	–$ 45		–$ 45		
(3)	–$ 633		–$ 633		

2.12 (Cement Plus; dual effects on balance sheet equation.) (Amounts in Millions)

Transaction	Assets	=	Liabilities	+	Shareholders' Equity
(1)	+$14,300 –$ 2,300		+$12,000		
(2)	+$ 3,000 –$ 3,000				
(3)	–$ 6,500				+$ 6,500
(4)			–$12,000		+$12,000

2.13 (Braskem S.A.; analyzing changes in accounts receivable.) (Amounts in Millions)

Accounts Receivable, Beginning of 2007	R$ 1,594.9
Plus Sales on Account during 2007	12,134.5
Less Cash Collections during 2007	(?)
Accounts Receivable, End of 2007	R$ 1,497.0

Cash collections during 2007 total R$12,232.4 million.

2.14 (Boeing Company; analyzing changes in inventory.) (Amounts in Millions)

Inventory, Beginning of 2007	$ 8,105
Plus Purchases or Production of Inventory during 2007	?
Less Cost of Goods Sold for 2007	(45,375)
Inventory, End of 2007	$ 9,563

Purchases or production of inventory during 2007 total $46,883 million.

2.15 (Ericsson; analyzing changes in inventory and accounts payable.) (Amounts in Millions)

Inventory, Beginning of 2007	SEK 21,470
Plus Purchases of Inventory during 2007	?
Less Cost of Goods Sold for 2007	(114,059)
Inventory, End of 2007	SEK 22,475

Purchases during 2007 total SEK115,064 million.

Accounts Payable, Beginning of 2007	SEK 18,183
Plus Purchases of Inventory on Account during 2007 from above	115,064
Less Cash Payments to Suppliers during 2007	(?)
Accounts Payable, End of 2007	SEK 17,427

Cash payments to suppliers during 2007 total SEK115,820 million.

2.16 (Kajima Corporation; analyzing changes in income taxes payable.) (Amounts in Millions of Yen)

Income Taxes Payable, Beginning of 2007	¥ 3,736
Plus Income Tax Expense for 2007 (.43 x ¥73,051)	31,412
Less Income Taxes Paid during 2007	(?)
Income Taxes Payable, End of 2007	¥ 14,310

Income taxes paid during 2007 total ¥20,838 million.

2.17 (Eaton Corporation; analyzing changes in retained earnings.) (Amounts in Millions)

Retained Earnings, Beginning of 2007	$ 2,796
Plus Net Income for 2007	?
Less Dividends Declared and Paid during 2007	(251)
Retained Earnings, End of 2007	$ 3,257

Net Income for 2007 totals $712 million.

2.18 (Bayer Group; relations between financial statements.) (Amounts in Millions)

a. $5,868 + $32,385 − $5,830 = a; a = $32,423.

b. $109 + b − $763 = $56; b = $710.

c. $14,723 − c + $2,155 = $12,911; c = $3,967.

d. $6,782 + $4,711 − d = $10,749; d = $744.

2.19 (Beyond Petroleum; relations between financial statements.) (Amounts in Millions)

a. a + $288,951 − $289,623 = $38,020; a = $38,692.

b. $2,635 + $10,442 − b = $3,282; b = $9,795.

c. $42,236 + $15,162 + c = $43,152; c = $14,246.

d. $88,453 + $21,169 − $8,106 = d; d = $101,516.

2.20 (Fujitsu Limited; journal entries for inventories and accounts payable.) (Amounts in Millions of Yen)

Merchandise Inventories.. 1,456,412
    Accounts Payable.. 1,456,412

Assets	=	Liabilities	+	Shareholders' Equity	(Class.)
+1,456,412		+1,456,412			

Cost of Goods Sold (¥408,710 + ¥1,456,412 −
  ¥412,387).. 1,452,735
    Merchandise Inventories.. 1,452,735

Assets	=	Liabilities	+	Shareholders' Equity	(Class.)
−1,452,735				−1,452,735	IncSt → RE

Accounts Payable (¥757,006 + $1,456,412 −
  ¥824,825).. 1,388,593
    Cash.. 1,388,593

Assets	=	Liabilities	+	Shareholders' Equity	(Class.)
−1,388,593		−1,388,593			

2.21 (Monana Company; journal entries for insurance.) (Amounts in Millions)

April 30, 2008
Insurance Expense.. 12
    Prepaid Insurance 12

Assets	=	Liabilities	+	Shareholders' Equity	(Class.)
−12				−12	IncSt → RE

Adjusting entry required for prepaid insurance consumed during April, 2008.

2.21 continued.

May 30, 2008
Insurance Expense 12
    Prepaid Insurance 12

Assets	=	Liabilities	+	Shareholders' Equity	(Class.)
–12				–12	IncSt → RE

Adjusting entry required for prepaid insurance consumed during May, 2008.

June 1, 2008
Prepaid Insurance 156
    Cash 156

Assets	=	Liabilities	+	Shareholders' Equity	(Class.)
+156					
–156					

To record payment of insurance for next 12 months.

June 30, 2008
Insurance Expense 13
    Prepaid Insurance 13

Assets	=	Liabilities	+	Shareholders' Equity	(Class.)
–13				–13	IncSt → RE

Adjusting entry required for prepaid insurance consumed during June, 2008 ($13 = $156/12 months).

July 31, 2008
Insurance Expense 13
    Prepaid Insurance 13

Assets	=	Liabilities	+	Shareholders' Equity	(Class.)
–13				–13	IncSt → RE

Adjusting entry required for prepaid insurance consumed during July, 2008.

2.22 (ABB Group; journal entries for prepaid rent.) (Amounts in Millions)

a. **Journal Entries for January, 2007:**
January 31, 2007
Rent Expense 247
   Prepaid Rent 247

Assets	=	Liabilities	+	Shareholders' Equity	(Class.)
–247				–247	IncSt → RE

To record the adjusting entry for the consumption of the prepaid portion of rent expense for the month of January.

January 31, 2007
Prepaid Rent 3,200
   Cash 3,200

Assets	=	Liabilities	+	Shareholders' Equity	(Class.)
+3,200					
–3,200					

To record the prepayment of rent for the next 12 months.

b. **Journal Entry in December, 2007:**
December 31, 2007
Rent Expense 2,933
   Prepaid Rent 2,933

Assets	=	Liabilities	+	Shareholders' Equity	(Class.)
–2,933				–2,933	IncSt → RE

To record the adjusting entry for the consumption of the prepaid portion of rent expense for the months of February through December.

Amount of Prepaid Rent consumed = [($3,200/12 months) x 11 months] = $2,933 million.

2.23 (Sappi Limited; journal entries for borrowing.) (Amounts in Millions)

a. Sappi repaid liabilities in fiscal 2007, in the amount of $1,634 + $1,200 − $1,828 = $1,006 million. To record the repayment, Sappi made the following journal entry:

Date of Repayment, Fiscal 2007
Noncurrent Financial Liabilities.................................. 1,006
   Cash..   1,006

Assets	=	Liabilities	+	Shareholders' Equity	(Class.)
−1,006		−1,006			

b. **Journal Entries:**

Fiscal Year 2007:
March 31, 2007
Cash 1,200
   Bank Loan Payable..   1,200

Assets	=	Liabilities	+	Shareholders' Equity	(Class.)
+1,200		+1,200			

To record the loan from the local bank.

September 30, 2007
Interest Expense [= $1,200 Million × .075 ×
   (180/360)].. 45
   Interest Payable...   45

Assets	=	Liabilities	+	Shareholders' Equity	(Class.)
		+45		−45	IncSt → RE

Adjusting entry to record interest expense earned but not yet paid at the end of fiscal year 2007.

Solutions

2.23 b. continued.

Fiscal Year 2008:
March 31, 2008
Interest Payable 45
Interest Expense 45
    Cash 90

Assets	=	Liabilities	+	Shareholders' Equity	(Class.)
–90		–45		–45	IncSt → RE

To record payment of interest for the first year.

September 30, 2008
Interest Expense [= $1,200 Million x .075 x
    (180/360)] 45
    Interest Payable 45

Assets	=	Liabilities	+	Shareholders' Equity	(Class.)
		+45		–45	IncSt → RE

Adjusting entry to record interest expense earned but not yet paid at the end of fiscal year 2008.

Fiscal Year 2009:
March 31, 2009
Interest Payable 45
Interest Expense 45
    Cash 90

Assets	=	Liabilities	+	Shareholders' Equity	(Class.)
–90		–45		–45	IncSt → RE

To record payment of interest for the second year.

March 31, 2009
Bank Loan Payable 1,200
    Cash 1,200

Assets	=	Liabilities	+	Shareholders' Equity	(Class.)
–1,200		–1,200			

To record repayment of the principal.

2.24 (Toyota Motor Company; journal entries related to the income statement.) (Amounts in Millions)

2007

| Accounts Receivable | 22,670 | |
| Revenues | | 22,670 |

Assets	=	Liabilities	+	Shareholders' Equity	(Class.)
+22,670				+22,670	IncSt → RE

To record product sales on account.

| Cost of Goods Sold | 18,356 | |
| Inventories | | 18,356 |

Assets	=	Liabilities	+	Shareholders' Equity	(Class.)
−18,356				−18,356	IncSt → RE

To record the cost of sales.

| Cash | 22,670 | |
| Accounts Receivable | | 22,670 |

Assets	=	Liabilities	+	Shareholders' Equity	(Class.)
−22,670					
+22,670					

To record the cash collected on sales made on account.

2.25 (Teva Pharmaceutical; journal entries related to the income statement.) (Amounts in Millions)

2007

| Accounts Receivable | 9,408 | |
| Revenues | | 9,408 |

Assets	=	Liabilities	+	Shareholders' Equity	(Class.)
+9,408				+9,408	IncSt → RE

To record product sales on account.

2.25 continued.

Cost of Goods Sold.. 6,531
    Inventories..   6,531

Assets	=	Liabilities	+	Shareholders' Equity	(Class.)
–6,531				–6,531	IncSt → RE

To record the cost of sales.

Cash.. 2,650
    Accounts Receivable..   2,650

Assets	=	Liabilities	+	Shareholders' Equity	(Class.)
–2,650					
+2,650					

To record the cash collected on sales made on account.

2.26 (Bostick Enterprises; journal entries to correct recording error.) (Amounts in Millions)

Entry Made:
Equipment Expense 120,000
    Cash   120,000

Assets	=	Liabilities	+	Shareholders' Equity	(Class.)
–120,000				–120,000	IncSt → RE

Correct Entries:
Equipment.. 120,000
    Cash   120,000

Assets	=	Liabilities	+	Shareholders' Equity	(Class.)
–120,000					
+120,000					

Depreciation Expense ($120,000/10)................................ 12,000
    Accumulated Depreciation..   12,000

Assets	=	Liabilities	+	Shareholders' Equity	(Class.)
–12,000				–12,000	IncSt → RE

2.26 continued.

Correcting Entry:

Equipment..	120,000	
Depreciation Expense	12,000	
Equipment Expense..		120,000
Accumulated Depreciation		12,000

Assets	=	Liabilities	+	Shareholders' Equity	(Class.)
+120,000				+120,000	IncSt → RE
–12,000				–12,000	IncSt → RE

2.27 (Bullseye Corporation; dual effects of transactions on balance sheet equation and journal entries.) (Amounts in Millions)

a.
Transaction Number	Assets	=	Liabilities	+	Shareholders' Equity
(1)	+ $ 960			+	$ 960
Subtotal	$ 960	=			$ 960
(2)	+ 1,500		+ $ 1,500		
Subtotal	$ 2,460	=	$ 1,500	+	$ 960
(3)	+ 3,200				
	+ 930				
	– 4,130				
Subtotal	$ 2,460	=	$ 1,500	+	$ 960
(4)	+ 860	=	+ 860		
Subtotal	$ 3,320	=	$ 2,360	+	$ 960
(5)	– 1,500		– 1,500		
Subtotal	$ 1,820	=	$ 860	+	$ 960
(6)	– 430		– 860	+	430
Total	$ 1,390	=	-0-	+	$ 1,390

b. (1)
Cash...	960.0	
Common Stock..		1.7
Additional Paid-in Capital		958.3

Assets	=	Liabilities	+	Shareholders' Equity	(Class.)
+960.0				+1.7	ContriCap
				+958.3	ContriCap

Issue 20 million shares of $0.0833 par value common stock for $960 million.

2.27 b. continued.

(2) Merchandise Inventory.. 1,500
    Accounts Payable... 1,500

Assets	=	Liabilities	+	Shareholders' Equity	(Class.)
+1,500		+1,500			

Purchase $1,500 million of inventory on account.

(3) Building.. 3,200
    Land... 930
    Cash... 4,130

Assets	=	Liabilities	+	Shareholders' Equity	(Class.)
+3,200					
+930					
–4,130					

Acquires building costing $3,200 million and land costing $930 million, and pays in cash.

(4) Building Fixtures 860
    Accounts Payable... 860

Assets	=	Liabilities	+	Shareholders' Equity	(Class.)
+860		–860			

Acquires building fixtures costing $860 million on account.

(5) Accounts Payable... 1,500
    Cash... 1,500

Assets	=	Liabilities	+	Shareholders' Equity	(Class.)
–1,500		–1,500			

Pays suppliers in Transaction (2).

2.27 b. continued.

(6) Accounts Payable.. 860.0
  Cash 430.0
  Common Stock 0.7
  Additional Paid-in Capital 429.3

Assets	=	Liabilities	+	Shareholders' Equity	(Class.)
–430.0		–860.0		+0.7	ContriCap
				+429.3	ContriCap

Pays suppliers of fixtures cash of $430 million in shares of common stock. Bullseye Corporation shares are trading at $50 per share, so it gave the supplier 8.6 million shares of common stock (= $430 million/$50 per share).

2.28 (Inheritance Brands; dual effects of transactions on balance sheet equation and journal entries.) (Amounts in Millions)

a.

Transaction Number		Assets	=	Liabilities	+	Shareholders' Equity
(1)		+ $ 550			+	$ 550
	Subtotal	$ 550	=			$ 550
(2)		– 400				
		+ 1,150		+ $ 750		
	Subtotal	$ 1,300	=	$ 750	+	$ 550
(3)		– 30				
		+ 30				
	Subtotal	$ 1,300	=	$ 750	+	$ 550
(4)		+ 400	=	+ 400		
	Subtotal	$ 1,700	=	$ 1,150	+	$ 550
(5)		– 400		– 400		
	Total	$ 1,300	=	$ 750	+	$ 550

b. (1) Cash.. 550.0
  Common Stock 31.25
  Additional Paid-in Capital 518.75

Assets	=	Liabilities	+	Shareholders' Equity	(Class.)
+550.0				+31.25	ContriCap
				+518.75	ContriCap

Issue 10 million shares of $3.125 par-value common stock for $55 per share.

2.28 b. continued.

(2) Land.. 250
    Building.. 900
        Cash 400
        Notes Payable.. 750

Assets	=	Liabilities	+	Shareholders' Equity	(Class.)
+250		+750			
+900					
–400					

Gives $400 million in cash and promises to pay the remainder in 2009 for land costing $250 million and a building costing $900 million.

(3) Prepaid Insurance.. 30
        Cash 30

Assets	=	Liabilities	+	Shareholders' Equity	(Class.)
+30					
–30					

Pays $30 million in advance to insurance company for coverage beginning next month.

(4) Merchandise Inventory.............................. 400
        Accounts Payable..................................... 400

Assets	=	Liabilities	+	Shareholders' Equity	(Class.)
+400		+400			

Purchases merchandise costing $400 million on account.

(5) Accounts Payable... 400
        Cash 400

Assets	=	Liabilities	+	Shareholders' Equity	(Class.)
–400		–400			

Pays cash to suppliers for merchandise on account.

2.29 (Callen Incorporated; preparing a balance sheet and an income statement.) (Amounts in Thousands of Euros)

a.
CALLEN, INCORPORATED
Balance Sheet

	Jan. 31, 2008	Jan. 31, 2007
Assets		
Cash	€ 30,536	€ 2,559
Merchandise Inventory	114,249	151,894
Other Current Assets	109,992	134,916
Total Current Assets	€ 254,777	€ 289,369
Property, Plant and Equipment (Net)	98,130	149,990
Other Noncurrent Assets	56,459	88,955
Total Assets	€ 409,366	€ 528,314
Liabilities and Shareholders' Equity		
Accounts Payable	€ 16,402	€ 14,063
Notes Payable to Banks	15,241	43,598
Other Current Liabilities	84,334	109,335
Total Current Liabilities	€ 115,977	€ 166,996
Long-Term Debt	31,566	38,315
Other Noncurrent Liabilities	19,859	27,947
Total Liabilities	€ 167,402	€ 233,258
Common Stock	€ 72,325	€ 72,325
Retained Earnings	169,639	222,731
Total Shareholders' Equity	€ 241,964	€ 295,056
Total Liabilities and Shareholders' Equity	€ 409,366	€ 528,314

b.
CALLEN, INCORPORATED
Income Statement

For the Year Ended:	Dec. 31, 2008
Sales	€ 695,623
Cost of Goods Sold	(382,349)
Selling Expenses	(72,453)
Administrative Expenses	(141,183)
Interest Expense	(2,744)
Income Taxes	(24,324)
Net Income	€ 72,570

c.
Retained Earnings, December 31, 2007	€ 222,731
Plus Net Income for 2008	72,570
Less Dividends Declared during 2008 (Plug)	(125,662)
Retained Earnings, December 31, 2008	€ 169,639

2.30 (ChemAsia Limited; preparing a balance sheet and an income statement.) (Amounts in Millions)

a.
ChemAsia, Limited
Income Statement
For the Year Ended December 31, 2008

Revenues:	
Net Operating Revenues	$ 835,037
Interest and Other Revenues	3,098
Total Revenues	$ 838,135
Less Expenses:	
Cost of Sales	$ (487,112)
Selling Expenses	(41,345)
General and Administrative Expenses	(49,324)
Other Operating Expenses	(64,600)
Interest Expense	(2,869)
Income Taxes	(49,331)
Total Expenses	$ (694,581)
Net Income	$ 143,554

b.
ChemAsia, Limited
Comparative Balance Sheet

	Dec 31, 2008	Dec. 31, 2007
Assets		
Noncurrent Assets:		
Intangible Assets	$ 20,022	$ 16,127
Oil and Gas Properties	326,328	270,496
Property, Plant and Equipment—Net	247,803	231,590
Other Noncurrent Assets	163,711	132,214
Total Noncurrent Assets	$ 757,864	$ 650,427
Current Assets:		
Inventories	$ 88,467	$ 76,038
Other Current Assets	20,367	13,457
Advances to Suppliers	20,386	12,664
Accounts Receivable	18,419	8,488
Cash	88,589	54,070
Total Current Assets	$ 236,228	$ 164,717
Total Assets	$ 994,092	$ 815,144

2.30 b. continued.

Liabilities and Shareholders' Equity

Noncurrent Liabilities:		
Long-Term Debt	$ 35,305	$ 30,401
Other Noncurrent Liabilities	42,062	36,683
Total Noncurrent Liabilities	$ 77,367	$ 67,084
Current Liabilities:		
Advances from Customers	$ 12,433	$ 11,590
Other Current Liabilities	84,761	90,939
Accounts Payable to Suppliers	104,460	77,936
Total Current Liabilities	$ 201,654	$ 180,465
Shareholders' Equity:		
Common Stock	$ 444,527	$ 354,340
Retained Earnings	270,544	213,255
Total Shareholders' Equity	$ 715,071	$ 567,595
Total Liabilities and Shareholders' Equity	$ 994,092	$ 815,144

c.
Retained Earnings, December 31, 2007	$ 213,255
Plus Net Income for Year Ending December 31, 2008	143,554
Subtract Dividends for Year Ending December 31, 2008 (Plug)	(86,265)
Retained Earnings, December 31, 2008	$ 270,544

2.31 (LBJ Group; miscellaneous transactions and adjusting entries.) (Amounts in Millions)

    a. (1)
Inventories	180,000	
Notes Payable		180,000

Assets	=	Liabilities	+	Shareholders' Equity	(Class.)
+180,000		+180,000			

    (2)
Interest Expense [= $180,000 x .08 x (60/360)]	2,400	
Interest Payable		2,400

Assets	=	Liabilities	+	Shareholders' Equity	(Class.)
		+2,400		–2,400	IncSt → RE

2.31 continued.

b. (1) Cash 842,000
       Advances from Customers 842,000

Assets	=	Liabilities	+	Shareholders' Equity	(Class.)
+842,000		+842,000			

c. (1) Equipment 1,400,000
       Cash 1,400,000

Assets	=	Liabilities	+	Shareholders' Equity	(Class.)
+1,400,000					
–1,400,000					

(2) Depreciation Expense [= 3/12 × ($1,400,000
    – $160,000)/10] 31,000
       Accumulated Depreciation 31,000

Assets	=	Liabilities	+	Shareholders' Equity	(Class.)
–31,000				–31,000	IncSt → RE

d. (1) Accounts Receivable 565,000
       Revenues 565,000

Assets	=	Liabilities	+	Shareholders' Equity	(Class.)
+565,000				+565,000	IncSt → RE

(2) Cost of Goods Sold 422,000
       Accumulated Depreciation 422,000

Assets	=	Liabilities	+	Shareholders' Equity	(Class.)
–422,000				–422,000	IncSt → RE

2.31 continued.

e. (1) Prepaid Insurance 360,000
    Cash.. 360,000

Assets	=	Liabilities	+	Shareholders' Equity	(Class.)
+360,000					
−360,000					

(2) Insurance Expense [= (4/12) x $360,000]........ 120,000
    Prepaid Insurance... 120,000

Assets	=	Liabilities	+	Shareholders' Equity	(Class.)
−120,000				−120,000	IncSt → RE

f. (1) Cash 1,040,000
    Common Stock Par Value............................... 40,000
    Additional Paid-in Capital............................... 1,000,000

Assets	=	Liabilities	+	Shareholders' Equity	(Class.)
+1,040,000				+40,000	ContriCap
				+1,000,000	ContriCap

(2) Accounts Payable..1,040,000
    Cash.. 1,040,000

Assets	=	Liabilities	+	Shareholders' Equity	(Class.)
−1,040,000		−1,040,000			

2.32 (Platinum Fields Limited; miscellaneous transactions and adjusting entries.) (Amounts in Millions)

a. (1) Cash 57,000
    Rental Fees Received in Advance.................. 57,000

Assets	=	Liabilities	+	Shareholders' Equity	(Class.)
+57,000		+57,000			

2.32 a. continued.

    (2) Rental Fees Received in Advance 19,000
          Rent Revenue [= (4/12) x R57,000]...............   19,000

Assets	=	Liabilities	+	Shareholders' Equity	(Class.)
		−19,000		+19,000	IncSt → RE

b. (1) Salary Expense.. 42,000
         Cash...   42,000

Assets	=	Liabilities	+	Shareholders' Equity	(Class.)
−42,000				−42,000	IncSt → RE

    (2) Salary Expense [= (1/2) x R42,000].................. 21,000
          Salaries Payable   21,000

Assets	=	Liabilities	+	Shareholders' Equity	(Class.)
		+21,000		−21,000	IncSt → RE

c. (1) Prepaid Insurance 960,000
         Cash...   960,000

Assets	=	Liabilities	+	Shareholders' Equity	(Class.)
+960,000					
−960,000					

    (2) Insurance Expense [= (8/24) x R960,000]........ 320,000
          Prepaid Insurance..   320,000

Assets	=	Liabilities	+	Shareholders' Equity	(Class.)
−320,000				−320,000	IncSt → RE

d. (1) Inventory.. 235,000
         Accounts Payable...   235,000

Assets	=	Liabilities	+	Shareholders' Equity	(Class.)
+235,000		+235,000			

2.32 continued.

e. (1) Equipment..728,000
       Cash..728,000

Assets	=	Liabilities	+	Shareholders' Equity	(Class.)
+728,000					
−728,000					

(2) Depreciation Expense [= (6/60 x R728,000]... 72,800
       Accumulated Depreciation...........................72,800

Assets	=	Liabilities	+	Shareholders' Equity	(Class.)
−72,800				−72,800	IncSt → RE

f. (1) Retained Earnings..1,143,000
       Dividends Payable.................................1,143,000

Assets	=	Liabilities	+	Shareholders' Equity	(Class.)
		+1,143,000		−1,143,000	RE

(2) Dividends Payable..1,143,000
       Cash...1,143,000

Assets	=	Liabilities	+	Shareholders' Equity	(Class.)
−1,143,000		−1,143,000			

2.33 (Hansen Retail Store; preparing income statement and balance sheet using accrual basis.)

a.
HANSEN RETAIL STORE
Income Statement
For the Year Ended December 31, 2008

Sales ($52,900 + $116,100)..	$ 169,000
Cost of Goods Sold ($125,000 − $15,400)............................	(109,600)
Salary Expense ($34,200 + $2,400).....................................	(36,600)
Utility Expense ($2,600 + $180)..	(2,780)
Depreciation Expense ($60,000/30)....................................	(2,000)
Interest Expense (.10 x $40,000)...	(4,000)
Net Income before Income Taxes	$ 14,020
Income Taxes at 40%...	(5,608)
Net Income	$ 8,412

2.33 continued.

b.
HANSEN RETAIL STORE
Balance Sheet
December 31, 2008

Assets

Cash ($50,000 + $40,000 – $60,000 – $97,400 + $52,900 + $54,800 – $34,200 – $2,600)	$ 3,500
Accounts Receivable ($116,100 – $54,800)	61,300
Inventories	15,400
Total Current Assets	$ 80,200
Building ($60,000 – $2,000)	58,000
Total Assets	$138,200

Liabilities and Shareholders' Equity

Accounts Payable ($125,000 – $97,400)	$ 27,600
Salaries Payable	2,400
Utilities Payable	180
Income Taxes Payable	5,608
Interest Payable	4,000
Loan Payable	40,000
Total Current Liabilities	$ 79,788
Common Stock	$ 50,000
Retained Earnings	8,412
Total Shareholders' Equity	$ 58,412
Total Liabilities and Shareholders' Equity	$138,200

2.34 (Regaldo Department Store; recording transactions and preparing a balance sheet.) (Amounts in Thousands)

a. T-accounts.

Cash (A)		Merchandise Inventory (A)		Prepaid Rent (A)	
(1) 500,000	20,000 (2)	(5) 200,000	8,000 (6)	(4) 60,000	
	4,000 (2)		3,200 (7)		
	60,000 (4)				
	156,800 (7)				
	12,000 (8)				
247,200		188,800		60,000	

2-23 Solutions

2.34 a. continued.

Prepaid Insurance (A)		Patent (A)		Accounts Payable (L)	
(8) 12,000		(2) 20,000		(6) 8,000	200,000 (5)
		(2) 4,000		(7) 160,000	
12,000		24,000			32,000

Common Stock (SE)	
	500,000 (1)
	500,000

b.
REGALDO DEPARTMENT STORES
Balance Sheet
January 31, 2008

Assets

Current Assets:	
Cash..	$ 247,200
Merchandise Inventory..	188,800
Prepaid Rent..	60,000
Prepaid Insurance...	12,000
Total Current Assets...	$ 508,000
Patent...	24,000
Total Assets..	$ 532,000

Liabilities and Shareholders' Equity

Current Liabilities:	
Accounts Payable..	$ 32,000
Total Current Liabilities..	$ 32,000
Shareholders' Equity:	
Common Stock..	$ 500,000
Retained Earnings...	0
Total Shareholders' Equity..	$ 500,000
Total Liabilities and Shareholders' Equity...................	$ 532,000

2.35 (Regaldo Department Stores; analysis of transactions and preparation of income statement and balance sheet.)

a. T-accounts.

Cash (A)			
√	247,200		
(3a)	62,900	32,400	(4)
(6)	84,600	2,700	(5)
		205,800	(7a)
		29,000	(7b)
√	124,800		

Accounts Receivable (A)			
√	0		
(3a)	194,600	84,600	(6)
√	110,000		

Inventory (A)			
√	188,800		
(2)	217,900	162,400	(3b)
		4,200	(7a)
√	240,100		

Prepaid Rent (A)			
√	60,000		
		30,000	(11)
√	30,000		

Prepaid Insurance (A)			
√	12,000	1,000	(12)
√	11,000		

Equipment (A)			
√	0		
(1)	90,000		
√	90,000		

Accumulated Depreciation (XA)			
		0	√
		1,500	(10)
		1,500	√

Patent (A)			
√	24,000		
		400	(13)
√	23,600		

Accounts Payable (L)			
		32,000	√
(7a)	210,000	217,900	(2)
(7b)	29,000		
		10,900	√

Note Payable (L)			
		0	√
		90,000	(1)
		90,000	√

Compensation Payable (L)			
		0	√
		6,700	(8)
		6,700	√

Utilities Payable (L)			
		0	√
		800	(9)
		800	√

2.35 a. continued.

Interest Payable (L)			Income Tax Payable (L)		
	0	√		0	√
	900	(14)		5,610	(15)
	900	√		5,610	√

Common Stock (SE)			Retained Earnings (SE)		
	500,000	√		0	√
				13,090	(16)
	500,000	√		13,090	√

	Sales Revenue (SE)				Cost of Goods Sold (SE)		
(16)	257,500	257,500	(3a)	(3b)	162,400	162,400	(16)

	Compensation Expense (SE)				Utilities Expense (SE)		
(4)	32,400			(5)	2,700		
(8)	6,700	39,100	(16)	(9)	800	3,500	(16)

	Depreciation Expense (SE)				Rent Expense (SE)		
(10)	1,500	1,500	(16)	(11)	30,000	30,000	(16)

	Insurance Expense (SE)				Patent Amortization Expense (SE)		
(12)	1,000	1,000	(16)	(13)	400	400	(16)

	Interest Expense (SE)				Income Tax Expense (SE)		
(14)	900	900	(16)	(15)	5,610	5,610	(16)

2.35 continued.

b.
REGALDO DEPARTMENT STORES
Income Statement
For the Month of February 2008

Sales Revenue	$ 257,500
Expenses:	
Cost of Goods Sold	$ 162,400
Compensation ($32,400 + $6,700)	39,100
Utilities ($2,700 + $800)	3,500
Depreciation	1,500
Rent	30,000
Insurance	1,000
Patent Amortization	400
Interest	900
Total Expenses	$ 238,800
Net Income before Income Taxes	$ 18,700
Income Tax Expense at 30%	(5,610)
Net Income	$ 13,090

2.35 continued.

c.
REGALDO DEPARTMENT STORES
Comparative Balance Sheet

	January 31, 2008	February 28, 2008
Assets		
Cash	$ 247,200	$ 124,800
Accounts Receivable	0	110,000
Inventories	188,800	240,100
Prepaid Rent	60,000	30,000
Prepaid Insurance	12,000	11,000
Total Current Assets	$ 508,000	$ 515,900
Equipment (at Cost)	$ 0	$ 90,000
Less Accumulated Depreciation	0	(1,500)
Equipment (Net)	$ 0	$ 88,500
Patent	24,000	23,600
Total Noncurrent Assets	$ 24,000	$ 112,100
Total Assets	$ 532,000	$ 628,000
Liabilities and Shareholders' Equity		
Accounts Payable	$ 32,000	$ 10,900
Notes Payable	0	90,000
Compensation Payable	0	6,700
Utilities Payable	0	800
Interest Payable	0	900
Income Tax Payable	0	5,610
Total Liabilities	$ 32,000	$ 114,910
Common Stock	$ 500,000	$ 500,000
Retained Earnings	0	13,090
Total Shareholders' Equity	$ 500,000	$ 513,090
Total Liabilities and Shareholders' Equity	$ 532,000	$ 628,000

2.36 (Zealock Bookstore; analysis of transactions and preparation of income statement and balance sheet.)

a. T-accounts.

	Cash (A)				Accounts Receivable (A)	
(1)	25,000	20,000	(3)	(8)	148,200	142,400 (10)
(2)	30,000	4,000	(4)			
(8)	24,600	10,000	(5)			
(10)	142,400	8,000	(6)			
(13)	850	16,700	(11)			
		139,800	(12)			
	24,350				5,800	

Solutions 2-28

2.36 a. continued.

Merchandise Inventory (A)					Prepaid Rent (A)			
(7)	160,000	140,000	(8)	(3)	20,000	10,000	(15)
		14,600	(9)				
	5,400				10,000		

Deposit with Suppliers (A)				Equipment (A)			
(6)	8,000			(4)	4,000		
				(5)	10,000		
	8,000				14,000		

Accumulated Depreciation (XA)				Note Payable (L)			
		400	(16)			30,000	(2)
		1,500	(17)				
		1,900				30,000	

Accounts Payable (L)				Advances from Customers (L)			
(9)	14,600	160,000	(7)			850	(13)
(12)	139,800						
		5,600				850	

Interest Payable (L)				Income Tax Payable (L)			
		900	(14)			1,320	(19)
		900				1,320	

Common Stock (SE)				Retained Earnings (SE)			
		25,000	(1)			1,980	(20)
		25,000				1,980	

Sales Revenue (SE)				Cost of Goods Sold (SE)			
(20)	172,800	172,800	(8)	(8)	140,000	140,000	(20)

Compensation Expense (SE)				Interest Expense (SE)			
(11)	16,700	16,700	(20)	(14)	900	900	(20)

2.36 a. continued.

Rent Expense (SE)				Depreciation Expense (SE)			
(15)	10,000	10,000	(20)	(16)	400	1,900	(20)
				(17)	1,500		

Income Tax Expense (SE)			
(19)	1,320	1,320	(20)

b. **ZEALOCK BOOKSTORE**
Income Statement
For the Six Months Ending December 31, 2008

Sales Revenue		$172,800
Less Expenses:		
Cost of Goods Sold	$140,000	
Compensation Expense	16,700	
Interest Expense	900	
Rent Expense	10,000	
Depreciation Expense	1,900	
Income Tax Expense	1,320	
Total Expenses	$170,820	
Net Income		$ 1,980

c. **ZEALOCK BOOKSTORE**
Balance Sheet
December 31, 2008

Assets

Current Assets:		
Cash		$ 24,350
Accounts Receivable		5,800
Merchandise Inventories		5,400
Prepaid Rent		10,000
Deposit with Suppliers		8,000
Total Current Assets		$ 53,550
Equipment		$ 14,000
Less Accumulated Depreciation		(1,900)
Equipment (Net)		$ 12,100
Total Assets		$ 65,650

2.36 c. continued.

Liabilities and Shareholders' Equity

Current Liabilities:
Accounts Payable	$ 5,600
Note Payable	30,000
Advances from Customers	850
Interest Payable	900
Income Tax Payable	1,320
Total Current Liabilities	$ 38,670

Shareholders' Equity:
Common Stock	$ 25,000
Retained Earnings	1,980
Total Shareholders' Equity	$ 26,980
Total Liabilities and Shareholders' Equity	$ 65,650

2.37 (Zealock Bookstore; analysis of transactions and preparation of comparative income statements and balance sheet.)

a. T-accounts.

Cash (A)			
√	24,350		
(3)	75,000	1,320	(1)
(4)	8,000	31,800	(2)
(7)	24,900	20,000	(5)
(9)	320,600	29,400	(10)
		281,100	(11)
		4,000	(12)
√	85,230		

Accounts Receivable (A)			
√	5,800		
(7)	327,950	320,600	(9)
√	13,150		

Merchandise Inventory (A)			
√	5,400		
(6)	310,000	286,400	(7)
		22,700	(8)
√	6,300		

Prepaid Rent (A)			
√	10,000		
(5)	20,000	20,000	(13)
√	10,000		

Deposit with Suppliers (A)			
√	8,000		
		8,000	(4)
√	0		

Equipment (A)		
√	14,000	
√	14,000	

2.37 a. continued.

Accumulated Depreciation (XA)				Note Payable (L)			
		1,900	√			30,000	√
		800	(14)	(2)	30,000	75,000	(3)
		3,000	(15)				
		5,700	√			75,000	√

Accounts Payable (L)				Advance from Customers (L)			
		5,600	√			850	√
(8)	22,700	310,000	(6)	(7)	850		
(11)	281,100						
		11,800	√			0	√

Interest Payable (L)				Income Tax Payable (L)			
		900	√			1,320	√
(2)	900	3,000	(16)	(1)	1,320	4,080	(17)
		3,000	√			4,080	√

Common Stock (SE)				Retained Earnings (SE)			
		25,000	√			1,980	√
				(12)	4,000	6,120	(18)
		25,000	√			4,100	√

Sales Revenue (SE)				Cost of Goods Sold (SE)			
(18)	353,700	353,700	(7)	(7)	286,400	286,400	(18)

Compensation Expense (SE)				Interest Expense (SE)			
(10)	29,400	29,400	(18)	(2)	900		
				(16)	3,000	3,900	(18)

Rent Expense (SE)				Depreciation Expense (SE)			
(13)	20,000	20,000	(18)	(14)	800		
				(15)	3,000	3,800	(18)

2.37 a. continued.

```
       Income Tax Expense (SE)
(17)        4,080  |  4,080    (18)
```

b. **ZEALOCK BOOKSTORE**
Comparative Income Statement
For 2008 and 2009

	2008	2009
Sales Revenue	$353,700	$172,800
Less Expenses:		
Cost of Goods Sold	$286,400	$140,000
Compensation Expense	29,400	16,700
Interest Expense	3,900	900
Rent Expense	20,000	10,000
Depreciation Expense	3,800	1,900
Income Tax Expense	4,080	1,320
Total Expenses	$347,580	$170,820
Net Income	$ 6,120	$ 1,980

c. **ZEALOCK BOOKSTORE**
Comparative Balance Sheet
December 31, 2008 and 2009

	2009	2008
Assets		
Current Assets:		
Cash	$ 85,230	$ 24,350
Accounts Receivable	13,150	5,800
Merchandise Inventories	6,300	5,400
Prepaid Rent	10,000	10,000
Deposit with Suppliers	--	8,000
Total Current Assets	$114,680	$ 53,550
Noncurrent Assets:		
Equipment	$ 14,000	$ 14,000
Less Accumulated Depreciation	(5,700)	(1,900)
Equipment (Net)	$ 8,300	$ 12,100
Total Assets	$122,980	$ 65,650

2.37 c. continued.

Liabilities and Shareholders' Equity

Current Liabilities:
Accounts Payable	$ 11,800	$ 5,600
Note Payable	75,000	30,000
Advances from Customers	--	850
Interest Payable	3,000	900
Income Tax Payable	4,080	1,320
Total Current Liabilities	$ 93,880	$ 38,670
Shareholders' Equity:		
Common Stock	$ 25,000	$ 25,000
Retained Earnings	4,100	1,980
Total Shareholders' Equity	$ 29,100	$ 26,980
Total Liabilities and Shareholders' Equity	$122,980	$ 65,650

2.38 (Portobello Co.; reconstructing the income statement and balance sheet.)

T-accounts to derive the amounts in the income statement and balance sheet appear below.

	Cash					Accounts Receivable		
√	18,600				√	33,000		
(4)	10,900	4,800	(3)		(15)	228,000	210,000	(14)
(14)	210,000	115,000	(5)					
		3,000	(10)					
		85,000	(17)					
		27,000	(19)					
√	4,700				√	51,000		

	Notes Receivable					Interest Receivable		
√	10,000				√	600		
		10,000	(4)				600	(4)
√	0				√	0		

	Merchandise Inventory					Prepaid Insurance		
√	22,000				√	4,500		
(6)	95,000	88,000	(8)				3,000	(1)
(7)	11,000							
√	40,000				√	1,500		

2.38 continued.

Advances to Employees			Prepaid Taxes		
√	0		√	0	
(17)	4,000		(19)	3,000	
√	4,000		√	3,000	

Computer System (at Cost)			Accumulated Depreciation—Computer System		
√	78,000			26,000	√
				13,000	(13)
√	78,000			39,000	√

Delivery Trucks			Accumulated Depreciation—Delivery Trucks		
√	0			0	√
(9)	60,000			4,500	(12)
√	60,000			4,500	√

Accounts Payable			Notes Payable		
	36,000	√		0	√
(5)	115,000	95,000 (6)		60,000	(9)
	16,000	√		60,000	√

Interest Payable			Dividend Payable		
	0	√		1,800	√
	2,000	(11)	(3)	4,800	6,000 (2)
	2,000	√		3,000	√

Salaries Payable			Taxes Payable		
	6,500	√		10,000	√
(17)	6,500		(19)	10,000	4,000 (20)
	1,300	(18)			
	1,300	√		4,000	√

Consulting Fee Payable			Advances from Customers		
	0	√		600	√
	4,800	(21)	(16)	600	1,400 (15)
	4,800	√		1,400	√

2.38 continued.

	Common Stock					Retained Earnings		
		40,000	√				45,800	√
		11,000	(7)	(2)	6,000		15,400	(22)
		51,000	√				55,200	√

	Sales Revenue					Interest Revenue		
		226,600	(15)	(22)	300		300	(4)
(22)	227,200	600	(16)					

	Cost of Goods Sold					Depreciation Expense		
(8)	88,000	88,000	(22)	(12)	4,500			
				(13)	13,000	17,500	(22)	

	Salary Expense					Tax Expense		
(17)	74,500			(19)	14,000			
(18)	1,300	75,800	(22)	(20)	4,000	18,000	(22)	

	Insurance Expense					Consulting Expense		
(1)	3,000	3,000	(22)	(21)	4,800	4,800	(22)	

	Interest Expense		
(10)	3,000		
(11)	2,000	5,000	(22)

Solutions

2.38 continued.

PORTOBELLO CO.
Income Statement
For the Year Ended December 31, 2008

Revenues:	
Sales	$227,200
Interest	300
Total Revenues	$227,500
Expenses:	
Cost of Goods Sold	$ 88,000
Depreciation	17,500
Salaries	75,800
Taxes	18,000
Insurance	3,000
Consulting	4,800
Interest	5,000
Total Expenses	$212,100
Net Income	$ 15,400

2.38 continued.

PORTOBELLO CO.
Balance Sheet
December 31, 2008

Assets

Current Assets:
Cash	$ 4,700
Accounts Receivable	51,000
Merchandise Inventories	40,000
Prepaid Insurance	1,500
Advances to Employees	4,000
Prepaid Property Taxes	3,000
Total Current Assets	$104,200

Noncurrent Assets:
Computer System—at Cost	$ 78,000	
Less Accumulated Depreciation	(39,000)	$ 39,000
Delivery Trucks	$ 60,000	
Less Accumulated Depreciation	(4,500)	55,500
Total Noncurrent Assets		$ 94,500
Total Assets		$198,700

Liabilities and Shareholders' Equity

Current Liabilities:
Accounts Payable	$ 16,000
Interest Payable	2,000
Dividend Payable	3,000
Salaries Payable	1,300
Taxes Payable	4,000
Consulting Fee Payable	4,800
Advances from Customers	1,400
Total Current Liabilities	$ 32,500
Note Payable	60,000
Total Liabilities	$ 92,500

Shareholders' Equity:
Common Stock	$ 51,000
Retained Earnings	55,200
Total Shareholders' Equity	$106,200
Total Liabilities and Shareholders' Equity	$198,700

2.39 (Computer Needs, Inc.; reconstructing the income statement and balance sheet.)

T-accounts.

	Cash		
√	15,600		
(A)	37,500	164,600	(D)
(B)	151,500	21,000	(G)
		3,388	(H)
		4,800	(I)
		6,000	(J)
√	4,812		

	Accounts Receivable		
√	32,100		
(C)	159,700	151,500	(B)
√	40,300		

	Inventory		
√	46,700		
(E)	172,100	158,100	(F)
√	60,700		

	Prepayments		
√	1,500		
(G)	300		
√	1,800		

	Property, Plant and Equipment		
√	59,700		
(J)	6,000		
√	65,700		

	Accumulated Depreciation		
		2,800	√
		3,300	(K)
		6,100	√

	Accounts Payable—Merchandise		
		37,800	√
(D)	164,600	172,100	(E)
		45,300	√

	Income Tax Payable		
		3,388	√
(H)	3,388	3,584	(L)
		3,584	√

	Other Current Liabilities		
		2,900	√
(G)	1,700		
		1,200	√

	Mortgage Payable		
		50,000	√
(I)	800		
		49,200	√

	Common Stock		
		50,000	√
		50,000	√

	Retained Earnings		
		8,712	√
		9,216	(M)
		17,928	√

2.39 continued.

Sales				Cost of Goods Sold			
		37,500	(A)	(F)	158,100	158,100	(M)
(M)	197,200	159,700	(C)				

Selling and Administrative Expense				Depreciation Expense			
(G)	19,000	19,000	(M)	(K)	3,300	3,300	(M)

Interest Expense				Income Tax Expense			
(I)	4,000	4,000	(M)	(L)	3,584	3,584	(M)

COMPUTER NEEDS, INC.
Income Statement
For the Years Ended December 31, 2007 and 2008

	2008	2007
Sales	$197,200	$152,700
Cost of Goods Sold	(158,100)	(116,400)
Selling and Administrative Expense	(19,000)	(17,400)
Depreciation Expense	(3,300)	(2,800)
Interest Expense	(4,000)	(4,000)
Income Taxes	(3,584)	(3,388)
Net Income	$ 9,216	$ 8,712

2.39 continued.

COMPUTER NEEDS, INC.
Balance Sheet
For the Years Ended December 31, 2007 and 2008

	2008	2007
Assets		
Cash	$ 4,812	$ 15,600
Accounts Receivable	40,300	32,100
Inventories	60,700	46,700
Prepayments	1,800	1,500
Total Current Assets	$107,612	$ 95,900
Property, Plant and Equipment:		
At Cost	$ 65,700	$ 59,700
Less Accumulated Depreciation	(6,100)	(2,800)
Net	$ 59,600	$ 56,900
Total Assets	$167,212	$152,800
Liabilities and Shareholders' Equity		
Accounts Payable—Merchandise	$ 45,300	$ 37,800
Income Tax Payable	3,584	3,388
Other Current Liabilities	1,200	2,900
Total Current Liabilities	$ 50,084	$ 44,088
Mortgage Payable	49,200	50,000
Total Liabilities	$ 99,284	$ 94,088
Common Stock	$ 50,000	$ 50,000
Retained Earnings	17,928	8,712
Total Shareholders' Equity	$ 67,928	$ 58,712
Total Liabilities and Shareholders' Equity	$167,212	$152,800

2.40 (Embotelladora; effect of errors on financial statements.)

	Assets	Liabilities	Shareholders' Equity
a.	U/S $60,000	NO	U/S $60,000
b.	NO	U/S $82,000	O/S $82,000
c.	U/S $95,958	NO	U/S $95,958
d.	O/S $ 3,100	NO	O/S $ 3,100
e.	NO	U/S $34,500	O/S $34,500
f.	NO	O/S $17,900	U/S $17,900

2.41 (Forgetful Corporation; effect of recording errors on financial statements.)

Note: The actual and correct entries appear below to show the effect and amount of the errors, but are not required.

a. **Actual Entry:**
Cash 1,400
    Sales Revenue 1,400

Assets	=	Liabilities	+	Shareholders' Equity	(Class.)
+1,400				+1,400	IncSt → RE

Correct Entry:
Cash 1,400
    Advance from Customer 1,400

Assets	=	Liabilities	+	Shareholders' Equity	(Class.)
+1,400		+1,400			

Liabilities understated by $1,400 and shareholders' equity overstated by $1,400.

b. **Actual Entry:**
Cost of Goods Sold 5,000
    Cash 5,000

Assets	=	Liabilities	+	Shareholders' Equity	(Class.)
−5,000				−5,000	IncSt → RE

2.41 b. continued.

Correct Entries:

Machine 5,000
   Cash 5,000

Assets	=	Liabilities	+	Shareholders' Equity	(Class.)
+5,000					
−5,000					

Depreciation Expense 500
   Accumulated Depreciation 500

Assets	=	Liabilities	+	Shareholders' Equity	(Class.)
−500				−500	IncSt → RE

Assets understated by $4,500 and shareholders' equity understated by $4,500.

c. **Actual Entry:**
None for accrued interest.

Correct Entry:
Interest Receivable ($2,000 x .12 x 60/360) 40
   Interest Revenue 40

Assets	=	Liabilities	+	Shareholders' Equity	(Class.)
+40				+40	IncSt → RE

Assets understated by $40 and shareholders' equity understated by $40.

d. The entry is correct as recorded.

e. **Actual Entry:**
None for declared dividend.

Correct Entry:
Retained Earnings 1,500
   Dividend Payable 1,500

Assets	=	Liabilities	+	Shareholders' Equity	(Class.)
		+1,500		−1,500	Dividend

Liabilities understated by $1,500 and shareholders' equity overstated by $1,500.

2.41 continued.

f. **Actual Entries:**

Machinery 50,000
    Accounts Payable 50,000

Assets	=	Liabilities	+	Shareholders' Equity	(Class.)
+50,000		+50,000			

Accounts Payable 50,000
    Cash 49,000
    Miscellaneous Revenue 1,000

Assets	=	Liabilities	+	Shareholders' Equity	(Class.)
−49,000		−50,000		+1,000	IncSt → RE

Maintenance Expense 4,000
    Cash 4,000

Assets	=	Liabilities	+	Shareholders' Equity	(Class.)
−4,000				−4,000	IncSt → RE

Correct Entries:

Machinery 50,000
    Accounts Payable 50,000

Assets	=	Liabilities	+	Shareholders' Equity	(Class.)
+50,000		+50,000			

Accounts Payable 50,000
    Cash 49,000
    Machinery 1,000

Assets	=	Liabilities	+	Shareholders' Equity	(Class.)
−49,000		−50,000			
−1,000					

Solutions

2.41 f. continued.

Machinery 4,000
  Cash 4,000

Assets	=	Liabilities	+	Shareholders' Equity	(Class.)
+4,000					
−4,000					

Assets understated by $3,000 and shareholders' equity understated by $3,000.

2.42 (Prima Company; working backwards to balance sheet at beginning of the period.)

A T-account method for deriving the solution appears below and on the following page. The end-of-year balance appears at the bottom of the T-account. The derived starting balance appears at the top. "p" indicates plug; "c" closing entry.

	Cash					Marketable Securities	
(p)	11,700				(p)	12,000	
(1)	47,000	128,000	(3)		(8)	8,000	
(2)	150,000	49,000	(4)				
		7,500	(5)				
		1,200	(6)				
		5,000	(7)				
		8,000	(8)				
Bal.	10,000				Bal.	20,000	

	Accounts Receivable					Merchandise Inventory	
(p)	22,000				(p)	33,000	
(10)	153,000	150,000	(2)		(9)	127,000	130,000 (11)
Bal.	25,000				Bal.	30,000	

	Prepayments for Miscellaneous Services					Land, Buildings, and Equipment	
(p)	1,700				(p)	40,000	
(4)	49,000	47,700	(14)				
Bal.	3,000				Bal.	40,000	

2.42 continued.

	Accounts Payable (for Merchandise)					Interest Payable		
		26,000	(p)				300	(p)
(3)	128,000	127,000	(9)	(6)	1,200	1,200	(15)
		25,000	Bal.				300	Bal.

	Taxes Payable					Note Payable		
		3,500	(p)				20,000	(p)
(5)	7,500	8,000	(13)					
		4,000	Bal.				20,000	Bal.

	Accumulated Depreciation				Common Stock		
		12,000	(p)			50,000	(p)
		4,000	(12)				
		16,000	Bal.			50,000	Bal.

	Retained Earnings					Sales		
		8,600	(p)				47,000	(1)
(7)	5,000	9,100	(16c)	(16c)	200,000	153,000	(10)
		12,700	Bal.					

	Cost of Goods Sold				Depreciation Expense		
(11)	130,000	130,000	(16c)	(12)	4,000	4,000	(16c)

	Tax Expense				Other Operating Expense		
(13)	8,000	8,000	(16c)	(14)	47,700	47,700	(16c)

	Interest Expense		
(15)	1,200	1,200	(16c)

2.42 continued.

Transactions spreadsheet.

Transactions, By Number and Description

Balance Sheet Accounts	Balance: Beginning of Period	1 Recog. Sales Rev.	2 Acct. Rec. Collected	3 Recog. Pur. Of Merchn.	4 Recog. COGS	5 Recog. Cash Pay. To Supp.	6 Recog. Depre. Exp.	7 Recog. Tax Exp.	8 Recog. Tax Paid	9 Recog. Prepay. Made	10 Recog. Oper. Exp.	11 Recog. Int. Exp.	12 Recog. Int. Paid	13 Recog. Div. Dec. and Paid	14 Record Mkt. Sec. Pur.	Balance: End of 2008
ASSETS																
Current Assets:																
Cash	11,700	47,000	150,000			−128,000			−7,500	−4,000			−1,200	−5,000	−8,000	10,000
Marketable Securities	12,000														8,000	20,000
Accounts Receivable	22,000	153,000	−150,000													25,000
Merchandise Inventory	33,000			127,000	−130,000											30,000
Prepayments for Miscellaneous Ser.	1,700									4,000	−47,700					3,000
Total Current Assets	80,400															88,000
Noncurrent Assets:																
Land, Building, & Equip.	40,000															40,000
Accumulated Depreciation	−12,000						−4,000									(16,000)
Total Noncurrent Assets	28,000															24,000
Total Assets	108,400															112,000
LIABILITIES AND SHAREHOLDERS' EQUITY																
Current Liabilities:																
Accounts Payable	26,000			127,000		−128,000										25,000
Interest Payable	300											1,200	−1,200			300
Taxes Payable	3,500							8,000	−7,500							4,000
Total Current Liabilities	29,800															29,300
Noncurrent Liabilities:																
Note Payable	20,000															20,000
Total Noncurrent Liabilities	20,000															20,000
Total Liabilities	49,800															49,300
Shareholders' Equity:																
Common Stock	50,000															50,000
Retained Earnings	8,600	200,000			−130,000		−4,000	−8,000			−47,700	−1,200		−5,000		12,700
Total Shareholders' Equity	58,600															62,700
Total Liabilities and Shareholders' Equity	108,400															112,000
Imbalance, if Any	−	−	−	−	−	−	−	−	−	−	−	−	−	−	−	
Income Statement Accounts		Sales Rev.			COGS		Depre. Exp.	Tax Exp.			Ot. Op. Exp.	Int. Exp.				

2-47 Solutions

2.42 continued.

PRIMA COMPANY
Balance Sheet
As of December 31, 2007

Assets

Cash		$ 11,700
Marketable Securities		12,000
Accounts Receivable		22,000
Merchandise Inventory		33,000
Prepayments		1,700
Total Current Assets		$ 80,400
Land, Buildings, and Equipment	$ 40,000	
Less Accumulated Depreciation	(12,000)	28,000
Total Assets		$108,400

Liabilities and Shareholders' Equity

Accounts Payable		$ 26,000
Interest Payable		300
Taxes Payable		3,500
Total Current Liabilities		$ 29,800
Notes Payable (6%)		20,000
Total Liabilities		$ 49,800
Common Stock		$ 50,000
Retained Earnings		8,600
Total Shareholders' Equity		$ 58,600
Total Liabilities and Shareholders' Equity		$108,400

2.43 (The Secunda Company; working backwards to cash receipts and disbursements.)

A T-account method for deriving the solution appears below and on the following page. After Entry (6), we have explained all revenue and expense account changes. Plugging for the unknown amounts determines the remaining, unexplained changes in balance sheet accounts. A "p" next to the entry number designates these entries. Note that the revenue and expense accounts are not yet closed to retained earnings, so dividends account for the decrease in the Retained Earnings account during the year of $10,000.

Cash					Accounts Receivable			
Bal.	20,000				Bal.	36,000		
(7)	85,000				(1)	100,000	85,000	(7p)
		2,000	(9)					
		81,000	(10)					
		3,000	(11)					
		10,000	(12)					
Bal.	9,000				Bal.	51,000		

Solutions
2-48

2.43 continued.

Merchandise Inventory				Prepayments			
Bal.	45,000			Bal.	2,000		
(8p)	65,000	50,000	(2)			1,000	(5)
Bal.	60,000			Bal.	1,000		

Land, Buildings, and Equipment				Cost of Goods Sold			
Bal.	40,000			Bal.	0		
				(2)	50,000		
Bal.	40,000			Bal.	50,000		

Interest Expense				Other Operating Expenses			
Bal.	0			Bal.	0		
(3)	3,000			(4)	2,000		
				(5)	1,000		
				(6p)	26,000		
Bal.	3,000			Bal.	29,000		

Accumulated Depreciation				Interest Payable			
		16,000	Bal.			1,000	Bal.
		2,000	(4)	(9p)	2,000	3,000	(3)
		18,000	Bal.			2,000	Bal.

Accounts Payable				Mortgage Payable			
		30,000	Bal.			20,000	Bal.
(10p)	81,000	26,000	(6)	(11p)	3,000		
		65,000	(8)				
		40,000	Bal.			17,000	Bal.

Common Stock				Retained Earnings			
		50,000	Bal.			26,000	Bal.
				(12p)	10,000		
		50,000	Bal.			16,000	Bal.

Sales			
		0	Bal.
		100,000	(1)
		100,000	Bal.

2.43 continued.

SECUNDA COMPANY
Cash Receipts and Disbursements Schedule

Receipts:		
Collections from Customers..............................		$85,000
Disbursements:		
Suppliers of Merchandise and Other Services..	$81,000	
Mortgage..	3,000	
Dividends	10,000	
Interest...	2,000	
Total Disbursements.......................................		96,000
Decrease in Cash		$11,000
Cash Balance, December 31, 2007........................		20,000
Cash Balance, December 31, 2008........................		$ 9,000

Solutions   2-50

2.43 continued.

Transactions spreadsheet.

Balance Sheet Accounts	Balance: Beginning of Period	Recog. Sales on Acct. 1	Cash Collect. From Cus. 2	Recog. COGS 3	Pur. Of Mer. On Acct. 4	Cash Pay. For Merchn. 5	Recog. Int. Exp. 6	Int. Paid 7	Recog. Depre. Exp. 8	Recog. Of Oper. Exp. 8	Cash Paid for Prepay. 9	Recog. Mort. Paid 10	Recog. Div. Dec. & Paid 11	Check on Ending Bal. Sheet Amts. 12	Balance: End of 2008
ASSETS															
Current Assets:															
Cash	20,000		85,000			-55,000		-2,000			-26,000	-3,000	-10,000	9,000	9,000
Accounts Receivable	36,000	100,000	-85,000											51,000	51,000
Merchandise Inventory	45,000			-50,000	65,000									60,000	60,000
Prepayments	2,000									-27,000	26,000			1,000	1,000
Total Current Assets	103,000													121,000	121,000
Noncurrent Assets:															
Land, Buildings, & Equip.	40,000													40,000	40,000
Accumulated Depreciation	-16,000								-2,000					-18,000	(18,000)
Total Noncurrent Assets	24,000													22,000	22,000
Total Assets	127,000													143,000	143,000
LIABILITIES AND SHAREHOLDERS' EQUITY															
Current Liabilities:															
Interest Payable	1,000						3,000	-2,000						2,000	2,000
Accounts Payable	30,000				65,000	-55,000								40,000	40,000
Total Current Liabilities	31,000													42,000	42,000
Noncurrent Liabilities:															
Mortgage Payable	20,000											-3,000		17,000	17,000
Total Noncurrent Liabilities	20,000													17,000	17,000
Total Liabilities	51,000													59,000	59,000
Shareholders' Equity:															
Common Stock	50,000													50,000	50,000
Retained Earnings	26,000	100,000		-50,000			-3,000		-2,000	-27,000			-10,000	34,000	34,000
Total Shareholders' Equity	76,000													84,000	84,000
Total Liabilities and Shareholders' Equity	127,000													143,000	143,000
Imbalance, if Any	-	-	-	-	-	-	-	-	-	-	-	-	-	-	-
Income Statement Accounts		Sales Rev.		COGS			Int. Exp.		Ot. Oper. Exp.	Ot. Oper. Exp.					

2.44 (Tertia Company; working backwards to income statements.)

A T-account method for deriving the solution appears below and on the following page. Transactions (1)–(9) correspond to the numbered cash transactions information. In Transactions (10)–(25), "p" indicates that the figure was derived by a "plug" and "c" indicates a closing entry. The final check is that the debit to close Income Summary in Transaction (25) matches the plug in the Retained Earnings account.

Cash					Accounts and Notes Receivable			
Bal.	40,000				Bal.	36,000		
(1)	144,000	114,000	(4)		(10p)	149,000	144,000	(1)
(2)	63,000	5,000	(5)					
(3)	1,000	500	(6)					
		57,500	(7)					
		1,200	(8)					
		2,000	(9)					
Bal.	67,800				Bal.	41,000		

Merchandise Inventory					Interest Receivable			
Bal.	55,000				Bal.	1,000		
(14)	121,000	126,500	(15p)		(11p)	700	1,000	(3)
Bal.	49,500				Bal.	700		

Prepaid Miscellaneous Services					Building, Machinery, and Equipment		
Bal.	4,000				Bal.	47,000	
(7)	57,500	56,300	(12p)				
Bal.	5,200				Bal.	47,000	

Accounts Payable (Miscellaneous Services)					Accounts Payable (Merchandise)			
		2,000	Bal.				34,000	Bal.
		500	(13p)		(4)	114,000	121,000	(14p)
		2,500	Bal.				41,000	Bal.

Property Tax Payable					Accumulated Depreciation		
		1,000	Bal.				10,000	Bal.
(8)	1,200	1,700	(16p)				2,000	(17p)
		1,500	Bal.				12,000	Bal.

Solutions 2-52

2.44 continued.

Mortgage Payable				Common Stock		
(5)	5,000	35,000	Bal.		25,000	Bal.
		30,000	Bal.		25,000	Bal.

Retained Earnings				Sales		
		76,000	Bal.		63,000	(2)
(9)	2,000	25,200	(18p)	(18c) 212,000	149,000	(10)
		99,200	Bal.			

Cost of Goods Sold				Interest Expense		
(15)	126,500	126,500	(18c)	(6)	500	500 (18c)

Interest Revenue				Miscellaneous Expenses		
(18c)	700	700	(11)	(12)	56,300	
				(13)	500	56,800 (18c)

Property Tax Expense				Depreciation Expense		
(16)	1,700	1,700	(18c)	(17)	2,000	2,000 (18c)

2.44 continued.

Transactions spreadsheet.

Balance Sheet Accounts	Balance: Beginning of Period	Collect. From Credit Cust. 1	Recog. Sales Rev. 2	Collect. Of Interest 3a	Recog. Int. Rev. 3b	Pay. To Sup. Of Merchn. 4	Pur. Of Merchn. 5	Recog. COGS 6	Repay. Of Mort. 7	Pay. Of Int. 8	Pay. For Misc. Ser. 9	Acq. Of Misc. Ser. 10	Pay. For Prop. Taxes 11	Recog. Prop. Tax Exp. 12	Dec. and Pay. Div. 13	Recog. Depre. Exp. 14	Check on Ending Bal. Sheet Amts. 15	Balance: End of 2008
ASSETS																		
Current Assets:																		
Cash	40,000	144,000	63,000	1,000		-114,000			-5,000	-500	-57,500		-1,200		-2,000		67,800	67,800
Accounts & Notes Rec.	36,000	-144,000	149,000														41,000	41,000
Merchandise Inventory	55,000						121,000	-126,500									49,500	49,500
Interest Receivable	1,000			-1,000	700												700	700
Prepaid Misc. Services	4,000										1,200						5,200	5,200
Total Current Assets	136,000																164,200	164,200
Noncurrent Assets:																		
Bldg., Mach., & Equipment	47,000																47,000	47,000
Accumulated Depreciation	-10,000															-2,000	(12,000)	(12,000)
Total Noncurrent Assets	37,000																35,000	35,000
Total Assets	173,000																199,200	199,200
LIABILITIES AND SHAREHOLDERS' EQUITY																		
Current Liabilities:																		
Accounts Pay. (miscellaneous ser.)	2,000										-56,300	56,800					2,500	2,500
Accounts Pay. (mer. pur.)	34,000					-114,000	121,000										41,000	41,000
Property Taxes Payable	1,000												-1,200	1,700			1,500	1,500
Total Current Liabilities	37,000																45,000	45,000
Noncurrent Liabilities:																		
Mortgage Payable	35,000								-5,000								30,000	30,000
Total Noncurrent Liabilities	35,000																30,000	30,000
Total Liabilities	72,000																75,000	75,000
Shareholders' Equity:																		
Common Stock	25,000																25,000	25,000
Retained Earnings	76,000		212,000		700			-126,500		-500		-56,800		-1,700	-2,000	-2,000	99,200	99,200
Total Shareholders' Equity	101,000																124,200	124,200
Total Liabilities and Shareholders' Equity	173,000																199,200	199,200
Imbalance, if Any		-	-	-	-	-	-	-	-	-	-	-	-	-	-	-	-	-
Income Statement Accounts			Sales Rev.		Int. Rev.			COGS		Int. Exp.	Mis. Ser. Exp.			Prop. Tax Exp.		Depre. Exp.		

2.44 continued.

TERTIA COMPANY
Statement of Income and Retained Earnings for 2008

Revenues:		
Sales..	$212,000	
Interest Revenue..	700	
Total Revenues..		$212,700
Expenses:		
Cost of Goods Sold...	$126,500	
Property Tax Expense..	1,700	
Depreciation Expense..	2,000	
Interest Expense	500	
Miscellaneous Expenses..	56,800	
Total Expenses..		187,500
Net Income...		$ 25,200
Less Dividends..		(2,000)
Increase in Retained Earnings......................................		$ 23,200
Retained Earnings, Beginning of Year		76,000
Retained Earnings, End of Year...................................		$ 99,200

2.45 (Preparing adjusting entries.)

a. The Prepaid Rent account on the year-end balance sheet should represent eight months of prepayments. The rent per month is $2,000 (= $24,000/12), so the balance required in the Prepaid Rent account is $16,000 (= 8 x $2,000). Rent Expense for 2006 is $8,000 (= 4 x $2,000 = $24,000 − $16,000).

Prepaid Rent...	16,000	
Rent Expense..		16,000

Assets	= Liabilities	+	Shareholders' Equity	(Class.)
+16,000			+16,000	IncSt → RE

To increase the balance in the Prepaid Rent account, reducing the amount in the Rent Expense account.

b. The Prepaid Rent account on the balance sheet for the end of 2007 should represent eight months of prepayments. The rent per month is $2,500 (= $30,000/12), so the required balance in the Prepaid Rent account is $20,000 (= 8 x $2,500). The balance in that account is already $16,000, so the adjusting entry must increase it by $4,000 (= $20,000 − $16,000).

2.45 b. continued.

Prepaid Rent 4,000
    Rent Expense 4,000

Assets	=	Liabilities	+	Shareholders' Equity	(Class.)
+4,000				+4,000	IncSt → RE

To increase the balance in the Prepaid Rent account, reducing the amount in the Rent Expense account.

The Rent Expense account will have a balance at the end of 2007 before closing entries of $26,000 (= $30,000 − $4,000). This amount comprises $16,000 (= $2,000 x 8) for rent from January through August and $10,000 (= $2,500 x 4) for rent from September through December.

c. The Prepaid Rent account on the balance sheet at the end of 2008 should represent two months of prepayments. The rent per month is $3,000 (= $18,000/6), so the required balance in the Prepaid Rent account is $6,000 (= 2 x $3,000). The balance in that account is $20,000, so the adjusting entry must reduce it by $14,000 (= $20,000 − $6,000).

Rent Expense 14,000
    Prepaid Rent 14,000

Assets	=	Liabilities	+	Shareholders' Equity	(Class.)
−14,000				−14,000	IncSt → RE

To decrease the balance in the Prepaid Rent account, increasing the amount in the Rent Expense account.

The Rent Expense account will have a balance at the end of 2008 before closing entries of $32,000 (= $18,000 + $14,000). This amount comprises $20,000 (= $2,500 x 8) for rent from January through August and $12,000 (= $3,000 x 4) for rent from September through December.

d. The Wages Payable account should have a credit balance of $4,000 at the end of April, but it has a balance of $5,000 carried over from the end of March. The adjusting entry must reduce the balance by $1,000, which requires a debit to the Wages Payable account.

2.45 d. continued.

Wages Payable... 1,000
    Wage Expense 1,000

Assets	=	Liabilities	+	Shareholders' Equity	(Class.)
		−1,000		+1,000	IncSt → RE

To reduce the balance in the Wages Payable account, reducing the amount in the Wage Expense account.

Wage Expense is $29,000 (= $30,000 − $1,000).

e. The Prepaid Insurance account balance of $3,000 represents four months of coverage. Thus, the cost of insurance is $750 (= $3,000/4) per month. The adjusting entry for a single month is as follows:

Insurance Expense... 750
    Prepaid Insurance 750

Assets	=	Liabilities	+	Shareholders' Equity	(Class.)
−750				−750	IncSt → RE

To recognize cost of one month's insurance cost as expense of the month.

f. The Advances from Tenants account has a balance of $25,000 carried over from the start of the year. At the end of 2007, it should have a balance of $30,000. Thus, the adjusting entry must increase the balance by $5,000, which requires a credit to the liability account.

Rent Revenue... 5,000
    Advance from Tenants... 5,000

Assets	=	Liabilities	+	Shareholders' Equity	(Class.)
		+5,000		−5,000	IncSt → RE

To increase the balance in the Advances from Tenants account, reducing the amount in the Rent Revenue account.

Rent Revenue for 2007 is $245,000 (= $250,000 − $5,000).

2.45 continued.

g. The Depreciation Expense for the year should be $2,000 (= $10,000/5). The balance in the Accumulated Depreciation account should also be $2,000; thus, the firm must credit Retained Earnings (Depreciation Expense) by $8,000 (= $10,000 − $2,000). The adjusting entry not only reduces recorded depreciation for the period but also sets up the asset account and its accumulated depreciation contra account.

Equipment..	10,000	
Accumulated Depreciation..		2,000
Depreciation Expense		8,000

Assets	= Liabilities	+	Shareholders' Equity	(Class.)
+10,000			+8,000	IncSt → RE
−2,000				

To reduce the recorded amount in Depreciation Expense from $10,000 to $2,000, setting up the asset and its contra account.

CHAPTER 3

BALANCE SHEET: PRESENTING AND ANALYZING RESOURCES AND FINANCING

Questions, Exercises, and Problems: Answers and Solutions

3.1　See the text or the glossary at the end of the book.

3.2　Conservatism emphasizes the early recognition of losses and delayed recognition of gains. Based on the conservatively reported earnings, a shareholder might sell shares of stock based on the assessment that the firm is not performing well. If the economic or "true" earnings of the firm are larger, the shareholder's assessment would result in a poor decision. Alternatively, shareholders might dismiss the management of a firm because they feel the firm is not performing well. It should be emphasized here that the principal objective of accounting reports as currently prepared is to present *fairly* the results of operations and the financial condition of the firm. Both U.S. GAAP and IFRS require reporting that results in the more conservative measurement of earnings.

3.3　One justification relates to the requirement that an asset or liability be measured with sufficient reliability. When there is an exchange between a firm and some other entity, there is market evidence of the economic effects of the transaction. The independent auditor verifies these economic effects by referring to contracts, cancelled checks and other documents underlying the transaction. If accounting recognized events without such a market exchange (for example, the increase in market value of a firm's assets), increased subjectivity would enter into the preparation of the financial statements.

3.4　The underlying principle is that acquisition cost includes all costs required to prepare an asset for its intended use. Assets provide future services. Costs that a firm must incur to obtain those expected services add value to the asset, and are included in the acquisition cost measurement of the asset.

3.5　The justification relates to the uncertainty as to the ultimate economic effects of the contracts. One party or the other may pull out of the contract. The accountant may not know the benefits and costs of the contract at the time of signing. Until one party or the other begins to perform under the contract, accounting usually gives no recognition. Accountants often disclose significant contracts of this nature in the notes to the financial statements.

3.6 Accountants record assets at acquisition cost. Cash discounts reduce acquisition cost and, therefore, the amount recorded for merchandise or equipment.

3.7
a. The contract between the investors and the construction company as well as cancelled checks provide evidence as to the acquisition cost.

b. Adjusted acquisition cost differs from the amount in Part *a.* by the portion of acquisition cost applicable to the services of the asset consumed during the first five years. There are several generally accepted methods of computing this amount (discussed in Chapter 9). A review of the accounting records for the office building should indicate how the firm calculated this amount.

c. There are at least two possibilities for ascertaining current replacement cost. One alternative is to consult a construction company to determine the cost of constructing a similar office building (that is, with respect to location, materials, size). The accountant would then adjust the current cost of constructing a new building downward to reflect the used condition of the five-year old office building. The current replacement cost amount could be reduced by 12.5% (= 5/40) if the asset's service potential decreases evenly with age. The actual economic decline in the value of the building during the first five years is likely to differ from 12.5% and, therefore, some other rate is probably appropriate. A second alternative for ascertaining current replacement cost is to consult a real estate dealer to determine the cost of acquiring a used office building providing services similar to the building that the investors own. The accountant might encounter difficulties in locating such a similar building.

d. The accountant might consult a local real estate dealer to ascertain the current market price, net of transactions cost, at which the investors might sell the building. There is always the question as to whether an interested buyer could be found at the quoted price. The accountant might also use any recent offers to purchase the building received by the investors.

e. The accountant might use the amount described in Part *d.* but exclude transactions cost when measuring fair value. The accountant might also measure fair value using the present value of the future net cash flows based on estimated rental receipts and operating expenses (excluding depreciation) for the building's remaining 35-year life. These cash flows are then discounted to the present using an appropriate rate of interest. The inputs to the fair value measurement are those that a market participant would use.

3.8 a. Liability—Receivable from Supplier or Prepaid Merchandise Orders.

b. Liability—Investment in Bonds.

c. Asset—Interest Payable.

d. Asset—Insurance Premiums Received in Advance.

e. Liability—Prepaid Rent.

3.9 a. Yes; amount of accrued interest payable.

b. Yes. Because of the indefiniteness of the time of delivery of the goods or services and the amount, the balance sheet reports a liability in the amount of the cash received.

c. No; accounting does not record executory promises.

d. Yes; at the present value, calculated using the yield rate at the time of issue, of the remaining coupon and principal payments.

e. Yes; at the expected, undiscounted value of future service costs arising from all sales made prior to the balance sheet date. The income statement includes warranty expense because of a desire to match all expenses of a sale with the sale; presumably, one reason the firm sold the product was the promise of free repairs. When recognizing the expense, the accountant credits a liability account to recognize the need for the future expenditures.

f. No. If the firm expected to lose a reasonably estimable amount in the suit, then it would show an estimated liability.

g. Yes, assuming statutes or contracts require the restoration. The present value of an estimate of the costs is the theoretically correct answer, but many accountants would use the full amount undiscounted.

h. No; viewed as executory.

i. Airlines recognize an expense and a liability for future services as passengers accumulate miles at regular fares, as those passengers reach award levels (for example, 30,000 flown miles). The measurement of the liability might be based on the estimated incremental cost of providing flights in exchange for miles, or on the estimated fair value of the flight services that passengers receive in exchange for accumulated miles.

3.10 a. The expected value of the liability is $90,000 in both cases (.90 × $100,000 = $90,000; .09 × $1 × 1,000,000 = $90,000). However, under both U.S. GAAP and IFRS, the liability from the lawsuit would be measured as $100,000, the most likely settlement amount.

b. The liability for the coupons would be measured at $90,000.

The inconsistency in the answers to Part *a.* and Part *b.* seems curious since the two situations differ only with respect to the number of possible outcomes (that is, all or nothing with respect to the lawsuit, whereas the coupon redemption rate conceivably ranges from one to one million).

3.11 a. In the definitions of assets and liabilities, *probable* is used to capture the idea that in commercial operations nothing can be entirely certain. It is used in its ordinary sense to refer to that which can be reasonably expected.

b. In the recognition criteria for liabilities with uncertain amount and/or timing, *probable* is used in U.S. GAAP to refer to a relatively high threshold of likelihood—a rule of thumb used in practice is approximately 80%. In IFRS, *probable* as recognition criterion for liabilities with uncertain amount and/or timing means "more likely than not"—approximately 51%.

3.12 (Aracruz Celulose; balance sheet formats.)

a. **U.S. GAAP Balance Sheet**. Assets and liabilities are listed on the balance sheet in order of decreasing liquidity, so the most liquid assets (liabilities) are shown first, under their respective categories.

ARACRUZ CELULOSE
Balance Sheet
For the Year Ended December 31, 2006
(Amounts in Thousands)

Assets

Current Assets:	
Cash and Short-Term Investments	$ 579,643
Accounts Receivable	285,795
Inventories	202,704
Other Current Assets	132,782
Total Current Assets	$ 1,200,924
Noncurrent Assets:	
Property, Plant and Equipment, Net	$ 2,151,212
Goodwill	192,035
Other Noncurrent Assets	451,757
Total Noncurrent Assets	$ 2,795,004
Total Assets	$ 3,995,928

3.12 a. continued.

Liabilities and Shareholders' Equity

Current Liabilities	$ 286,819
Noncurrent Liabilities:	
Long-Term Debt	$ 1,155,050
Other Long-Term Liabilities	350,761
Total Noncurrent Liabilities	1,505,811
Shareholders' Equity:	
Common Stock (No Par)	$ 295,501
Preferred Stock	614,496
Retained Earnings	1,293,301
Total Shareholders' Equity	$ 2,203,298
Total Liabilities and Shareholders' Equity	$ 3,995,928

b. **IFRS Balance Sheet.** Note that IFRS permits firms discretion as to how they list assets and liabilities on their balance sheet. One acceptable format is identical to that shown in Part *a.*, the other is to list assets and liabilities in increasing order of liquidity, as shown below.

ARACRUZ CELULOSE
Balance Sheet
For the Year Ended December 31, 2006
(Amounts in Thousands)

Assets

Noncurrent Assets:	
Other Noncurrent Assets	$ 451,757
Goodwill	192,035
Property, Plant and Equipment, Net	2,151,212
Total Noncurrent Assets	$ 2,795,004
Current Assets:	
Other Current Assets	$ 132,782
Inventories	202,704
Accounts Receivable	285,795
Cash and Short-Term Investments	579,643
Total Current Assets	$ 1,200,924
Total Assets	$ 3,995,928

Liabilities and Shareholders' Equity

Shareholders' Equity:	
Common Stock (No Par)	$ 295,501
Preferred Stock	614,496
Retained Earnings	1,293,301
Total Shareholders' Equity	$ 2,203,298
Noncurrent Liabilities:	
Other Long-Term Liabilities	$ 350,761
Long-Term Debt	1,155,050
Total Noncurrent Liabilities	$ 1,505,811
Current Liabilities	$ 286,819
Total Liabilities and Shareholders' Equity	$ 3,995,928

3.13 (Delhaize Group; balance sheet formats.)

DELHAIZE GROUP
Balance Sheet
For the Year Ended December 31, 2007
(Amounts in Millions of Euros)

Assets

Current Assets:	
Cash and Cash Equivalents	€ 248.9
Receivables	564.6
Inventories	1,262.0
Other Current Assets	121.5
Total Current Assets	€ 2,197.0
Noncurrent Assets:	
Property, Plant and Equipment	€ 3,383.1
Intangible Assets	552.1
Goodwill	2,445.7
Other Noncurrent Assets	244.0
Total Noncurrent Assets	€ 6,624.9
Total Assets	€ 8,821.9

Liabilities and Shareholders' Equity

Current Liabilities:	
Accounts Payable	€ 1,435.8
Accrued Expenses	375.7
Income Tax Payable	58.7
Short-Term Borrowings	41.5
Long-Term Debt, Current Portion	108.9
Obligations under Finance Lease, Current Portion	39.0
Provisions	41.8
Other Current Liabilities	119.3
Total Current Liabilities	€ 2,220.7
Noncurrent Liabilities:	
Long-Term Debt	€ 1,911.7
Obligations under Finance Leases	595.9
Provisions	207.2
Other Noncurrent Liabilities	210.4
Total Noncurrent Liabilities	€ 2,925.2
Total Liabilities	€ 5,145.9
Shareholders' Equity:	
Share Capital	€ 50.1
Share Premium	2,698.9
Retained Earnings	2,355.3
Other Reserves and Adjustments	(1,428.3)
Total Shareholders' Equity	€ 3,676.0
Total Liabilities and Shareholders' Equity	€ 8,821.9

3.14 (Classifying financial statement accounts.) (Unless indicated, classifications do not differ between U.S. GAAP and IFRS.)

a. NA.

b. NI (revenue).

c. CC.

d. NI (U.S. GAAP); NI and NA (IFRS). Under U.S. GAAP, all R&D expenditures are expensed in the period incurred. Under IFRS, the portion of R&D associated with research is expensed in the period incurred; development (D) expenditures are capitalized as a noncurrent asset on the firm's balance sheet, if the expenditures are on a product that has reached a sufficient stage (called technological feasibility).

e. NA.

f. CA.

g. X.

h. NI (expense).

i. CA.

j. CL.

k. X (U.S. GAAP); X or NA (IFRS). Under U.S. GAAP, an increase in the value of the land would not be recognized as a gain until the firm sells the land. Under IFRS, the firm has the option to revalue the land upward prior to sale.

l. RE.

m. CL.

n. NL.

o. CL.

3.15 (Genting Group; balance sheet relations.)

The missing items appear in boldface type below (amounts in millions of ringgit, RM).

	2007	2006	2005	2004
Current Assets	RM 10,999.2	RM **9,507.3**	RM 7,202.2	RM 6,882.6
Noncurrent Assets	**19,179.7**	18,717.4	11,289.1	9,713.9
Total Assets	RM **30,178.9**	RM 28,224.7	RM **18,491.3**	RM 16,596.5
Current Liabilities	RM **2,919.9**	RM 4,351.3	RM 1,494.2	RM 1,755.2
Noncurrent Liabilities	5,721.7	**7,206.5**	7,995.1	3,540.7
Shareholders' Equity	21,537.3	16,666.9	9,002.0	**11,300.6**
Total Liabilities and Shareholders' Equity	RM 30,178.9	RM **28,224.7**	RM 18,491.3	RM **16,596.5**

3.16 (Kajima; balance sheet relations.)

The missing items appear in boldface type below (amounts in billions of yen).

	2007	2006	2005	2004
Current Assets	¥ 1,323	¥ 1,133	¥ **1,100**	¥ 1,110
Noncurrent Assets	**784**	773	703	**760**
Total Assets	¥ **2,107**	¥ **1,906**	¥ 1,803	¥ 1,870
Current Liabilities	¥ 1,318	¥ 1,148	¥ 1,172	¥ 1,172
Noncurrent Liabilities	437	460	411	467
Total Liabilities	¥ **1,755**	¥ **1,608**	¥ 1,583	¥ **1,639**
Shareholders' Equity	**352**	298	220	**231**
Total Liabilities and Shareholders' Equity	¥ **2,107**	¥ **1,906**	¥ **1,803**	¥ **1,870**

3.17 (Metso; balance sheet relations.)

The missing items appear in boldface type below (amounts in millions of euros).

	2007	2006	2005	2004
Current Assets	€ 3,357	€ 2,995	€ 2,477	€ 2,097
Noncurrent Assets	**1,897**	1,973	**1,427**	**1,473**
Total Assets	€ **5,254**	€ **4,968**	€ **3,904**	€ **3,570**
Current Liabilities	€ **2,706**	€ 2,610	€ 1,802	€ 1,466
Noncurrent Liabilities	957	**908**	810	1,109
Total Liabilities	€ **3,663**	€ **3,518**	€ **2,612**	€ **2,575**
Contributed Capital	€ **681**	€ 711	€ 739	€ 634
Retained Earnings	910	739	553	361
Total Shareholders' Equity	€ **1,591**	€ **1,450**	€ **1,292**	€ **995**
Total Liabilities and Shareholders' Equity	€ 5,254	€ 4,968	€ 3,904	€ 3,570

3.18   (Ford Models; asset and liability recognition and measurement.)

Accounting does not normally recognize mutually unexecuted contracts as assets or liabilities. This contract between Danielle Evans and Ford Models is partially executed to the extent that Ford Models provides the car at the time of signing. Because the modeling agency will receive the services of Danielle Evans beginning next year, it recognizes an asset, Advances on Contracts, of $70,000 on its balance sheet at the time of signing.

3.19   (Duke University; asset recognition and measurement.)

The expenditures do not qualify as an asset because: (1) Duke University cannot point to a specific future economic benefit that it controls (employees can choose to work elsewhere even though doing so sacrifices the tuition benefit), and (2) there is not a reasonably reliable measurement attribute for this benefit.

3.20   (Trader Joe's; asset measurement.)

The acquisition cost of the refrigeration system includes the purchase price of $1.3 million, the modification costs of $120,000, and the cost to transport and install the unit in the store of $55,000, for a total of $1,475,000. The insurance premium and the salary of the repairperson are operating expenses and are not part of the acquisition cost of the refrigeration system. Trader Joe's would show the amount paid for the insurance premium as a prepaid asset on its balance sheet (Prepaid Insurance). The salary of the repairperson is not recognized as an asset.

3.21   (Nordstrom; recognition of a loss contingency.)

a. Nordstrom should recognize the contingency as soon as it is probable that it has incurred a loss and it can reasonably estimate the amount of the loss. Whether the store recognizes a loss at the time of the injury on July 5, 2007, depends on the strength of the case the store feels it has against the customer's claims. If the cause of the accident was an escalator malfunction, then Nordstrom may determine it is probable that it has incurred a liability. If, on the other hand, the customer fell while running up the clearly identified down side of the escalator, then Nordstrom may determine that it is probable that it has not incurred a liability. Attorneys, not accountants, must make these probability assessments.

If Nordstrom does not recognize a loss at the time of the injury, the next most likely time is June 15, 2008, when the jury renders its verdict. Unless attorneys for the store conclude that it is probable that the court will reverse the verdict on appeal, Nordstrom should recognize the loss at this time.

3.21 a. continued.

If attorneys feel that the grounds for appeal are strong, then the next most likely time to record the loss is on April 20, 2009, when the jury in the lower court reaches the same verdict as previously. This is the latest time in this case, at which the store should recognize the loss. If the store had recognized a loss on June 15, 2008, in the amount of $400,000, it would recognize only the extra damage award of $100,000 on April 20, 2009.

b. Under IFRS, the threshold for recognition is also probable but the meaning differs, such that a lower probability (more than 50%) will result in liability recognition under IFRS than under U.S. GAAP (more than approximately 80%).

3.22 (Nestlé; asset recognition and measurement.)

a. Both U.S. GAAP and IFRS would recognize Investment in Bond (noncurrent asset), CHF800 million. Nestlé would record the bond at acquisition cost, not the amount it will receive at maturity.

b. Both U.S. GAAP and IFRS would recognize Prepaid Insurance (current asset); CHF240 million would be recorded initially. At Nestlé's year-end, the balance in the Prepaid Insurance account would reflect the two months usage of the insurance, reducing the balance to CHF200 [= CHF240 − (CHF240 x 2/12)] million.

c. Both U.S. GAAP and IFRS would recognize Option to Purchase Land (noncurrent asset), CHF6 million.

d. Neither U.S. GAAP nor IFRS recognizes the employment contract, a mutually unexecuted contract, as an asset.

e. Under U.S. GAAP, Nestlé would record only the costs of obtaining the patent as an asset on its balance sheet, Patent (noncurrent asset), CHF0.5 million. The remaining CHF80 million is an expense of the period. Under IFRS, Nestlé would recognize Research Expense of CHF48 (= 60% x CHF80) million in the period incurred and record a Development Asset (noncurrent asset) at the acquisition cost of CHF32 million (= 40% of CHF80 million) as an asset on its balance sheet, which it would depreciate over the useful life of the product. Under IFRS, Nestlé would also recognize the patent as an asset on its balance sheet, Patent (noncurrent asset), CHF0.5 million.

f. Under both U.S. GAAP and IFRS, Nestlé would not recognize the cocoa beans as an asset until it receives the inventory.

3.23 (Ryanair Holdings; asset recognition and measurement.)

a. Under both U.S. GAAP and IFRS, a decision on the part of Ryanair's board of directors does not give rise to an asset.

b. Under both U.S. GAAP and IFRS, Ryanair's placing of an order does not give rise to an asset.

c. Under both U.S. GAAP and IFRS, Ryanair's payment gives rise to an asset on their balance sheet, Deposit on Aircraft (noncurrent asset), €60 million.

d. Under both U.S. GAAP and IFRS, Ryanair's purchase gives rise to an asset, Landing Rights (noncurrent asset), €50 million.

e. Under both U.S. GAAP and IFRS, Ryanair's purchase gives rise to an asset on their balance sheet, Equipment (noncurrent asset), €77 million. Ryanair would also record a liability, Mortgage Note Payable (noncurrent), HK$65 million.

f. Under both U.S. GAAP and IFRS, Ryanair's purchase gives rise to an asset, Equipment (noncurrent asset), €160 million. The carrying, or book, value of the aircraft on the seller's books is not relevant to Ryanair's recording of the purchase.

3.24 (Hana Microelectronic Public Company Limited; liability recognition and measurement.)

a. Under both U.S. GAAP and IFRS, this arrangement is a mutually unexecuted contract; as such, it does not give rise to a liability on Hana Microelectronics balance sheet.

b. Under both U.S. GAAP and IFRS, Hana Microelectronics would record Advances from Customers (current liability), Bt168 million.

c. Under both U.S. GAAP and IFRS, Hana Microelectronics would record Advances from Customers (current liability), Bt84 million and Advances from Customers (noncurrent liability), Bt84 million.

d. Under both U.S. GAAP and IFRS, common stock does not meet the definition of a liability because the firm need not repay the funds in a particular amount at a particular time.

e. Under both U.S. GAAP and IFRS, Hana Microelectronic would record Notes Payable (current liability), Bt8 million, and Notes Payable (noncurrent liability), Bt16 million.

3.24 continued.

    f. Under both U.S. GAAP and IFRS, this arrangement is mutually unexecuted and, therefore, does not give rise to a liability.

    g. Under both U.S. GAAP and IFRS, this arrangement is mutually unexecuted and, therefore, does not give rise to a liability.

3.25 (Berlin Philharmonic; liability recognition and measurement.)

    a. Under both U.S. GAAP and IFRS, the Berlin Philharmonic would record Advances from Customers (current liability), €3,040,000.

    b. Under both U.S. GAAP and IFRS, the Berlin Philharmonic does not recognize a liability because it has not yet received benefits obligating it to pay.

    c. Under both U.S. GAAP and IFRS, the Berlin Philharmonic would record Accounts Payable (current liability), €185,000.

    d. Under both U.S. GAAP and IFRS, the Berlin Philharmonic would not normally recognize a liability for an unsettled lawsuit unless payment is probable and the entity can reliably estimate the loss. Because the suit has not yet come to trial, it is unclear whether any liability exists.

    e. Under both U.S. GAAP and IFRS, the Berlin Philharmonic would not recognize a liability for this mutually unexecuted contract.

    f. Under both U.S. GAAP and IFRS, accounting normally does not recognize a liability for mutually unexecuted contracts. Thus, at the time of contract signing, the Berlin Philharmonic would record no liability. In 2012, however, the firm would record a liability for the portion of the yearly compensation earned by Sir Simon Rattle each month, or Salary Payable (current liability), €0.167 million per month.

3.26 (Beyond Petroleum; liability recognition and measurement.)

Under both U.S. GAAP and IFRS, the recognition of a loss contingency requires that a loss be probable. Although U.S. GAAP does not define probable, a rule of thumb used in practice defines probable as greater than or equal to 80%; under IFRS, the threshold for probable is 51% (more likely than not). The measurement of the loss contingency depends first on whether it meets the recognition criterion; only if the loss is probable will it be measured and reported on the balance sheet. The measurement depends on which set of accounting standards is applied.

3.26 continued.

a. Refer to the above discussion of the recognition criteria under both U.S. GAAP and IFRS. The information given indicates that engineers view the probability of loss to be 10%. Because this probability does not meet the threshold percentages under U.S. GAAP or IFRS, no liability will be recorded under either set of accounting standards.

b. The probability of loss is now 51%. This meets the probable threshold under IFRS, but not under U.S. GAAP. Therefore, IFRS will show a liability on the balance sheet, but U.S. GAAP would not. The amount of the liability shown under IFRS would be the "best" estimate of the amount of future cash outflows. In this example, the best estimate could be either the outcome with the highest probability of occurrence, $5 million (with probability 51%) or it could be the expected loss $2.55 million (= 0.51 x $5 million + 0.49 x $0). IFRS provides enough latitude to permit either of these "best" estimates.

c. Under the environmentalists' estimates, there is a 100% probability of loss. Thus, both U.S. GAAP and IFRS would record a liability. The amount of the liability would vary under the two accounting approaches. Under U.S. GAAP, the firm would record the most likely amount of damages, or $4,000 million, because this is the estimate with the highest probability of occurrence (45% is greater than either 35% or 20%). Under IFRS, the firm would record the "best" estimate. The best estimate could be either the outcome with the highest probability of occurrence, $4,000 million (with probability 45%) or it could be the expected loss $1,910 million (= 0.45 x $4,000 million + 0.35 x $300 million + 0.20 x $25 million). IFRS provides enough latitude to permit either of these "best" estimates.

d. Under the environmentalists' estimates, the probability of loss is 85%. This exceeds the threshold for recognition of a liability under both U.S. GAAP and IFRS. Under U.S. GAAP, the amount recorded will be $5,000 million because this is the outcome with the highest probability of occurrence. The amount recorded under IFRS is the best estimate, which in this example is also likely to be $5,000 million.

3.27 (Magyar Telekom; effect of recording errors on balance sheet equation.) (Amounts in Millions)

Transaction Number	Assets	=	Liabilities	+	Shareholders' Equity
(1)	No		No		No
(2)	O/S HUF 900		O/S HUF 900		No
(3)	U/S HUF 14,500		U/S HUF 14,500		No
(4)	No[a]		No		No
(5)	U/S HUF 6,000		U/S HUF 6,000		No
(6)	U/S HUF 1,200		No		U/S HUF 1,200
(7)	No		No		No

[a]The value of total assets is correctly stated; the problem is that rather than debiting Property for the insurance payment, the firm should have debited Prepaid Insurance.

3.28 (Sivensa; effect of recording errors on balance sheet equation.) (Amounts in Thousands)

Transaction Number	Assets	=	Liabilities	+	Shareholders' Equity
(1)	U/S $ 8,000		U/S $ 8,000		No
(2)	O/S $ 4,000		O/S $ 4,000		No
(3)	U/S $ 800		U/S $ 800		No
(4)	O/S $ 1,000		O/S $ 1,000		No
(5)	U/S $ 2,500		No		U/S $2,500
(6)	O/S $ 4,900[a] U/S $ 4,900[a]		No		No

[a]The response "No" is also acceptable here.

Solutions 3-14

3.29 (Cathay Pacific; balance sheet format, terminology, and accounting methods.) [Amounts in Millions of HK Dollars (HKD)]

a.
CATHAY PACIFIC AIRWAYS LIMITED
Balance Sheet, U.S. GAAP
(Amounts in Millions of HKD)

	December 31, 2007	December 31, 2006
Assets		
Current Assets:		
Cash and Cash Equivalents[a]	HKD 21,649	HKD 15,624
Trade and Other Receivables	11,376	8,735
Inventory[b]	882	789
Assets Pledged Against Current Liabilities[c]	910	1,352
Total Current Assets	34,817	26,500
Noncurrent Assets:		
Investments in Associates	10,054	8,826
Fixed Assets	62,388	57,602
Other Long-Term Receivables and Investments	3,519	3,406
Intangible Assets	7,782	7,749
Assets Pledged Against Noncurrent Liabilities[d]	7,833	8,164
Total Noncurrent Assets	91,576	85,747
Total Assets	HKD 126,393	HKD 112,247
Liabilities and Shareholders' Equity		
Current Liabilities:		
Trade and Other Payables	HKD 14,787	HKD 10,999
Current Portion of Long-Term Liabilities	4,788	7,503
Unearned Transportation Revenue	6,254	4,671
Income Taxes Payable[e]	2,475	2,902
Total Current Liabilities	28,304	26,075
Noncurrent Liabilities:		
Long-Term Liabilities	40,323	33,956
Retirement Benefit Obligations	268	170
Deferred Tax Liability[f]	6,771	6,508
Total Noncurrent Liabilities	47,362	40,634
Total Liabilities	75,666	66,709
Minority Interests	178	152
Shareholders' Equity:		
Share Capital	788	787
Reserves	49,761	44,599
Total Shareholders' Equity	50,549	45,386
Total Liabilities and Shareholders' Equity[g]	HKD 126,393	HKD 112,247

Footnotes appear on following page.

3.29 a. continued.

Terminology (differences from account names reported by Cathay Pacific).

[a] Liquid Funds.
[b] Stock.
[c] Related Pledged Security Deposits (Current Portion of Long-Term Debt).
[d] Related Pledged Security Deposits (Noncurrent Portion of Long-Term Debt).
[e] Taxation.
[f] Deferred Taxation.
[g] Funds Attributable to Cathay Pacific Shareholders.

b.

CATHAY PACIFIC AIRWAYS LIMITED
Balance Sheet, IFRS
(Amounts in Millions of HKD)

	December 31, 2007	December 31, 2006
Assets		
Noncurrent Assets:		
Intangible Assets	HKD 7,782	HKD 7,749
Fixed Assets	62,388	57,602
Assets Pledged Against Noncurrent Liabilities[d]	7,833	8,164
Investments in Associates	10,054	8,826
Other Long-Term Receivables and Investments	3,519	3,406
Total Noncurrent Assets	91,576	85,747
Current Assets:		
Inventory[b]	882	789
Assets Pledged Against Current Liabilities[c]	910	1,352
Trade and Other Receivables	11,376	8,735
Cash and Cash Equivalents[a]	21,649	15,624
Total Current Assets	34,817	26,500
Total Assets	HKD 126,393	HKD 112,247

3.29 b. continued.

Liabilities and Shareholders' Equity

Noncurrent Liabilities:		
Long-Term Liabilities...............................	HKD 40,323	HKD 33,956
Retirement Benefit Obligations...........	268	170
Deferred Tax Liability[f].............................	6,771	6,508
Total Noncurrent Liabilities.............	47,362	40,634
Current Liabilities:		
Income Taxes Payable[e]........................	2,475	2,902
Trade and Other Payables....................	14,787	10,999
Current Portion of Long-Term Liabilities...	4,788	7,503
Unearned Transportation Revenue...	6,254	4,671
Total Current Liabilities...................	28,304	26,075
Total Liabilities...................................	75,666	66,709
Shareholders' Equity:		
Minority Interests..................................	178	152
Share Capital...	788	787
Reserves..	49,761	44,599
Total Shareholders' Equity...............	50,727	45,538
Total Liabilities and Shareholders' Equity[g]...	HKD 126,393	HKD 112,247

Terminology (differences from account names reported by Cathay Pacific).

[a] Liquid Funds.

[b] Stock.

[c] Related Pledged Security Deposits (Current Portion of Long-Term Debt).

[d] Related Pledged Security Deposits (Noncurrent Portion of Long-Term Debt).

[e] Taxation.

[f] Deferred Taxation.

[g] Funds Attributable to Cathay Pacific Shareholders.

3.30 (Infosys Technologies Limited; balance sheet format.)

a. Infosys Technologies Limited, U.S. GAAP formatted balance sheet.

INFOSYS TECHNOLOGIES LIMITED
Balance Sheet
(In Millions of Rs. Crore)

	March 31, 2008	March 31, 2007
Assets		
Current Assets:		
Cash and Cash Equivalents	Rs 6,429	Rs 5,470
Accounts Receivable	3,093	2,292
Other Current Assets	2,705	1,199
Total Current Assets	Rs 12,227	Rs 8,961
Noncurrent Assets:		
Investments	Rs 964	Rs 839
Property, Plant and Equipment	3,931	3,107
Deferred Tax Assets	99	79
Total Noncurrent Assets	Rs 4,994	Rs 4,025
Total Assets	Rs 17,221	Rs 12,986
Liabilities and Shareholders' Equity		
Current Liabilities	Rs 1,483	Rs 1,162
Provisions	2,248	662
Total Liabilities	Rs 3,731	Rs 1,824
Shareholders' Equity:		
Contributed Capital	Rs 286	Rs 286
Retained Earnings	13,204	10,876
Total Shareholders' Equity	Rs 13,490	Rs 11,162
Total Liabilities and Shareholders' Equity	Rs 17,221	Rs 12,986

3.30 continued.

b. Infosys Technologies Limited, IFRS formatted balance sheet.

INFOSYS TECHNOLOGIES LIMITED
Balance Sheet
(In Millions of Rs. Crore)

	March 31, 2008	March 31, 2007
Assets		
Noncurrent Assets:		
Property, Plant and Equipment	Rs 3,931	Rs 3,107
Deferred Tax Assets	99	79
Investments	964	839
Total Noncurrent Assets	Rs 4,994	Rs 4,025
Current Assets:		
Other Current Assets	Rs 2,705	Rs 1,199
Accounts Receivable	3,093	2,292
Cash and Cash Equivalents	6,429	5,470
Total Current Assets	Rs 12,227	Rs 8,961
Total Assets	Rs 17,221	Rs 1,824
Liabilities and Shareholders' Equity		
Provisions	Rs 2,248	Rs 662
Current Liabilities	1,483	1,162
Total Liabilities	Rs 3,731	Rs 1,824
Shareholders' Equity:		
Contributed Capital	Rs 286	Rs 286
Retained Earnings	13,204	10,876
Total Shareholders' Equity	Rs 13,490	Rs 11,162
Total Liabilities and Shareholders' Equity	Rs 17,221	Rs 12,986

3.31 (Ericsson; balance sheet format, terminology, and accounting methods.)

ERICCSON
U.S. GAAP Balance Sheet
For the Year Ended December 31, 2007
(Amounts in SEK Millions)

Assets

Current Assets:
Cash and Cash Equivalents	SEK	28,310
Short-Term Investments		29,406
Trade Receivables		60,492
Customer Financing, Current		2,362
Other Current Receivables		15,062
Inventories		22,475
Total Current Assets	SEK	158,107

Noncurrent Assets:
Equity in Joint Ventures	SEK	10,903
Other Investments in Shares		738
Customer Financing, Noncurrent		1,012
Other Financial Assets, Noncurrent		2,918
Deferred Tax Assets		11,690
Property, Plant and Equipment		8,404
Intellectual Property Rights, Brands		23,958
Goodwill		22,826
Total Noncurrent Assets	SEK	82,449
Total Assets	SEK	240,556

Liabilities and Shareholders' Equity

Current Liabilities:
Trade Payables	SEK	17,427
Borrowings, Current		5,896
Provisions, Current		8,858
Other Current Liabilities		44,995
Total Current Liabilities	SEK	77,176

Noncurrent Liabilities:
Provisions, Noncurrent	SEK	368
Borrowings, Noncurrent		21,320
Post-Employment Benefits		6,188
Deferred Tax Liabilities		2,799
Other Noncurrent Liabilities		1,714
Total Noncurrent Liabilities	SEK	32,389
Total Liabilities	SEK	109,565
Minority Interest		940
Shareholders' Equity		130,051
Total Liabilities and Equity	SEK	240,556

3.31 continued.

1. U.S. GAAP does not permit the capitalization of development costs. Removal of these costs reduces assets by SEK3,661 million, and reduces shareholders' equity (Retained Earnings) by SEK3,661 million.

2. U.S. GAAP does not permit the upward revaluation of land. In 2007, this upward revaluation led to land being stated at a value SEK900 million higher on Ericsson's balance sheet than would have been permitted under U.S.GAAP. The upward revaluation would also have been included as an unrealized gain, in Ericsson's shareholders' equity. To conform to U.S. GAAP, removal of the upward revaluation of the land would, therefore, reduce assets and shareholders' equity by SEK900 million for 2007.

3. Both U.S. GAAP and IFRS require assessments for impairment of noncurrent assets. Thus, the write down of the equipment in 2007 from SEK2,400 to SEK1,600 would also exist under U.S. GAAP.

4. From the information provided, the probability of loss is 60% for the patent infringement lawsuit. Thus, the lawsuit meets the IFRS threshold for recognition; it does not, however, meet the probable standard under U.S. GAAP (80%). Thus, under U.S. GAAP, Ericsson would not have recognized a liability for this lawsuit. Under IFRS, Ericsson would have recognized the "best" estimate as the amount of the liability. This best estimate was likely SEK500, since this is the amount of expected damages with the largest probability of occurring. Another best estimate that is possible is the expected value of the range of estimates, or SEK994 million. Whatever the best estimate, the amount would need to be removed from current provisions, and added back to shareholders' equity, to derecognize this liability under U.S. GAAP. The balance sheet shown above displays a best estimate of SEK500.

Summary Calculations for Shareholders' Equity:

Balance per Ericsson Balance Sheet, 2007 (IFRS)	SEK 134,112
Removal of Capitalized Development Costs That Would Be Expensed Under U.S. GAAP	(3,661)
Removal of Upward Revaluation of Land That Would Not Have Been Made under U.S. GAAP	(900)
Removal of Lawsuit Expense That Would Not Have Met the Standard for Recognition Under U.S. GAAP	500
Balance per Ericsson Balance Sheet, 2007 U.S. GAAP	SEK 130,051

3.32 (Texas Steakhouse; interpreting balance sheet changes.)

a. The principal assets of a restaurant are property, plant and equipment. These assets comprise two-thirds of the assets of Texas Steakhouse. Accounts receivable represent a small percentage of total assets because this restaurant either sells for cash or customers use third-party credit cards. Inventories likewise comprise a small percentage of total assets because of the need to turn over food products quickly. The firm used long-term financing to finance its investments in property, plant, and equipment. The surprising observation is that Texas Steakhouse used primarily shareholders' equity financing instead of long-term debt financing. Long-term debt financing is usually less costly as a source of funds. It appears that the firm obtained most of the funds needed for the acquisition of property, plant, and equipment from the retention of assets generated by earnings instead of issuing common stock.

b. The common-size percentage for cash increased significantly between 2007 and 2008 and the common-size percentage for other assets decreased significantly. One possible explanation is that the firm sold off other assets (perhaps investments in securities) for cash. The common-size percentage for common stock decreased and the common-size percentage for retained earnings increased. Perhaps the firm was very profitable during 2008 and retained a higher proportion of earnings, instead of paying a larger dividend. The firm may also have bought back some of its common stock with the assets generated by earnings.

c. The percentages in the common-size balance sheet are not independent of each other. A decrease in the dollar amount of property, plant, and equipment may result in an increasing, decreasing, or stable proportion for this balance sheet item, depending on the changes in other assets.

Solutions

3.33 (Cemex; common-size balance sheet and interpreting balance sheet changes.)

a. The common size balance sheet for Cemex for years 2007 and 2006 are shown below.

	2007		2006	
Assets				
Current Assets:				
Cash and Investments...............	$ 8,670	1.6%	$ 18,494	5.3%
Trade Receivables Less Allowance for Doubtful Accounts..	20,719	3.8%	16,525	4.7%
Other Accounts Receivable.......	9,830	1.8%	9,206	2.6%
Inventories, Net........................	19,631	3.6%	13,974	4.0%
Other Current Assets................	2,394	0.5%	2,255	0.6%
Total Current Assets............	$ 61,244	11.3%	$ 60,454	17.2%
Noncurrent Assets:				
Investments in Associates........	$ 10,599	2.0%	$ 8,712	2.5%
Other Investments in Noncurrent Accounts Receivable.....	10,960	2.0%	9,966	2.8%
Property, Machinery and Equipment, Net.......................	262,189	48.3%	201,425	57.4%
Goodwill, Intangible Assets and Deferred Charges............	197,322	36.4%	70,526	20.1%
Total Noncurrent Assets..	$481,070	88.7%	$290,629	82.8%
Total Assets.........................	$542,314	100.0%	$351,083	100.0%
Liabilities and Shareholders' Equity:				
Current Liabilities:				
Short-Term Debt Including Current Maturities of Long-Term Debt...............................	$ 36,257	6.7%	$ 14,657	4.2%
Trade Payables...........................	23,660	4.4%	20,110	5.7%
Other Accounts Payable and Accrued Expenses..................	23,471	4.3%	17,203	4.9%
Total Current Liabilities...	$ 83,388	15.4%	$ 51,970	14.8%

3.33 a. continued.

Noncurrent Liabilities:				
Long-Term Debt	$180,654	33.3%	$73,674	21.0%
Pension and Other Retirement Benefits	7,650	1.4%	7,484	2.1%
Deferred Income Tax Liability	50,307	9.3%	30,119	8.6%
Other Noncurrent Liabilities	16,162	3.0%	14,725	4.2%
Total Noncurrent Liabilities	$254,773	47.0%	$126,002	35.9%
Total Liabilities	$338,161	62.4%	$177,972	50.7%
Minority Interest	$ 40,985	7.6%	$ 22,484	6.4%
Shareholders' Equity:				
Common Stock	$ 4,115	0.8%	$ 4,113	1.2%
Additional Paid-in Capital	63,379	11.7%	56,982	16.2%
Less Other Equity Reserves	(104,574)	(19.3%)	(91,244)	(26.0%)
Retained Earnings	200,248	36.9%	180,776	51.5%
Total Shareholders' Equity	$163,168	30.1%	150,627	42.9%
Total Liabilities and Shareholders' Equity	$542,314	100.0%	$351,083	100.0%

b. The largest asset is property, plant, and equipment, which represents the generating and distribution capacity of the construction company. Long-term financing dominates the financing side of the balance sheet, with the largest proportion coming from long-term debt.

c. Between 2006 and 2007, Cemex decreased the percentage of tangible noncurrent assets and increased the percentage of intangible noncurrent assets on its balance sheet. In particular, property, plant and equipment decreased from 57.4% to 48.3% of total assets and intangible assets (including goodwill) increased from 20.1% to 36.4% of total assets. The net increase in noncurrent assets was financed by increased debt, as evidenced by the increase in the common size percentage of long-term borrowings from 21.0% to 33.3% of total assets. These data indicate that Cemex's capital expenditures were largely financed through increases in long term debt.

3.34 (Relating market value to book value of shareholders' equity.)

a. (1) **Coke**—One important asset missing from the balance sheet of Coke is the value of its brand names. Coke follows generally accepted accounting principles (U.S.GAAP) in expensing the cost of developing and maintaining its brand names each year (for example, product development, quality control, advertising). The future benefits of these expenditures are too difficult to identify and measure with sufficient precision to justify recognizing an asset. Coke also reports its property, plant, and equipment at acquisition

3.34 a. continued.

cost (adjusted downward for depreciation) instead of current market values. Acquisition cost valuations are more objective and easier to audit than current market valuations.

(2) **Bristol**—Bristol engages in research and development to discover new drugs. U.S. GAAP requires firms to expense research and development expenditures immediately. The future benefits of these expenditures are too uncertain to justify recognizing an asset. Thus, the value of patents and technologies developed by Bristol, as well as the value of the research scientists employed by Bristol, do not appear on its balance sheet.

(3) **Bankers Trust**—The market-to-book value ratio for Bankers is 1.0. Most of the assets and liabilities of Bankers are monetary items and turn over frequently. Thus, the market values and book values closely conform.

(4) **International Paper (IP)**—IP reports its forestlands on the balance sheet at acquisition cost. IP likely acquired the land many years ago. The acquisition cost of the land is considerably less than its current market value. Also, IP follows general industry practice and expenses the annual cost of maintaining its forest lands. Thus, the value of forest lands increases each year as trees grow. The market incorporates this value increase into its price of the common stock of IP even though U.S. GAAP does not reflect the value increase on the balance sheet. The value increase is too difficult to measure objectively to justify substituting market values for acquisition cost.

(5) **Disney**—Disney depreciates the cost of film inventory over its expected useful life. Fortunately for Disney and other film production companies, the value of old films has increased in recent years with the growth of cable networks. Thus, the market value of some of Disney's films exceeds their book values. The market-to-book value ratio reflects this under valuation. Also, Disney reports its property, plant and equipment at acquisition cost (adjusted downward for depreciation) instead of current market values. The land underlying its theme parks has likely increased in value since the date of acquisition, but the accounting records do not reflect the value increase under U.S. GAAP.

b. (1) **Coke**—Coke's current assets are less than its current liabilities. This relation indicates short-term liquidity risk. The high market-to-book value ratio suggests that the market value (selling price) of its inventory exceeds the book value, so current assets probably equal

3.34 b. continued.

or exceed current liabilities at market value. Shareholders' equity represents a higher proportion of long-term financing than long-term debt. One explanation for the relatively low proportion of long-term debt is that Coke is very profitable (suggested by the high market-to-book value ratio) and therefore generates most of its needed cash from operations. Further support for the internal generation of cash is the high proportion of retained earnings and significant treasury stock purchases. Another explanation for the relatively low proportion of long-term debt relates to the investments in its bottlers. Chapter 13 discusses the accounting for intercorporate investments. Because Coke owns less than 50% of the outstanding common stock of these bottlers, it does not consolidate them. Thus, the assets and the financing of the bottlers are "off balance sheet." These bottlers may carry significantly more long-term debt than Coke.

(2) **Bristol**—The interesting insight from studying Bristol's capital structure is the relatively small proportion of long-term debt. The products of Bristol are subject to technological obsolescence. Competitors could develop technologically superior drugs that would replace those of Bristol in the market. Given this product risk, Bristol probably does not want to add the financial risk that fixed interest and principal payments on debt create.

(3) **Bankers Trust**—Bankers relies heavily on short-term sources for financing, principally deposits and short-term borrowing. Customers can withdraw their funds on no, or very short, notice. Thus, Bankers must maintain a relatively liquid balance sheet. Most of its assets are in cash, short-term marketable securities, and loans. The loans are less liquid than cash and marketable securities but tend to have predictable cash flows. Note that shareholders' equity makes up approximately 5% of liabilities plus shareholders' equities. Such a low percentage is common for commercial banks. Banks carry high proportions of liabilities because of the high liquidity of their assets.

(4) **International Paper (IP)**—IP carries a high proportion of noncurrent assets and matches this with a high proportion of long-term financing. IP uses approximately equal proportions of long-term liabilities and shareholders' equity to finance its noncurrent assets. The sales of paper products vary with movements through economic cycles. During recessionary periods, demand slackens and firms reduce prices in order to utilize capital-intensive manufacturing facilities. Paper companies do not want too much debt in

3.34 b. continued.

their capital structures that could force them into bankruptcy during these times. On the other hand, when the economy is booming, the profits and cash flows of paper companies increase significantly. Firms spread the cost of their capital-intensive plants over larger volumes of output. In these cases, shareholders benefit from debt in the capital structure (a phenomenon known as *financial leverage*, discussed in Chapter 5). Thus, the approximately equal proportions of long-term debt and shareholders' equity reflect these opposing considerations.

(5) **Disney**—Disney reports a significant excess of current assets over current liabilities. Interpreting this excess involves two opposing considerations. Some of Disney's films continue to generate revenues and cash flows, even though the films carry a zero book value on Disney's books. On the other hand, Disney accumulates the cost of films in process in the inventory account without knowing whether or not the films will be a commercial success. Disney uses a higher proportion of shareholders' equity than long-term debt in its long-term financing structure. Its property, plant and equipment can serve as collateral for long-term borrowing. Its predictable revenue and cash flows from theme parks also argues for a high proportion of long-term debt relative to shareholders' equity. Perhaps Disney did not want to use up its borrowing capacity in case it had the opportunity to make an acquisition (such as Capital Cities/ABC) and needed to borrow to finance the transaction.

3.35 (Relating market value to book value of shareholders' equity.)

a. (1) **Pfizer**—Pharmaceutical firms make ongoing expenditures on research and development (R&D) to develop new products. Some of these expenditures result in profitable new products, while other expenditures do not provide any future benefit. The difficulty encountered in trying to identify whether or not a particular R&D expenditure results in a future benefit has led accounting standard setters to require the immediate expensing of R&D costs in the year incurred. Thus, the valuable patents for pharmaceutical products and the value of potential products in the research pipeline do not appear on the balance sheet of Pfizer. The market does place a value on these technologies in deciding on an appropriate market price for the firm's stock.

Students might suggest approaches that technology firms could follow to measure the value of their technology resources. One approach might be to study the past success record of discovering new technologies. For example, if 20% of expenditures in the past

3.35 a. continued.

resulted in valuable technologies, the firm might report 20% of the expenditures on R&D each period as an asset. If these new technologies provided benefits for, say, seven years on average, then the firm would amortize the amount recognized as an asset over seven years. An alternative approach would be to use the prices paid recently when acquiring firms purchase target firms that have similar technologies. Each of these approaches involves a degree of subjectivity that has led standard setters to require the immediate expensing of R&D expenditures in the year incurred.

(2) **Nestlé**—The products of Nestlé carry a high degree of brand recognition, which leads loyal customers to purchase Nestlé products on a regular basis and new customers to try its products. The value of the Nestlé name and its other brand names is created through advertising, quality control, and new product introductions. Nestlé follows GAAP in expensing these expenditures each year. Thus, the value of the brand name does not appear on the balance sheet as an asset. If the brand name did appear on the balance sheet, assets and shareholders' equity would be larger and the market-to-book value ratio would be closer to 1.0.

One might ask how Nestlé might value its brand names if it were permitted to recognize these valuable resources as assets. One approach might be to determine the profit margin (that is, net income divided by sales) that Nestlé realizes on sales of its products relative to the profit margin of competitors. Nestlé would then multiply the excess profit margin times the number of units expected to be sold in future years to measure its excess profitability. It would then discount the future excess earnings to a present value. An alternative approach is to identify the prices paid recently by firms acquiring other branded consumer products companies to ascertain the approximate price paid for identifiable assets and the portion paid for brand names. Each of these approaches involves a degree of subjectivity and opens the door for firms to cast their balance sheets in the most favorable light possible. Accounting standard setters in most countries recognize this potential source of bias and require firms to expense brand development costs in the year expenditures are made.

(3) **Promodes**—Promodes is the largest grocery store chain in France and likely has some brand name recognition that does not appear on its balance sheet. In addition, the stores of Promodes are valued at acquisition cost adjusted downward for depreciation to date. The land and perhaps the store buildings probably have market values that exceed their book values. Standard setters in most countries require firms to account for land and buildings using acquisition costs instead of current market values because of the subjectivity

3.35 a. continued.

in the latter valuations. This real estate is probably easier to value than brand names and technological know how because of active real estate markets. Thus, the market-to-book value ratio probably reflects brand recognition and undervalued fixed assets.

(4) **Deutsche Bank**—Most of the assets of a commercial bank are reported on the balance sheet at current market values. Marketable securities are revalued to market value at each balance sheet date. Loans receivable are stated net of estimated uncollectibles and should therefore reflect cash-equivalent values. Deposits and short-term borrowing on the liability side of the balance sheet appear at current cash-equivalent values. Thus, the market-to-book value ratio should be approximately 1.0. The ratio of 1.7 for Deutsche Bank suggests the presence of intangibles that do not appear on the balance sheet. Possibilities include the size and dominant influence of Deutsche Bank in the German economy, technologically sophisticated information systems, and superior work force. The financial consulting capabilities of its investment banking employees are a valuable resource that does not appear on the balance sheet as an asset.

(5) **British Airways**—The aircraft and ground facilities of British Airways appear at acquisition cost net of depreciation to date. The market values of these fixed assets likely exceed their book values. In addition, British Airways has landing and gateway rights that appear on the balance sheet only to the extent that the firm has paid amounts up front. In most cases, British Airways pays fees periodically as it uses these facilities. Thus, no asset appears on the balance sheet.

(6) **New Oji Paper Co.**—The balance sheet of New Oji Paper Co. includes a high proportion of intercorporate investments in securities and property, plant, and equipment. GAAP in Japan reports these assets at acquisition cost, with plant and equipment adjusted downward for depreciation to date. The market value of land probably exceeds its book value. The market values of securities in Japan have decreased significantly in recent years but may still exceed their book values if the investments were made many years ago. Note that the market-to-book value ratio does not exceed 1.0 by as much as the consumer products and pharmaceutical companies with brand recognition.

b. (1) **Pfizer**—One question related to Pfizer is why it would use such a small percentage of long-term debt financing. Pharmaceutical firms face product obsolescence and legal liability risks. They tend not to add financial risk from having a high proportion of long-term debt on

3.35 b. continued.

the balance sheet. Although this exercise does not provide the needed information, Pfizer is very profitable and generates sufficient cash flow from operations that it does not need much external financing.

A second question related to Pfizer is the large percentage for other noncurrent liabilities on the balance sheet. This amount includes its healthcare benefit obligation to employees and deferred income taxes. Students generally have not studied these two items sufficiently to generate much discussion.

A third question related to Pfizer is its high proportion of treasury stock. Economic theory would suggest that if the market fairly values a firm prior to a stock buyback, then the market price of the stock should not change. The economic value of the firm should decrease by the amount of cash paid out. The number of shares of common stock outstanding should decline proportionally and the stock price should remain the same. However, the effect of stock buybacks generally is to increase the market price of the stock. One possible explanation for the market price increase is that the market views the buyback as a positive signal by management about the firm's future prospects. Management knows about the firm's future plans and might feel that the market is underpricing the firm, given these future plans. The buyback signals this positive information and the market price increases.

(2) **Nestlé**— Nestlé, like Pfizer, has highly predictable cash flows from its brand name products and generates sufficient cash flows in the long term to reduce the need for long-term debt financing. Nestlé, however, extends credit to customers and must carry inventory for some period of time before sale. It uses suppliers and short-term borrowing to finance this working capital.

(3) **Promodes**—The majority of the assets of Promodes is short-term receivables and inventories. The majority of its financing is likewise short-term. Thus, firms attempt to match the term structure of their financing to the term structure of their assets.

(4) **Deutsche Bank**—Deutsche Bank obtains the vast majority of its funds from depositors and short-term borrowing. Such a high proportion of short-term financing might appear risky. However, a large portion of its assets is in highly liquid cash and short-term investments. A large portion is also in loans to businesses and consumers. Although loans are generally not as liquid as cash and investments, they do have predictable cash flows. The large number of borrowers also diversifies the risk of Deutsche Bank on these loans. The low level of risk on the asset side of the balance sheet and the stability of the deposit base means that banks need only a small proportion of shareholders' equity.

3.35 b. continued.

(5) **British Airways**—The majority of the assets of British Airways is in flight and ground support equipment. British Airways matches these long-term assets with long-term financing, either in the form of long-term debt or shareholders' equity. The heavier use of debt financing stems from its lower cost and the availability of the equipment to serve as collateral for the borrowing. Lenders generally prefer that firms have more current assets than current liabilities. The excess current liabilities of British Airways stem from advance sales of airline tickets (appears in Other Current Liabilities). British Airways will satisfy this liability by providing transportation services rather than paying cash. Thus, the net current liability position is not of particular concern.

(6) **New Oji Paper Co.**—The balance sheet of Oji portrays some relationships that are typical of Japanese companies. First, note the high proportion of investments in securities. Many Japanese companies are part of corporate groups (called "Kieretsus"). The investments in firms in the corporate groups tend to represent 20% to 30% of these other companies and appear as intercorporate investments on the balance sheet. Secondly, note the relatively high proportion of short-term bank borrowing. Most corporate groups have a commercial bank as a member. This commercial bank is not likely to force a member of the group into bankruptcy if it is unable to repay a loan at maturity. The bank will more likely simply extend the term of the loan. Short-term borrowing is usually less costly than long-term borrowing and helps explain the high proportion of short-term borrowing on the balance sheet.

3.36 (Identifying industries using common-size balance sheet percentages).

Firm (1) has a high percentage of receivables among its assets and substantial borrowing in its capital structure. This mix of assets and financing is typical of the finance company, Household International. We ask students why the capital markets allow a finance company to have such a high proportion of borrowing in its capital structure. The answer is threefold: (1) finance companies have contractual rights to receive cash flows in the future from borrowers; the cash flow tends to be highly predictable, (2) finance companies lend to many different individuals, which diversifies their risk, and (3) borrowers often pledge collateral to back up the loan, which provides the finance companies with an alternative for collecting cash if borrowers default on their loans. The relative mix of current liabilities and long-term debt suggests that loans with maturities longer than one year exceed loans maturing within the next year, since companies attempt to match the maturities of their debt with the maturities of their assets.

3.36 continued.

Firms (2) and (3) have a high proportion of their assets in property, plant, and equipment. Commonwealth Edison and Newmont Mining are both capital intensive. These firms differ primarily with respect to their financing. Firm (2) has a higher proportion of long-term debt and Firm (3) has a higher proportion of financing from shareholders' equity. Commonwealth Edison has essentially a monopoly position in its market area and is subject to regulation with respect to rates charged. The reasonably assured cash flows permit it to take on more debt than Newmont Mining. Newmont Mining faces uncertainties with respect to the amount of gold and other minerals that it will discover and the price it will obtain for gold and minerals sold. Its high proportion of fixed costs in its cost structure means that its earnings can vary significantly as revenues increase and decrease over time. This larger business risk for Newmont Mining suggest that it should take on less long-term debt than Commonwealth Edison. Thus, Firm (2) is Commonwealth Edison and Firm (3) is Newmont Mining.

This leaves Hewlett Packard and May Department Stores and Firms (4) and (5). Firms (4) and (5) both have substantial receivables and inventories, which we would expect for both firms. Firm (4) has a lower proportion of property, plant, and equipment than Firm (5). Hewlett-Packard outsources the manufacturing of components and then assembles the components in its factories. The outsourcing reduces somewhat its need for fixed assets. May Department Stores, on the other hand, has fixed assets from its retail stores. This suggests that Firm (4) is Hewlett-Packard and Firm (5) is May Department Stores. The financing provides additional evidence for this pairing. Technological change reduces the product life cycles of computers and printers. Long-term lenders are reluctant to lend when substantial uncertainty exists about the long-term sales potential of a firm's products. The land and buildings of department stores serve as collateral for borrowing and permit a higher level of long-term debt in the capital structure. Firm (4) has a lower proportion of long-term debt than Firm (5), consistent with Firm (4) being Hewlett-Packard and Firm (5) being May Department Stores.

CHAPTER 4

INCOME STATEMENT: REPORTING THE RESULTS OF OPERATING ACTIVITIES

Questions, Exercises, and Problems: Answers and Solutions

4.1 See the text or the glossary at the end of the book.

4.2 Revenues measure the inflow of net assets from operating activities and expenses measure the outflow of net assets consumed in the process of generating revenues. Thus, recognizing revenues and expenses always involves a simultaneous entry in an asset and/or liability account. Likewise, adjusting entries almost always involve an entry in at least one income statement and one balance sheet account.

4.3 Cost is the economic sacrifice made to acquire goods or services. When the good or service acquired has reliably measurable future benefits to a firm, the cost is an asset. When the firm consumes the good or service, the cost is an expense.

4.4 Current accounting practice takes the viewpoint of shareholders by reporting the amount of net income available to shareholders after subtracting from revenues all expenses incurred in generating the revenue by claimants (for example, employees, lenders, governments) other than shareholders.

4.5 The assets and income from operations that a firm has decided to discontinue (and dispose of or abandon) will not be part of that firm's future performance. Thus, separating the two income components allows users to form better predictions of future earnings.

4.6 The revenues must be earned (the firm must have achieved substantial performance) and the amount to be received must qualify as an asset (there must be a future economic benefit and the amount must be measured with sufficient reliability). Therefore, the firm must have a reasonable expectation that it will collect the amount owed from the customer.

4.7 The matching convention assigns expenses to the related revenues. If the firm pays cash to acquire goods in a period before the goods are sold and collects the cash, then under a cash basis system, the expense will appear in a different accounting period than the related revenues.

4.8 Revenues are part of the ongoing central operations of the firm, so they are relatively persistent and sustainable. In contrast, gains arise from relatively infrequent transactions, and there can be no assurance that a gain will recur in any future period. Therefore, separating the two income components allows users of financial reports to focus on the portion of income that is more likely to continue (revenues), separately from the portion that would not be expected to recur (gains), and thereby aids prediction.

4.9 The profit margin percentage, because it uses only sales revenues and net income, which are not affected by differences in display and format. Settings where the profit margins of two firms may not be comparable occur when one firm nets certain expenses (such as bad debt expense) directly against revenues, while another shows it as a separate expense.

4.10 Firms do not necessarily recognize revenues when they receive cash or recognize expenses when they disburse cash. Thus, net income will not necessarily equal cash flow from operations each period. Furthermore, firms disburse cash to acquire property, plant and equipment, repay debt, and pay dividends. Thus, net income and cash flows usually differ. A profitable firm will likely borrow funds in order to remain in business, but eventually operations must generate cash to repay the borrowing.

4.11 (Neiman Marcus; revenue recognition.)

	February	March	April
a.	--	--	$ 800
b.	--	$ 2,160	--
c.	$39,200	--	--
d.	--	$ 59,400	--
e.	--	$ 9,000	$ 9,000
f.	--	$ 9,000	$ 9,000

4.12 (Fonterra Cooperative Group Limited; revenue recognition.)

a. No. Fonterra has not yet delivered the milk and, therefore, has not achieved substantial performance.

b. No. Fonterra would recognize NZ$5,000 as an Advance from Customer, a current liability. When Fonterra delivered the milk, it would recognize the revenue.

4.12 continued.

c. Yes. Fonterra would likely recognize revenues at this point of NZ$26,000, assuming the likelihood of the purchaser returning the milk is small.

d. No. Fonterra would clearly not recognize revenue on hearing that some of the milk delivered was spoiled. The question is how they record the non-sale of this milk. Typically, the firm would debit Selling, General and Administrative Expense for NZ$6,000 to reflect the fact that spoiled milk is a normal cost of business. Fonterra would credit Accounts Receivable for NZ$6,000 to reflect the portion of the sales for which the customer will not pay. Chapter 7 discusses other treatments for such sales returns.

e. No. Accrual accounting usually recognizes revenue when a firm sells goods or services. Fonterra has only developed a technology that may or may not result in future sales.

f. No. Fonterra does not recognize revenues at the signing of the contracts. Fonterra recognizes revenues when it has performed all that it needs to do as stipulated in the contracts.

4.13 (Sun Microsystems; expense recognition.)

	June	July	August
a.	--	$15,000	$15,000
b.	$4,560	--	--
c.	--	$5,800	$6,300
d.	$600	$600	$600
e.	--	--	--
f.	--	--	$4,500
g.	$6,600	--	--

4.14 (Tesco Plc.; expense recognition.)

a. None (this is a September expense).

b. £20,000 (= £1,200,000/60) in depreciation expense.

c. £25,000 (= £300,000/12) in property tax expense.

d. £13,600 (= £3,500 + £15,500 − £5,400) in office supply expense.

4.14 continued.

    e. £4,000 in maintenance and repairs expense (the repair does not extend the life beyond that originally expected).

    f. None, the firm will include the deposit in the acquisition cost of the land.

    g. £100,000 in rent expense; the remaining £100,000 is in prepaid rent.

4.15   (Bombardier Corporation; relating net income to balance sheet changes.)

    a. Net Income = [($1,040 – $765) + $30 – $12] = $293 million.

    b. Net Income = [($20,562 – $18,577) – ($17,444 – $15,844) – ($2,078 – $1,968) + $30 – $12] = $293 million.

4.16   (Magyar Telekom; relating net income to balance sheet changes.) (Amounts in Millions of HUF)

    a. Assets = Liabilities + Shareholders' Equity.

    HUF1,131,595 = HUF538,428 + (HUF128,728 + HUF67,128 + Retained Earnings).

    Retained Earnings = HUF397,311.

    b.

	2007
Retained Earnings, Beginning of Year (Part a. above)	HUF 397,311
Plus Net Income (Plug)	60,155
Plus Adjustment	307
Less Dividends Declared and Paid	(72,729)
Retained Earnings, End of Year	HUF 385,044

4.17   (Lenovo Group Limited; income statement relations.) (Amounts in Thousands)

The missing items appear in boldface type below:

	2008	2007
Sales	$ 16,351,503	$ 13,978,309
Cost of Goods Sold	(13,901,523)	(12,091,433)
Gross Profit	$ **2,449,980**	$ 1,886,876
Selling and Administrative Expense	(1,103,713)	(1,033,296)
Advertising Expense	(595,902)	(488,150)
Research and Development Expense	(229,759)	(196,225)
Other Income (Expense)	**11,715**	18,130
Profit before Taxes	$ 532,321	$ 187,335
Income Tax Expense	(47,613)	(26,197)
Net Income	$ 484,708	$ **161,138**

4.18   (ABB; income statement relations.) (Amounts in Millions)

The missing items appear in boldface below:

	2007	2006	2005
Sales of Products	$ 24,816	$ **19,503**	$ 17,622
Sales of Services	4,367	3,778	3,342
Cost of Products Sold	(17,292)	(13,967)	(13,205)
Cost of Services Sold	**(2,923)**	(2,570)	(2,305)
Gross Profit	$ 8,968	$ 6,744	$ **5,454**
Selling and Administrative Expenses	(4,975)	(**4,326**)	(3,780)
Other Operating Income (Expense)	**30**	139	37
Earnings before Interest and Taxes	$ 4,023	$ 2,557	$ **1,711**
Interest and Dividend Income	273	147	**153**
Interest and Other Financial Expense	(286)	(**307**)	(407)
Other Non-Operating Income (Expense)	**342**	(321)	(258)
Income before Taxes	$ 4,352	$ 2,076	$ 1,199
Income Tax Expense	(595)	(**686**)	(464)
Net Income	$ 3,757	$ 1,390	$ **735**

4.19   (James John Corporation; income and equity relations.) (Amounts in Millions)

The missing items appear in boldface below:

JAMES JOHN CORPORATION
Comparative Balance Sheets
March 31, 2008, 2007, and 2006

	March 31,		
	2008	2007	2006
Common Stock	$ 1.1[a]	$ 1.1[a]	$ 1.1
Accumulated Other Comprehensive Income	40.5	(27.2)	0.0
Retained Earnings	1,742.3	**1,379.2**[b]	1,090.3
Treasury Stock	**(321.5)**[c]	(87.1)	(80.0)
Additional Paid-in Capital	872.5	783.6	**664.3**
Total Shareholders' Equity	$ 2,334.9	$ 2,049.6	$ 1,675.7

Calculations:

[a]No new stock issuance implies same balance in common stock for 2007 and 2008 as the balance in this account in 2006.

[b]Retained Earnings, End of 2007 = Retained Earnings, End of 2006 + Net Income, 2007 − Dividend Declared, 2007 = $1,090.3 + $308.5 − $19.6 = $1,379.2.

4.19 continued.

[c]Treasury Shares, 2008 = Treasury Shares, 2007 + Repurchases, 2008 = $(87.1) + $(234.4) = $(321.5).

4.20 (Colgate Palmolive Company; income and equity relations.) (Amounts in Millions)

The missing items appear in boldface below:

COLGATE PALMOLIVE COMPANY
Comparative Balance Sheets
December 31, 2007, 2006, and 2005

	December 31,		
	2007	2006	2005
Income Statement Information:			
Net Income	$ 1,737.4	$ 1,353.4	$ 1,351.4
Other Comprehensive Income	414.4	**(276.5)**[d]	1.5
Balance Sheet Information:			
Common Stock	$ **732.9**[a]	$ **732.9**[a]	$ 732.9
Accumulated Other Comprehensive Income	**(1,666.8)**[e]	(2,081.2)	(1,804.7)
Unearned Compensation	(218.9)	(251.4)	(283.3)
Preferred Stock	197.5	222.7	253.7
Retained Earnings	10,627.5	**9,643.7**[b]	8,968.1
Treasury Stock	**(8,903.7)**[f]	**(8,073.9)**[c]	(7,581.0)
Additional Paid-in Capital	1,517.7	1,218.1	**1,064.4**
Total Shareholders' Equity	$ **2,286.2**	$ **1,410.9**	$ 1,350.1
Other Information:			
Dividends Declared and Paid	$ **753.6**[g]	$ 677.8	$ 607.2
Share Repurchases	829.8	492.9	615.6
Common Shares Issued	0	0	0

Calculations:

[a]No new shares issued, so common stock stays the same.

[b]Retained Earnings, End of 2006 = Retained Earnings, End of 2005 + Net Income, 2006 − Dividend Declared, 2006 = $8,968.1 + $1,353.4 − $677.8 = $9,643.7.

[c]Treasury Shares, 2006 = Treasury Shares, 2005 + Repurchases, 2006 = $(7,581.0) + $(492.9) = $(8,073.9).

4.20 continued.

[d]Accumulated Other Comprehensive Income, End of 2006 = Accumulated Other Comprehensive Income, End of 2005 + Other Comprehensive Income, 2006. $(2,081.2) = $(1,804.7) + Other Comprehensive Income, 2006. Other Comprehensive Income, 2006 = $(276.5).

[e]Accumulated Other Comprehensive Income, End of 2007 = Accumulated Other Comprehensive Income, End of 2006 + Other Comprehensive Income, 2007. Accumulated Other Comprehensive Income, End of 2007 = $(2,081.2) + $414.4 = $(1,666.8).

[f]Treasury Shares, 2007 = Treasury Shares, 2006 + Repurchases, 2007 = $(8,073.9) + $(829.8) = $(8,903.7).

[g]Retained Earnings, End of 2007 = Retained Earnings, End of 2006 + Net Income, 2007 – Dividends Declared, 2007. $10,627.5 = $9,643.7 + $1,737.4 – Dividends Declared, 2007. Dividends Declared, 2007 = $753.6.

4.21 (MosTechi Corporation; accumulated other comprehensive income relations.) (Amounts in Millions of Yen)

The missing items appear in boldface below:

MOSTECHI CORPORATION
Comparative Balance Sheets
March 31, 2008, 2007, and 2006

	March 31, 2008	March 31, 2007	March 31, 2006
Common Stock	¥ 626,907	¥ 624,124	¥ 621,709
Accumulated Other Comprehensive Income	**(115,493)**[b]	**(156,437)**[a]	(385,675)
Retained Earnings	**1,700,133**[c]	1,602,654	1,506,082
Treasury Stock	**(3,470)**	(3,127)	(6,000)
Additional Paid-in Capital	1,143,423	1,136,638	1,134,222
Total Shareholders' Equity	**¥3,351,500**	**¥3,203,852**	¥2,870,338

Calculations:

[a]Accumulated Other Comprehensive Income, End of 2007 = Accumulated Other Comprehensive Income, End of 2006 + Other Comprehensive Income, 2007 = ¥(385,675) + ¥229,238 = ¥(156,437).

[b]Accumulated Other Comprehensive Income, End of 2008 = Accumulated Other Comprehensive Income, End of 2007 + Other Comprehensive Income, 2008 = ¥(156,437) + ¥40,944 = ¥(115,493).

4.21 continued.

[c]Retained Earnings, End of 2008 = Retained Earnings, End of 2007 + Net Income, 2008 − Dividends Declared, 2008 + Adjustment, 2008 = ¥1,602,654 + ¥126,328 − ¥25,042 − ¥3,807 = ¥1,700,133.

4.22 (Solaronx Company; accumulated other comprehensive income relations.) (Amounts in Millions)

The missing items appear in boldface below:

SOLARONX COMPANY
Comparative Balance Sheets
December 31, 2008, 2007, and 2006

	December 31,		
	2008	2007	2006
Common Stock	$ 5	$ 5	$ 5
Accumulated Other Comprehensive Income	**(2,514)**[e]	**(1,950)**[b]	(1,919)
Retained Earnings	**4,329**[f]	3,475[c]	2,998
Treasury Stock	(816)	(543)	(73)
Additional Paid-in Capital	10,097	9,722	9,540
Total Shareholders' Equity	$ **11,101**[g]	$ **10,709**[d]	$ 10,551[a]

Calculations:

[a]Total Shareholders' Equity, End of 2006 = $5 − $1,919 + $2,998 − $73 + $9,540 = $10,551.

[b]Accumulated Other Comprehensive Income, End of 2007 = Accumulated Other Comprehensive Income, End of 2006 + Other Comprehensive Income, 2007 = $(1,919) + $(31) = $(1,950).

[c]Comprehensive Income, End of 2007 = Net Income, 2007 + Other Comprehensive Income, 2007. $840 = Net Income, 2007 + $(31). Net Income, 2007 = $871.

Retained Earnings, End of 2007 = Retained Earnings, End of 2006 + Net Income, 2007 − Dividends Declared, 2007 = $2,998 + Net Income, 2007 − $394.

Retained Earnings, End of 2007 = $2,998 + $871 − $394 = $3,475.

[d]Total Shareholders' Equity, End of 2007 = $5 − $1,950 + $3,475 − $543 + $9,722 = $10,709.

4.22 continued.

    ^{e}Accumulated Other Comprehensive Income, End of 2008 = Accumulated Other Comprehensive Income, End of 2007 + Other Comprehensive Income, 2008 + Adjustment, 2008 = $(1,950) + $774 – $1,338 = $(2,514).

    ^{f}Comprehensive Income, 2008 = Net Income, 2008 + Other Comprehensive Income, 2007. $2,057 = Net Income, 2008 + $774. Net Income, 2008 = $1,283.

    Retained Earnings, End of 2008 = Retained Earnings, End of 2007 + Net Income, 2008 – Dividends Declared, 2008 = $3,475 + $1,283 – $429.

    Therefore, Retained Earnings, End of 2008 = $3,475 + $1,283 – $429 = $4,329.

    ^{g}Total Shareholders' Equity, End of 2008 = $5 – $2,514 + $4,329 – $816 + $10,097 = $11,101.

4.23   (Bayer Group; discontinued operations.)

    a. In 2007, 51% [= €2,410/(€2,410 + €2,306)] of Bayer's income came from discontinued operations, compared to 9% [= €169/(€169 + €1,526)] in 2006.

    b. In 2007, less than 0.2% (= €84/€51,378) of Bayer's total assets were associated with discontinued operations, compared to 5.2% (= €2,925/€55,891) in 2006.

    c. The large decline in Bayer's assets held for discontinued operations is due to the fact that Bayer disposed of the assets in 2007. The assets are no longer owned by Bayer and, therefore, no longer a part of Bayer's balance sheet at the end of 2007. The income those assets generated during the year prior to disposal is, however, part of Bayer's income for 2007.

4.24 (Orascom Telecom Holding S.A.E.; discontinued operations.) (Amounts in Thousands of Egyptian Pounds)

The missing items appear in boldface type below:

ORASCOM TELECOM HOLDING S.A.E.
Comparative Balance Sheets
December 31, 2007 and 2006

	December 31, 2007	December 31, 2006
Income from Continuing Operations (before Taxes)	£ 9,293,448	£ 4,456,900
Less Taxes on Income from Continuing Operations	(2,571,426)	**(861,187)**
Income from Continuing Operations (after Tax)	£ **6,722,022**	£ 3,595,713
Income from Discontinued Operations (Net of Tax)	**5,213,066**	1,020,213
Net Income	£ 11,935,088	£ **4,615,926**
Assets Held for Discontinued Operations	£ **5,144,015**	£ 7,327,709
Assets Used in Continuing Operations	34,348,838	**26,882,037**
Total Assets	£ **39,492,853**	£ 34,209,746

Solutions

4.25 (Cemex S.A.B.; income statement formats.)

The missing items appear in boldface type below:

CEMEX S.A.B.
IFRS Income Statements
December 31, 2007 and 2006

	December 31, 2007	December 31, 2006
Net Sales	$ 236,669	$ 213,767
Cost of Sales	(157,696)	**(136,447)**
Gross Profit	$ **78,973**	$ 77,320
Administrative and Selling Expenses	(33,120)	(28,588)
Distribution Expenses	(13,405)	**(14,227)**
Other Expenses, Net	(3,281)	(580)
Operating Income	$ **29,167**	$ 33,925
Financial Expenses	(8,809)	**(5,785)**
Financial Income	862	536
Income (Expense) from Financial Instruments	2,387	(161)
Other Financial Income (Expense)	6,647	4,905
Equity in Income of Associates	1,487	1,425
Profit before Income Tax	$ 31,741	$ 34,845
Income Tax	(4,796)	**(5,697)**
Consolidated Profit	$ **26,945**	$ **29,148**
Portion of Profit Attributable to Minority Interest	$ 837	$ 1,293
Portion of Profit Attributable to Cemex Shareholders	$ **26,108**	$ 27,855

4.26 (GoodLuck Brands; income statement formats.)

GoodLuck Brands
Income Statements
For 2008, 2007, and 2006

	2008	2007	2006
Net Sales	$ 8,769.0	$ 7,061.2	$ 6,145.2
Cost of Products Sold	4,618.9	3,843.0	3,342.1
Excise Taxes on Spirits and Wine	514.0	326.5	299.7
Advertising, Selling and Administrative Costs	2,070.1	1,694.4	1,433.6
Amortization of Intangibles	43.5	33.4	35.4
Restructuring Charges	21.2	--	9.8
Operating Income	$ 1,501.3	$ 1,163.9	$ 1,024.6
Interest Expense	332.4	158.9	77.3
Other Financial Expense (Income)	(40.2)	78.9	(47.0)
Net Financial Expense (Income)	$ 292.2	$ 237.8	$ 40.3
Profit before Taxes	$ 1,209.1	$ 926.1	$ 994.3
Less Income Taxes	311.1	324.5	261.1
Income from Continuing Operations	$ 898.0	$ 601.6	$ 733.2
Income from Discontinued Operations, Net of Tax	--	39.5	67.8
Net Profit	$ 898.0	$ 641.1	$ 801.0
Portion of Profit Owned by Minority Interests	$ 67.9	$ 20.0	$ 17.2
Portion of Profit Owned by Shareholders	$ 830.1	$ 621.1	$ 783.8

4.27 (Broyo Corporation; correcting errors in income statement transactions.) (Amounts in Millions of Pounds)

a. Broyo should not have recognized revenue on this transaction because it has yet to perform on the contract. Revenues are overstated by €200 and Cost of Goods Sold is overstated by €160, so income is overstated by €40.

b. Broyo should not have recorded the advance from customer as revenues. It is a liability (Advance from Customer). Revenues are, therefore, overstated by €20.

c. Broyo should have recorded Revenues of €45, and Cost of Goods Sold of €36, for a gross profit of €9.

d. Because the expenditures do not qualify as capitalized development costs, they should have been expensed not capitalized. Broyo's income in 2008 is, therefore, overstated by €11.

4.27 continued.

 e. Broyo had performed all of its obligations with the customer, so on December 1, 2008, it should have recognized Revenues of €266, and Cost of Goods Sold of €250. Because they did not, Revenues are understated by €266, Cost of Goods Sold is understated by €250, and Gross Profit is understated by €16.

 f. The sale of a plant is not a recurring part of Broyo's business. Therefore, it should not be included as part of Revenues and Cost of Goods Sold, which pertain to recurring transactions. Revenues are, therefore, overstated by €100, and Cost of Goods Sold is overstated by €80. The sale of the plant generated a gain of €20, which should have been included in Other Operating Income.

4.28 (Dragon Group International Limited; correcting errors in income statement transactions.)

 a. In 2007, Dragon Group's revenues are overstated by $1,000. These revenues should have been recognized in 2006.

 b. Dragon Group had not performed its obligations under the agreement as of February 2. Thus, it should not have recognized revenues at that time. However, Dragon Group did perform those obligations by the end of the fiscal year (in September). As a result, its revenues and expenses are correctly stated for 2007 for this transaction.

 c. Dragon Group correctly recorded the results of this transaction as a separate line item, below gross profit on its income statement.

 d. Because the firm should have capitalized the development costs, expenses for 2007 are overstated by $1,232.

 e. Interest income on investments is not part of Dragon Group's normal recurring operations. It should not have been recorded as revenues, but as a component of Financial Costs. Net Revenues are, therefore, overstated by $230, and financial income is understated by $230.

 f. Dragon Group should have expensed the advertising costs in 2007. Because it did not, Selling and Marketing Costs are understated by $15,000.

4.29 (Standard Denim and Blue Label Jeans; interpreting common-size income statements.)

a. The decreasing cost of goods sold to sales percentages for both firms suggest a common explanation. One possibility is that the economy was doing well and both firms were able to increase selling prices and thereby their profit margins. Another possibility is that the firms were able to purchase merchandise in larger quantities or pay more quickly to take advantage of discounts. A third possibility is that the firms implemented more effective inventory control systems, thereby reducing obsolescence and the need to reduce selling prices to move their merchandise. Another possibility is that sales grew rapidly and the firms were able to spread their relatively fixed occupancy costs over a larger sales base.

b. Blue Label Jeans relies more heavily on in-store promotions, which tend to increase its cost of goods sold to sales percentages, whereas Standard Denim relies more on advertising to stimulate sales, which Standard Denim includes in selling and administrative expenses.

c. The increasing selling and administrative expenses to sales percentages for both firms suggest a common explanation. One possibility is that the specialty retailing industry became more competitive over this period (from new entrants and from the Internet) and the firms had to increase marketing expenses to compete. This explanation, however, is inconsistent with a more attractive pricing environment suggested in Part a. above. Another possibility is that both firms experienced increased administrative expenses as they introduced new store concepts and opened new stores.

d. The explanation in Part b. applies here as well. Standard Denim includes its promotion costs in selling and administrative expenses, whereas more of those of Blue Label Jeans appear in cost of goods sold.

e. The interest expense to sales percentage decreased for Standard Denim and increased for Blue Label Jeans. One possible explanation is Standard Denim reduced the amount of debt outstanding or grew it at a slower pace than that of Blue Label Jeans. Another possibility is that the market viewed Standard Denim as increasingly less risky, permitting it to borrow at lower interest rates. On the other hand, the market viewed Blue Label Jeans as more risky and required it to pay a higher interest rate. These two possibilities are not independent. Perhaps Standard Denim was able to borrow at a lower rate because it reduced the amount of debt in its capital structure. The higher interest rate for Blue Label Jeans may reflect increased risk from an increased proportion of debt in its capital structure.

4.29 continued.

    f.   Both firms experienced increased net income relative to sales. Both firms should therefore experience increased income tax expense relative to sales. A more meaningful way to interpret income taxes is to relate income tax expense to income before income taxes. The latter is the base on which governments impose income taxes. Consider the following:

	Standard Denim			Blue Label Jeans		
	2008	2007	2006	2008	2007	2006
(1) Income before Income Taxes (Plug)..............	16.3%	14.6%	12.4%	6.9%	6.5%	5.8%
(2) Income Tax Expense............	(6.6)	(5.5)	(4.2)	(2.4)	(2.3)	(2.0)
(3) Net Income......	9.7%	9.1%	8.2%	4.5%	4.2%	3.8%
(2)/(1)........................	40.5%	37.7%	33.9%	34.8%	35.4%	34.5%

The income tax expense to income before income taxes percentages for Standard Denim continually increased while those of Blue Label Jeans remained relatively stable. One possible explanation is that Standard Denim expanded its operations into other countries and perhaps experienced higher income tax rates in those countries than it experiences in the United States.

4.30   (Lyle's Lemonade Company and CitraPop; interpreting common-size income statements.)

    a.   The creation, manufacture, and distribution of beverages involve six principal activities:

        (1) Research and development to create the beverage, which generally involves developing the formula for the syrup.

        (2) Promoting the beverage through advertising and other means.

        (3) Manufacturing the syrup.

        (4) Mixing water with the syrup to manufacture the beverage.

        (5) Placing the beverage in a container.

        (6) Distributing the beverage to retail and other outlets.

Lyle's Lemonade primarily engages in the first three activities and its independent bottlers engage in the last three activities. CitraPop engages more heavily in all six activities. The lower cost of goods sold to

4.30 a. continued.

sales percentage for Lyle's Lemonade might suggest that the market views the first three activities as higher value added than the last three, permitting Lyle's Lemonade to extract a relatively high price from its bottlers for the syrup sold to them. CitraPop's cost of goods sold to sales percentage reflects both the higher value added of the first three activities and the lower value added of the last three activities. Another possible explanation is that Lyle's Lemonade dominates its bottlers and can extract a higher price because of the bottlers' reliance on Lyle's Lemonade for most of their purchases.

b. The beverage industry, particularly for cola beverages, is relatively mature. The increasing selling and administrative expense to sales percentages for Lyle's Lemonade might reflect increased advertising to gain market share or to introduce new beverages. Note that both firms experienced poor sales results in 2006. Perhaps Lyle's Lemonade increased advertising expenditures in 2007 and 2008 to stimulate sales. The decreasing percentages are consistent with not increasing advertising in light of the 2006 sales results. Note that sales growth for CitraPop in 2007 and 2008 is less than the corresponding rates for Lyle's Lemonade, suggesting less aggressiveness on the part of CitraPop.

c. One possibility is that both firms reduced their levels of interest-bearing debt, which reduced interest expense. Another possibility is that declining interest rates permitted both firms to borrow at lower rates.

d.

	Lyle's Lemonade Company			**CitraPop**		
	2008	2007	2006	2008	2007	2006
(1) Income before Income Taxes (Plug)	28.1%	32.3%	27.9%	20.3%	18.8%	17.5%
(2) Income Tax Expense	(7.8)	(9.6)	(10.0)	(6.5)	(6.4)	(5.6)
(3) Net Income	20.3%	22.7%	17.9%	13.8%	12.4%	11.9%
(2)/(1)	27.8%	29.7%	35.8%	32.0%	34.0%	32.0%

Lyle's Lemonade tax burden by this measure is less than that of CitraPop in 2007 and 2008. The income tax is a tax on income before taxes and not on sales. Thus, this measure more accurately reflects the income tax burden. The larger income tax expense to sales percentages for Lyle's Lemonade results from Lyle's Lemonade having higher income before taxes to sales percentages.

4.31   (Ericsson; interpreting common-size income statements.)

Ericsson's profit margin declined from 16.0% in 2005, to 14.7% in 2006, to 11.8% in 2007. The decline results primarily from increases in the cost of goods sold to sales percentage and in the selling and administrative expense to sales percentage. One possible explanation for the increase in both cost of sales (as a percentage of sales) and selling and administrative expenses (as a percentage of sales) is that the markets that Ericsson competes in became more competitive over these three years. Competition might force selling prices to not increase at the same rate that costs increase.

4.32   (Thales Group; interpreting common-size income statements.)

The principal reason for the increasing profit margin was the increase in 2007 of the portion of income attributable to gains on disposals of assets: 3.5% in 2007 compared to 0.2% in 2006 and 1.5% in 2005. To approximate the effect the gain in 2007 had on Thales profit margin, remove the gain of €432.1 million in 2007. We recalculate the profit margin (without the gain) to be 3.7% (= €456.6/€12,295.6), which is similar to the profit margins in 2005 and 2006.

4.33   (Identifying industries using common-size income statement percentages.)

Exhibit 4.11 indicates that two firms have relatively low profit margins, two firms have medium profit margins, and two firms have relatively large profit margins. Low barriers to entry, extensive competition, and commodity products characterize firms with low profit margins. The likely candidates for Firms (1) and (2) are Kelly Services and Kroger Stores. The office services offered by Kelly Services are clerical in nature and not particularly unique. Kelly Services serves essentially as an intermediary between the employee and the customer, offering relatively little value added. Grocery products are commodities, with little, if any, differentiation between grocery stores. Firms (1) and (2) differ primarily with respect to depreciation and interest expense. Grocery stores require retail and warehouse space. Kelly Services should require relatively little space, since its employees work on the customers' premises. Thus, Firm (1) is Kroger Stores and Firm (2) is Kelly Services.

Firms with the highest profit margin should operate in industries with high barriers to entry, relatively little competition, and differentiated products. Electric utilities have operated until recently as regulated utilities and require extensive amounts of capital to build capital-intensive plants. Regulation and capital serve as barriers to entry. Tiffany's offers brand name products. The brand names serve as an entry barrier. Customers also perceive its products to be differentiated. Thus, Firm (5) and Firm (6) are likely to be Commonwealth Edison and Tiffany & Co. in some order. Firm (5) has considerably more depreciation and interest expense than Firm (6) and Firm (6) has considerably more selling and administrative expenses than Firm (5). Thus, Firm (5) is Commonwealth Edison and Firm (6) is Tiffany & Co.

4.33 continued.

This leaves Hewlett-Packard and Delta Airlines with medium profit margins. Hewlett-Packard offers products that are somewhat differentiated and with some brand name appeal. However, competition in the computer industry and rapid technological change drive down profit margins. Delta Airlines offers a commodity product, but the need for capital to acquire airplanes serves as a barrier to entry. Thus, these two firms have some characteristics of firms with relatively low profit margins and some characteristics of firms with relatively high profit margins. Firm (3) appears to have considerably more debt in its capital structure than Firm (4). The short product life cycles in the computer industry tend to drive down their use of debt. The aircraft of Delta Airlines can serve as collateral for borrowing. Thus, one would expect Delta Airlines to have a higher amount of borrowing. This clue suggests that Firm (3) is Delta Airlines and Firm (4) is Hewlett-Packard.

4.34 (SeaBreeze, Inc.; classification and interpretation of income statements.)

a. The ¥10,000 in Gains on Sales of Assets should not have been included in Sales Revenues because the gains do not reflect a transaction that the firm is regularly engaged in as part of its business model. The gain should have been recorded below the gross margin line, and identified as a non-recurring item. Gross Profit would decline by ¥10,000.

b. Net Financial Income of ¥13,800 should have been reported below the gross profit line, because it is not part of the normal, core part of the firm's operations. Removing Net Financial Income will reduce gross profit by ¥13,800.

c. The firm included a ¥6,000 writedown of inventory in Selling, General and Administrative Expenses. Normally in this industry, such a writedown is included in Cost of Sales. Adding the writedown to Cost of Sales would cause Gross Profit to decrease by ¥6,000.

d. The firm included research and development expenditures of ¥34,000 in Cost of Sales. None of the expenditures related to proven technologies (and so were correctly not capitalized). So, while the expenditures should be expensed on the income statement, R&D is typically not part of Cost of Sales. Removing the R&D from Cost of Sales would cause Gross Profit to increase by ¥34,000.

e. The results of discontinued operations should be shown separately on the income statement, below the margin line. Removing discontinued operations will cause Gross Profit to decline by ¥22,000.

Each of the above transactions belongs in the income statement (implying that net income is calculated correctly), but is not correctly displayed in the income statement (implying that gross profit may be calculated incorrectly).

4.34 continued.

A summary of the effects of reclassifying the items on gross profit and net income is provided below:

	Gross Profit	Net Income
Original Amount	¥ 154,039	¥ 31,921
Effect of (a)	(10,000)	No effect on Net Income
Effect of (b)	(13,800)	No effect on Net Income
Effect of (c)	(6,000)	No effect on Net Income
Effect of (d)	34,000	No effect on Net Income
Effect of (e)	(22,000)	No effect on Net Income
Revised Amount	¥ 136,239	¥ 31,921

4.35 (Dyreng Plc.; classification and interpretation of income statements.)

a. Dyreng should not have recognized any revenues (nor any costs) of this project in 2008 because it had performed no work. 2008 Revenues are overstated by €240, causing both Gross Profit and Pre-tax Profit from Continuing Operations to be overstated by this amount.

b. 2008 Revenues are overstated by €700. The revenues and associated costs should have been recorded in 2007 when the work was performed. The receipt of cash is irrelevant to the timing of the revenue recognition. 2008 Gross Profits and Pre-tax Profit from Continuing Operations are overstated by €40 (= €700 – €660).

c. The sale of the office building was not a normal part of Dyreng's operations. It should not, therefore, have been included in Sales or Cost of Sales. The net effect of the sale, a loss of €40, should have been included in Other Operating Income. Gross Profit is understated by €40, but Pre-tax Profit from Continuing Operations is correctly stated.

d. Other Operating Income is overstated by €45. Gross Profit is correctly stated, but Pre-tax Profit from Continuing Operations is overstated by €45.

e. Dyreng performed all work in 2008, and so should have recognized Revenues of €450 and Cost of Sales of €230. 2008 Gross Profits and Pre-tax Profit from Continuing Operations are both understated by €220 (= €450 – €230).

f. The sale of the advertising space is not a normal part of Dyreng's business model. It should, therefore, have been included as a Source of Other Operating Income, not as a Reduction to Cost of Sales. In addition, only half of the amount should have been recognized because Dyreng has not performed completely on this obligation. Gross Profit is, therefore, overstated by €960, whereas Pre-tax Profit from Continuing Operations is over-stated by €480.

4.35 continued.

A summary of the effects of reclassifying the items on gross profit and net income is provided below:

	Gross Profit	Pre-tax Profit
Original Amount	€ 4,795.3	€ 604.5
Effect of (a)	(240.0)	(240.0)
Effect of (b)	(700.0)	(700.0)
Effect of (c)	40.0	No effect
Effect of (d)	No effect	(45.0)
Effect of (e)	220.0	220.0
Effect of (f)	(960.0)	(480.0)
Revised Amount	€ 3,155.3	€ (640.5)

4.36 (Calculation of tax rates.)

a. 2007: $7,712/$87,548 = 8.8%; 2008: $8,093/$88,396 = 9.2%.

b. 2007: $11,757/$87,548 = 13.4%; 2008: $11,534/$88,396 = 13.0%.

c. 2007: $4,045/$11,757 = 34.4%; 2008: $3,441/$11,534 = 29.8%.

d. The improved profitability clearly relates to an improved income tax position. The ratio of income before income taxes to revenues computed in Part b. indicates that profitability before taxes decreased between 2007 and 2008.

CHAPTER 5

STATEMENT OF CASH FLOWS: REPORTING THE EFFECTS OF OPERATING, INVESTING, AND FINANCING ACTIVITIES ON CASH FLOWS

Questions, Exercises, and Problems: Answers and Solutions

5.1 See the text or the glossary at the end of the book.

5.2 One can criticize a single income statement using a cash basis of accounting from two standpoints: (1) it provides a poor measure of operating performance each period because of the inaccurate matching of revenues and expenses (see discussion in Chapter 3), and (2) it excludes important investing (acquisitions and sales of long-lived assets) activities and financing (issuance or redemption of bonds or capital stock) activities of a firm that affect cash flow.

5.3 Accrual accounting attempts to provide a measure of operating performance that relates inputs to output without regard to when a firm receives or disburses cash. Accrual accounting also attempts to portray the resources of a firm and the claims on those resources without regard to whether the firm holds the resource in the form of cash. Although accrual accounting may satisfy user's needs for information about operating performance and financial position, it does not provide sufficient information about the cash flow effects of a firm's operating, investing, and financing activities. The latter is the objective of the statement of cash flows.

5.4 The statement of cash flows reports changes in the investing and financing activities of a firm. Significant changes in property, plant, and equipment affect the maturity structure of assets on the balance sheet. Significant changes in long-term debt or capital stock affect both the maturity structure of equities as well as the mix of debt versus shareholder financing.

5.5 The indirect method reconciles net income, the primary measure of a firm's profitability, with cash flow from operations. Some argue that the relation between net income and cash flow from operations is less evident when a firm reports using the direct method. More likely, the frequent use of the indirect method prior to the issuance of FASB *Statement No. 95*

5.5 continued.

probably explains its continuing popularity. Why might accountants have preferred the indirect method before FASB *Statement No. 95*? We have heard the following, but cannot vouch for this from first-hand experience: The direct method's format resembles the income statement. Where the income statement has a line for revenues, the direct method has a line for cash collections from customers. Where the income statement has a line for cost of goods sold, the direct method might have a line for payments to suppliers of income. Where the income statement has a line for income tax expense, the direct method has a line for income tax payments. The old-timers thought the resemblance of the two statements, the income statement and the direct method presentation in the statement of cash flows, would cause confusion. They were likely right, but we think its confusion is less than the confusion resulting from the indirect method. Some argue that preparing the direct method costs more. But you can see how easy preparing the direct method's version is; you learn how in this chapter. We have told those who say it's costly that they can hire any one of our students to do this for under $100. Are yours available?

5.6 The classification in the statement of cash flows parallels that in the income statement, where interest on debt is an expense but payments on the principal amount of the debt are not an expense but a reduction in a liability. This is, in our opinion, a feeble explanation. The overarching rule seems to be that 'if it's in the income statement, it's operating.' We think that repayment of principal on borrowings and interest on borrowings are both financing transactions, but we are in the minority.

5.7 The classification in the statement of cash flows parallels that in the income statement, where interest on debt is an expense but dividends are a distribution of earnings, not an expense. This is, in our opinion, a feeble explanation. The overarching rule seems to be that 'if it's in the income statement, it's operating.' We think that dividends on shares and interest on borrowings are both financing transactions, but we are in the minority.

5.8 Firms generally use accounts payable directly in financing purchases of inventory and other operating costs. Firms might use short-term bank financing indirectly in financing accounts receivable, inventories, or operating costs or use it to finance acquisitions of noncurrent assets or reductions in long-term financing. Thus, the link between short-term bank financing and operations is less direct and may not even relate to operating activities. To achieve consistency in classification, the FASB stipulates that changes in short-term bank loans are financing activities. This is not compelling. We suspect the opposite treatment could be justified.

5.9 This is an investing and financing transaction whose disclosure helps the statement user understand why property, plant and equipment and long-term debt changed during the period. Because the transaction does not affect cash directly, however, firms must distinguish it from investing and

5.9 continued.

financing transactions that do affect cash flow. The rules used to allow the firm to report this single transaction as though it were two—the issue of debt for cash and the use of cash to acquire the property—and the appearance of both of these two in the so-called funds statement, the predecessor sometimes called the Statement of Changes in Financial Position.

5.10 Both are correct, but the writer's point is not expressed clearly. Depreciation expense is a charge to operations, but does not require cash. If revenues precisely equal total expenses, there will be a retention of net funds in the business equal to the amount of the depreciation. As long as replacement of the depreciating assets is not necessary, it is possible to finance considerable expansion without resorting to borrowing or the issuance of additional stock.

The "reader" is correct in saying that depreciation in itself is not a source of cash and that the total cash available would not have increased by adding larger amounts to the depreciation accounts. The source of cash is sales to customers.

When one considers income tax effects, however, depreciation expenses do save cash because taxable income and, hence, income tax expense using cash are lower than they would be in the absence of depreciation charges.

5.11 The firm must have increased substantially its investment in accounts receivable or inventories or decreased substantially its current liabilities.

5.12 The firm might be capital intensive and, therefore, subtracted substantial amounts of depreciation expense in computing net income. This depreciation expense is added back to net income in computing cash flow from operations. In addition, the firm might have decreased significantly its investment in accounts receivable or inventories or increased its current liabilities.

5.13 Direct Method: The accountant classifies the entire cash proceeds from the equipment sale as an investing activity. Indirect Method: As above, the entire cash proceeds appear as an investing activity. Because the calculation of cash flow from operations starts with net income (which includes the gain on sale of equipment), the accountant must subtract the gain to avoid counting cash flow equal to the gain twice, once as an operating activity and once as an investing activity.

5.14 (Microsoft; derive sales revenue from data in the statement of cash flows and balance sheet.) (Amounts in Millions)

Cash Collections for the Year		$ 33,551
Accounts Receivable, End of Year	$ 5,334	
Accounts Receivable, Beginning of Year	5,196	
Add: Increase in Receivables		138
Sales for the Year		$ 33,689

5.15 (General Electric; derive cost of goods sold from data in the statement of cash flows.) (Amounts in Millions)

Cash Payments for Inventories for the Year	$ 64,713
Subtract: Increase in Inventories for the Year	(1,753)
Cost of Goods Sold for the Year	$ 62,960

5.16 (Ann Taylor Stores; derive cost of goods sold from data in the statement of cash flows.) (Amounts in Millions)

Cash Payments for Inventories for the Year	$ 646.9
Add: Increase in Accounts Payable for Inventories	5.9
Subtract: Increase in Inventories for the Year	(5.7)
Cost of Goods Sold for the Year	$ 647.1

5.17 (AMR; derive wages and salaries expense from data in the statement of cash flows.) (Amounts in Millions)

Cash Payments for Wages and Salaries for the Year	$ 8,853
Subtract: Decrease in Wages and Salaries Payable during the Year	(21)
Wages and Salaries Expense for the Year	$ 8,832

5.18 (Johnson & Johnson; derive cash disbursements for dividends.) (Amounts in Millions)

Net Income for the Year		$ 5,030
Retained Earnings, End of Year	$ 28,132	
Retained Earnings, Beginning of Year	(26,571)	
Subtract: Increase in Retained Earnings		(1,561)
Dividends Declared for the Year		$ 3,469
Subtract: Increase in Dividends Payable during the Year		(233)
Cash Paid for Dividends during the Year (Financing Activity)		$ 3,236

Refer to Exhibit 5.16. Line (10) increases and Line (11) decreases by $3,236.

Solutions

5.19 (Gillette; effect of borrowing and interest on statement of cash flows.) (Amounts in Millions)

Cash 250.00
    Bonds Payable 250.00

Change in Cash	=	Change in Liabilities	+	Change in Shareholders' Equity	−	Change in Non-cash Assets
+250.0 Finan		+250.0				

October 1 bond issue. Refer to Exhibit 5.16. Line (11) increases by $250. Line (8) increases by $250.

Interest Expense 3.75
    Interest Payable [(.06/12) x $250.00 x 3 Months] 3.75

Change in Cash	=	Change in Liabilities	+	Change in Shareholders' Equity	−	Change in Non-cash Assets
		+3.75		−3.75		

Refer to Exhibit 5.16. Line (3) decreases by $3.75. Line (4) increases by $3.75.

5.20 (Radio Shack; effect of income taxes on statement of cash flows.) (Amounts in Millions)

Income Tax Expense 161.5
Income Taxes Payable 18.0
    Cash 179.5

Change in Cash	=	Change in Liabilities	+	Change in Shareholders' Equity	−	Change in Non-cash Assets
−179.5 Opns		−18.0		−161.5		

18.0 = 78.1 − 60.1. Refer to Exhibit 5.16. Line (2) increases by $179.5. Line (3) decreases by $161.5. Line (5) increases by $18.0. Line (11) decreases by $179.5.

5.21 (Effect of rent transactions on statement of cash flows.)

Rent Expense 1,200
    Prepaid Rent   1,200

Change in Cash	=	Change in Liabilities	+	Change in Shareholders' Equity	–	Change in Non-cash Assets
				–1,200		–1,200

January rent expense.

Prepaid Rent 18,000
    Cash   18,000

Change in Cash	=	Change in Liabilities	+	Change in Shareholders' Equity	–	Change in Non-cash Assets
–18,000 Opns						+18,000

Payment on February 1.

Rent Expense 16,500
    Prepaid Rent   16,500

Change in Cash	=	Change in Liabilities	+	Change in Shareholders' Equity	–	Change in Non-cash Assets
				–16,500		–16,500

Rent expense for February through December; $18,000/12 per month = $1,500. 11 x $1,500 = $16,500.

All of these combine as:
Rent Expense 17,700
Prepaid Rent   300
    Cash   18,000

Change in Cash	=	Change in Liabilities	+	Change in Shareholders' Equity	–	Change in Non-cash Assets
–18,000 Opns				–17,700		+300

All transactions of the year. Refer to Exhibit 5.16. Line (2) increases by $18,000. Line (3) decreases by $17,700. Line (5) increases by $300. Line (11) decreases by $18,000.

Solutions

5.22 (Information Technologies; calculating components of cash inflow from operations.) (Amounts in Thousands)

Sales for the Year...	$ 14,508
Add: Decrease in Receivables..	782
Cash Collections from Customers for the Year........................	$ 15,290

5.23 (Information Technologies; calculating components of cash outflow from operations.) (Amounts in Thousands)

a.
Cost of Goods Sold for the Year..	$ 11,596
Subtract: Increase in Accounts Payable for Inventories.....	(90)
Subtract: Decrease in Inventories for the Year......................	(66)
Cash Payments for Inventories for the Year...........................	$ 11,440

b.
Other Expenses, Total..	$ 2,276
Subtract: Decrease in Prepayments for Other Costs...............	(102)
Add: Decrease in Wages and Salaries Payable during the Year..	240
Cash Payments to Employees and Suppliers of Other Services for the Year	$ 2,414

5.24 (Spread sheet for understanding the relation between changes in income statement items and changes in items in the statement of cash flows.)

a. S1 changes from $10 to $12.

b. Lines [1], [2], and [4] of the statement of cash flows do not change.
Line [3] changes from $7 to $11.
Line [5] changes from ($1) to ($5)
S1 does not change.

c. Lines [1], [3], and [5] do not change.
Line [2] changes from ($15) to ($17).
Line [4] changes from $4 to $2.
S1 changes from $10 to $8.

5.25 (American Airlines; working backwards from changes in buildings and equipment account.) (Amounts in Millions)

Buildings and Equipment (Original Cost)		**Accumulated Depreciation**	
Balance, 1/1..............................	$16,825	Balance, 1/1..........................	$ 4,914
Outlays during Year.............	1,314	Depreciation during Year..	1,253
	$18,139		$ 6,167
Balance, 12/31........................	17,369	Balance, 12/31......................	5,465
Retirements during Year	$ 770	Retirements during Year...	$ 702

Proceeds = Book Value at Retirement
= $770 − $702
= $68.

5.26 (Southwest Airlines; preparing a statement of cash flows from changes in balance sheet accounts.)

a.
SOUTHWEST AIRLINES
Statement of Cash Flows
For the Year
(Amounts in Thousands)

Operations:		
Net Income	$	474,378
Additions:		
Depreciation Expense		264,088
Decrease in Accounts Receivable		15,351
Increase in Other Current Liabilities		114,596
Subtractions:		
Increase in Inventories		(15,117)
Increase in Prepayments		(16,776)
Decrease in Accounts Payable		(660)
Cash Flow from Operations	$	835,860
Investing:		
Acquisition of Property, Plant and Equipment	$	(1,134,644)
Increase in Other Non-operating Assets		(8,711)
Cash Flow from Investing	$	(1,143,355)
Financing:		
Increase in Long-term Debt	$	244,285
Increase in Common Stock		96,991
Payment of Dividends[a]		(133,499)
Increase in Non-operating Liabilities		140,026
Cash Flow from Financing	$	347,803
Net Change in Cash	$	40,308
Cash, Beginning of Year		378,511
Cash, End of Year	$	418,819

[a] Net Income of $474,378 less Increase in Retained Earnings of $340,879 = Dividends of $133,499.

b. Cash flow from operations exceeds net income primarily because of the addback for depreciation expense and increases in other current liabilities, so Southwest Airlines relied on long-term debt and common stock to make up the needed amount.

5.27 (Bamberger Enterprises; calculating and interpreting cash flow from operations.)

a.
Net Income	$ 290
Additions:	
Depreciation Expense	210
Decrease in Accounts Receivable	780
Decrease In Inventories	80
Decrease in Prepayments	100
Increase in Accounts Payable	90
Subtraction:	
Decrease in Other Current Liabilities	(240)
Cash Flow from Operations	$ 1,310

b. Bamberger Enterprises decreased its noncash current assets, particularly accounts receivable, generating positive cash flows. Although it repaid other current liabilities, the reduction in accounts receivable dominated and caused cash flow from operations to exceed net income.

5.28 (Finnish cellular phone manufacturer; calculating and interpreting cash flow from operations.) (Amounts in Millions of €)

a.
	2008	2007	2006	2005
Net Income	€ 3,847	€ 2,542	€ 1,689	€ 1,032
Depreciation Expense	1,009	665	509	465
(Inc.) Dec. in Accounts Receivable	(2,304)	(982)	(1,573)	(272)
(Inc.) Dec. in Inventories	(422)	(362)	(103)	(121)
(Inc.) Dec. in Prepayments	49	(33)	(17)	77
Inc. (Dec.) in Accounts Payable	458	312	140	90
Inc. (Dec.) in Other Current Liabilities	923	867	1,049	450
Cash Flow from Operations	€ 3,560	€ 3,009	€1,694	€ 1,721

b. The addback for depreciation, a noncash expense, causes cash flow from operations to exceed net income each year, except 2008. Inventories increased in line with increases in net income. The company increases its accounts payable to finance the increased inventories. The firm also increased other current liabilities to finance growing operations. Variations in the relation between net in-

5.28 b. continued.

come and cash flow from operations result from variations in accounts receivable. Unusually large increases in accounts receivable in 2006 and 2008 cause cash flow from operations to approximately equal net income in 2006 and to be less than net income in 2008. The variations in accounts receivable might result from a conscious effort by Finnish to vary credit terms to stimulate sales. It may also reflect conditions in the economy that cause its customers to delay payments in some years.

5.29 (Marketing Communications; calculating and interpreting cash flows.)

a.
MARKETING COMMUNICATIONS
Comparative Statement of Cash Flows
(Amounts in Millions)

	2008	2007	2006
Operations			
Net Income	$ 499	$ 363	$ 279
Depreciation and Amortization	226	196	164
(Inc.) Dec. in Accounts Receivable	(514)	(648)	(238)
(Inc.) Dec. in Inventories	(98)	(13)	(35)
(Inc.) Dec. in Prepayments	(125)	10	(64)
Inc. (Dec.) in Accounts Payable	277	786	330
Inc. (Dec.) in Other Current Liabilities	420	278	70
Cash Flow from Operations	$ 685	$ 972	$ 506
Investing			
Acquisition of Property, Plant and Equipment	$ (150)	$ (130)	$ (115)
Acquisition of Investments in Securities	(885)	(643)	(469)
Cash Flow from Investing	$ (1,035)	$ (773)	$ (584)
Financing			
Long-term Debt Issued	$ 599	$ 83	$ 208
Common Stock Issued (Reacquired)	(187)	(252)	42
Dividends Paid	(122)	(104)	(88)
Cash Flow from Financing	$ 290	$ (273)	$ 162
Change in Cash	$ (60)	$ (74)	$ 84

5.29 continued.

b. Interpreting cash flow from operations for a marketing services firm requires a comparison of the change in accounts receivable from clients and accounts payable to various media. Marketing services firms act as agents between these two constituents. In Year 2006 and Year 2007, the increase in accounts payable slightly exceeded the increase in accounts receivable, indicating that Marketing Communications used the media to finance its accounts receivable. In Year 2008, however, accounts payable did not increase nearly as much as accounts receivable. It is unclear whether the media demanded earlier payment, whether the media offered incentives to pay more quickly, or some other reason. As a consequence, cash flow from operations decreased in Year 2008. Cash flow from operations continually exceeds expenditures on property, plant, and equipment. This relation is not surprising, given that marketing services firms are not capital intensive. Marketing Communications invested significantly in other entities during the three years. The classification of these investments as noncurrent suggests that they were not made with temporarily excess cash but as a more permanent investment. Cash flow from operations was not sufficient to finance both capital expenditures and these investments, except in Year 2007. The firm relied on long-term debt to finance the difference. Given the marketing services firms are labor-intensive, one might question the use of debt instead of equity financing for these investments. In fact, Marketing Communications repurchased shares of its common stock in Year 2007 and Year 2008. Thus, the capital structure of the firm became more risky during the three years.

5.30 (Largay Corporation; effects of gains and losses from sales of equipment on cash flows.) (Amounts in Thousands)

	a.	b.	c.
Operations:			
Net Income	$ 100	$ 102	$ 98
Depreciation Expense	15	15	15
Gain on Sale of Equipment	--	(2)	--
Loss on Sale of Equipment	--	--	2
Changes in Working Capital Accounts	(40)	(40)	(40)
Cash Flow from Operations	$ 75	$ 75	$ 75
Investing:			
Sale of Equipment	$ 10	$ 12	$ 8
Acquisition of Buildings and Equipment	(30)	(30)	(30)
Cash Flow from Investing	$ (20)	$ (18)	$ (22)
Financing:			
Repayment of Long-term Debt	$ (40)	$ (40)	$ (40)
Change in Cash	$ 15	$ 17	$ 13
Cash, Beginning of Year	27	27	27
Cash, End of Year	$ 42	$ 44	$ 40

5.30 continued.

The instructor should note for the students that Cash Flow from Operations remains constant. Income changes, but the gain or loss on sale of equipment is not an operating source or use of cash.

5.31 (Effect of various transactions on statement of cash flows.)

Note to instructors: If you use transparencies in class, it is effective to flash onto the screen the answer transparency for some problem showing a comprehensive statement of cash flows. Then you can point to the lines affected as the students attempt to answer the question. It helps them by letting them see the possibilities. We use this question for in-class discussion. We seldom assign it for actual homework. A favorite form of question for examinations is to present a schematic statement of cash flows and to ask which lines certain transactions affect and how much. When we use this problem in class, we invariably tell students that it makes a good examination question; this serves to strengthen their interest in the discussion.

a. Amortization Expense... 600
    Patent... 600

Change in Cash	=	Change in Liabilities	+	Change in Shareholders' Equity	–	Change in Non-cash Assets
				–600		–600

(3) Decreases by $600; reduces net income through amortization expense.

(4) Increases by $600; amount of expense is added back to net income in deriving cash flow from operations.

No effect on net cash flow from operations or cash.

b. Factory Site.. 50,000
    Common Stock... 50,000

Change in Cash	=	Change in Liabilities	+	Change in Shareholders' Equity	–	Change in Non-cash Assets
				+50,000		+50,000

The transaction does not appear in the statement of cash flows because it does not affect cash. The firm must disclose information about the transaction in a supplemental schedule or note.

5.31 continued.

c. Inventory.. 7,500
    Accounts Payable... 7,500

Change in Cash	=	Change in Liabilities	+	Change in Shareholders' Equity	−	Change in Non-cash Assets
		+7,500				+7,500

(4) Increases by $7,500; operating increase in cash from increase in Accounts Payable.

(5) Increases by $7,500; operating decrease in cash for increase in inventory.

The net effect of these two transactions is to leave cash from operations unchanged, because the amounts added and subtracted change in such a way as to cancel out each other.

d. Inventory.. 6,000
    Cash.. 6,000

Change in Cash	=	Change in Liabilities	+	Change in Shareholders' Equity	−	Change in Non-cash Assets
−6,000 Opns						+6,000

(2) Increases by $6,000; use of cash in operations.

(5) Increase the subtraction by $6,000; increase in Inventory account, subtracted.

(11) Decreases by $6,000.

The net effect is to reduce cash from operations and cash by $6,000 the cash expenditure for an operating asset, inventory.

e. Fire Loss.. 1,500
    Inventory... 1,500

Change in Cash	=	Change in Liabilities	+	Change in Shareholders' Equity	−	Change in Non-cash Assets
				−1,500		−1,500

5.31 e. continued.

(3) Decreases by $1,500; net income goes down.

(4) Increases by $1,500; additions go up because inventory, not cash, was destroyed. OK to show as a reduction to a subtraction for Line (5).

No net effect on cash flow including cash flow from operations or cash.

f. Cash 1,450
  Accounts Receivable 1,450

Change in Cash	=	Change in Liabilities	+	Change in Shareholders' Equity	–	Change in Non-cash Assets
+1,450 Opns						–1,450

(1) Increases by $1,450 for collection of cash from customers.

(4) Increases by $1,450; operating increase in cash reflected by decrease in the amount of Accounts Receivable. OK to show as a reduction in the subtraction on Line (5).

(11) Increases by $1,450.

Cash flow from operations increases by $1,450, which causes cash to increase by $1,450.

g. Cash 10,000
  Bonds Payable 10,000

Change in Cash	=	Change in Liabilities	+	Change in Shareholders' Equity	–	Change in Non-cash Assets
+10,000 Finan		+10,000				

(8) Increases by $10,000; increase in cash from security issue.

(11) Increases by $10,000.

5.31 continued.

h. Cash.. 4,500
    Equipment (Net).. 4,500

Change in Cash	=	Change in Liabilities	+	Change in Shareholders' Equity	–	Change in Non-cash Assets
+4,500 Invst						–4,500

(6) Increases by $4,500; increase in cash from sale of noncurrent asset.

(11) Increases by $4,500.

5.32 (Heidi's Hide-Out; inferring cash flows from trial balance data.)

a.
Sales Revenue from Retail Customers	$ 120,000
Less Increase in Accounts Receivable from Retail Customers ($8,900 – $8,000)	(900)
Plus Increase in Advances from Retail Customers ($10,000 – $9,000)	1,000
Cash Collected from Retail Customers	$ 120,100

b.
Rent Expense	$ (33,000)
Less Increase in Advances to Landlords ($5,600 – $5,000)	(600)
Less Decrease in Rent Payable to Landlords ($5,300 – $6,000)	(700)
Cash Paid to Landlords	$ (34,300)

c.
Wage Expense	$ (20,000)
Less Increase in Advances to Employees ($1,500 – $1,000)	(500)
Less Decrease in Wages Payable to Employees ($1,800 – $2,000)	(200)
Cash Paid to Employees	$ (20,700)

d.
Cost of Retail Merchandise Sold	$ (90,000)
Plus Decrease in Inventory of Retail Merchandise ($10,000 – $11,000)	1,000
Less Increase in Advances to Suppliers of Retail Merchandise ($10,500 – $10,000)	(500)
Less Decrease in Accounts Payable to Suppliers of Retail Merchandise ($7,700 – $8,000)	(300)
Cash Paid to Suppliers of Retail Merchandise	$ (89,800)

5.33 (Digit Retail Enterprises, Inc.; inferring cash flows from balance sheet and income statement data.)

a.
Sales Revenue	$ 270,000
Less Increase in Accounts Receivable ($38,000 – $23,000)	(15,000)
Less Decrease in Advances from Customers ($6,100 – $8,500)	(2,400)
Cash Received from Customers during the Year	$ 252,600

b.
Cost of Goods Sold	$ (145,000)
Less Increase in Merchandise Inventory ($65,000 – $48,000)	(17,000)
Acquisition Cost of Merchandise Purchased during the Year	$ (162,000)

c.
Acquisition Cost of Merchandise Purchased during the Year (from Part b.)	$ (162,000)
Plus Increase in Accounts Payable—Merchandise Suppliers ($20,000 – $18,000)	2,000
Cash Paid for Acquisitions of Merchandise during the Year	$ (160,000)

d.
Salaries Expense	$ (68,000)
Plus Increase in Salaries Payable ($2,800 – $2,100)	700
Cash Paid to Salaried Employees during the Year	$ (67,300)

e.
Insurance Expense	$ (5,000)
Less Increase in Prepaid Insurance ($12,000 – $9,000)	(3,000)
Cash Paid to Insurance Companies during the Year	$ (8,000)

f.
Rent Expense	$ (12,000)
Plus Decrease in Prepaid Rent ($0 – $2,000)	2,000
Plus Increase in Rent Payable ($3,000 – $0)	3,000
Cash Paid to Landlords for Rental of Space during the Year	$ (7,000)

g.
Increase in Retained Earnings ($11,800 – $11,500)	$ 300
Less Net Income	(9,600)
Dividend Declared	$ (9,300)
Less Decrease in Dividend Payable ($2,600 – $4,200)	(1,600)
Cash Paid for Dividends during the Year	$ (10,900)

5.33 continued.

h.
Depreciation Expense		$ (20,000)
Plus Increase in Accumulated Depreciation ($35,000 – $20,000)		15,000
Accumulated Depreciation of Property, Plant and Equipment Sold		$ (5,000)
Cost of Property, Plant and Equipment Sold ($100,000 – $90,000)		10,000
Book Value of Property, Plant and Equipment Sold		$ 5,000
Plus Gain on Sale of Property, Plant and Equipment		3,200
Cash Received from Sale of Property, Plant and Equipment		$ 8,200

5.34 (Hale Company; preparing and interpreting a statement of cash flows using a T-account work sheet.)

a.
HALE COMPANY
Statement of Cash Flows
For the Year

Operations:		
Net Income	$ 44,000	
Additions:		
Depreciation Expense	54,000	
Increase in Accounts Payable	5,000	
Subtractions:		
Increase in Accounts Receivable	(13,000)	
Increase in Inventory	(11,000)	
Decrease in Interest Payable	(2,000)	
Cash Flow from Operations		$77,000
Investing:		
Sale of Equipment	$ 5,000	
Acquisition of Equipment	(55,000)	
Cash Flow from Investing		(50,000)
Financing:		
Dividends	$ (10,000)	
Retirement of Portion of Mortgage Payable	(11,000)	
Cash Flow from Financing		(21,000)
Net Change in Cash		$ 6,000
Cash, January 1		52,000
Cash, December 31		$58,000

5.34 a. continued.

The amounts in the T-account work sheet below are in thousands.

	Cash	
√	52	

Operations

Net Income	(1)	44	13	(5)	Increase in Accounts Receivable
Depreciation	(3)	54			
Increase in Accounts Payable	(8)	5	11	(6)	Increase in Inventory
			2	(9)	Decrease in Interest Payable

Investing

Sale of Equipment	(4)	5	55	(7)	Acquisition of Equipment

Financing

		10	(2)	Dividends
		11	(10)	Decrease in Mortgage Payable

√	58	

Accounts Receivable			Inventory			Land	
√	93		√	151		√	30
(5)	13		(6)	11			
√	106		√	162		√	30

Buildings and Equipment (Cost)			Accumulated Depreciation			Accounts Payable	
√	790			460	√	136	√
(7)	55	15 (4)	(4) 10	54	(3)	5	(8)
√	830			504	√	141	√

5.34 a. continued.

Interest Payable		Mortgage Payable		Common Stock	
	10 √		120 √		250 √
(9) 2		(10) 11			
	8 √		109 √		250 √

Retained Earnings	
	140 √
(2) 10	44 (1)
	174 √

5.34 continued.

b. Deriving Direct Method Cash Flow from Operations Using Data from T-Account Work Sheet (All Dollar Amounts in Thousands)

1. Copy Income Statement and Cash Flow from Operations; see Column (a) in the display below.

2. Copy Information from T-Account Work Sheet Next to Related Income Statement Item; see Columns (b) and (c) in the display below.

3. Sum Across Rows to Derive Direct Receipts and Expenditures; see Column (d) in the display below.

Operations	Indirect Method	Changes in Related Balance Sheet Accounts from T-Account Work Sheet	Direct Method	From Operations: Receipts less Expenditures
	(a)	(b)	(c)	(d)
Revenues.............	$1,200	$ (13)	= Accounts Receivable Increase	$ 1,187	Receipts from Customers
Cost of Goods Sold......	(788)	5	= Accounts Payable Increase	(794)	Payments for Merchandise
		(11)	= Merchandise Inventory Increase		
Wages and Salaries......	(280)	--	= Other Current Liabilities Increase	(280)	Payments for Wages and Salaries
Depreciation Expense....	(54)	54	(Expense Not Using Cash)	--	
Interest Expense..........	(12)	(2)	= Interest Payable Decrease	(14)	Payments for Interest
Income Tax Expense.....	(22)	--	= Income Taxes Payable Increase	(22)	Payments for Income Taxes
Net Income..................	$ 44	$ 44	Totals	$ 77	= Cash Flow from Operations Derived via Direct Method
		$ 77	= Cash Flow from Operations Derived via Indirect Method		

Solutions

5.34 continued.

    c. Statement of Cash Flows presenting the direct method and a reconciliation of income to cash flows from operations.

HALE COMPANY
Statement of Cash Flows
For the Year

Operating Activities:
  Sources of Cash:
    Cash Received from Customers .... $ 1,187,000
  Uses of Cash:
    Payments to Suppliers .... (794,000)
    Payments to Employees .... (280,000)
    Interest Payments .... (14,000)
    Tax Payments .... (22,000)
  Cash Flow from Operations .... $ 77,000

Reconciliation of Net Income to Cash from Operations:	
Net Income	$ 44,000
Depreciation	54,000
Changes in Operating Accounts:	
Accounts Receivable	(13,000)
Inventory	(11,000)
Accounts Payable	5,000
Interest Payable	(2,000)
Cash from Operations	$ 77,000

Investing Activities:
  Cash Used for New Acquisition of Equipment ..... $ (55,000)
  Cash Received from Disposition of Equipment   5,000
Net Cash Provided by (Used for) Investing ....   (50,000)
Financing Activities:
  Cash Used for Dividends .... $ (10,000)
  Cash Used to Pay Portion of Mortgage .... (11,000)
Net Cash Provided by (Used for) Financing ....   (21,000)
Net Change in Cash for Year .... $ 6,000
Cash, January 1   52,000
Cash, December 31 .... $ 58,000

    d. Cash flow from operations was sufficient to finance acquisitions of equipment during the year. The firm used the excess cash flow to pay dividends and retire long-term debt.

5.35 (Dickerson Manufacturing Company; preparing and interpreting a statement of cash flows using a T-account work sheet.)

a.
DICKERSON MANUFACTURING COMPANY
Statement of Cash Flows
For the Year

Operations:		
Net Income	$ 568,000	
Additions:		
Depreciation	510,000	
Loss on Sale of Machinery	5,000	
Increase in Accounts Payable	146,000	
Increase in Taxes Payable	16,000	
Increase in Short-Term Payables	138,000	
Subtractions:		
Increase in Accounts Receivable	(106,000)	
Increase in Inventory	(204,000)	
Cash Flow from Operations		$ 1,073,000
Investing:		
Sale of Machinery	$ 25,000	
Acquisition of Land	(36,000)	
Acquisition of Buildings and Machinery	(1,018,000)	
Cash Flow from Investing		(1,029,000)
Financing:		
Issue of Common Stock	$ 32,000	
Dividends Paid	(60,000)	
Bonds Retired	(50,000)	
Cash Flow from Financing		(78,000)
Net Change in Cash		$ (34,000)
Cash, January 1		358,000
Cash, December 31		$ 324,000

5.35 a. continued.

The amounts in the T-account work sheet below are in thousands.

	Cash		
√	358		

Operations					
Net Income	(1)	568	106	(5)	Increase in Accounts Receivable
Depreciation Expense	(3)	510			
Loss on Sale of Equipment	(4)	5	204	(6)	Increase in Inventory
Increase in Accounts Payable	(9)	146			
Increase in Taxes Payable	(10)	16			
Increase in Other Short-Term Payables	(11)	138			

Investing					
Sale of Machinery	(4)	25	1,018	(7)	Acquisition of Buildings and Machinery
			36	(8)	Acquisition of Land

Financing					
Issue of Common Stock	(13)	32	60	(2)	Dividends
			50	(12)	Retirement of Bonds

√	324	

Accounts Receivable			Inventory		
√	946		√	1,004	
(5)	106		(6)	204	
√	1,052		√	1,208	

Buildings and Machinery				Accumulated Depreciation—Buildings and Machinery			
√	8,678					3,974	√
(7)	1,018	150	(4)	(4)	120	510	(3)
√	9,546					4,364	√

5.35 a. continued.

Land				Accounts Payable		
√	594				412	√
(8)	36				146	(9)
√	630				558	√

Taxes Payable				Other Short-Term Payables		
		274	√		588	√
		16	(10)		138	(11)
		290	√		726	√

Bonds Payable				Common Stock		
		1,984	√		1,672	√
(12)	50				32	(13)
		1,934	√		1,704	√

Retained Earnings			
		2,676	√
(2)	60	568	(1)
		3,184	√

b. Dickerson Manufacturing Company is heavily capital intensive. Its cash flow from operations exceeds net income because of the depreciation expense addback. Cash flow from operations appears substantial, but so are its expenditures for building and equipment. The firm's relatively low dividend payout rate suggests that it expects large capital expenditures to continue.

5.36 (GTI, Inc.; preparing and interpreting a statement of cash flows using a T-account work sheet.) (Amounts in Thousands)

a.

T-Account Work Sheet for 2007

			Cash			
	√	430				

Operations

Net Income	(1)	417		168	(3)	Increase in Accounts Receivable
Depreciation Expense	(6)	641				
Amortization Expense	(8)	25		632	(4)	Increase in Inventories
				154	(5)	Increase in Prepayments
				769	(10)	Decrease in Accounts Payable
				299	(12)	Decrease in Other Current Liabilities
				37	(14)	Decrease in Other Noncurrent Liabilities

Investing

				1,433	(7)	Acquisition of Property, Plant, and Equipment
				391	(9)	Acquisition of Patent

Financing

Issue of Notes Payable	(11)	220		12	(2)	Dividends Paid
Increase in Long-term Debt	(13)	2,339				
Increase in Preferred Stock	(15)	289				
Increase in Common Stock	(16)	9				
	√	475				

5.36 a. continued.

Accounts Receivable				Inventories			
√	3,768			√	2,334		
(3)	168			(4)	632		
√	3,936			√	2,966		

Prepayments				Property, Plant and Equipment (Net)			
√	116			√	3,806		
(5)	154			(7)	1,433	641	(6)
√	270			√	4,598		

Other Noncurrent Assets				Accounts Payable			
√	193					1,578	√
(9)	391	25	(8)	(10)	769		
√	559					809	√

Notes Payable to Banks				Other Current Liabilities			
		11	√			1,076	√
		220	(11)	(12)	299		
		231	√			777	√

Long-Term Debt				Other Noncurrent Liabilities			
		2,353	√			126	√
		2,339	(13)	(14)	37		
		4,692	√			89	√

Preferred Stock				Common Stock			
		0	√			83	√
		289	(15)			2	(16)
		289	√			85	√

Additional Paid-in Capital				Retained Earnings			
		4,385	√			1,035	√
		7	(16)	(2)	12	417	(1)
		4,392	√			1,440	√

Solutions

5.36 a. continued.

T-Account Work Sheet for 2008

Cash

√	475				

Operations

Decrease in Accounts Receivable	(3)	1,391	2,691	(1)	Net Loss
Decrease in Inventories	(4)	872	13	(10)	Decrease in Accounts Payable (Inventory)
Decrease in Prepayments	(5)	148	82	(12)	Decrease in Other Current Liabilities
Depreciation Expense	(6)	625			
Amortization Expense	(8)	40			
Increase in Other Non-current Liabilities	(14)	24			

Investing

Sale of Patents	(9)	63	54	(7)	Acquisition of Property, Plant, and Equipment

Financing

Issue of Notes Payable to Banks	(11)	2,182	8	(2)	Dividends Paid
Increase in Common Stock	(15)	3	2,608	(13)	Decrease in Long-Term Debt
√		367			

5.36 a. continued.

Accounts Receivable				Inventories			
√	3,936			√	2,966		
		1,391	(3)			872	(4)
√	2,545			√	2,094		

Prepayments				Property, Plant and Equipment (Net)			
√	270			√	4,598		
		148	(5)	(7)	54	625	(6)
√	122			√	4,027		

Other Noncurrent Assets				Accounts Payable			
√	559					809	√
		40	(8)	(10)	13		
		63	(9)				
√	456					796	√

Notes Payable to Banks				Other Current Liabilities			
		231	√			777	√
		2,182	(11)	(12)	82		
		2,413	√			695	√

Long-Term Debt				Other Noncurrent Liabilities			
		4,692	√			89	√
(13)	2,608					24	(14)
		2,084	√			113	√

Preferred Stock				Common Stock			
		289	√			85	√
						1	(15)
		289	√			86	√

Additional Paid-in Capital				Retained Earnings			
		4,392	√			1,440	√
		2	(15)	(1)	2,691		
				(2)	8		
		4,394	√	√	1,259		

5.36 continued.

b.
GTI, INC.
Statement of Cash Flows
For 2007 and 2008

	2008	2007
Operations:		
Net Income (Loss)	$ (2,691)	$ 417
Depreciation Expense	625	641
Amortization Expense	40	25
Inc. (Dec.) in Other Noncurrent Liabilities	24	(37)
(Inc.) Dec. in Accounts Receivable	1,391	(168)
(Inc.) Dec. in Inventories	872	(632)
(Inc.) Dec. in Prepayments	148	(154)
Inc. (Dec.) in Accounts Payable to Suppliers of Inventory	(13)	(769)
Inc. (Dec.) in Other Current Liabilities	(82)	(299)
Cash Flow from Operations	$ 314	$ (976)
Investing:		
Sale of Patents	$ 63	$ --
Acquisition of Property, Plant and Equipment	(54)	(1,433)
Acquisition of Patents	--	(391)
Cash Flow from Investing	$ 9	$ (1,824)
Financing:		
Inc. (Dec.) in Notes Payable to Banks	$ 2,182	$ 220
Inc. (Dec.) in Long-Term Debt	(2,608)	2,339
Increase in Preferred Stock	--	289
Increase in Common Stock	3	9
Dividends Paid	(8)	(12)
Cash Flow from Financing	$ (431)	$ 2,845
Net Change in Cash	$ (108)	$ 45
Cash, Beginning of Year	475	430
Cash, End of Year	$ 367	$ 475

c. Deriving Direct Method Cash Flow from Operations Using Data from T-Account Work Sheet
(All Dollar Amounts in Thousands)

2007
1. Copy Income Statement and Cash Flow from Operations; see Column (a) in the display below.
2. Copy Information from T-Account Work Sheet Next to Related Income Statement Item; see Columns b) and (c) in the display below.
3. Sum Across Rows to Derive Direct Receipts and Expenditures; see Column (d) in the display below.

Operations, 2007	(a)	Indirect Method (b)	Changes in Related Balance Sheet Accounts from T-Account Work Sheet (c)	Direct Method (d)	From Operations: Receipts less Expenditures 2007
Revenues............	$ 22,833	$ (168)	= Accounts Receivable Increase	$ 22,665	Receipts from Customers
Cost of Goods Sold	(16,518)	(769)	= Accounts Payable for Inventories Decrease	(17,919)	Payments for Inventories
		(632)	= Inventory Increase		
Selling and Administrative Expenses......	(4,849)	641	(Expense Not Using Cash)	(4,673)	Payments for Selling and Administrative Services
		25	(Expense Not Using Cash)		
		(154)	= Increase in Prepayments		
		(299)	= Decrease in Other Current Liabilities		
		(37)	= Decrease in Other Noncurrent Liabilities		
Interest Expense......	(459)		- Interest Payable (no change in balance sheet)	(459)	Payments for Interest
Income Tax Expense.	(590)		= Income Taxes Payable Increase	(590)	Payments for Income Taxes
Net Income..........	$ 417	$ 417	Totals............	$ (976) =	Cash Flow from Operations Derived via Direct Method
		$ (976)	= Cash Flow from Operations Derived via Indirect Method		

Solutions 5-30

5.36 continued.

    d. Cash flow from operations was negative during 2007, despite positive net income, primarily because GTI reduced accounts payable and other current liabilities. The increases in receivables, inventories, and prepayments suggest that GTI grew during 2007 relative to 2006. One usually finds in these cases that current operating liabilities increase as well. The reduction in these current liabilities occurred either because GTI chose to use cash to liquidate these obligations or because creditors forced the firm to repay. GTI obtained the cash needed to finance the operating cash flow shortfall and capital expenditures by increasing short- and long-term debt and issuing preferred stock.

       GTI experienced a net loss in 2008 but its cash flow from operations turned positive. The firm reduced receivables, inventories and prepayments with only minor reductions in current operating liabilities. The small reductions in current operating liabilities relative to the declines in current operating assets reflect either a stretching of short-term creditors or a return to a normal level of current operating liabilities after the repayment made in 2007. GTI dramatically decreased capital expenditures in 2008 and replaced long-term debt with short-term borrowing.

5.37 (CVS Caremark Corporation; interpreting a statement of cash flows based on the direct method for presenting cash flow from operations.)

		2007
a.	Net Revenues	$ 76,329.5
	Less Cash Receipts from Revenues	(61,986.3)
	Increase in Accounts Receivable	$ 14,343.2
b.	Cash Paid for Inventory	$ 45,772.6
	Increase in Accounts Payable for Inventory	181.4
	Purchases for Inventory	$ 45,954.0
	Less Cost of Revenues	(60,221.8)
	Change (Decrease) in Inventories for the Year	$(14,267.8)

    Beginning Inventory + Purchases − COGS = Ending Inventory
    Purchases − COGS = Ending Inventory − Beginning Inventory
    Change in Inventory = Purchases − COGS

c.	Amount Paid for Interest	$ 468.2
	Interest Expense	(434.6)
	Payment Exceeded Expenses by	$ 33.6

    d. The company acquired another large company. In fact, CVS acquired Caremark.

5.38 (CVS Caremark Corporation; interpreting a statement of cash flows based on the direct method for presenting cash flow from operations.)

a.
	2006
Net Revenues	$ 43,821.4
Less Cash Receipts from Revenues	(43,273.7)
Increase in Accounts Receivable	$ 547.7

b.
Cost of Revenues	$ 32,079.2
Increase in Inventories for the Year	624.1
Purchases for Inventory	$ 32,703.3
Less Cash Paid for Inventory	(31,422.1)
Increase in Accounts Payable for Inventory	$ 1,281.2

Beginning Inventory + Purchases – COGS = Ending Inventory
Purchases – COGS = Ending Inventory – Beginning Inventory
Purchases = Ending Inventory – Beginning Inventory + COGS

Purchases – Cash Paid = Increase in Accounts Payable

c.
Amount Paid for Interest	$ 228.1
Interest Expense	(215.8)
Payment Exceeded Expenses by	$ 12.3

d. (Repeats Part *d.* of preceding problem.) The company acquired another large company. In fact, CVS acquired Caremark.

5.39 (Nordstrom Inc.; Derive cash flow from operations presented with the direct method from annual report presentation that uses the indirect method.)

Deriving Direct Method Cash Flow from Operations Using Data from T-Account Work Sheet
(All Dollar Amounts in Millions)

Fiscal Year 2006 Operations	(a)	Indirect Method (b)	Changes in Related Balance Sheet Accounts from T-Account Work Sheet (c)	Direct Method (d)	
Net Sales	$ 8,560.7	$ 17.1	= Provision for Bad Debt Expense	$ 8,577.8	Receipts from Customers
		(61.3)	= Accounts Receivable Increase	(61.3)	
				$ 8,516.5	
Cost of Goods Sold	(5,353.9)	(38.6)	= Merchandise Inventories Increase	$ (5,392.5)	Payments to Suppliers of Merchandise
		84.3	= Accounts Payable Increase	84.3	
				(5,308.2)	
Selling General and Administrative Expenses	(2,296.9)	248.2	= Depreciation and Amortization, Net not Using Cash this Period	248.2	Payments for S, G & A
		37.4	= Stock-Based Compensation Expense	(2,259.5)	
		(4.7)	= Prepaid Expenses Increase	(4.7)	
		48.7	= Accrued Salaries, Wages and Related Benefits Increase	48.7	
				(1,967.3)	
Interest Expense	(42.8)			$ (42.8)	Payments for Interest
				(42.8)	
Other Income, Net	238.5	128.0	= Asset Backed Securities Decrease (Increase)	$ 366.5	New Receipts for Other Items
		(7.7)	= Other Assets Increase	(7.7)	
		23.5	= Other Current Liabilities Increase	23.5	
		30.7	= Deferred Property Incentives Increase	30.7	
		17.3	= Other Liabilities Increase	17.3	
				430.3	
Income Tax Expense	(427.6)	(58.3)	= Deferred Income Tax Benefits	$ (485.9)	Payments for Income Taxes
		43.6	= Tax Benefits from Stock-Based Payments	43.6	
		(38.3)	= Excess Stock Benefits from Stock-Based Payments	(38.3)	
		(5.5)	= Income Taxes Payable Decrease	(5.5)	
				(486.1)	
Net Income	$ 678.0	$ 678.0			
		$ 1,142.4	= Cash Flow from Operations Derived via Indirect Method	$ 1,142.4	Cash Flow from Operations Derived via the Direct Method

5.40 (Nordstrom Inc.; Derive cash flow from operations presented with the direct method from annual report presentation that uses the indirect method.)

Deriving Direct Method Cash Flow from Operations Using Data from T-Account Work Sheet
(All Dollar Amounts in Millions)

Fiscal Year 2005 Operations	(a)	Indirect Method (b)	Changes in Related Balance Sheet Accounts from T-Account Work Sheet (c)	Direct Method (d)	
Net Sales	$ 7,722.8	$ 20.9	= Provision for Bad Debt Expense	$ 7,743.7	
		(15.1)	= Accounts Receivable Increase	(15.1)	
				$ 7,728.6	Receipts from Customers
Cost of Goods Sold	(4,888.0)	(20.8)	= Merchandise Inventories Increase	$ (4,908.8)	
		31.7	= Accounts Payable Increase	31.7	
				(4,877.1)	Payments to Suppliers of Merchandise
Selling General and Administrative Expenses	(2,100.7)	242.9	= Depreciation and Amortization, Net not Using Cash this Period	242.9	
		13.3	= Stock-Based Compensation Expense	(2,087.4)	
		(1.0)	= Prepaid Expenses Increase	(1.0)	
		(11.3)	= Accrued Salaries, Wages and Related Benefits Increase	(11.3)	
				(1,856.8)	Payments for S, G & A
Interest Expense	(45.3)			$ (45.3)	Payments for Interest
Other Income, Net	196.4	(135.8)	= Asset Backed Securities Decrease (Increase)	$ 60.6	
		(3.5)	= Other Assets Increase	(3.5)	
		38.8	= Other Current Liabilities Increase	38.7	
		49.5	= Deferred Property Incentives Increase	49.5	
		19.3	= Other Liabilities Increase	19.3	
				164.6	New Receipts for Other Items
Income Tax Expense	(333.9)	(11.2)	= Deferred Income Tax Benefits	$ (345.1)	
		41.1	= Tax Benefits from Stock-Based Payments	41.1	
		—	= Excess Stock Benefits from Stock-Based Payments		
		(33.9)	= Income Taxes Payable Decrease	(33.9)	
				(337.9)	Payments for Income Taxes
Net Income	$ 551.3	$ 551.3			
		$ 776.2	= Cash Flow from Operations Derived via Indirect Method	$ 776.2	Cash Flow from Operations Derived via the Direct Method

Solutions 5-34

5.41 (Quinta Company; working backwards through the statement of cash flows.)

QUINTA COMPANY
Condensed Balance Sheet
January 1, 2008
($ in 000's)

Assets

Current Assets:		
Cash...	$ 20	
Accounts Receivable.......................................	190	
Merchandise Inventories.................................	280	
Total Current Assets..................................		$ 490
Land...		50
Buildings and Equipment.....................................	$ 405	
Less Accumulated Depreciation.......................	(160)	245
Investments..		140
Total Assets...		$ 925

Liabilities and Shareholders' Equity

Current Liabilities:		
Accounts Payable..	$ 255	
Other Current Liabilities..................................	130	
Total Current Liabilities............................		$ 385
Bonds Payable..		60
Common Stock...		140
Retained Earnings..		340
Total Liabilities and Shareholders' Equity.........		$ 925

Shown below are T-accounts for deriving the solution. Entries (1)–(13) are reconstructed from the statement of cash flows. Changes for the year are appropriately debited or credited to end-of-year balances to get beginning-of-year balances. T-account amounts are shown in thousands.

Cash			Accounts Receivable		Merchandise Inventories	
	20			190		280
(1)	200	30 (4)	(4)	30	(5)	40
(2)	60	40 (5)				
(3)	25	45 (6)				
(7)	40	130 (10)				
(8)	15	200 (13)				
(9)	10					
(11)	60					
(12)	40					
√	25		√	220	√	320

5-35 Solutions

5.41 continued.

Land		Buildings and Equipment		Accumulated Depreciation	
50		405			160
	10 (9)	(10) 130	35 (8)	(8) 20	60 (2)
√ 40		√ 500			200 √

Investments		Accounts Payable		Other Current Liabilities	
140			255		130
	40 (7)		25 (3)	(6) 45	
√ 100			280 √		85 √

Bonds Payable		Common Stock		Retained Earnings	
	60		140		340
	40 (12)		60 (11)	(13) 200	200 (1)
	100 √		200 √		340 √

Shown on the following page is the Transactions Spreadsheet. Entries (1)–(13) are reconstructed from the statement of cash flows. Changes for the year are appropriately debited or credited to end-of-year balances to get beginning-of-year balances. Amounts are shown in thousands.

5.41 continued.

Following, we show the Transaction Spreadsheet for those who prefer to work problems with it, not with T-accounts.

Transactions spreadsheet.

Balance Sheet Accounts	Balance: Beginning of Period (Derived)	1 Net Income for Year	2 Depreciation Expense	3 Increase in Accounts Payable	4 Increase in Accounts Receivable	5 Increase in Merchandise Inventories	6 Decrease in Other Current Liabilities	7 Sale of Investments	8 Sale of Buildings and Equipment	9 Sale of Land	10 Acquire New Buildings and Equipment	11 Issue Common Stock	12 Issue Bonds Payable	13 Dividends Paid in Cash	Balance: End of Period (Given)
ASSETS															
Current Assets:															
Cash	20	200	60	25	−30	−40	−45	40	15	10	−130	60	40	−200	25
Accounts Receivable	190				30										220
Merchandise Inventories	280					40									320
Total Current Assets	490														565
Noncurrent Assets:															
Land	50									−10					40
Building and Equipment	405								−35		130				500
Accumulated Depreciation	−160		−60						20						(200)
Investments	140							−40							100
Total Noncurrent Assets	435														440
Total Assets	925														1,005
LIABILITIES AND SHAREHOLDERS' EQUITY															
Current Liabilities:															
Accounts Payable	255			25											280
Other Current Liabilities	130						−45								85
Total Current Liabilities	385														365
Noncurrent Liabilities:															
Bonds Payable	60												40		100
Total Noncurrent Liabilities	60														100
Total Liabilities	445														465
Shareholders' Equity:															
Common Stock	140											60			200
Retained Earnings	340	200												−200	340
Total Shareholders' Equity	480														540
Total Liabilities and Shareholders' Equity	925														1,005
Imbalance, if Any		-	-	-	-	-	-	-	-	-	-	-	-	-	-
Income Statement Accounts		Income Summary													

5.42   (Swoosh Shoes, Inc.; interpreting the statement of cash flows.)

   a. Swoosh Shoes' growth in sales and net income led to increases of account receivable and inventories. Swoosh Shoes, however, did not increase its accounts payable and other current operating liabilities to help finance the buildup in current assets. Thus, its cash flow from operations decreased.

   b. Swoosh Shoes increased its acquisitions of property, plant and equipment to provide the firm with operating capacity to sustain its rapid growth. Swoosh Shoes also acquired investments in securities of other firms. It is not clear from the statement of cash flows whether the investments represented short-term investments of temporarily excess cash (a current asset) or long-term investments made to develop an operating relation with another firm (noncurrent asset).

   c. Swoosh Shoes used cash flow from operations during 2006 and 2007 to finance its investing activities. The excess cash flow after investing activities served to repay short- and long-term debt and pay dividends. Cash flow from operations during 2008 was insufficient to finance investing activities. Swoosh Shoes engaged in short-term borrowing to make up the shortfall and finance the payment of dividends.

   d. Operating cash flows should generally finance the payment of dividends. Either operating cash flows or long-term sources of capital should generally finance acquisitions of property, plant and equipment. Thus, Swoosh Shoes' use of short-term borrowing seems inappropriate. One might justify such an action if Swoosh Shoes (1) expected cash flow from operations during 2009 to return to its historical levels, (2) expected cash outflows for property, plant and equipment to decrease during 2009, or (3) took advantage of comparatively low short-term borrowing rates during 2008 and planned to refinance this debt with long-term borrowing during 2009.

5.43   (Spokane Corporation; interpreting the statement of cash flows.) (We have based this problem on the actual financial statements of the former Boise Cascade Corporation.)

   a. Forest products companies are capital intensive. Depreciation is therefore a substantial non-cash expense each year. The addback for depreciation converts a net loss each year into positive cash flow from operations. Note that cash flow from operations increased each year as the net loss decreased.

   b. Spokane Corporation had substantial changes in its property, plant and equipment during the three years. It likely built new, more efficient production facilities and sold off older, less efficient facilities.

5.43 continued.

c. For the three years combined, Spokane Corporation reduced its long-term debt and replaced it with preferred stock. The sales of forest products are cyclical. When the economy is in a recession, as apparently occurred during the three years, the high fixed cost of capital-intensive manufacturing facilities can result in net losses. If Spokane Corporation is unable to repay debt on schedule during such years, it causes expensive financial distress or even bankruptcy. Firms have more latitude with respect to dividends on preferred stock than interest on debt. Thus, a shift toward preferred stock and away from long-term debt reduces the bankruptcy risk of Spokane Corporation. Note that Spokane Corporation continued to pay, and even increase, dividends despite operating at a net loss. Most shareholders prefer less rather than more fluctuation in their dividends over the business cycle.

5.44 (Interpreting statement of cash flow relations.)

American Airlines—Property, plant and equipment comprises a large proportion of the total assets of American Airlines. Depreciation expense is a major expense for the airline. The firm operated at a net loss for the year, but the addback for depreciation resulted in a positive cash flow from operations. Cash flow from operations was not sufficient to fund capital expenditures on new property, plant and equipment. American Airlines is apparently growing since its capital expenditures exceed depreciation expense for the year. The firm financed its capital expenditures in part with cash flow from operations and in part with the issuance of additional long-term debt and capital stock. The net effect of the cash flow from financing is a reduction in liabilities and an increase in capital stock (actually preferred stock). Operating at a net loss increases the risk of bankruptcy. Perhaps American Airlines reduced the amount of debt in its capital structure to reduce fixed payment claims and substituted preferred stock that generally requires dividend payments only when declared by the board of directors.

American Home Products—Because of patent protection, pharmaceutical companies tend to generate relatively high profit margins and significant cash flows from operations. Although the manufacturing process for pharmaceutical products is capital intensive, cash flow from operations is usually sufficient to fund capital expenditures. American Home Products used the excess cash flow to pay dividends and repurchase capital stock. The firm also borrowed short-term funds and invested the proceeds in the acquisition of another business. Borrowing short term to finance investments in long-term assets is usually undesirable, because the firm must repay the debt before the long-term assets generate sufficient cash flow. Perhaps American Home Products needed to borrow short term to consummate the acquisition, with the expectation of refinancing the short-term debt with long-term borrowing soon after the

5.44 continued.

acquisition. Alternatively, American Home Products might have anticipated a decline in long-term rates in the near future and borrowed short term until long-term rates actually declined.

Interpublic Group—An advertising agency serves as a link between clients desiring advertising time and space and various media with advertising time and space to sell. Thus, the principal asset of an advertising agency is accounts receivable from clients and the principal liability is accounts payable to various media. Interpublic Group reports an increase in accounts receivable of $66 million and an increase in accounts payable of $59 million. Thus, the firm appeared to manage its receivables/payables position well. Advertising agencies lease most of the physical facilities used in their operations. They purchase equipment for use in designing and producing advertising copy. Thus, they must make some capital expenditures. Cash flow from operations, however, is more than sufficient to finance acquisitions of equipment. Interpublic Group used the excess cash flow plus the proceeds of additional short- and long-term borrowing to pay dividends, repurchase capital stock, and increase cash on the balance sheet.

Procter & Gamble—Procter & Gamble's brand names create high profit margins and cash flows from operations. Cash flow from operations is more than adequate to finance capital expenditures. Note that capital expenditures significantly exceed depreciation, suggesting that the firm is still in a growth mode. The firm used the excess cash flow to repay short- and long-term debt and to pay dividends.

Reebok—Cash flow from operations for Reebok is less than net income plus depreciation, a somewhat unusual relationship for a seasoned firm. Reebok increased its accounts receivable and inventories during the year but did not stretch its accounts payable commensurably. The financing section of the statement of cash flows suggests that Reebok might have used short-term debt to finance some of its working capital needs. Cash flow from operations was still more than sufficient to fund capital expenditures. One explanation for the sufficiency of cash flow from operations to cover capital expenditures is that Reebok is not very capital intensive. The relation between depreciation expense and net income supports this explanation. Reebok outsources virtually all of its manufacturing. Reebok used the excess cash flows from operating and investing activities to pay dividends and repurchase its capital stock.

Texas Instruments—Like American Home Products and Upjohn (discussed later), Texas Instruments invests heavily in technology to create a competitive advantage. Patents and copyrights on computer hardware, software, and other products serve as a barrier to entry by competitors and provide Texas Instruments with an attractive profit margin. Texas Instruments differs from the two pharmaceutical compan-

5.44 continued.

ies with respect to the amount of depreciation relative to net income. Despite generating less than one-half of the net income of American Home Products, Texas Instruments has more than twice the amount of depreciation expense and capital expenditures. Thus, Texas Instruments is likely more capital intensive than the other two technology-based companies. Note that the changes in individual working capital accounts are relatively large, compared to the amount of net income. These relations suggest, although do not prove, that the operations of Texas Instruments grew significantly during the year. Cash flow from operations was sufficient to fund capital expenditures and increase the balance of cash on the balance sheet. Note that Texas Instruments issued capital stock during the year and repaid long-term debt. The amounts involved, however, are small.

Limited Brands—Current assets and current liabilities dominate the balance sheets of retailers. Thus, working capital management is of particular importance. Limited Brands increased its current liabilities in line with increases in accounts receivable and inventories. Thus, cash flow from operations approximately equals net income plus depreciation. Limited Brands invested most of the cash flow from operations in additional property, plant and equipment, the acquisition of other businesses, the repayment of short-term debt, and the payment of dividends.

Upjohn—This problem includes Upjohn primarily to compare and contrast it with American Home Products, also a pharmaceutical company. Both companies generated sufficient cash flow from operations to fund capital expenditures and pay dividends. Upjohn sold a portion of its business during the year and invested the proceeds in marketable securities.

5.45 (Fierce Fighters Corporation; interpreting direct and indirect methods.)

(We have taken these data from the statements of cash flows of Northrop Grumman Corporation, which was for many years the only large company to use the direct method for present cash flows from operations. As we write this, they are still one of few. We use the particular years here, which were 1999, 2000, and 2001, because of the steady progression downwards, about ten percent per year, in cash flow from operations.)

a. We think this is hopeless. We cannot write a coherent explanation of the decline from these data alone, at least not without further analysis.

5.45 continued.

    b. Some academics think that even the question is nonsense—that is, trying to explain changes in the data which themselves explain changes in cash. The statement of cash flows explains the change in the cash account from year to year. Consider that the statement of income and retained earnings explains the change in Retained Earnings from year to year. Most analysts think it sensible comparing income statements from one year to the next, to understand the causes of the change in income (which itself explains the causes of part of the changes in Retained Earnings). We think it sensible comparing statements of cash flows from one year to the next to explain the causes of the changes in cash flow from operations (which itself explains the causes of part of the changes in Cash).

       In this case, the decline in cash flow from operations appears to result from a decreased margin of collections from customers for sales. The focus must be on what is going on with long-term and other sales contracts. From 2007 to 2008, we see increased payments to supplie4rs and employees that the analysis should investigate. We cannot be sure what is happening, but we can see where to inquire. Focus on those contracts, not on the changes in balance sheet operating accounts.

    c. A reader can more easily interpret the direct method. The fundamental problem with the indirect method is that not a single number is itself a cash flow. So, changes in those numbers from year to year do not illuminate.

5.46   (Issues in manipulating cash flows from operations.)

    a. This will increase cash flow from operations, assuming that had the maintenance been done this period, the firm would have paid for it this period. This may be an unsound management practice, as improper maintenance will increase long-run costs. Most managers would likely consider this ethical, but likely unwise.

    b. This will not increase cash flow from operations. It will conserve cash, but when the firm spends the cash, it appears as an investing use, not an operating use. This can be an unsound management practice.

    c. There is a continuing race between clever financial managers and accounting standard setters about transactions such as this. Most simple transactions of this sort will not increase cash flow from operations, but will generate investing or financing cash flows. Chapter 13 discusses some of these complications. The Special Purpose Entities (created in 1990, but curtailed in 2003) enabled firms to treat some financing transactions as though they were oper-

5.46 c. continued.

ating. Many financial managers think it is a badge of honor to devise transactions that will comply with accounting rules while showing larger operating cash flows.

d. Not paying on time for items related to employment activities will, in the short run, increase cash flow from operations. Suppliers will catch on and will likely demand different payment terms, or higher prices, to compensate them for the slower payments. Many firms appear to engage in this practice without qualm. Others say: bargain hard for low price and delayed payments, but once you make a deal, pay on time.

e. Same issues as in Part *d.* above.

f. This will increase cash flow from operations in the period of sale, but will reduce it in the next period when the customers get cash refunds. This practice is fraud and will result in overstated revenue and income, as well as increased cash flow from operations. Such side agreements, often written by sales staff into so-called *side letters*, are illegal. Even ethical managers sometimes cannot detect side letters offered by sales staff to customers.

This page is intentionally left blank

CHAPTER 6

INTRODUCTION TO FINANCIAL STATEMENT ANALYSIS

Questions, Exercises, and Problems: Answers and Solutions

6.1   See the text or the glossary at the end of the book.

6.2   The increase in the cost of goods sold to sales percentage could result from increases in the purchase prices of inventory items or increases in the cost of theft or product obsolescence which the firm could not pass on to the customers by way of higher prices. The increase in the cost of goods sold to sales percentage could result from increased competition or weak economic conditions which forced the firm to lower prices. The increase in the cost of goods sold to sales percentage could result from a combination of factors affecting both the numerator and denominator. Thus, interpreting a change in this expense percentage requires careful analysis.

6.3   The adjustment in the numerator of rate of return on assets is for the *incremental* effect on *net* income of having versus not having interest expense. Because interest expense reduces taxable income and, therefore, income taxes otherwise payable, the tax savings from interest expense incrementally affect net income. The computation of the numerator must, therefore, incorporate this tax effect.

6.4   Assets other than accounts receivable, inventory, or fixed assets must have increased at a faster rate than the increase in sales. Perhaps the firm issued debt or common stock, thereby increasing cash or marketable securities. Perhaps the firm made a corporate acquisition using its common stock as consideration and recognized intangible assets.

6.5   The profit margin for ROA ignores how a firm has financed its assets (that is, the extent of debt versus equity financing), whereas the profit margin for ROCE takes the mix of financing into account. A firm with increased pricing power in its markets, more efficient inventory controls, or benefits of economies of scale for administrative costs might experience increases in its profit margin for ROA. However, if interest rates increased or the firm engaged in substantial new borrowing, its profit margin for ROCE could decline because of increased financing costs.

6.6 The first company apparently has a relatively small profit margin and must rely on turnover to generate a satisfactory rate of return. A discount department store is an example. The second company, on the other hand, has a larger profit margin and does not need as much turnover as the first company to generate a satisfactory rate of return.

6.7 Management strives to keep its inventories at a level that is neither too low so that it loses sales nor too high so that it incurs high storage costs. Thus, there is an optimal level of inventory for a particular firm in a particular period and an optimal inventory turnover ratio.

6.8 The rate of return on common shareholders' equity exceeds the rate of return on assets when the latter rate exceeds the return required by creditors and preferred shareholders (net of tax effects). In this situation, financial leverage is working to the benefit of the common shareholders. The rate of return on common shareholders' equity will be less than the return on assets when the latter rate is less than the return required by creditors and preferred shareholders. This situation generally occurs during periods of very poor earnings performance.

6.9 This statement suggests that the difference between the rate of return on assets and the after-tax cost of debt is positive but small. Increasing the amount of debt will require a higher interest rate that will eliminate this positive difference and financial leverage will work to the disadvantage of the common shareholders.

6.10 Financial leverage involves using debt capital that has a smaller after-tax cost than the return a firm can generate from investing the capital in various assets. The excess return belongs to the common shareholders. A firm cannot continually increase the amount of debt in the capital structure without limit. Increasing the debt level increases the risk to the common shareholders. These shareholders will not tolerate risk levels that they consider too high. Also, the cost of borrowing increases as a firm assumes larger proportions of debt. Sooner or later, the excess of the rate of return on assets over the after-tax cost of borrowing approaches zero or even becomes negative. Financial leverage then works to the disadvantage of the common shareholders.

6.11 (CBRL Group and McDonald's; calculating and disaggregating rate of return on assets.) (Amounts in Millions)

a. **CBRL Group:** $\dfrac{\$76 + (1 - .35)(\$59)}{\$1,473} = 7.8\%$.

  McDonald's: $\dfrac{\$2,335 + (1 - .35)(\$417)}{\$29,183} = 8.9\%$.

6.11 continued,

b.

	Rate of Return on Assets	=	Profit Margin for ROA	x	Total Assets Turnover Ratio

CBRL Group:

$$\frac{\$76+(1-.35)(\$59)}{\$1,473} = \frac{\$76+(1-.35)(\$59)}{\$2,352} \times \frac{\$2,352}{\$1,473}$$

$$7.8\% = 4.9\% \times 1.6$$

McDonald's:

$$\frac{\$2,335+(1-.35)(\$417)}{\$29,183} = \frac{\$2,335+(1-.35)(\$417)}{\$22,787} \times \frac{\$22,787}{\$29,183}$$

$$8.9\% = 11.4\% \times .8$$

c. McDonald's has a higher ROA, the result of a higher profit margin for ROA offset by a lower total assets turnover. McDonald's higher profit margin for ROA might result from its larger size, permitting it to benefit from spreading fixed costs over a larger sales base. McDonald's also generates revenues from franchise fees, which increase net income but not sales revenue. McDonald's lower total assets turnover might result from having the land and buildings of some of its franchisees on its balance sheet but not including the sales of these franchisees in its sales.

6.12 (Abercrombie & Fitch and Family Dollar Stores; profitability analysis for two types of retailers.) (Amounts in Millions)

Company A is the specialty retailer (Abercrombie & Fitch) because of its higher profit margin and lower total assets turnover, relative to Company B (Family Dollar Stores). The specialized, branded products of Abercrombie & Fitch permit it to price its products for a higher profit margin. Family Dollar Stores' prices are lower and thereby it generates a faster turnover of merchandise.

6.12 continued.

	Rate of Return On Assets	=	Profit Margin for ROA	x	Total Assets Turnover Ratio
Company A:	$\dfrac{\$476+(1-.35)(\$1)}{\$2,458}$	=	$\dfrac{\$476+(1-.35)(\$1)}{\$3,750}$	x	$\dfrac{\$3,750}{\$2,458}$
	19.4%	=	12.7%	x	1.5
Company B:	$\dfrac{\$243+(1-.35)(\$17)}{\$2,574}$	=	$\dfrac{\$243+(1-.35)(\$17)}{\$6,834}$	x	$\dfrac{\$6,834}{\$2,574}$
	9.9%	=	3.7%	x	2.7

6.13 (Exxon Mobil; calculating and disaggregating rate of return on common shareholders' equity.) (Amounts in Millions)

a.

Year	Numerator	Denominator	Rate of Return on Common Shareholders' Equity
2005	$ 36,130	$106,471	33.9%
2006	39,500	112,515	35.1%
2007	40,610	117,803	34.5%

b. **Profit Margin for ROCE**

Year	Numerator	Denominator	Profit Margin for ROCE
2005	$ 36,130	$370,680	9.7%
2006	39,500	377,635	10.5%
2007	40,610	404,552	10.0%

Total Assets Turnover

Year	Numerator	Denominator	Total Assets Turnover
2005	$370,680	$201,796	1.84
2006	377,635	213,675	1.77
2007	404,552	230,549	1.75

Capital Structure Leverage Ratio

Year	Numerator	Denominator	Capital Structure Leverage Ratio
2005	$201,796	$106,471	1.90
2006	213,675	112,515	1.90
2007	230,549	117,803	1.96

6.13 continued.

c. The rate of return on common shareholders' equity was relatively steady during the three years. The profit margin for ROCE and the capital leverage ratio increased but the total assets turnover decreased. Sales increased at a higher rate in 2007 than in 2006 but the profit margin for ROCE declined. Part of the explanation for the decreased profit margin for ROCE might relate to higher interest expense from the higher capital structure leverage ratio. Exxon Mobil might have increased expenditures on exploration or development of petroleum resources in 2007, which lowered net income. The higher sales level should have provided Exxon Mobil with benefits of economies of scale, but any such benefits were offset by higher other expenses.

6.14 (Harley Davidson and Starbucks; profitability analysis for two companies.) (Amounts in Millions)

a.

	Rate of Return on Assets	=	Profit Margin for ROA	x	Total Assets Turnover
Company A:	$\dfrac{\$476}{\$2,458}$	=	$\dfrac{\$476}{\$3,750}$	x	$\dfrac{\$3,750}{\$2,458}$
	19.4%	=	12.7%	x	1.5
Company B:	$\dfrac{\$934}{\$5,594}$	=	$\dfrac{\$934}{\$6,143}$	x	$\dfrac{\$6,143}{\$5,594}$
	16.7%	=	15.2%	x	1.1

b.

	Rate of Return on Common Shareholders' Equity	=	Profit Margin for ROCE	x	Total Assets Turnover	x	Capital Structure Leverage Ratio
Company A:	$\dfrac{\$476}{\$2,256}$	=	$\dfrac{\$476}{\$3,750}$	x	$\dfrac{\$3,750}{\$2,458}$	x	$\dfrac{\$2,458}{\$2,256}$
	21.1%	=	12.7%	x	1.5	x	1.1
Company B:	$\dfrac{\$934}{\$2,566}$	=	$\dfrac{\$934}{\$6,143}$	x	$\dfrac{\$6,143}{\$5,594}$	x	$\dfrac{\$5,594}{\$2,566}$
	36.4%	=	15.2%	x	1.1	x	2.2

6.14 continued.

    c. Company A is Starbucks and Company B is Harley Davidson. Starbucks typically leases the space for its restaurants and, therefore, has few fixed assets. It sells for cash and, therefore, has few accounts receivable. It will maintain some inventory, but the need for freshness of its foods suggests a rapid turnover. Thus, we would expect Starbucks to have the fastest total assets turnover. Harley Davidson needs fixed assets to manufacture its motor cycles. The smaller profit margins for Starbucks are somewhat of a surprise. Competition from other coffee shops and supermarkets with fresh ground coffees probably dampens its profit margins. Starbucks' low capital structure leverage ratio reflects its lack of assets to use as collateral for borrowing. The manufacturing of motorcycles is essentially an assembly operation, but Harley Davidson needs facilities for the assembly operation. These assets serve as collateral for borrowing.

6.15 (Intel and Verizon Communications; profitability analysis for two companies.) (Amounts in Millions)

a.

	Rate of Return on Assets	=	Profit Margin for ROA	x	Total Assets Turnover
Company A:	$\frac{\$6,986}{\$52,010}$	=	$\frac{\$6,986}{\$38,334}$	x	$\frac{\$38,334}{\$52,010}$
	13.4%	=	18.2%	x	.74
Company B:	$\frac{\$6,999}{\$187,882}$	=	$\frac{\$6,999}{\$93,469}$	x	$\frac{\$93,469}{\$187,882}$
	3.7%	=	7.5%	x	.50

b.

	Rate of Return on Common Shareholders' Equity	=	Profit Margin for ROCE	x	Total Assets Turnover	x	Capital Structure Leverage Ratio
Company A:	$\frac{\$6,976}{\$39,757}$	=	$\frac{\$6,976}{\$38,334}$	x	$\frac{\$38,334}{\$52,010}$	x	$\frac{\$52,010}{\$39,757}$
	17.5%	=	18.2%	x	.7	x	1.3
Company B:	$\frac{\$5,510}{\$49,558}$	=	$\frac{\$5,510}{\$93,469}$	x	$\frac{\$93,469}{\$187,882}$	x	$\frac{\$187,882}{\$49,558}$
	11.1%	=	5.9%	x	.5	x	3.8

6.15 continued.

c. Company A is Intel and Company B is Verizon Communications. Both of these firms are fixed-asset intensive, so their total assets turnovers are small. Their ROAs and ROCEs differ with respect to profit margin and capital structure leverage. Semiconductors are technology-intensive products and can command high profit margins if the products are on the technology edge. Telecommunication services, on the other hand, are commodity products and are difficult to differentiate from competitors. The technological intensity of semiconductors leads to short product life cycles. Firms in this industry tend not to take on substantial debt because of the short product life cycles. Telecommunication services are somewhat less technology intensive, at least with respect to the need to create the technologies. Firms in the telecommunications industry have capital-intensive fixed assets that can serve as collateral for borrowing and a somewhat more stable revenue stream, relative to semiconductors.

6.16 (Dell, Inc. and Sun Microsystems; analyzing accounts receivable for two companies.) (Amounts in Millions)

a. **Dell, Inc.** **Sun Microsystems**

$$\frac{\$61,133}{.5(\$6,152+\$7,693)} \qquad \frac{\$13,873}{.5(\$2,702+\$2,964)}$$

= 8.8 Times per Year. = 4.9 Times per Year.

b. $\frac{365}{8.8} = 41.5$ days. $\frac{365}{4.9} = 74.5$ days.

c. Dell, Inc. sells primarily to individuals who pay with credit cards. Dell, Inc. collects these accounts receivable quickly. Sun Microsystems sells to businesses. Customers may require Sun Microsystems to finance their purchases. Customers may also delay paying Sun Microsystems until their computers are set up and working properly. Sun Microsystems may also offer liberal credit terms as an inducement to businesses to purchase its computers.

6.17 (Mattel; analyzing inventories over three years.) (Amounts in Millions)

a.
Year	Numerator	Denominator	Inventory Turnover
2005	$ 2,806	$ 415	6.76
2006	3,038	380	7.99
2007	3,193	406	7.86

6.17 continued.

b.
Year	Numerator	Denominator	Days Inventory Held
2005	365	6.76	54.0
2006	365	7.99	45.7
2007	365	7.86	46.4

c.
Year	Numerator	Denominator	Cost of Goods Sold Percentage
2005	$ 2,806	$ 5,179	54.2%
2006	3,038	5,650	53.8%
2007	3,193	5,970	53.5%

d. Mattel experienced an increasing inventory turnover and a decreasing cost of goods sold to sales percentage between 2005 and 2006. Toys are trendy products. Mattel's products might have received rapid market acceptance, so that it was both able to move products more quickly and to achieve a higher gross margin on products sold. The faster turnover for trendy products means that Mattel would not need to mark down products in order to sell them or to incur additional storage costs. Mattel's cost of goods sold to sales percentage declined further in 2007 but its inventory turnover declined. Sales increased 9.1% [= ($5,650/$5,179) – 1] between 2005 and 2006 but only 5.7% [= ($5,970/$5,650) – 1] between 2006 and 2007. Perhaps Mattel increased inventory levels in 2007 expecting a larger sales increase than actually occurred. The unsold inventory resulted in a decrease in the inventory turnover rate.

6.18 (The Walt Disney Company; analyzing fixed asset turnover over three years.) (Amounts in Millions)

a.
Year	Numerator	Denominator	Fixed Asset Turnover
2005	$31,374	$15,362	2.04
2006	33,747	16,174	2.09
2007	35,510	16,270	2.18

b. The fixed asset turnover increased during the three-year period. Disney reduced its capital expenditures in 2006 and its capital expenditures in 2007 were not as large as in 2005. Its capital expenditures each year do not differ significantly from its depreciation expense. Thus, Disney seems to be approximately maintaining its level of investment in fixed assets, while its sales grow. Thus, the fixed asset turnover increases.

6.19 (Relating profitability to financial leverage.)

a.

Case	Net Income Plus After-Tax Interest Expense[a]	After-Tax Interest Expense[b]	Net Income[c]	Rate of Return on Common Shareholders' Equity
A	$12	$6.0	$ 6	$ 6/$100 = 6%
B	$16	$6.0	$10	$10/$100 = 10%
C	$16	$7.2	$ 8.8	$ 8.8/$80 = 11%
D	$ 8	$6.0	$ 2	$ 2/$100 = 2%
E	$12	$3.0	$ 9	$ 9/$100 = 9%
F	$10	$3.0	$ 7	$ 7/$100 = 7%

[a]Numerator of the rate of return on assets. In Case A, $12 = .06 × $200.

[b]After-tax cost of borrowing times interest-bearing debt. In Case A, $6.0 = .06 × $100.

[c]Net income plus after-tax interest expense minus after-tax interest expense. In Case A, $6 = $12 − $6.

b. Leverage works successfully in Cases B, C, E, and F with respect to total debt. With respect to interest-bearing debt, leverage works successfully in Cases B and C.

6.20 (Company A/Company B; interpreting changes in earnings per share.)

a. **Company A Earnings per Share:**

2008 .... $\dfrac{\$100{,}000}{100{,}000 \text{ Shares}} = \$1$ per Share.

2009 .... $\dfrac{\$100{,}000}{100{,}000 \text{ Shares}} = \$1$ per Share.

Company B Earnings per Share:

2008 .... $\dfrac{\$100{,}000}{100{,}000 \text{ Shares}} = \$1$ per Share.

2009 .... $\dfrac{.10 \times (\$1{,}000{,}000 + \$100{,}000)}{100{,}000 \text{ Shares}} = \$1.10$ per Share.

6.20 continued.

  b. Company A: No growth.
     Company B: 10% annual growth.

  c. Company B: This result is misleading. Comparisons of growth in earnings per share are valid only if firms employ equal amounts of assets in the business. Both the rate of return on assets and on shareholders' equity are better measures of growth performance. Earnings per share results do not, in general (as in this problem), take earnings retention into account.

6.21 (NIKE; calculating and interpreting short-term liquidity ratios.) (Amounts in Millions)

  a. **Current Ratio**

Year End	Numerator	Denominator	Current Ratio
2004	$5,528	$2,031	2.72
2005	6,351	1,999	3.18
2006	7,346	2,613	2.81
2007	8,077	2,584	3.13

  Quick Ratio

Year End	Numerator	Denominator	Quick Ratio
2004	$3,349	$2,031	1.65
2005	4,087	1,999	2.04
2006	4,686	2,613	1.79
2007	5,342	2,584	2.07

  b. **Cash Flow from Operations to Current Liabilities Ratio**

Year	Numerator	Denominator	Cash Flow from Operations to Current Liabilities Ratio
2005	$1,571	$2,015.0[a]	78.0%
2006	1,668	2,306.0[b]	72.3%
2007	1,879	2,598.5[c]	72.3%

[a] .5($2,031 + $1,999) = $2,015.0.
[b] .5($1,999 + $2,613) = $2,306.0.
[c] .5($2,613 + $2,584) = $2,598.5.

6.21 b. continued.

Accounts Receivable Turnover Ratio

Year	Numerator	Denominator	Accounts Receivable Turnover Ratio
2005	$13,740	$2,191.0[a]	6.27
2006	14,955	2,322.5[b]	6.44
2007	16,326	2,439.0[c]	6.69

[a].5($2,120 + $2,262) = $2,191.0.
[b].5($2,262 + $2,383) = $2,322.5.
[c].5($2,383 + $2,495) = $2,439.0.

Inventory Turnover Ratio

Year	Numerator	Denominator	Inventory Turnover Ratio
2005	$7,624	$1,730.5[a]	4.41
2006	8,368	1,944.0[b]	4.30
2007	9,165	2,099.5[c]	4.37

[a].5($1,650 + $1,811) = $1,730.5.
[b].5($1,811 + $2,077) = $1,944.0.
[c].5($2,077 + $2,122) = $2,099.5.

Accounts Payable Turnover Ratio

Year	Numerator	Denominator	Accounts Payable Turnover Ratio
2005	$7,785[a]	$777.5[d]	10.01
2006	8,634[b]	863.5[e]	10.00
2007	9,210[c]	996.0[f]	9.25

[a]$7,624 + $1,811 − $1,650 = $7,785.   [d].5($780 + $775) = $777.5.
[b]$8,368 + $2,077 − $1,811 = $8,634.   [e].5($775 + $952) = $863.5.
[c]$9,165 + $2,122 − $2,077 = $9,210.   [f].5($952 + $1,040) = $996.0.

c. The short-term liquidity risk of Nike did not change significantly during the three-year period. The current and quick ratios fluctuated but are well above 1.0. Its cash flow from operations to current liabilities ratio declined slightly but is well above the 40% benchmark for a healthy company. Nike increased its accounts receivable turnover each year, providing operating cash flows. Its inventory turnover was relatively

6.21 c. continued.

stable. Although the accounts payable turnover decreased between 2006 and 2007, providing operating cash flows, it does not appear that the slower rate of paying suppliers is due to a shortage of liquid assets. Another factor affecting the assessment of short-term liquidity risk is the increased profit margin, net income divided by revenues, between 2005 and 2006. The increasing profit margin ultimately provides more cash than if the profit margin had remained stable.

6.22 (Nestle; calculating and interpreting short-term liquidity ratios.) (Amounts in Millions of Euros)

a. **Current Ratio**

Year End	Numerator	Denominator	Current Ratio
2004	€ 22,828	€ 18,811	1.21
2005	26,865	23,063	1.16
2006	21,933	20,178	1.09
2007	21,610	26,175	0.83

Quick Ratio

Year End	Numerator	Denominator	Quick Ratio
2004	€ 17,527	€ 18,811	0.93
2005	20,381	23,063	0.88
2006	16,185	20,178	0.80
2007	15,053	26,175	0.58

b. **Cash Flow from Operations to Current Liabilities Ratio**

Year	Numerator	Denominator	Cash Flow from Operations to Current Liabilities Ratio
2005	€ 8,461	€ 20,937.0[a]	40.4%
2006	9,197	21,620.5[b]	42.5%
2007	11,030	23,176.5[c]	47.6%

[a].5(€18,811 + €23,063) = €20,937.0.
[b].5(€23,063 + €20,178) = €21,620.5.
[c].5(€20,178 + €26,175) = €23,176.5.

6.22 b. continued.

Accounts Receivable Turnover Ratio

Year	Numerator	Denominator	Accounts Receivable Turnover Ratio
2005	€ 73,135	€ 8,416.5[a]	8.69
2006	78,533	9,124.5[b]	8.61
2007	89,625	9,186.0[c]	9.76

[a].5(€7,640 + €9,193) = €8,416.5.
[b].5(€9,193 + €9,056) = €9,124.5.
[c].5(€9,056 + €9,316) = €9,186.0.

Inventory Turnover Ratio

Year	Numerator	Denominator	Inventory Turnover Ratio
2005	€ 30,435	€ 4,897.5[a]	6.21
2006	32,474	5,119.0[b]	6.34
2007	37,530	5,295.0[c]	7.09

[a].5(€4,545 + €5,250) = €4,897.5.
[b].5(€5,250 + €4,988) = €5,119.0.
[c].5(€4,988 + €5,602) = €5,295.0.

Accounts Payable Turnover Ratio

Year	Numerator	Denominator	Accounts Payable Turnover Ratio
2005	€ 31,140[a]	€ 6,511.0[d]	4.78
2006	32,212[b]	7,480.5[e]	4.31
2007	38,144[c]	8,188.0[f]	4.66

[a]€30,435 + €5,250 − €4,545 = €31,140.
[b]€32,474 + €4,988 − €5,250 = €32,212.
[c]€37,530 + €5,602 − €4,988 = €38,144.
[d].5(€5,871 + €7,151) = €6,511.0.
[e].5(€7,151 + €7,810) = €7,480.5.
[f].5(€7,810 + €8,566) = €8,188.0.

6.22 continued.

c. The current and quick ratios both declined during the last four years, with a significant decline in 2007. The gradual decline over time occurs in part because of the increase in the accounts receivable and inventory turnovers. The significant decline in 2007 occurs because of the increase in bank loans. Offsetting these signals of increased risk, however, is an increase in the cash flow from operations to current liabilities ratio, related in part to the increased rate of accounts receivable and inventory turnovers. This ratio also increased because of increased profitability. The ratio of net income to revenues was 8.9% (= €6,498/€73,135) in 2005 and 9.9% (= €8,874/€89,625) in 2007. The cash flow from operations to current liabilities ratio exceeded the 40% threshold for healthy companies in all three years. The levels of the current and quick ratios were marginal prior to the end of 2007 and at an undesirable level at the end of 2007. Thus, the short-term liquidity ratios provide mixed signals of risk. The increased profitability coupled with improved accounts receivable and inventory turnover ratios suggest the overall short-term liquidity risk of Nestle is low.

6.23 (Tokyo Electric; calculating and interpreting long-term liquidity ratios.) (Amounts in Billions of Japanese Yen)

a. **Long-Term Debt Ratio**

Year End	Numerator	Denominator	Long-Term Debt Ratio
2004	¥7,391	¥11,540 + ¥2,360	53.2%
2005	7,150	11,247 + 2,502	52.0%
2006	6,278	10,814 + 2,780	46.2%
2007	5,871	10,488 + 3,034	43.4%

Debt-Equity Ratio

Year End	Numerator	Denominator	Debt-Equity Ratio
2004	¥7,391	¥2,360	313.2%
2005	7,150	2,502	285.8%
2006	6,278	2,780	225.8%
2007	5,871	3,034	193.5%

6.23 continued.

b. **Cash Flow from Operations to Total Liabilities Ratio**

Year	Numerator	Denominator	Cash Flow from Operations to Total Liabilities Ratio
2005	¥ 1,411	.5(¥ 11,540 + ¥ 11,247)	12.4%
2006	936	.5(¥ 11,247 + ¥ 10,814)	8.5%
2007	1,074	.5(¥ 10,814 + ¥ 10,488)	10.1%

Interest Coverage Ratio

Year	Numerator	Denominator	Interest Coverage Ratio Earned
2005	¥ 538	¥ 165	3.3
2006	635	161	3.9
2007	651	155	4.2

c. The proportion of long-term debt in the capital structure declined during the three-year period, but still appears to be at a high level. The cash flow from operations to average total liabilities ratio is low, relative to the 20% level commonly found for healthy firms. The interest coverage ratio was low in 2005 but improved by 2007. If this firm were a manufacturer, we would probably conclude that its long-term liquidity risk level is high. However, Tokyo Electric has a monopoly position in its service area. Regulators would not likely allow the firm to experience bankruptcy. Its protected status allows it to carry heavier levels of debt than a nonregulated manufacturing firm.

6.24 (Arcelor Mittal; calculating and interpreting long-term liquidity ratios.) (Amounts in Millions of Euros)

a. **Long-Term Debt Ratio**

Year End	Numerator	Denominator	Long-Term Debt Ratio
2004	€ 1,206	€ 7,760 + € 4,301	10.0%
2005	6,760	17,448 + 11,264	23.5%
2006	16,416	53,114 + 31,947	19.3%
2007	15,106	52,749 + 38,662	16.5%

6.24 a. continued.

Debt-Equity Ratio

Year End	Numerator	Denominator	Debt-Equity Ratio
2004	€ 1,206	€ 4,301	28.0%
2005	6,760	11,264	60.0%
2006	16,416	31,947	51.4%
2007	15,106	38,662	39.1%

b. **Cash Flow from Operations to Total Liabilities Ratio**

Year	Numerator	Denominator	Cash Flow from Operations to Total Liabilities Ratio
2005	€ 6,034	.5(€ 7,760 + € 17,448)	47.9%
2006	6,828	.5(€ 17,448 + € 53,114)	19.4%
2007	8,539	.5(€ 53,114 + € 52,749)	16.1%

Interest Coverage Ratio

Year	Numerator	Denominator	Interest Coverage Ratio Earned
2005	€ 4,160	€ 404	10.3
2006	6,624	895	7.4
2007	11,538	676	17.1

c. The long-term debt levels increased significantly during 2005 but steadily declined during 2006 and 2007. Despite the decline in the debt ratios, the cash flow from operations to total liabilities ratio declined during the three-year period and was less than the 20% benchmark for a healthy company at the end of 2007. The interest coverage ratio is at a healthy level in all three years. This problem illustrates the difficulties encountered interpreting financial ratios based on average amounts for a year when a significant increase occurs in the numerator or denominator. This problem also shows the importance of assessing profitability in concert with assessing risk. Although the long-term debt ratios appear low for a capital-intensive company, steel companies experience variations in sales with changes in economic activity. Because of their high levels of fixed costs, net income will vary with changes in sales and decrease the level of long-term debt considered desirable.

6.25 (Effect of various transactions on financial statement ratios.)

Transaction	Rate of Return on Common Shareholders' Equity	Current Ratio	Liabilities to Assets Ratio
a.	No Effect	(1)	Increase
b.	Increase	Increase	Decrease
c.	No Effect	No Effect	No Effect
d.	No Effect	(2)	Decrease
e.	No Effect	Increase	No Effect
f.	Increase	Decrease	Increase
g.	Decrease	Increase	Decrease
h.	No Effect	Decrease	Increase

(1) The current ratio remains the same if it was one to one prior to the transaction, decreases if it was greater than one, and increases if it was less than one.

(2) The current ratio remains the same if it was equal to one prior to the transaction, increases if it was greater than one, and decreases if it was less than one.

6.26 (Effect of various transactions on financial statement ratios.)

Transaction	Earnings per Common Share	Working Capital	Quick Ratio
a.	Increase	Increase	Increase
b.	No Effect	Decrease	Decrease
c.	No Effect	No Effect	Decrease
d.	No Effect	Increase	Increase
e.	No Effect	No Effect	Increase
f.	Decrease	Increase	Decrease

6.27 (Target Corporation; calculating and interpreting profitability and risk ratios in a time series setting.) (Amounts in Millions)

a. 1. Rate of Return on Assets $= \dfrac{\$2,849 + (1-.35)(\$669)}{.5(\$38,599 + \$46,373)} = 7.7\%$.

2. Profit Margin for Rate of Return on Assets $= \dfrac{\$2,849 + (1-.35)(\$669)}{\$61,471} = 5.3\%$.

3. Total Assets Turnover $= \dfrac{\$61,471}{.5(\$38,599 + \$46,373)} = 1.4$ times.

4. Other Revenues/Sales $= \dfrac{\$1,918}{\$61,471} = 3.1\%$.

5. Cost of Goods Sold/Sales $= \dfrac{\$41,895}{\$61,471} = 68.2\%$.

6. Selling and Administrative Expense/Sales $= \dfrac{\$16,200}{\$61,471} = 26.4\%$.

7. Interest Expense/Sales $= \dfrac{\$669}{\$61,471} = 1.1\%$.

8. Income Tax Expense/Sales $= \dfrac{\$1,776}{\$61,471} = 2.9\%$.

9. Accounts Receivable Turnover Ratio $= \dfrac{\$61,471}{.5(\$6,194 + \$8,054)} = 8.6$ times.

10. Inventory Turnover Ratio $= \dfrac{\$41,895}{.5(\$6,254 + \$6,780)} = 6.4$ times.

11. Fixed Asset Turnover $= \dfrac{\$61,471}{.5(\$22,681 + \$25,908)} = 2.5$ times.

12. Rate of Return on Common Shareholders' Equity $= \dfrac{\$2,849}{.5(\$15,633 + \$15,307)} = 18.4\%$.

Solutions

6.27 a. continued.

13. Profit Margin for Return on Common Shareholders' Equity $= \dfrac{\$2{,}849}{\$61{,}471} = 4.6\%$.

14. Capital Structure Leverage Ratio $= \dfrac{.5(\$38{,}599 + \$46{,}373)}{.5(\$15{,}633 + \$15{,}307)} = 2.7$.

15. Current Ratio $= \dfrac{\$18{,}906}{\$11{,}782} = 1.6$.

16. Quick Ratio $= \dfrac{\$2{,}450 + \$8{,}054}{\$11{,}782} = .9$.

17. Accounts Payable Turnover Ratio $= \dfrac{(\$41{,}895 + \$6{,}780 - \$6{,}254)}{.5(\$6{,}575 + \$6{,}721)} = 6.4$ times.

18. Cash Flow from Operations to Current Liabilities Ratio $= \dfrac{\$4{,}125}{.5(\$11{,}117 + \$11{,}782)} = 36.0\%$.

19. Liabilities to Assets Ratio $= \dfrac{\$31{,}066}{\$46{,}373} = 67.0\%$.

20. Long-Term Debt Ratio $= \dfrac{\$16{,}939}{\$46{,}373} = 36.5\%$.

21. Debt-Equity Ratio $= \dfrac{\$16{,}939}{\$15{,}307} = 110.7\%$.

22. Cash Flow from Operations to Total Liabilities Ratio $= \dfrac{\$4{,}125}{.5(\$22{,}966 + \$31{,}066)} = 15.3\%$.

23. Interest Coverage Ratio $= \dfrac{(\$2{,}849 + \$1{,}776 + \$669)}{\$669} = 7.9$ times.

6.27 continued.

    b. **Rate of Return on Assets (ROA)**
The ROA of Target Corporation increased between the fiscal years ended January 31, 2006 and 2007 and then decreased between fiscal years ended January 31, 2007 and 2008. The improved ROA between 2006 and 2007 results from an increased profit margin for ROA. The decreased ROA between 2007 and 2008 results from both a decreased profit margin for ROA and a decreased total assets turnover.

    Profit Margin for ROA The changes in the profit margin for ROA result primarily from changes in the selling and administrative expense to sales percentage. Sales increased 12.9% between 2006 and 2007 but only 6.2% between 2007 and 2008. Most administrative expenses and some selling expenses are relatively fixed in amount. Variations in sales growth cause this expense percentage to vary as well.

    Total Assets Turnover The total assets turnover declined between 2007 and 2008. Target Corporation experienced declines in all three individual asset turnovers. These declines are also likely due to the significant decline in the growth rate in sales in 2008. Customers perhaps purchased more on credit and did not pay as quickly. Target Corporation geared its inventory levels expecting a higher growth rate in sales than actually occurred, slowing the inventory turnover. The firm opened new stores expecting a larger growth in sales than occurred, slowing the fixed asset turnover.

    c. **Rate of Return on Common Shareholders' Equity**
ROCE follows the same path as ROA, increasing between 2006 and 2007 and then decreasing between 2007 and 2008. The profit margin for ROCE increased between 2006 and 2007 and decreased between 2007 and 2008, primarily for the same reasons as the variations in the profit margin for ROA. The total assets turnover declined between 2007 and 2008 for the reasons discussed in Part b. above. The capital structure leverage ratio declined between 2006 and 2007 and increased between 2007 and 2008. The decreased capital structure leverage ratio between 2006 and 2007 resulted primarily from the retention of earnings. Total liabilities changed only slightly between the end of 2006 and 2007, but shareholders' equity increased because of the retention of earnings. The capital structure leverage ratio increased between 2007 and 2008 for two principal reasons: an increase in long-term debt and the repurchase of common stock. The increased capital structure leverage ratio in 2008 moderated the decline in ROA and resulted in a smaller decline in ROCE than would have otherwise been the case.

6.27 continued.

    d. **Short-Term Liquidity Risk**

    The current and quick ratios of Target Corporation vary inversely with changes in the accounts receivable and inventory turnovers. Increased turnovers for these assets between 2006 and 2007 resulted in declines in the current and quick ratios, whereas decreased turnovers for these assets between 2007 and 2008 resulted in increases in the current and quick ratios. When turnovers increase, the firm turns accounts receivable and inventories into cash more quickly, which the firm can use to pay current liabilities, invest in new stores, or pay dividends. When turnovers decrease, the opposite occurs. The levels of the current and quick ratios are not at troublesome levels in any year. The cash flow from operations to current liabilities ratio declined between 2006 and 2008 and was less than the 40% benchmark in 2008. The decline below 40% in 2008 occurred because of decreases in the accounts receivable and inventory turnovers and an increase in the accounts payable turnover. Either the sales growth rate will return to more normal levels in 2009 or Target Corporation will adjust its accounts receivable and inventory policies for a lower level of sales growth. Thus, Target Corporation does not exhibit high short-term liquidity risk.

    e. **Long-Term Solvency Risk**

    The debt ratios declined between 2006 and 2007 and increased between 2007 and 2008, as Part *b.* discusses. The cash flow from operations to total liabilities declined between 2007 and 2008 for the reasons discussed in Part *d.* Although this ratio is below the 20% benchmark in 2008, it is likely the result of the slower rate of sales growth experienced in that year. The interest coverage ratio declined in all three years but is not at a level in any year that would suggest high long-term liquidity risk. Thus, Target Corporation does not exhibit high long-term liquidity risk.

6.28   (Carrefour, Target, and Wal-Mart; profitability and risk analysis in a cross section setting.)

    a. Wal-Mart's advantage over Target Corporation on ROA is a higher total assets turnover that more than offsets a lower profit margin for ROA.

    Profit Margin for ROA: Target Corporation's advantage on the profit margin for ROA results from a higher other revenues to sales percentage and a lower cost of goods sold to sales percentage, offset by a higher selling and administrative expense to sales percentage, a higher advertising expense to sales percentage, and a larger tax burden. Possible explanations for these differences in the revenue and expenses percentage are as follows:

6.28 a. continued.

- Higher Other Revenues to Sales Percentage for Target Corporation: Target Corporation offers its own credit card, which generates interest revenues. Wal-Mart sells for cash or permits customers to use third party credit cards. Wal-Mart collects cash within three days of sales, whereas Target Corporation collects cash in approximately 40 days of sale. This longer period of outstanding accounts receivable for Target Corporation provides interest on customers' unpaid balances.

- Lower Cost of Goods Sold to Sales Percentage for Target Corporation: Target sells a higher proportion of brand name and trend merchandise than Wal-Mart, enabling higher markups on cost when setting selling prices. Wal-Mart's size likely permits it to purchase merchandise for a lower per unit cost than Target Corporation but Wal-Mart passes this cost savings to customers through lower prices. Target Corporation also provides for a more pleasant shopping experience (wider aisles, less inventory per square foot, more employees to provide customer service), also permitting it to mark up selling prices and thereby lower the cost of goods sold to sales percentage relative to Wal-Mart.

- Higher selling and administrative expenses to sales percentage for Target Corporation: Several factors might explain this higher percentage. First, Target Corporation is significantly smaller than Wal-Mart, so Target Corporation must spread relatively fixed administrative costs over a smaller sales base. Note that the fixed assets per square foot for Target Corporation and Wal-Mart are similar but Target Corporation does not generate the sales per square foot that Wal-Mart achieves. Second, Target Corporation has lower sales per employee, suggesting that it hires more sales personnel to offer customers a more pleasant shopping experience. Third, Target Corporation incurs costs in administrating its credit card operation (credit granting and collection, uncollectible accounts).

- Higher advertising expense to sales percentage for Target Corporation: Target Corporation likely advertises its brand name and trend merchandise, whereas everyday lower prices attract customers to Wal-Mart.

6.28 a. continued.

- Higher tax burden for Target Corporation: We measure tax burden by relating income tax expense to income before income taxes.

  Target:
  2006: 3.2%/(5.3% + 3.2%) = 37.6%
  2007: 3.3%/(5.5% + 3.3%) = 37.5%
  2008: 3.3%/(5.3% + 3.3%) = 38.4%

  Wal-Mart:
  2006: 2.0%/(4.0% + 2.0%) = 33.3%
  2007: 2.0%/(3.9% + 2.0%) = 33.9%
  2008: 2.0%/(3.8% + 2.0%) = 34.5%

  Target Corporation derives all of its income from within the United States, whereas Wal-Mart might derive some of its income in lower tax rate countries abroad.

  Total Assets Turnover: Wal-Mart's advantage on total assets turnover results from faster accounts receivable, inventory and fixed assets turnovers. Explanations for the faster asset turnovers are as follows:

- Faster accounts receivable turnover for Wal-Mart: Wal-Mart does not have its own credit card and collects from third party credit card companies within three days of sale.

- Faster inventory turnover for Wal-Mart: Wal-Mart has an everyday low price strategy, which emphasizes turnover over profit margin. Wal-Mart derives a higher percentage of its sales from superstores than does Target Corporation. These superstores carry perishable grocery products which turn over more quickly than household products.

- Faster fixed asset turnover for Wal-Mart: Wal-Mart has approximately the same cost of fixed assets per square foot as Target Corporation but generates much higher sales per square foot. The latter results from its aggressive pricing policies and higher inventory per square foot.

6.28 continued.

b. Wal-Mart's advantage over Carrefour on ROA is a higher profit margin for ROA and a higher total assets turnover.

Profit Margin for ROA: Wal-Mart's advantage on profit margin for ROA results from a lower cost of goods sold to sales percentage and a lower advertising expense to sales percentage offset by a lower other revenues to sales percentage, a higher selling and administrative expense to sales percentage, and a higher income tax burden. Possible explanations for differences in these revenue and expense percentages are as follows:

- Lower cost of goods sold to sales percentage for Wal-Mart: One possible explanation is that Wal-Mart has a higher proportion of non-grocery products in its sales mix that have a higher markup on cost than do grocery products. The differences in the inventory turnovers of Wal-Mart and Carrefour provide some support for this explanation. Another possibility is that the retailing market in the United States, Wal-Mart's emphasis, is less competitive than in Europe, Carrefour's emphasis.

- Lower advertising expense to sales percentage for Wal-Mart: Less competition in Wal-Mart's principal markets and an established reputation for everyday low prices might permit Wal-Mart to advertise less. A more competitive European market might require Carrefour to advertise more. Also, Carrefour has a larger number of store brands than Wal-Mart. Carrefour must conduct advertising for each store brand, in contrast to Wal-Mart's fewer store brands.

- Lower other revenues to sales percentage for Wal-Mart: The problem data indicate that Carrefour derives license fees from firms using the Carrefour name, which might account for its higher other revenues to sales percentage.

- Higher selling and administrative expenses to sales percentage for Wal-Mart: One would expect the larger size of Wal-Mart to provide it with economies of scale in spreading fixed administrative costs over a larger sales base and result in a lower selling and administrative expense to sales percentage. Also, the larger number of different store concepts for Carrefour should increase its administrative cost relative to Wal-Mart. Thus, the explanation for the higher selling and administrative expense for Wal-Mart must lie elsewhere. One possibility is that compensation levels for Carrefour are higher than those for Wal-Mart. Carrefour, however, has higher sales per employee, offsetting any compensation cost disadvantage. Another possibility is that these firms include different cost items in

6.28 b. continued.

cost of goods sold and in selling and administrative expenses. Note that the combined amounts for these two expense percentages are approximately the same for these two firms, supportive of this explanation.

- Higher tax burden for Wal-Mart. The calculation of the tax burdens is as follows:

Carrefour:
2006:   1.3%/(3.1% + 1.3%) = 29.5%
2007:   1.3%/(3.1% + 1.3%) = 29.5%
2008:   1.2%/(2.9% + 1.2%) = 29.3%

Wal-Mart:
2006:   2.0%/(4.0% + 2.0%) = 33.3%
2007:   2.0%/(3.9% + 2.0%) = 33.9%
2008:   2.0%/(3.8% + 2.0%) = 34.5%

The problem does not provide sufficient information to explain these differences in average tax burdens. These firms operate with a different geographical sales mix, which could account for the differences.

Total Assets Turnover We examine each of the companies' individual asset turnovers to understand Wal-Mart's advantage on total assets turnover.

- Larger accounts receivable turnover for Wal-Mart: Carrefour likely has accounts receivable for fees from licensees, which slows its accounts receivable turnover. Wal-Mart's advantage on the accounts receivable turnover will not likely explain its larger total asset turnover because accounts receivable comprise only 2% of its assets.

- Smaller inventory turnover for Wal-Mart: Wal-Mart may have a smaller percentage of grocery products in its sales mix than Carrefour. Also, Wal-Mart has much larger stores than Carrefour but derives much smaller sales per square foot. Carrefour seems to emphasize turnover of inventory. The slower inventory turnover will not explain the larger total asset turnover for Wal-Mart.

6.28 b. continued.

- Similar fixed asset turnovers for Wal-Mart and Carrefour. The cost per square foot of store space is significantly larger for Carrefour than for Wal-Mart, due perhaps to more costly land or higher building costs of smaller stores. Yet, Carrefour derives larger sales per square foot than Wal-Mart, largely offsetting any cost disadvantage on the cost of land and buildings.

- Other assets comprise a lower percentage of total assets for Wal-Mart. Both firms have grown by acquiring established retail chains. Such acquisitions result in the recognition of intangibles and goodwill. Carrefour apparently has grown more by acquisition than Wal-Mart, as both the higher proportion of other assets and the larger number of store brands indicate. These other assets lower the total assets turnover of Carrefour.

c. The advantage from using financial leverage stems from two principal factors: (1) an excess of ROA over the after-tax cost of borrowing, and (2) the proportion of borrowing in the capital structure. Although the case does not permit calculation of the after-tax cost of borrowing, one would expect that Wal-Mart and Target Corporation would have the advantage here because of their higher ROAs than Carrefour. Carrefour has significantly more debt in its capital structures than Wal-Mart and Target Corporation. We can assess the leveraging impact of these two factors by computing the ratio of ROCE/ROA. The ratios for the three companies are as follows:

	2006	2007	2008
Carrefour:			
23.6%/4.5%	5.2%		
20.8%/4.4%		4.7%	
18.6%/4.3%			4.3%
Target:			
17.7%/7.8%	2.3%		
18.7%/8.5%		2.2%	
18.4%/7.7%			2.4%
Wal-Mart:			
22.2%/9.1%	2.4%		
21.2%/8.8%		2.4%	
20.4%/8.6%			2.4%

Thus, Carrefour appears to use financial leverage more effectively than Target and Wal-Mart. One might question Carrefour's greater use of financial leverage, given its weaker profitability. Question *d.* addresses the risk levels of these firms.

6.28 continued.

d. Carrefour is the most risky, with Target Corporation and Wal-Mart showing low levels of risk.

Short-term Liquidity Risk: Carrefour has the lowest current ratios and those ratios are significantly less than 1.0. Its cash flow from operations to current liabilities ratios are smaller than the desired 40% level. It stretches its creditors longer than Target Corporation or Wal-Mart. The longer days accounts payable for Carrefour might result from different credit terms provided by suppliers or from less of an ability to pay suppliers. Wal-Mart's short-term liquidity ratios are at healthy levels in general. One might question its low quick ratio. However, Wal-Mart essentially sells for cash, so has few accounts receivable.

Long-term Liquidity Risk: Carrefour's ratios are not at healthy levels. Its debt levels are the highest of the three firms. Although Carrefour reduced its debt levels during the three-year period, they are still extremely high. Its cash flow from operations to total liabilities ratios are less than the 20% benchmark in all three years. Its interest coverage ratio is at a satisfactory level.

6.29 (The Gap and Limited Brands; calculating and interpreting profitability and risk ratios.)

The financial statement ratios on pages 6-29, 6-30, and 6-31 form the basis for the responses to the questions raised.

a. Limited Brands has a higher ROA in the fiscal year ended January 31, 2008, the result of a higher profit margin for ROA, offset by a lower total assets turnover. The higher profit margin for ROA results from a higher other revenues to sales percentage and a lower selling and administrative expenses to sales percentage. The higher other revenues results primarily from gains on the divestment of stores. The analyst would need to examine previous years to see if Limited Brands regularly sells stores or if the gains in fiscal year 2008 are unusual. The lower selling and administrative expense to sales percentage for Limited Brands is unexpected, given its smaller size and need to emphasize its more fashion-oriented product line. The lower cost of goods sold to sales percentage for The Gap occurs because its clothes are more standardized than those of Limited Brands, perhaps permitting lower manufacturing costs (for example, from quantity discounts on materials, fewer machine setups, less training of employees). The Gap probably also incurs fewer inventory writedowns from obsolescence because its clothing line is less fashion oriented.

6.29 a. continued.

The slower total asset turnover of Limited Brands is not due to either inventories or fixed assets, because Limited Brands has faster turnover ratios for these assets. Accounts receivable comprises such a small proportion of the total assets of Limited Brands that the differences in the accounts receivable turnover ratios exert very little influence on the total assets turnover. The difference in total assets turnover relates to the proportion of Other Noncurrent Assets on the balance sheet of each company. Other Noncurrent Assets averages 4.9% of total assets for The Gap for the two years, whereas it averages 35.2% of total assets for Limited Brands. Other Noncurrent Assets likely relates to goodwill and other intangibles from corporate acquisitions. These items increase total assets and reduce the total assets turnover.

The larger rate of return on assets of Limited Brands carries over to the rate of return on common shareholders' equity. In addition to larger operating profitability, Limited Brands carries substantially more financial leverage, enhancing its profitability advantage over The Gap.

b. The current and quick ratios vary considerably between fiscal 2007 and fiscal 2008, but neither company appears risky by these measures. Limited Brands pays its suppliers more quickly than The Gap. The cash flow from operations to average current liabilities ratios for The Gap and Limited Brands both exceed the 40% benchmark, particularly for The Gap. Although neither company appears to have much short-term liquidity risk, the ratios for Limited Brands are not as strong as those of The Gap.

c. Limited Brands has higher levels of debt than The Gap. Its cash flow from operations to total liabilities ratio is less than the 20% benchmark. Its interest coverage ratio is less than that of The Gap but not at a troublesome level. Thus, Limited Brands has higher long-term liquidity risk.

6.29 a. continued.

		The Gap	Limited Brands
1.	Rate of Return on Assets	$= \dfrac{\$867 + (1-.35)(\$26)}{.5(\$7,838 + \$8,544)} = 10.8\%$	$= \dfrac{\$718 + (1-.35)(\$149)}{.5(\$7,437 + \$7,093)} = 11.2\%$
2.	Profit Margin for Return on Assets	$= \dfrac{\$867 + (1-.35)(\$26)}{\$15,763} = 5.6\%$	$= \dfrac{\$718 + (1-.35)(\$149)}{\$10,134} = 8.0\%$
3.	Total Assets Turnover	$= \dfrac{\$15,763}{.5(\$7,838 + \$8,544)} = 1.9$ times per year.	$= \dfrac{\$10,134}{.5(\$7,437 + \$7,093)} = 1.4$ times per year.
4.	Other Revenues/Sales	$= \dfrac{\$117}{\$15,763} = .7\%$	$= \dfrac{(\$146 + 230)}{\$10,134} = 3.7\%$
5.	Cost of Goods Sold to Sales	$= \dfrac{\$10,071}{\$15,763} = 63.9\%$	$= \dfrac{\$6,592}{\$10,134} = 65.0\%$
6.	Selling and Administration Expenses to Sales	$= \dfrac{\$4,377}{\$15,763} = 27.8\%$	$= \dfrac{\$2,640}{\$10,134} = 26.1\%$
7.	Interest Expenses to Sales	$= \dfrac{\$26}{\$15,763} = .2\%$	$= \dfrac{\$149}{\$10,134} = 1.5\%$
8.	Income Tax Expenses to Sales	$= \dfrac{\$539}{\$15,763} = 3.4\%$	$= \dfrac{\$411}{\$10,134} = 4.1\%$
9.	Accounts Receivable Turnover	$= \dfrac{\$15,763}{.5(\$0 + \$0)} = $ N/A.	$= \dfrac{\$10,134}{.5(\$355 + \$176)} = 38.2$ times per year.
10.	Inventory Turnover	$= \dfrac{\$10,071}{.5(\$1,575 + \$1,796)} = 6.0$ times per year.	$= \dfrac{\$6,592}{.5(\$1,251 + \$1,770)} = 4.4$ times per year.

6.29 a. continued.

11. Fixed Asset Turnover
$$= \frac{\$15,763}{.5(\$3,267+\$3,197)} = 4.9 \text{ times per year.}$$
$$= \frac{\$10,134}{.5(\$1,862+\$1,862)} = 5.4 \text{ times per year.}$$

12. Rate of Return on Common Shareholders' Equity
$$= \frac{\$867}{.5(\$4,274+\$5,174)} = 18.4\%.$$
$$= \frac{\$718}{.5(\$2,219+\$2,955)} = 27.8\%.$$

13. Profit Margin for Return on Common Shareholders' Equity
$$= \frac{\$867}{\$15,763} = 5.5\%.$$
$$= \frac{\$718}{\$10,134} = 7.1\%.$$

14. Capital Structure Leverage Ratio
$$= \frac{.5(\$7,838+\$8,544)}{.5(\$4,274+\$5,174)} = 1.7.$$
$$= \frac{.5(\$7,437+\$7,093)}{.5(\$2,219+\$2,955)} = 2.8.$$

15. Current Ratio:
January 31, 2007
$$= \frac{\$5,029}{\$2,272} = 2.2.$$
$$= \frac{\$2,771}{\$1,709} = 1.6.$$
January 31, 2008
$$= \frac{\$4,086}{\$2,433} = 1.7.$$
$$= \frac{\$2,919}{\$1,374} = 2.1.$$

16. Quick Ratio:
January 31, 2007
$$= \frac{\$2,644}{\$2,272} = 1.2.$$
$$= \frac{(\$500+\$176)}{\$1,709} = .4.$$
January 31, 2008
$$= \frac{\$1,939}{\$2,433} = .8.$$
$$= \frac{(\$1,018+\$355)}{\$1,374} = 1.0.$$

17. Days Accounts Receivable
$$= \frac{365}{0} = \text{N/A.}$$
$$= \frac{365}{38.2} = 9.6.$$

18. Days Inventory
$$= \frac{365}{4.1} = 89.0.$$
$$= \frac{365}{4.4} = 83.0.$$

19. Accounts Payable Turnover
$$= \frac{(\$10,071+\$1,796-\$1,575)}{.5(\$1,006+\$772)} = 11.6.$$
$$= \frac{(\$6,592+\$1,770-\$1,251)}{.5(\$517+\$593)} = 12.8.$$

6.29 a. continued.

20.	Days Accounts Payable	$= \dfrac{365}{11.6} = 31.5.$
		$= \dfrac{365}{12.8} = 28.5.$
21.	Cash Flow from Operations to Current Liabilities	$= \dfrac{\$2,081}{.5(\$2,433+\$2,272)} = 88.5\%.$
		$= \dfrac{\$765}{.5(\$1,374+\$1,709)} = 49.6\%.$
22.	Liabilities to Assets Ratio: January 31, 2007	$= \dfrac{\$3,370}{\$8,544} = 39.4\%.$
		$= \dfrac{\$4,138}{\$7,093} = 58.3\%.$
	January 31, 2008	$= \dfrac{\$3,564}{\$7,838} = 45.5\%.$
		$= \dfrac{\$5,218}{\$7,437} = 70.2\%.$
23.	Long-Term Debt Ratio: January 31, 2007	$= \dfrac{\$188}{\$8,544} = 2.2\%.$
		$= \dfrac{\$1,665}{\$7,093} = 23.5\%.$
	January 31, 2008	$= \dfrac{\$50}{\$7,838} = .6\%.$
		$= \dfrac{\$2,905}{\$7,437} = 39.1\%.$
24.	Debt-Equity Ratio: January 31, 2007	$= \dfrac{\$188}{\$5,174} = 3.6\%.$
		$= \dfrac{\$1,665}{\$2,955} = 56.3\%.$
	January 31, 2008	$= \dfrac{\$50}{\$4,274} = 1.2\%.$
		$= \dfrac{\$2,905}{\$2,219} = 130.9\%.$
25.	Cash Flow from Operations to Total Liabilities	$= \dfrac{\$2,081}{.5(\$3,564+\$3,370)} = 60.0\%.$
		$= \dfrac{\$765}{.5(\$5,218+\$4,138)} = 16.4\%.$
26.	Interest Coverage Ratio	$= \dfrac{(\$867+\$539+\$26)}{\$26} = 55.1 \text{ times.}$
		$= \dfrac{(\$718+\$411+\$149)}{\$149} = 8.6 \text{ times.}$

6.30 (GlaxoSmithKline plc; interpreting profitability and risk ratios.)

a. The increasing profit margin for ROA results from an increase in the investment income to sales percentage and to a decrease in the selling and administrative expense to sales percentage. The problem does not provide sufficient information to interpret the increasing investment income percentage. Growth in sales perhaps permits the firm to spread relatively fixed administrative expenses over a larger sales base and, thereby, reduce the selling and administrative expense to sales percentage.

b. The decreased total assets turnover in 2007 results from declines in the accounts receivable, inventory, and fixed asset turnovers. Sales grew at only 6.3% in 2007, after growing 7.6% in 2005 and 8.5% in 2006. Perhaps the firm expected faster growth in sales in 2007 than occurred and geared its plant capacity, inventory levels, and credit policies to such a faster growth.

c. Financial leverage works to the advantage of the common shareholders whenever the rate of return on assets exceeds the after-tax cost of borrowing. Because ROCE exceeds ROA, ROA must exceed the after-tax cost of borrowing. Thus, financial leverage worked to the advantage of the common shareholders in 2007. Financial leverage did not work as much to the advantage of the common shareholders in 2007 as it did in 2006, both because of the decline in ROA in 2007 and the decrease in the capital structure leverage ratio.

d. The slower accounts receivable and inventory turnovers should have led to an increase in these current assets. A decline in the current ratio likely therefore occurs because of increased current liabilities. The days accounts payable declined between 2006 and 2007 and, therefore, is not the cause of an increase in current liabilities. Observe that the liabilities to assets ratio increased 5.8 percentage points (= 68.0% − 62.2%), whereas the long-term debt ratio increased 4.1 percentage points (= 22.8% − 18.7%). The remaining increase in the liabilities to assets ratio likely relates to increases in current liabilities.

e. The two cash flow ratios declined between 2005 and 2006 and increased between 2006 and 2007. The debt ratios indicate that both total debt and long-term debt decreased between 2005 and 2006 and increased between 2006 and 2007. These changes in debt levels should have had the opposite effects on the cash flow ratios than those observed. Thus, the decline in the cash flow ratio between 2005 and 2006 likely resulted from a decline in cash flow from operations and the increase between 2006 and 2007 likely resulted from an increase in cash flow from operations. The problem does not provide sufficient information to examine cash flow from operations further.

6.31 (Scania; interpreting profitability and risk ratios.)

a. The increase in the profit margin for ROA results from decreases in the cost of goods sold to sales percentage and the selling and administrative expense to sales percentage. Both of these expenses include depreciation and other fixed costs. Scania experienced rapid sales growth in all three years and likely benefited from economies of scale as it spread these fixed costs over a larger sales base. Investment and net financing income as a percentage of revenues both declined and would not account for the increased profit margin for ROA.

b. Economies of scale (see the discussion in Part *a.* above) explains the decreased cost of goods sold to sales percentage but not the increasing inventory turnover. Any benefits from economies of scale affect both the numerator and denominator of the inventory turnover ratio. One possibility is that the firm instituted just-in-time manufacturing, which reduced raw materials and finished goods inventories and lowered inventory-carrying costs. Another possibility is that the sales mix shifted to higher margin, made-to-order vehicles. The high growth rates in sales also suggest that Scania enjoyed pricing advantages for its products and experienced little difficulty in selling its products quickly.

c. The growth rate in sales in 2007 was higher than in 2005 and 2006. Perhaps Scania had geared its productive capacity for 2007 for sales growth of approximately 12%. With a 19.4% sales growth in 2007, Scania had to utilize its plant capacity more intensely, driving up the fixed asset turnover. Another possibility is that Scania enjoyed pricing advantages in its markets and was able to increase sales revenue without having to raise production levels.

d. Scania must have experienced increases in cash, investments, or other assets besides accounts receivable, inventories, or fixed assets. The firm's annual report indicates that other noncurrent assets increased during these years.

e. Cash flow from operations likely increased as a result of the increase in the accounts receivable and inventory turnovers and the decrease in the days accounts payable. The explanation does not appear to be in the denominator of these cash flow ratios because total liabilities to assets did not change significantly and the long-term debt ratio declined.

6.31 continued.

    f. The increase in the accounts receivable and inventory turnovers moderated the increase in current assets for these two items, thereby affecting the numerator of these ratios. The firm might have sold marketable securities and used the cash proceeds to acquire property, plant and equipment, pay dividends, or other purposes. Current liabilities likely increased as a percentage of total assets, given that the liabilities to assets ratio increased 2.6 percentage points (= 72.9% − 70.3%) whereas the long-term debt ratio increased only 1.4 percentage points (= 21.7% − 20.3%).

    g. Financial leverage works to the advantage of the common shareholders whenever the rate of return on assets exceeds the after-tax cost of borrowing. Given that ROCE exceeds ROA each year, the after-tax cost of borrowing must be less than ROA. The capital structure leverage ratio increased over the three year period, so Scania made increasing use of financial leverage to enhance ROCE.

6.32   (Detective analysis; identify company.)

There are various approaches to this exercise. One approach begins with a particular company, identifies unique financial characteristics (for example, steel companies have a high proportion of property, plant, and equipment among their assets), and then searches the common-size financial data to identify the company with that unique characteristic. Another approach begins with the common-size data, identifies unusual financial statement relationships (for example, Firm (12) has a high proportion of cash, marketable securities, and receivables among its assets), and then looks over the list of companies to identify the one most likely to have that unusual financial statement relationship. This teaching note employs both approaches.

6.32 continued.

Firm (12) — The high proportions of cash, marketable securities, and receivables for Firm (12) suggest that it is Fortis, the Dutch insurance and banking company. Insurance companies receive cash from premiums each year and invest the funds in various investment vehicles until needed to pay insurance claims. They recognize premium revenue from the cash received and investment income from investments each year. They must match against this revenue an appropriate portion of the expected cost of insurance claims from policies in force during the year. Fortis includes this amount on the line labeled Operating Expenses in Exhibit 6.33. Operating revenues also includes interest revenue on loans made. One might ask: Why does Fortis have such a high proportion of financing in the form of current liabilities? This balance sheet category includes the estimated cost of claims not yet paid from insurance in force. It also includes deposits by customers to its banks. One might also ask: What types of quality of earnings issues arise for a company like Fortis? One issue relates to the measurement of insurance claims expense each period. The ultimate cost of claims will not be known with certainty until customers make claims and the firm makes settlements. Prior to that time, Fortis must estimate what that cost will be. The need to make such estimates creates the opportunity to manage earnings and lowers the quality of earnings. Another issue relates to estimated uncollectible loans. Fortis recognizes interest revenue from loans each year and must match against this revenue the cost of any loans that will not be repaid. The need to make such estimates also provides management with an opportunity to manage earnings and therefore lowers the quality of earnings.

Firms (2), (3), (5), and (9) — There are four firms with research and development (R&D) expenses, (2), (3), (5) and (9). These are likely to be Nestle, Roche Holding, Sun Microsystems, and Toyota Motor in some combination.

Roche Holding and Sun Microsystems are more technology oriented and therefore likely to have a higher percentage of R&D to sales. This suggests that they are Firms (2) and (9) in some combination. The inventories of Firm (9) turn over more slowly at 1.4 times per year (= 27.2/20) than those of Firm (2) at 16.1 times per year (= 45.2/2.8). Firm (9) is also more capital intensive than firm (2). This suggests that Firm (2) is Sun Microsystems and Firm (9) is Roche Holdings. Sun uses only 11.8 cents in fixed assets for each dollar of sales generated. These ratios are consistent with Sun's strategy of outsourcing most of its manufacturing operations. The inventory turnover of Roche is consistent with the making of fewer production runs for each pharmaceutical product to gain production efficiencies. The manufacture of pharmaceuticals is highly automated, consistent with the slower fixed asset turnover of Roche. These two firms have the highest profit margins of the twelve firms studied. Sun is a technology leader in engineering workstations and servers. Roche sells products protected by patents. These advantages permit the firms to achieve high profit margins. Roche has a very high proportion of its assets

6.32 continued.

in cash and marketable securities. It generates interest revenue from these investments, which it includes in other revenues. It is interesting to observe the relatively small cost of goods sold to sales percentage for Roche. The manufacturing cost of pharmaceutical products primarily includes the cost of the chemical raw materials, which machines combine into various drugs. Pharmaceutical firms must price their products significantly above manufacturing costs to recoup their investments in R&D. Note also that Sun has very little long-term debt in its capital structure. Computer products have short product life cycles. Lenders are reluctant to lend for a long period because of the concern for technological obsolescence. Computer companies that outsource their production also have few assets that can serve as collateral for long-term borrowing.

This leaves Firms (3) and (5) as Nestle and Toyota Motor in some combination. Firm (5) has a larger amount of receivables relative to sales than Firm (3), consistent with Toyota Motor providing financing for its customers' purchases of automobiles. Nestle will have receivables from wholesalers and distributors of its food products as well, but not to the extent of the multi-year financing of automobiles. The inventory turnover of Firm (3) is 4.5 times a year (= 44.5%/9.9%), whereas the inventory turnover of Firm (5) is 10.6 times a year (= 68%/6.4%). One might at first expect a food processor to have a much higher inventory turnover than an automobile manufacturer, suggesting that Firm (3) is Toyota Motor and Firm (5) is Nestle. Toyota Motor, however, has implemented just-in-time inventory systems, which speed its inventory turnover. Nestle tends to manufacture chocolates to meet seasonal demands, and therefore carries inventory somewhat longer than one might expect. Firm (3) has a much higher percentage of selling and administrative expense to sales than Firm (5). Both of these firms advertise their products heavily. It is difficult to know why one would have a substantially different percentage than the other. The profit margin of Firm (3) is substantially higher than that of Firm (5). The auto industry is more competitive than at least the chocolate side of the food industry. However, other food products encounter extensive competition. Firm (5) has a high proportion of intercorporate investments. Japanese companies tend to operate within groups, called *kieretsu*. The members of the group make investments in the securities of other firms within the group. This would suggest that Firm (5) is Toyota Motor. Another characteristic of Japanese companies is their heavier use of debt in their capital structures. One of the members of these Japanese corporate groups is typically a bank, which lends to group members as needed. With this more-or-less assured source of funds, Japanese firms tend to take on more debt. Although the ratios give somewhat confusing signals, Firm (3) is Nestle and Firm (5) is Toyota Motor.

6.32 continued.

Firms (10) and (11)—Firms (10) and (11) are unique in that they are both very fixed-asset intensive. Electric utilities and telecommunication firms both utilize fixed assets in the delivery of their services. Firm (11) is the most fixed-asset intensive of the two firms and carries a higher proportion of long-term debt. Electric-generating plants are more fixed-asset intensive than the infrastructure needed for distribution of telecommunication services. This would suggest that Firm (10) is Deutsche Telekon and Firm (11) is Tokyo Electric Power. The telecommunication industry is going through deregulation whereas Tokyo Electric Power still has a monopoly position in Japan. Thus, the selling and administrative expense to operating revenues percentage for Deutsche Telekon is substantially higher than for Tokyo Electric Power.

Firms (6) and (8)—Two of the remaining industries are also capital intensive, but not to the extent of Deutsche Telekon and Tokyo Electric Power. These firms are Accor, a hotel group, and Arbed-Acier, a steel manufacturer. Firms (6) and (8) require the next highest fixed assets per dollar of sales after Firms (10 and (11). Thus, Firms (6) and (8) are Accor and Arbed-Acier in some combination. Firm (8) has virtually no inventories, whereas Firm (6) has substantial inventories. This suggests that Firm (6) is Arbed-Acier, the steel company, and Firm (8) is Accor, the hotel group. Accor has grown in recent years by acquiring established hotel chains. Accor allocates a portion of the purchase price to goodwill in its acquisitions, which accounts for its higher percentage for Other Assets. Steel products are commodities, whereas hotels have some brand recognition appeal. These factors may explain the higher profit margin for Firm (6) than for Firm (8).

Firm (7)—Firm (7) has an unusually high proportion of its assets in receivables and in current liabilities. Although this pattern would be typical for a commercial bank, we identified Firm (12) earlier as the financial institution. The pattern is also typical for an advertising agency, which creates and sells advertising copy for clients (for which it has a current receivable) and purchasing time and space on various media to display it (for which it has a current liability). Additional evidence that Firm (7) is Interpublic Group is the high percentage for Other Assets, representing goodwill from acquisitions. Firm (7) also has a relatively high profit margin percentage, reflective of its ability to differentiate its creative services.

Firm (1)—Firm (1) is distinguished by its high cost of goods sold to sales and small profit margin percentages. This pattern suggests commodity products with low value added. Of the remaining firms, this characterizes a grocery business. Firm (1) is Carrefour. Its combination of a rapid receivables turnover of 11.8 times per year (= 100/8.5) and rapid inventory turnover of 8.9 times per year (= 87.8/9.9) are also consistent with a grocery business. Current liabilities comprise more than half of its financing. Current assets make up a similarly high proportion of its current assets.

6.32 continued.

> **Firm (4)** — The remaining firm is Firm (4), which is Marks & Spencer the department store chain. Firm (4) has substantial receivables, consistent with having a credit card.

6.33 (Target Corporation; preparing pro forma financial statements requires Appendix 6.1.)

a. See attached pro forma financial statements and related financial ratios.

b. Target Corporation needs to increase borrowing. Cash flow from operations is positive in each year. Thus, the financing need does not appear to be short term. Although Target Corporation increases long-term debt at the growth rate in property, plant and equipment, the amount invested in property, plant and equipment at the end of fiscal 2008 of $25,908 million is larger than long-term debt at the end of fiscal 2008 of $16,939. Growing long-term debt at the same growth rate as property, plant and equipment does not adequately finance the fixed assets. If we assume that long-term debt increases at 2 times the growth rate in property, plant and equipment, long-term debt (after reclassifications to current liabilities), grows 20% (= 2 times 10%) annually and provides adequate cash.

c. The pro forma financial statement ratios indicate a decreasing ROCE. The projected profit margin for ROCE and total assets turnover ratios are stable. The declining ROCE results from a declining capital structure leverage ratio. Even if we grow long-term debt at 2 times the growth rate in property, plant and equipment (see Part *b.* above), the capital structure leverage ratio and ROCE decline. The reason for the declining capital structure leverage ratio is that retained earnings grows faster than borrowing. Still further increases in borrowing to stabilize the capital structure leverage ratio results in too much cash on the balance sheet. Target Corporation would then need to increase its dividends or repurchase common stock with the excess cash. To stabilize the capital structure leverage ratio, Target Corporation needs to increase borrowing, increase the growth rate in dividends, or repurchase common stock.

6.33 a. continued.

The following pro forma financial statements were generated by a spreadsheet program that rounds to many decimal places. Rounding causes some of the sub-totals and totals to differ from the sum of the amounts that comprise them.

TARGET CORPORATION
PRO FORMA INCOME STATEMENT
YEAR ENDED JANUARY 31
(Amounts in Millions)

	2008	2009	2010	2011	2012	2013
Sales Revenue	$ 61,471	$ 67,003	$ 73,034	$ 79,607	$ 86,771	$ 94,581
Other Revenues	1,918	2,010	2,191	2,388	2,603	2,837
Total Revenues	$ 63,389	$ 69,013	$ 75,225	$ 81,995	$ 89,374	$ 97,418
Expenses:						
Cost of Goods Sold	$ 41,895	$ 45,629	$ 49,736	$ 54,212	$ 59,091	$ 64,409
Selling and Administration	16,200	17,421	18,989	20,698	22,561	24,591
Interest	669	934	911	906	894	913
Income Taxes	1,776	1,911	2,124	2,348	2,595	2,852
Total Expenses	$ 60,540	$ 65,895	$ 71,760	$ 78,164	$ 85,141	$ 92,766
Net Income	$ 2,849	$ 3,118	$ 3,465	$ 3,831	$ 4,233	$ 4,652
Less Dividends	442	513	595	690	800	928
Increase in Retained Earnings	$ 2,407	$ 2,606	$ 2,870	$ 3,141	$ 3,433	$ 3,724

Assumptions:

Growth Rate of Sales	9.0%	
Other Revenues	3.0%	of sales
Cost of Goods Sold	68.1%	of sales
Selling and Administration Expense	26.0%	of sales
Interest Expense	5.0%	on average amount of interest bearing debt
Income Tax Rate	38.0%	of income before income taxes
Dividends	16.0%	growth rate

6.33 a. continued.

TARGET CORPORATION
PRO FORMA BALANCE SHEET
JANUARY 31
(Amounts in Millions)

	2008	2009	2010	2011	2012	2013
Cash	$ 2,450	$ 1,778	$ 768	$ 680	$ (668)	$ 292
Accounts Receivable	8,054	8,779	9,569	10,430	11,369	12,392
Inventories	6,780	7,390	8,055	8,780	9,571	10,432
Prepayments	1,622	1,768	1,927	2,101	2,290	2,496
Total Current Assets	$ 18,906	$ 19,715	$ 20,319	$ 21,991	$ 22,561	$ 25,612
Property, Plant and Equipment	25,908	28,499	31,349	34,484	37,932	41,725
Other Assets	1,559	1,559	1,559	1,559	1,559	1,559
Total Assets	$ 46,373	$ 49,773	$ 53,227	$ 58,033	$ 62,052	$ 68,896
Accounts Payable	$ 6,721	$ 7,507	$ 8,001	$ 8,902	$ 9,523	$ 10,561
Notes Payable	0	0	0	0	0	0
Current Portion—Long-Term Debt	1,964	1,951	1,251	2,236	107	2,251
Other Current Liabilities	3,097	3,376	3,680	4,011	4,372	4,765
Total Current Liabilities	$ 11,782	$ 12,833	$ 12,932	$ 15,149	$ 14,001	$ 17,577
Long-Term Debt	16,939	16,487	16,759	15,976	17,456	16,725
Other Noncurrent Liabilities	2,345	2,556	2,786	3,037	3,310	3,608
Total Liabilities	$ 31,066	$ 31,876	$ 32,477	$ 34,162	$ 34,767	$ 37,910
Common Stock	$ 68	$ 68	$ 68	$ 68	$ 68	$ 68
Additional Paid-in Capital	2,656	2,656	2,656	2,656	2,656	2,656
Retained Earnings	12,761	15,367	18,237	21,378	24,812	28,536
Accumulated Other Comprehensive Income	(178)	(194)	(211)	(231)	(251)	(274)
Total Shareholders' Equity	$ 15,307	$ 17,897	$ 20,750	$ 23,872	$ 27,284	$ 30,986
Total Liabilities and Shareholders' Equity	$ 46,373	$ 49,773	$ 53,227	$ 58,033	$ 62,052	$ 68,896

(See Following Page for Assumptions)

6.33 a. continued.

(Assumptions for Pro Forma Balance Sheet)

Assumptions:

Cash...........................	PLUG
Accounts Receivable....	Sales Growth Rate
Inventory.....................	Sales Growth Rate
Prepayments.................	Sales Growth Rate
Property, Plant and Equipment..................	10.0% Growth Rate
Other Assets.................	0.0% Growth Rate
Accounts Payable Turnover.....................	6.4 6.5 6.5 6.5 6.5 6.5
Merchandise Purchases........................	46,240 50,401 54,937 59,882 65,271
Average Payables.........	7,114 7,754 8,452 9,213 10,042
Notes Payable...............	No change
Other Current Liabilities....................	Sales Growth Rate
Long-Term Debt...........	Property, Plant and Equipment Growth Rate
Other Noncurrent Liabilities....................	Sales Growth Rate
Common Stock, APIC...........................	0.0% Growth Rate
Accumulated Other Comprehensive Income.......................	Sales Growth Rate

6.33 a. continued.

TARGET CORPORATION
PRO FORMA STATEMENT OF CASH FLOWS
FOR THE YEAR ENDED JANUARY 31
(Amounts in Millions)

Cash Flow Statement	2008	2009	2010	2011	2012	2013
Operations:						
Net Income	$ 2,849	$ 3,118	$ 3,465	$ 3,831	$ 4,233	$ 4,653
Depreciation	1,659	1,825	2,007	2,208	2,429	2,672
Other	485	195	213	232	253	275
(Inc.)/Dec. in Accounts Receivable	(602)	(725)	(790)	(861)	(939)	(1,023)
(Inc.)/Dec. in Inventory	(525)	(610)	(665)	(725)	(790)	(861)
(Inc.)/Dec. in Prepayments	(38)	(146)	(159)	(173)	(189)	(206)
Inc./(Dec.) in Accounts Payable	111	786	495	901	621	1,038
Inc./(Dec.) in Other Current Liabilities	186	279	304	331	361	393
Cash Flow from Operations	$ 4,125	$ 4,722	$ 4,869	$ 5,743	$ 5,979	$ 6,940
Investing:						
Acquisition of Property, Plant, and Equipment	$ (4,369)	$ (4,416)	$ (4,857)	$ (5,343)	$ (5,877)	$ (6,465)
Other Investing	0	0	0	0	0	0
Cash Flow from Investing	$ (4,369)	$ (4,416)	$ (4,857)	$ (5,343)	$ (5,877)	$ (6,465)
Financing:						
Inc./(Dec.) in Short-Term Borrowing	$ 500	$ 0	$ 0	$ 0	$ 0	$ 0
Inc./(Dec.) in Long-Term Borrowing	6,291	(465)	(427)	201	(649)	1,413
Inc./(Dec.) in Common Stock	(2,598)	0	0	0	0	0
Dividends	(442)	(513)	(595)	(690)	(800)	(928)
Other Financing	(44)	0	0	0	0	0
Cash Flow from Financing	$ 3,707	$ (978)	$ (1,022)	$ (489)	$ (1,449)	$ 485
Change in Cash	$ 1,637	$ (672)	$ (1,010)	$ (88)	$ (1,348)	$ 960
Cash, Beginning of Year	813	2,450	1,778	768	680	(668)
Cash, End of Year	$ 2,450	$ 1,778	$ 768	$ 680	$ (668)	$ 292
Cash Balance from Balance Sheet	2,450	1,778	768	680	(668)	292
Difference	$ 0	$ 0	$ 0	$ 0	$ 0	$ 0

(See Following Page for Assumptions)

6.33 a. continued.

(Assumptions for Pro Forma Statement of Cash Flows)

Assumptions:

Depreciation Growth Rate	Same as Property, Plant, and Equipment
Other Operating Addbacks	Change in Other Noncurrent Liabilities and Change in Accumulated Other Comprehensive Income
Other Investing Cash Flows	Change in Other Noncurrent Assets
Other Financing Cash Flows	Zero

TARGET CORPORATION
PRO FORMA FINANCIAL RATIOS

	2008	2009	2010	2011	2012	2013
Rate of Return on Assets	7.7%	7.7%	7.8%	7.9%	8.0%	8.0%
Profit Margin for ROA	5.3%	5.5%	5.5%	5.5%	5.5%	5.5%
Total Assets Turnover	1.4	1.4	1.4	1.4	1.4	1.4
Cost of Goods Sold/Sales	68.2%	68.1%	68.1%	68.1%	68.1%	68.1%
Selling and Administrative Expenses/Sales	26.4	26.0%	26.0%	26.0%	26.0%	26.0%
Interest Expense/Sales	1.1%	1.4%	1.2%	1.1%	1.0%	1.0%
Income Tax Expense/Sales	2.9%	2.9%	2.9%	2.9%	3.0%	3.0%
Accounts Receivable Turnover Ratio	8.6	8.0	8.0	8.0	8.0	8.0
Inventory Turnover Ratio	6.4	6.4	6.4	6.4	6.4	6.4
Fixed Assets Turnover Ratio	2.5	2.5	2.4	2.4	2.4	2.4
Rate of Return on Common Equity	18.4%	18.8%	17.9%	17.2%	16.6%	16.0%
Profit Margin for ROCE	4.6%	4.7%	4.7%	4.8%	4.9%	4.9%
Capital Structure Leverage Ratio	2.7	2.9	2.7	2.5	2.3	2.2
Current Ratio	1.60	1.54	1.57	1.45	1.61	1.46
Quick Ratio	0.89	0.82	0.80	0.73	0.76	0.72
Cash Flow from Operations/Current Liabilities	36.0%	38.4%	37.8%	40.9%	41.0%	44.0%
Accounts Payable Turnover Ratio	6.4	6.5	6.5	6.5	6.5	6.5
Liabilities to Assets Ratio	67.0%	64.0%	61.0%	58.9%	56.0%	55.0%
Long-Term Debt Ratio	36.5%	33.1%	31.5%	27.5%	28.1%	24.3%
Debt-Equity Ratio	110.7%	92.1%	80.8%	66.9%	64.0%	54.0%
Cash Flow from Operations/Total Liabilities	15.3%	15.0%	15.1%	17.2%	17.3%	19.1%
Interest Coverage Ratio	7.9	6.4	7.1	7.8	8.6	9.2

This page is intentionally left blank

CHAPTER 7

REVENUE RECOGNITION, RECEIVABLES, AND ADVANCES FROM CUSTOMERS

Questions, Exercises, and Problems: Answers and Solutions

7.1 See the text or the glossary at the end of the book.

7.2 The cost recovery method defers revenue recognition past the point where the seller has delivered goods to the customer. It is used when there is considerable uncertainty about the amount of cash to be collected (the collection period is lengthy and there is no reasonable basis for estimating the amount of cash to be collected). There is typically no uncertainty about the cost to the seller, because the customer typically has possession of the goods. The completed contract method is applied to long-term contracts in which the outcome (either the cost or the amount to be collected) is uncertain. The cost recovery method recognizes revenues equal to cash received and sets expenses equal to revenues until all costs are recovered, while the completed contract recognizes neither revenue nor expense until the entire contract is completed. The completed contract recognizes revenue at the point where the seller delivers the promised item to the customer.

7.3 Both approaches apply accounting criteria to determine the amount and timing of revenue recognition when an arrangement with a customer (a contract) is not yet complete. The percentage-of-completion method uses the cost of work performed to date as the criterion. The accounting for a multiple element arrangement first determines the number of separable components (or deliverables) in the contract; the criterion for revenue recognition timing is the performance of a deliverable and the amount is based on the relative fair value of the deliverable, compared to the contract price as a whole.

7.4 The gross amount of accounts receivable is the amount owed by customers. The allowance account provides a rough estimate of the credit quality of those customers; changes in the allowance shed light on changes in the credit quality of customers.

7.5 a. This statement is valid. Most businesses ought not to set credit policies so stringent that they have no uncollectible accounts. To do so would require extremely careful screening of customers, which is costly, and the probable loss of many customers who will take their business

7.5 a. continued

elsewhere. So long as the revenues collected from credit sales exceed the sum of both selling costs and the cost of goods sold on credit, then the firm should not be concerned if some percentage of its accounts receivable are uncollectible.

b. When the larger uncollectible accounts result from a credit granting policy that increases income overall. A business might liberalize its credit policy by granting to a group of customers, who were not previously granted this privilege, the right to buy on account, with the intent of generating net revenues from the new credit customers that exceed the cost of goods sold to them and the selling expenses of executing the sales. The extension of credit to new customers can increase net income even though it results in more uncollectible accounts.

c. When the net present value of the receipts from selling to new customers is larger than the net present value of the costs of putting goods into their hands.

7.6 If a firm computes the Bad Debt Expense figure at the end of the accounting period but writes off specific accounts receivable during the period as information about uncollectible accounts becomes available, then the Allowance for Uncollectibles will have a debit balance whenever the amount of accounts written off during the period exceeds the opening credit balance in the Allowance account. Firms prepare balance sheets only after making adjusting entries. Both the Bad Debt Expense and the Allowance for Uncollectibles accounts must be brought up to date with appropriate adjusting entries before preparing the balance sheet. Because the Allowance for Uncollectibles account is an asset contra, it will always show a credit (or perhaps a zero) balance after making adjusting entries.

7.7 Manufacturing firms typically do not identify a customer or establish a firm selling price until they sell products. Thus, these firms do not satisfy the criteria for revenue recognition while production is taking place. In contrast, construction companies usually identify a customer and establish a contract price before construction begins. In addition, the production process for a manufacturing firm is usually much shorter than for a construction firm. The recognition of revenue at the time of production or at the time of sale does not result in a significantly different pattern of income for a manufacturing firm. For a construction company, the pattern of income could differ significantly.

7.8 Under the installment method, accountants recognize proportionate parts of the costs incurred as expenses each period as they recognize proportionate parts of the selling price as revenues. Under the cost-recovery-first method, costs match dollar-for-dollar with revenues until revenues equal total costs. Thus, the income patterns differ because of the *expense*-recognition pattern, not the revenue-recognition pattern.

7.9 Application of the installment method requires a reasonably accurate estimate of the total amount of cash the firm expects to receive from customers, but a firm cannot use this method unless cash collections are uncertain. The cost-recovery-first method does not require such an estimate.

7.10 There are two principal explanations. First, the obligation to customers in the event the firm does not publish the magazines is $45,000. Second, recognition of a liability of $32,000 requires a remaining credit of $13,000 to some other account. Recognizing the $13,000 as income is inappropriate because the publisher has not yet rendered the required services. Including the $13,000 is some type of Deferred Income account (a liability) has the same effect on total liabilities as reporting the Advance from Customers at $45,000.

7.11 Both customer returns and bad debts ultimately affect the net cash collected from customers. In accounting for estimated sales returns, the firm debits a contra revenue account (thus reducing net revenues) and in accounting for bad debt expense, the firm typically debits an expense account, which does not affect net revenues. The accounting is similar in that income is reduced in the period in which sales occur, not in the period in which the customer returns an item or a when a customer's account is determined to be uncollectible.

7.12 Deferred Gross Margin is the difference between the Account Receivable from the customer (the amount of cash that the firm will collect and recognize as sales revenue if the customer pays all that is owed) and the seller's cost (the amount that will be recognized as cost of goods sold). Thus, the amount recognized as Deferred Gross Margin will be recognized as the margin on the sale if the customer pays in full. Conceptually, Deferred Gross Margin is not a liability, because the seller has no further obligations to the customer. As a practical matter, many firms classify this account as a liability or between liabilities and equity.

7.13 (Revenue recognition for various types of businesses.)

We have found this question to be an excellent one for class discussion because it forces the student to think about both revenue *and* expense timing and measurement questions. It also generates active student interest. Some of the items are relatively obvious while others require more discussion.

a. Time of sale.

b. Probably as work progresses using the percentage-of-completion method. Students normally assume the sale is to the United States Government. We ask them if it would make any difference if the sale was to a relatively weak government in Africa or South America. This question gets at the issue of whether the amount of cash the firm will receive is subject to reasonably accurate estimation.

7.13 continued

    c.   Probably as the firm collects cash using the installment method.

    d.   At the time of sale.

    e.   At the time the firm picks citrus products and delivers them to customers. We ask students if their response would change if the citrus firm had a five-year contract at a set price to supply a particular quantity of citrus products to a citrus processor. The issue here is whether, given uncertainties about future weather conditions, the citrus grower will be able to make delivery on the contract.

    f.   AICPA *Statement of Position 79-4* stipulates that the firm should not recognize revenue until it meets all of the following conditions:

        1. The firm knows the sales price.

        2. The firm knows the cost of the film or can reasonably estimate the loss.

        3. The firm is reasonably assured as to the collectibility of the selling price.

        4. A licensee has accepted the film in accordance with the license agreement.

        5. The film is available (that is, the licensee can exercise the right to use the film and all conflicting licenses have expired).

    Revenue recognition from the sale of rights to the television network is appropriate as soon as the firm meets these conditions even though the license period is three years. The firm cannot recognize revenues from the sale of subsequent rights to others until the three-year licensing period has expired. An important question in this example is when to recognize the production costs as an expense. Should the firm recognize all of the costs as an expense on the initial sale to the television network? Or, should it treat some portion of the costs as an asset, matched against future sales of license rights? Most accountants would probably match all of the costs against revenue from the television network license agreement, unless the firm has signed other license agreements for periods beginning after the initial three-year period at the same time as the television license agreement.

    g.   At the time of sale of each house to a specific buyer.

7.13 continued

h. At the time of sale to a specific buyer at a set price. This will vary, depending on who owns the whiskey during the aging process. We pose the following situation: Suppose a particular whiskey producer has an on-going supplier relationship with a whiskey distributor. The quantity purchased by the distributor and the price set depend on supply and demand conditions at the time aged whiskey is brought to the market. The supplier always purchases some minimum quantity. When should the firm recognize revenue? This question gets at the issue of measuring revenue in a reasonably reliable manner. You may also want to discuss the following other wrinkle. Suppose the whiskey producer doubles capacity. The firm cannot sell any of the whiskey produced from this new capacity for six years. What should the firm do with the costs of this new capacity?

i. As time passes and the firm lets borrowers use funds.

j. The alternatives here are (1) as customers make reservations, (2) as customers make some formal commitments to confirm their reservations, or (3) as the agency receives cash from commissions. The second alternative is probably best. However, past experience may provide sufficient evidence as to the proportion of reservations that customers ultimately confirm to justify earlier recognition.

k. At the completion of the printing activity.

l. The issue here is whether to recognize revenue when the firm sells stamps to food stores or when customers turn in the stamps for redemption. One might argue for revenue recognition at the time of sale of the stamps, since the seller must have some estimate of the redemption rate in setting the price for the sale of the stamps.

m. At the time, the wholesaler delivers food products to stores.

n. The issue here is whether to recognize revenue while the livestock is growing. A grower of timber faces a similar issue. For the reasons Part *h.* above discusses, it is probably best to await the time of delivery to a specific customer at an agreed upon price.

o. Probably during each period in a manner similar to the percentage-of-completion method. In practice firms use several methods.

7.14 (Income recognition for various business arrangements.)

a. Company A is selling software and access to data and other software. At the time of initial delivery of the software, Company A has been paid, so the price is fixed and collectability is not a problem. However, Company A has a two-year obligation remaining, to provide both an active website and updates. If the firm can reasonably disaggregate the initial selling price into the portion applicable to the software and the portion applicable to the later services, then it could recognize the software sales as revenues at the time of delivery and then recognize the remaining selling price over the two-year period as customers use the web-accessed services. If not, then recognizing the revenue ratably over the two-year period seems more appropriate. In addition, IFRS would require that Company A be able to reliably measure its costs to be incurred.

b. The issue in this case for Company B is the ability of the SAPs to pay for the software. Their ability to pay depends on the number of customers they sign up and the collection of cash from these customers. Although Company B has performed and has transferred the risks and rewards of ownership to the customer, there is uncertainty about the amount of cash that will be collected. Therefore, Company B may apply a revenue recognition method that is based on cash collections.

c. The issue with Company C is whether it satisfies the criterion that revenues must be "earned" at the beginning of the two-year period (collectibility of cash is not an issue). That is, Company C may have to recognize revenue as it performs its obligation to provide access over two years.

d. Assuming that collectibility is not an issue, Company D will earn the fee over the period during which it performs its obligation to provide the customer with access to the auction site. If this period is short (less than one accounting period) then Company D should be able to recognize the fee at the time of initial listing. The timing of its recognition of the transaction fee depends on the predictability of buyers backing out on the purchase, because this affects the amount of cash that Company D will ultimately collect. If the probability of buyers backing out is either low or highly predictable or both, then recognizing the transaction fee at the time of the transaction is appropriate. If Company D cannot reliably measure the amount of revenue that it will ultimately earn on the transaction fee, it should delay the recognition of the transaction fee until the transaction is completed.

7.14 continued

e. Company E should recognize the fee paid by the supplier as revenue, not the selling price of the product as revenue and the cost of the good as cost of goods sold. Company E bears none of the risk of purchasing and holding the product in this case. The timing of revenue recognition is determined by the point at which Company E has performed all of its obligations.

f. Company F assumes more product risk in this case than in Part e. and has many of the characteristics of a retailer. It assumes the risk of not selling the specified minimum number of units and pays to store and ensure those units. It could probably justify recognizing revenue for the specified minimum number of units each month and cost of goods sold expense for the cost of those units.

g. Company G has performed its obligation to the customer at the time it delivers the computer. However, the amount of cash that Company G will collect is uncertain, and has to be estimated. The issue for Company G is its ability to estimate at the time of the initial sale of the computer the cost of rebates that it will have to be paid to the Internet service provider after the time of the sale. If this amount is highly predictable, then Company G can justify recognizing the full selling price as revenue at the time of sale and the initial 10% cost of the rebate and any additional later cost of reallocated rebates as an expense. However, if linked computer/Internet sales are a new arrangement, Company G may have difficulty estimating the cost of reallocated rebates. The $400 rebate appears to be a substantial amount relative to the selling price of the personal computer. The arrangement seems to be more to stimulate sales of the Internet service provider than those of Company G, given the .90/.10 cost-sharing percentages. If predictability of the reallocated rebate cost is highly uncertain, than recognizing the selling price minus $360 (= .9 x $400) as revenue at the time of sale of the computer and the remaining $360 ratably over the three-year period seems appropriate. Actual costs of any reallocated rebates would be recognized as incurred each year.

h. Collectibility of the revenue is not an issue. However, Company H has not performed its obligations at the inception of the contract. Company H performs its obligations to the customer during the one-year contract period. It should recognize one-twelfth of the annual fee each month, as time passes and the contract provisions are satisfied.

i. Assuming that Company I has performed its obligations, the issue for Company I is the ability to measure the cash-equivalent value of the common stock. Company I has clearly received an asset from the customer; the issue is determining a reliable measurement for that asset.

7.14 continued

j. This is a barter transaction. To justify recognizing revenue from advertising space sold and expense for advertising space purchased, these companies would need to demonstrate evidence of a price that they would charge for a cash sale of the advertising space to other customers, with some reasonable expectation of being able to collect this price. The best evidence to support such an expectation would be actual cash transactions at this price. This transaction has zero effect on earnings, because the amount of expense for space purchased equals the amount of revenue for space sold. Some companies may like to show this transaction as offsetting revenue and expenses; for example, if a start up company with no income is valued in the stock market as a multiple of sales, this transaction would affect that firm's market valuation.

7.15 (Meaning of allowance for uncollectible accounts.)

a. This characterization of the allowance account is incorrect. The allowance account normally has a credit balance and assets have debit balances. Firms do not set aside assets in an amount equal to the credit balance in the allowance account.

b. This characterization of the allowance account is incorrect for the same reasons as in Part *a.* above. Firms do not set aside cash in an amount equal to the balance in the allowance account.

c. This characterization of the allowance account is incorrect. The balance in the allowance accounts is an estimate of the amount from sales on account in all periods, not just the current period, that firms have not yet collected nor expect to collect.

d. This characterization of the allowance account is incorrect.

e. This characterization of the allowance account is correct.

f. This characterization of the allowance account is incorrect. The issue with uncollectible accounts is nonpayment of amounts owed not obligations to accept returns of goods from customers.

g. Although the allowance account normally has a credit balance, like liabilities, firms do not owe amounts to anyone if customers fail to pay.

h. This characterization of the allowance account for the same reasons as in Part *f.* above.

i. This characterization is incorrect. The balance in the allowance account is an estimate of the amount of sales in all periods, not just the

7.15 i. continued

current period, that firms have not yet collected and never expect to collect. A portion of the balance in the allowance account does likely result from recognizing bad debt expense during the current period. However, the balance also includes portions of bad debt expense of earlier periods as well. There is no way to know how much of the balance in the allowance account relates to provisions made during the current period versus earlier periods.

j. This characterization is incorrect. Deferred revenues, commonly called advances from customers, have credit balances and are liabilities. The firm owes cash to those making advances if the firm does not deliver the goods and services as promised. The firm does not receive cash when it credits the allowance for uncollectibles account, nor does it owe cash to customers.

k. This characterization is incorrect. When firms credit the allowance account, they debit bad debt expense, a part of the retained earnings account. Thus, the allowance account indirectly links with retained earnings but is not an accurate characterization of its nature.

7.16 (Pret a Manger; revenue recognition at end and after time of sale.)

a. Journal entry to record original transaction; customer pays in cash:

Cash.. 8.40
   Sales Revenue... 8.40

Assets	=	Liabilities	+	Shareholders' Equity	(Class.)
+8.40				+8.40	IncSt → RE

b. Journal entry to record transaction that includes card; customer pays in cash:

Cash.. 48.40
   Advances from Customer (Card)........................... 40.00
   Sales Revenue... 8.40

Assets	=	Liabilities	+	Shareholders' Equity	(Class.)
+48.40		+40.00		+8.40	IncSt → RE

7.16 continued

c. Journal entry to record transaction; customer pays with card:

Advances from Customer (Card)................................. 8.40
   Sales Revenue... 8.40

Assets	=	Liabilities	+	Shareholders' Equity	(Class.)
		−8.40		+8.40	IncSt → RE

7.17 (Bed, Bath & Beyond; revenue recognition at and after time of sale.)

Cash 556.5
   Sales Revenue... 280.0
   Advances from Customer (Gift Certificate)............ 250.0
   Sales Taxes Payable... 26.5

Assets	=	Liabilities	+	Shareholders' Equity	(Class.)
		+250.0			
+556.5		+26.5		+280.0	IncSt → RE

7.18 (Marks and Spencer; revenue recognition at time of sale.)

a. Journal entry to recognize revenues and expenses:

Accounts Receivable, Gross... 9,022.0
Cost of Goods Sold... 5,535.2
   Sales Revenue... 9,022.0
   Merchandise Inventory... 5,535.2

Assets	=	Liabilities	+	Shareholders' Equity	(Class.)
+9,022.0				+9,022.0	IncSt → RE
−5,535.2				−5,535.2	IncSt → RE

b. Journal entry to recognize sales returns and bad debts expense (combined):

Sales Returns.. 90.22
Bad Debt Expense.. 135.33
   Allowance for Doubtful Accounts and Sales
     Returns... 225.55

7.18 b. continued

Assets	=	Liabilities	+	Shareholders' Equity	(Class.)
				−90.22	IncSt → RE
−225.55				−135.33	IncSt → RE

c. Beginning Balance, Allowance .... £   1.10
   Sales Returns 90.22
   Bad Debt Expense 135.33
   Less Ending Balance, Allowance ....   (3.30)
      Total Returns and Writeoffs .... £ 223.35

7.19   (Lentiva, revenue recognition at time of sale.)

Fair Value of Laptop Component (= $1,500 × 50,000
   Laptops) .... $ 75,000,000
Fair Value of Training Component (= $100 × 50,000
   Laptops)   5,000,000
      Total .... $ 80,000,000

Journal Entries on January 1, 2008

Cash 15,000,000
Accounts Receivable 60,000,000
   Sales Revenue   70,312,500
   Advances from Customer   4,687,500

Assets	=	Liabilities	+	Shareholders' Equity	(Class.)
+15,000,000		+4,687,500		+70,312,500	IncSt → RE

To record the sale of the laptops and training services.

The laptop sales meet the criteria for recognizing revenue equaling $70,312,500 [= ($75,000,000/$80,000,000) × $75,000,000]. The training revenue equaling $4,687,500 [= ($5,000,000/$80,000,000) × $75,000,000] is deferred and will be earned as training services are delivered.

Inventory 60,000,000
   Cost of Goods Sold   60,000,000

Assets	=	Liabilities	+	Shareholders' Equity	(Class.)
−60,000,000				−60,000,000	IncSt → RE

To record the cost of the laptop sales.

7.19 continued

Journal Entries on December 31, 2008

Advances from Customer	2,343,750	
Cost of Training Services	1,250,000	
Sales Revenue		2,343,750
Salaries Payable		1,250,000

Assets	=	Liabilities	+	Shareholders' Equity	(Class.)
		−2,343,750		+2,343,750	IncSt → RE
		+1,250,000		−1,250,000	IncSt → RE

To record the revenues and expenses for training services provided during 2008. Revenues equal $2,343,750 (= $4,687,500/2 years); Expenses equal $1,250,000 [= ($50 per laptop × 50,000 laptops)/2 years].

Journal Entries on December 31, 2009

Advances from Customer	2,343,750	
Cost of Training Services	1,250,000	
Sales Revenue		2,343,750
Salaries Payable		1,250,000

Assets	=	Liabilities	+	Shareholders' Equity	(Class.)
		−2,343,750		+2,343,750	IncSt → RE
		+1,250,000		−1,250,000	IncSt → RE

To record the revenues and expenses for training services provided during 2009. Revenues equal $2,343,750 (= $4,687,500/2 years); Expenses equal $1,250,000 [= ($50 per laptop × 50,000 laptops)/2 years].

7.20 (Morrison's Cafeteria; journal entries for coupons.)

a. **January**

Cash	50,100	
Sales Revenue		48,000
Coupon Liability		2,100

Assets	=	Liabilities	+	Shareholders' Equity	(Class.)
+50,100		+2,100		−48,000	IncSt → RE

7.20 a. continued

Coupon Liability 1,600
    Sales Revenue 1,600

Assets	=	Liabilities	+	Shareholders' Equity	(Class.)
		−1,600		+1,600	IncSt → RE

February
Cash 50,700
    Sales Revenue 48,500
    Coupon Liability 2,200

Assets	=	Liabilities	+	Shareholders' Equity	(Class.)
+50,700		+2,200		−48,500	IncSt → RE

Coupon Liability 2,300
    Sales Revenue 2,300

Assets	=	Liabilities	+	Shareholders' Equity	(Class.)
		−2,300		+2,300	IncSt → RE

March
Cash 52,400
    Sales Revenue 50,000
    Coupon Liability 2,400

Assets	=	Liabilities	+	Shareholders' Equity	(Class.)
+52,400		+2,400		+50,000	IncSt → RE

Coupon Liability 2,100
    Sales Revenue 2,100

Assets	=	Liabilities	+	Shareholders' Equity	(Class.)
		−2,100		+2,100	IncSt → RE

b. The Coupon Liability account has a balance of $4,700 (= $4,000 + $2,100 − $1,600 + $2,200 − $2,300 + $2,400 − $2,100) on March 31.

7.21 (Abson Corporation; journal entries for service contracts.)

a. **1/31/08–3/31/08**
Cash 180,000
  Service Contract Fees Received in Advance 180,000

Assets	=	Liabilities	+	Shareholders' Equity	(Class.)
+180,000		−180,000			

To record sale of 300 annual contracts.

3/31/08
Service Contract Fees Received in Advance 22,500
  Contract Revenues 22,500

Assets	=	Liabilities	+	Shareholders' Equity	(Class.)
		−22,500		+22,500	IncSt → RE

To recognize revenue on 200 contracts sold during the first quarter; 1.5/12 x $180,000.

1/01/08–3/31/08
Service Expenses 32,000
  Cash (and Other Assets and Liabilities) 32,000

Assets	=	Liabilities	+	Shareholders' Equity	(Class.)
−32,000				−32,000	IncSt → RE

4/01/08–6/30/08
Cash 300,000
  Service Contract Fees Received in Advance 300,000

Assets	=	Liabilities	+	Shareholders' Equity	(Class.)
+300,000		−300,000			

To record the sale of 500 annual contracts.

Solutions

7.21 a. continued

6/30/08
Service Contract Fees Received in Advance............ 82,500
   Contract Revenues 82,500

Assets	=	Liabilities	+	Shareholders' Equity	(Class.)
		−82,500		+82,500	IncSt → RE

To recognize revenue on 500 contracts sold during the
second quarter and 300 contracts outstanding from
the first quarter:
  First Quarter:
     3/12   x $180,000 = $ 45,000
  Second Quarter:
     1.5/12 x $300,000 =   37,500
                                    $ 82,500

4/01/08–6/30/08
Service Expenses 71,000
   Cash (and Other Assets and Liabilities)................. 71,000

Assets	=	Liabilities	+	Shareholders' Equity	(Class.)
−71,000				−71,000	IncSt → RE

7/01/08–9/30/08
Cash.. 240,000
   Service Contract Fees Received in Advance 240,000

Assets	=	Liabilities	+	Shareholders' Equity	(Class.)
+240,000		−240,000			

To record the sale of 400 annual contracts.

7.21 a. continued

9/30/08
Service Contract Fees Received in Advance............ 150,000
    Contract Revenues 150,000

Assets	=	Liabilities	+	Shareholders' Equity	(Class.)
		−150,000		+150,000	IncSt → RE

To recognize revenue on 400 contracts sold during the third quarter and 800 contracts outstanding from sales in prior quarters:
  First Quarter Sales:
    3/12 x $180,000 = $ 45,000
  Second Quarter Sales:
    3/12 x $300,000 =   75,000
  Third Quarter Sales:
    1.5/12 x $240,000 =   30,000
                              = $ 150,000

7/01/08–9/30/08
Service Expenses 105,000
    Cash (and Other Assets and Liabilities)................. 105,000

Assets	=	Liabilities	+	Shareholders' Equity	(Class.)
−105,000				−105,000	IncSt → RE

b. Balances in Service Contract Fees Received in Advance Account:

January 1, 2008	--
Less First Quarter Expirations...	$ (22,500)
Plus First Quarter Sales..	180,000
March 31, 2008...	$ 157,500
Less Second Quarter Expirations...	(82,500)
Plus Second Quarter Sales...	300,000
June 30, 2008...	$ 375,000
Less Third Quarter Expirations...	(150,000)
Plus Third Quarter Sales...	240,000
September 30, 2008..	$ 465,000
Less Fourth Quarter Expirations...	(195,000)
Plus Fourth Quarter Sales...	120,000
December 31, 2008...	$ 390,000

7.21 b. continued

OR

Contracts	x	Balance Remaining	x	$600	=	Amount
300	x	1.5/12	x	$600	=	$ 22,500
500	x	4.5/12	x	$600	=	112,500
400	x	7.5/12	x	$600	=	150,000
200	x	10.5/12	x	$600	=	105,000
						$ 390,000

7.22 (Diversified Technologies; allowance method for uncollectible accounts.)

a. $5,076 (= .04 x $126,900).

b. Accounts Receivable Gross ($126,900 − $94,300 − $2,200)... $ 30,400
Less Allowance for Uncollectible Accounts ($5,076 − $2,200)... (2,876)
Accounts Receivable Net.. $ 27,524

7.23 (York Company; aging accounts receivable.)

Bad Debt Expense... 9,050
  Allowance for Uncollectible Accounts........................... 9,050

Assets	=	Liabilities	+	Shareholders' Equity	(Class.)
−9,050				−9,050	IncSt → RE

The Allowance account requires a balance of $25,050 [= (.005 x $1,200,000) + (.01 x $255,000) + (.10 x $75,000) + (.30 x $30,000)]. The adjusting entry *increases* the Allowance account by $9,050 (= $25,050 − $16,000) and recognizes Bad Debt Expense for the period by the same amount.

7.24 (Dove Company; aging accounts receivable.)

Bad Debt Expense... 3,700
  Allowance for Uncollectible Accounts........................... 3,700

Assets	=	Liabilities	+	Shareholders' Equity	(Class.)
−3,700				−3,700	IncSt → RE

The Allowance account requires a balance of $20,900 [= (.005 x $400,000) + (.01 x $90,000) + (.10 x $40,000) + (.70 x $20,000)]. The required charge for Bad Debt Expense is, therefore, $3,700 (= $20,900 − $17,200).

7.25 (Hamilia S.A.; aging accounts receivable.)

Allowance for Uncollectible Accounts 21,500
    Bad Debt Expense 21,500

Assets	=	Liabilities	+	Shareholders' Equity	(Class.)
+21,500				+21,500	IncSt → RE

The Allowance account requires a balance of €75,100 [= (.005 x €980,000) + (.03 x €130,000) + (.15 x €102,000) + (.75 x €68,000)]. The adjusting entry *decreases* the Allowance account by €21,500 (= €96,600 − €75,100) and recognizes a credit to Bad Debt Expense by the same amount.

7.26 (Seward Corporation; reconstructing events when using the allowance method.)

a. Accounts Receivable 240,000
    Sales Revenue 240,000

Assets	=	Liabilities	+	Shareholders' Equity	(Class.)
+240,000				+240,000	IncSt → RE

b. Bad Debt Expense 4,800
    Allowance for Uncollectible Accounts 4,800

Assets	=	Liabilities	+	Shareholders' Equity	(Class.)
−4,800				−4,800	IncSt → RE

7.26 continued.

c. Allowance for Uncollectible Accounts ($8,700 + $4,800 − $9,100) 4,400
      Accounts Receivable 4,400

Assets	=	Liabilities	+	Shareholders' Equity	(Class.)
+4,400					
−4,400					

d. Cash ($82,900 + $240,000 − $4,400 − $87,300) 231,200
      Accounts Receivable 231,200

Assets	=	Liabilities	+	Shareholders' Equity	(Class.)
+231,200					
−231,200					

7.27 (Pandora Company; allowance method: reconstructing journal entry from events.)

Bad Debt Expense 3,700
    Allowance for Uncollectible Accounts 3,700

Assets	=	Liabilities	+	Shareholders' Equity	(Class.)
−3,700				−3,700	IncSt → RE

Writeoff of $2,200 + Ending Balance of Allowance of $5,000 − Beginning Balance of $3,500 = $3,700.

7.28 (Milton Corporation; allowance method: reconstructing journal entries from events.)

Accounts Receivable 75,000,000
    Sales Revenue 75,000,000

Assets	=	Liabilities	+	Shareholders' Equity	(Class.)
+75,000,000				+75,000,000	IncSt → RE

$750,000 is 1% of Sales Revenue; Sales Revenue = $750,000/.01.

7.28 continued.

Bad Debt Expense.. 750,000
    Allowance for Uncollectible Accounts..................... 750,000

Assets	=	Liabilities	+	Shareholders' Equity	(Class.)
–750,000				–750,000	IncSt → RE

Allowance for Uncollectible Accounts ($1,400,000 +
  $750,000 – $1,550,000)... 600,000
    Accounts Receivable.. 600,000

Assets	=	Liabilities	+	Shareholders' Equity	(Class.)
+600,000					
–600,000					

Cash ($15,200,000 + $75,000,000 – $600,000 –
  $17,600,000)... 72,000,000
    Accounts Receivable.. 72,000,000

Assets	=	Liabilities	+	Shareholders' Equity	(Class.)
+72,000,000					
–72,000,000					

7.29 (Reconstructing events from journal entries.)

a. Estimated bad debt expense for the period is $2,300 using the allowance method.

b. A firm writes off specific customers' accounts totaling $450 as uncollectible under the allowance method.

c. A firm realizes that its expected uncollectibles in the future are less than the amount already reserved in the allowance for uncollectibles. It records an adjustment to Bad Debt Expense for $200 to reduce the balance in the Allowance for Uncollectibles to the necessary (lower) amount.

7.30 (Heath Company; journal entries for the allowance method.)

a. **2006**

Bad Debt Expense (.03 x $340,000).............................. 10,200
    Allowance for Uncollectible Accounts................... 10,200

Assets	=	Liabilities	+	Shareholders' Equity	(Class.)
−10,200				−10,200	IncSt → RE

Allowance for Uncollectible Accounts......................... 1,800
    Accounts Receivable.. 1,800

Assets	=	Liabilities	+	Shareholders' Equity	(Class.)
+1,800					
−1,800					

2007

Bad Debt Expense (.03 x $450,000).............................. 13,500
    Allowance for Uncollectible Accounts................... 13,500

Assets	=	Liabilities	+	Shareholders' Equity	(Class.)
−13,500				−13,500	IncSt → RE

Allowance for Uncollectible Accounts......................... 8,300
    Accounts Receivable.. 8,300

Assets	=	Liabilities	+	Shareholders' Equity	(Class.)
+8,300					
−8,300					

2008

Bad Debt Expense (.03 x $580,000).............................. 17,400
    Allowance for Uncollectible Accounts................... 17,400

Assets	=	Liabilities	+	Shareholders' Equity	(Class.)
−17,400				−17,400	IncSt → RE

7.30 a. continued.

Allowance for Uncollectible Accounts................ 14,100
    Accounts Receivable... 14,100

Assets	=	Liabilities	+	Shareholders' Equity	(Class.)
+14,100					
−14,100					

b. Yes. Uncollectible accounts arising from sales in 2006, 2007, and 2008 total $42,600, which equals 3.1% (= $42,600/$1,370,000) of total sales on account during the three year period.

7.31 (Schneider Corporation; journal entries for the allowance method.)

a. **2006**
Bad Debt Expense (.02 x $750,000)............................ 15,000
    Allowance for Uncollectible Accounts................... 15,000

Assets	=	Liabilities	+	Shareholders' Equity	(Class.)
−15,000				−15,000	IncSt → RE

Allowance for Uncollectible Accounts........................ 1,300
    Accounts Receivable... 1,300

Assets	=	Liabilities	+	Shareholders' Equity	(Class.)
+1,300					
−1,300					

2007
Bad Debt Expense (.02 x $1,200,000)........................ 24,000
    Allowance for Uncollectible Accounts................... 24,000

Assets	=	Liabilities	+	Shareholders' Equity	(Class.)
−24,000				−24,000	IncSt → RE

Allowance for Uncollectible Accounts........................ 11,200
    Accounts Receivable... 11,200

Assets	=	Liabilities	+	Shareholders' Equity	(Class.)
+11,200					
−11,200					

7.31 a. continued.

2008

Bad Debt Expense (.02 x $2,400,000)............ 48,000
    Allowance for Uncollectible Accounts 48,000

Assets	=	Liabilities	+	Shareholders' Equity	(Class.)
–48,000				–48,000	IncSt → RE

Allowance for Uncollectible Accounts............ 23,600
    Accounts Receivable................................. 23,600

Assets	=	Liabilities	+	Shareholders' Equity	(Class.)
+23,600					
–23,600					

b. Yes. The actual loss experience is 1.9% (= $82,500/$4,350,000) of sales on account for sales during 2006 through 2008.

7.32 (Fujitsu Limited; reconstructing events when using the allowance method.)

a. Accounts Receivable 5,100,163
    Sales Revenue.. 5,100,163

Assets	=	Liabilities	+	Shareholders' Equity	(Class.)
+5,100,163				+5,100,163	IncSt → RE

b. Bad Debt Expense (.01 x ¥5,100,163)........... 51,002
    Allowance for Uncollectible Accounts 51,002

Assets	=	Liabilities	+	Shareholders' Equity	(Class.)
–51,002				–51,002	IncSt → RE

c. Allowance for Uncollectible Accounts............ 50,877
    Accounts Receivable................................. 50,877

Assets	=	Liabilities	+	Shareholders' Equity	(Class.)
+50,877					
–50,877					

¥50,877 = ¥6,781 + ¥51,002 – ¥6,906.

7.32 continued.

 d. Cash.. 4,880,538
   Accounts Receivable..   4,880,538

Assets	=	Liabilities	+	Shareholders' Equity	(Class.)
+4,880,538					
–4,880,538					

¥4,880,538 = ¥885,300 + ¥5,100,163 – ¥50,877 – ¥1,054,048.

7.33 (WollyMartin; effects of transactions involving suppliers and customers on cash flows.)

 a. €127,450 = €130,000 – (€8,600 – €8,000) + (€750 – €700) – €2,000
     = €130,000 – €600 + €50 – €2,000.

 b. €84,700 = €85,000 – (€7,500 – €7,000) + (€11,200 – €11,000)
     = €85,000 – €500 + $200.

7.34 (Shannon Construction Company; percentage-of-completion and completed contract methods of income recognition.)

Percentage-of-Completion Method

Year	Degree of Completion	Revenue	Expense	Income
2007	$1,200,000/$4,800,000 = 25.0%	$1,500,000	$1,200,000	$ 300,000
2008	$3,000,000/$4,800,000 = 62.5%	3,750,000	3,000,000	750,000
2009	$ 600,000/$4,800,000 = 12.5%	750,000	600,000	150,000
		$6,000,000	$4,800,000	$1,200,000

Completed Contract Method

Year	Revenue	Expense	Income
2007	--	--	--
2008	--	--	--
2009	$6,000,000	$4,800,000	$1,200,000
	$6,000,000	$4,800,000	$1,200,000

7.35 (Raytheon; percentage-of-completion and completed contract methods of income recognition.)

Percentage-of-Completion Method

Year	Degree of Completion	Revenue	Expense	Income
2006	$200/$700 = 28.6%	$ 257.4	$ 200	$ 57.4
2007	$200/$700 = 28.6%	257.4	200	57.4
2008	$300/$700 = 42.8%	385.2	300	85.2
		$ 900.0	$ 700	$ 200.0

Completed Contract Method

Year	Revenue	Expense	Income
2006	--	--	--
2007	--	--	--
2008	$ 900	$ 700	$ 200
	$ 900	$ 700	$ 200

7.36 (Cunningham Realty Partners; installment and cost recovery methods of income recognition.)

Installment Method

Year	Revenue	(PLUG) Expense[b]	Income[a]
2008	$ 30,000	$ 20,000	$10,000
2009	30,000	20,000	10,000
2010	30,000	20,000	10,000
2011	30,000	20,000	10,000
	$120,000	$ 80,000	$40,000

[a]Income = Gross Margin Percentage x Cash Received, or ($40,000/$120,000) x $30,000 = $10,000.

[b]Expense = Revenue – Income = $30,000 – $10,000 = $20,000.

Cost-Recovery-First Method

Year	Revenue	Expense	Income
2008	$ 30,000	$ 30,000	$ -0-
2009	30,000	30,000	-0-
2010	30,000	20,000	10,000
2011	30,000	-0-	30,000
	$120,000	$ 80,000	$40,000

7.37 (Boeing; installment and cost recovery methods of income recognition.) (Amounts in Millions)

Installment Method

Year	Revenue	(PLUG) Expense[b]	Income[a]
2007	$ 24	$ 19	$ 5
2008	24	19	5
2009	24	19	5
	$ 72	$ 57	$ 15

[a] Income = Gross Margin Percentage x Cash Received, or ($15/$72) x $24 = $5 million.

[b] Expense = Revenue – Income = $24 – $5 = $19 million.

Cost-Recovery-First Method

Year	Revenue	Expense	Income
2007	$ 24	$ 24	$ -0-
2008	24	24	-0-
2009	24	9	15
	$ 72	$ 57	$ 15

7.38 (Nordstrom; revenue recognition at and after time of sale.)

a. **December 2008**

Cash 8,000,000
Accounts Receivable 24,000,000
    Advances from Customers (Gift Cards) 12,000,000
    Sales Revenue 20,000,000

Assets	=	Liabilities	+	Shareholders' Equity	(Class.)
+8,000,000					
+24,000,000		+12,000,000		+20,000,000	IncSt → RE

Cost of Goods Sold 7,200,000
    Merchandise Inventory 7,200,000

Assets	=	Liabilities	+	Shareholders' Equity	(Class.)
–7,200,000				–7,200,000	IncSt → RE

Solutions

7.38 continued.

b. **Adjusting Entries for December 2008**

Bad Debt Expense.. 240,000
Sales Returns... 400,000
    Allowance for Uncollectibles and Returns.............   640,000

Assets	=	Liabilities	+	Shareholders' Equity	(Class.)
–640,000				–240,000	IncSt → RE
				–400,000	IncSt → RE

c. **Nordstrom Earned Income before Taxes**

Sales Revenue.. $ 20,000,000
Less Sales Returns.. (400,000)
Net Sales Revenue... $ 19,600,000
Cost of Goods Sold.. (7,200,000)
Bad Debt Expense.. (240,000)
Income before Taxes... $ 12,160,000

d. **January 2009**

Advances from Customers (Gift Cards)..................... 6,000,000
Cost of Goods Sold... 3,600,000
    Sales Revenue...   6,000,000
    Merchandise Inventory...   3,600,000

Assets	=	Liabilities	+	Shareholders' Equity	(Class.)
–3,600,000		–6,000,000		–3,600,000	IncSt → RE
				+6,000,000	IncSt → RE

Sales Returns.. 120,000
    Allowance for Uncollectibles and Sales Returns..   120,000

Assets	=	Liabilities	+	Shareholders' Equity	(Class.)
–120,000				–120,000	IncSt → RE

To record estimated sales returns of $120,000 [= .02 x ($6,000,000)] on merchandise purchased with gift cards during January 2009.

7.39 (Hilton Hotels; revenue recognition at or after time of sale.)

a. **February 2, 2008:** Journal entry to record internet special reservation for four nights at $150 per night.

Cash.. 600
    Advances from Customer...   600

Assets	=	Liabilities	+	Shareholders' Equity	(Class.)
+600		+600			

February 20, 2008: Journal entry to record revenue after services supplied.

Advances from Customer.. 600
    Sales Revenue...   600

Assets	=	Liabilities	+	Shareholders' Equity	(Class.)
		−600		+600	IncSt → RE

b. **February 2, 2008:** Journal entry to record internet special reservation for four nights at $150 per night.

Cash.. 600
    Advances from Customer...   600

Assets	=	Liabilities	+	Shareholders' Equity	(Class.)
+600		+600			

February 14, 2008: Journal entry to record revenue after customer cancels the reservation.

Advances from Customers.. 600
    Sales Revenue...   600

Assets	=	Liabilities	+	Shareholders' Equity	(Class.)
		−600		+600	IncSt → RE

7.39 continued.

c. **February 2, 2008:** Journal entry to record refundable room reservation for four nights at $220 per night.

Cash.. 880
    Advances from Customer.. 880

Assets	=	Liabilities	+	Shareholders' Equity	(Class.)
+880		+880			

February 20, 2008: Journal entry to record revenue after services supplied.

Advances from Customer... 880
    Sales Revenue.. 880

Assets	=	Liabilities	+	Shareholders' Equity	(Class.)
		−880		+880	IncSt → RE

d. **February 2, 2008:** Journal entry to record refundable room reservation for four nights at $220 per night.

Cash.. 880
    Advances from Customer.. 880

Assets	=	Liabilities	+	Shareholders' Equity	(Class.)
+880		+880			

February 14, 2008: Journal entry to record cancellation of refundable room reservation.

Advances from Customer... 880
    Cash.. 880

Assets	=	Liabilities	+	Shareholders' Equity	(Class.)
−880		−880			

7.39 continued.

e. **February 2, 2008:** Journal entry to record refundable room reservation for four nights at $220 per night.

Cash.. 880
   Advances from Customer.. 880

Assets	=	Liabilities	+	Shareholders' Equity	(Class.)
+880		+880			

February 16, 2008: Journal entry to record revenue (for one night) after customer cancels the reservation after 3 p.m., and to refund the remaining three nights.

Advances from Customer... 880
   Sales Revenue.. 220
   Cash 660

Assets	=	Liabilities	+	Shareholders' Equity	(Class.)
–660		–880		+220	IncSt → RE

7.40 (Stone Pest Control; revenue recognition at and after time of sale.)

a. **January 4, 2008:** Journal entry to record revenue for pest control services rendered.

Cash.. 80
   Sales Revenue... 80

Assets	=	Liabilities	+	Shareholders' Equity	(Class.)
+80				+80	IncSt → RE

b. **January 4, 2008:** Journal entry to record pest control services rendered for cash.

Cash.. 180
   Sales Revenue... 180

Assets	=	Liabilities	+	Shareholders' Equity	(Class.)
+180				+180	IncSt → RE

7.40 continued.

c. The contract has three elements: quarterly service (fair value of $320 = $80 per service x 4 service calls per year), termite inspection (fair value of $100), and interim service calls at request of customer (fair value = expected value if sold separately = $80 given one visit expected). The total fair value of the contract is $500 (= $320 + $100 + $80). The portion of the contract associated with the service calls is 64% (= $320/$500), or 16% for each service call (= $80/$500); the portion associated with the interim service requests is 16% (= $80/$500); the portion associated with the termite inspection is 20% (= $100/$500).

January 4, 2008: Journal entry to record contract for pest control services.

Cash.. 300
    Advances from Customer...   300

Assets	=	Liabilities	+	Shareholders' Equity	(Class.)
+300		+300			

Advances from Customers... 108
    Sales Revenue..   108

Assets	=	Liabilities	+	Shareholders' Equity	(Class.)
		−108		+108	IncSt → RE

To record sales for first quarterly service call and termite inspection of $108 [= (16% x $300) + (20% x $300)].

d. and e.

Stone should recognize the portion of the contract price associated with the interim service calls, $48 (= 16% x $300) pro rata over the life of the contract. Specifically, Stone should record the following journal entry at the end of each month, January–December.

Advances from Customer... 4
    Sales Revenue..   4

Assets	=	Liabilities	+	Shareholders' Equity	(Class.)
		−4		+4	IncSt → RE

To recognize sales for interim service calls of $4 (= $48/12 months).

7.40 d. and e. continued.

Stone would not recognize incremental revenue on April 30, 2008 when it sprays for ants.

7.41 (Kajima Corporation; analyzing changes in accounts receivable.) (Amounts in Millions)

a.

	2007	2006	2005
(1) Sales on Account			
Accounts Receivable ...	1,891,466	1,775,274	1,687,380
Sales Revenue	1,891,466	1,775,274	1,687,380

Assets	=	Liabilities	+	Shareholders' Equity	(Class.)
+1,891,466				+1,891,466	IncSt → RE
+1,775,274				+1,775,274	IncSt → RE
+1,687,380				+1,687,380	IncSt → RE

	2007	2006	2005
(2) Provision for Estimated Uncollectible Accounts			
Bad Debt Expense	1,084	3,152	2,999
Allowance for Uncollectible Accounts	1,084	3,152	2,999

Assets	=	Liabilities	+	Shareholders' Equity	(Class.)
–1,084				–1,084	IncSt → RE
–3,152				–3,152	IncSt → RE
–2,999				–2,999	IncSt → RE

7.41 a. continued.

(3) Write Off of Actual Bad Debts

	2007	2006	2005
Allowance for Uncollectible Accounts	6,471[a]	820[b]	8,099[c]
Accounts Receivable			
	6,471	820	8,099

[a] ¥10,673 + ¥1,084 − ¥5,286 = ¥6,471.
[b] ¥8,341 + ¥3,152 − ¥10,673 = ¥820.
[c] ¥13,441 + ¥2,999 − ¥8,341 = ¥8,099.

Assets	=	Liabilities	+	Shareholders' Equity	(Class.)
+6,471/−6,471					
+820/−820					
+8,099/−8,099					

(4) Collection of Cash from Customers

	2007	2006	2005
Cash	1,723,338[d]	1,761,584[e]	1,606,456[f]
Accounts Receivable			
	1,723,338	1,761,584	1,606,456

[d] ¥468,387 + ¥1,891,466 − ¥6,471 − ¥630,044 = ¥1,723,338.
[e] ¥455,517 + ¥1,775,274 − ¥820 − ¥468,387 = ¥1,761,584.
[f] ¥382,692 + ¥1,687,380 − ¥8,099 − ¥455,517 = ¥1,606,456.

Assets	=	Liabilities	+	Shareholders' Equity	(Class.)
+1,723,338/−1,723,338					
+1,761,584/−1,761,584					
+1,606,456/−1,606,456					

7.41 continued.

b. | | 2007 | 2006 | 2005 |

(1) **Accounts Receivable Turnover**
2007: ¥1,891,466/.5(¥624,758 + ¥457,714)... 3.49
2006: ¥1,775,274/.5(¥457,714 + ¥447,176)...   3.92
2005: ¥1,687,380/.5(¥447,176 + ¥369,251)...   4.13

(2) **Bad Debt Expense/Revenues**
2007: ¥1,084/¥1,891,466.................................... 0.06%
2006: ¥3,152/¥1,775,274..   0.18%
2005: ¥2,999/¥1,687,380..   0.18%

(3) **Allowance for Uncollectible Accounts/ Gross Accounts Receivable at End of Year**
2007: ¥5,286/¥630,044....................................... 0.84%
2006: ¥10,673/¥468,387......................................   2.28%
2005: ¥8,341/¥455,517..   1.83%

(4) **Accounts Written Off/Average Gross Accounts Receivable**
2007: ¥6,471/.5(¥630,044 + ¥468,387)........... 1.18%
2006: ¥820/.5(¥468,387 + ¥455,517) 0.18%
2005: ¥8,099/.5(¥455,517 + ¥382,692)...........   1.93%

c. The accounts receivable turnover ratio decreased during the three-year period from 4.13 (in 2005) to 3.92 (in 2006) to 3.49 (in 2007). The firm decreased the amount of accounts written off between 2005 and 2006, from 1.54% to 0.18%, leading to a decrease in the allowance account relative to the gross accounts receivable. The firm decreased its provision for estimated uncollectible accounts in 2007 (the percentage of bad debt expense to sales declined from 0.18% in 2005 and 2006 to 0.06% in 2007), consistent with the build up in the allowance account. The accounts written off as a percentage of gross accounts receivable increased in 2007, from 0.18% in 2006 to 1.47% in 2007, perhaps because credit conditions worsened in that year. The latter is consistent with the decrease in the accounts receivable turnover ratio, from 3.92 in 2006 to 3.49 in 2007.

7.42 (Polaris Corporation; analyzing changes in accounts receivable.) (Amounts in Millions)

a.

	2008	2007	2006	2005
Allowance for Uncollectible Accounts, Beginning of Year........	$138.1	$115.1	$111.0	$97.8
Plus Bad Debt Expense.....................	36.8	40.1	20.1	20.1
Less Accounts Written Off (Plug)...	(2.9)	(17.1)	(16.0)	(6.9)
Allowance for Uncollectible Accounts, End of Year..................	$172.0	$138.1	$115.1	$111.0

b.

	2008	2007	2006	2005
Accounts Receivable, Gross at Beginning of Year...........................	$605.6	$599.2	$566.7	$539.5
Plus Sales on Account[a].....................	3,660.1	3,221.6	2,809.7	2,479.1
Less Accounts Written Off...............	(2.9)	(17.1)	(16.0)	(6.9)
Less Cash Collections from Credit Customers (Plug)...........................	(3,582.4)	(3,198.1)	(2,761.2)	(2,445.0)
Accounts Receivable, Gross at End of Year...	$680.4	$605.6	$599.2	$566.7

[a]Total Sales x 0.75.

c.

	2008	2007	2006	2005
Cash Collections from Cash Sales[a]...	$1,220.0	$1,073.9	$936.6	$826.4
Cash Collections from Credit Customers (from Part b.)....................	3,582.4	3,198.1	2,761.2	2,445.0
Total Cash Collected from Customers............................	$4,802.4	$4,272.0	$3,697.8	$3,271.4

[a]Total Sales x 0.25.

d.

Total Sales/Average Accounts Receivable, Net:	2008	2007	2006	2005
$4,880.1/.5($508.4+ $467.5)........	10.00			
$4,295.4/.5($467.5 + $484.1).......		9.03		
$3,746.3/.5($484.1 + $455.7).......			7.97	
$3,305.4/.5($455.7 + $441.7).......				7.37

7.43 (Aracruz Celulose; analyzing changes in accounts receivable.) (Amounts in Thousands)

a. Carrying Value = Accounts Receivable, Net.
For 2007: $361,603 (= $365,921 – $4,318).
For 2006: $285,795 (= $290,429 – $4,634).

7.43 continued.

    b. Total Amount Customers Owe = Accounts Receivable, Gross.
       For 2007: $365,921.
       For 2006: $290,429.

    c. Journal Entries for Bad Debt Expense:

2007
Bad Debt Expense.. 117
    Allowance for Uncollectible Accounts 117

Assets	= Liabilities	+	Shareholders' Equity	(Class.)
–117			–117	IncSt → RE

Bad Debt Expense equals $117 (= $4,318 + $433 – $4,634).

2006
Bad Debt Expense.. 592
    Allowance for Uncollectible Accounts 592

Assets	= Liabilities	+	Shareholders' Equity	(Class.)
–592			–592	IncSt → RE

Bad Debt Expense equals $592 (= $4,634 + $25 – $4,067).

7.44 Metso Corporation; analyzing disclosures of accounts receivable.) (Amounts in Millions)

    a. Carrying Value = Accounts Receivable, Net.
       For 2007: €1,274.
       For 2006: €1,218.

    b. Total Amount Customers Owe = Accounts Receivable, Gross.
       For 2007: €1,310 = €1,274 + €36.
       For 2006: €1,253 = €1,218 + €35.

7.44 continued.

    c. Journal Entries for Writeoffs:

2007
Allowance for Doubtful Accounts................................. 5
    Accounts Receivable, Gross......................................   5

Assets	= Liabilities	+	Shareholders' Equity	(Class.)
−5				
+5				

Writeoff equals €5 (= €35 + €13 − €7 − €36).

2006
Allowance for Doubtful Accounts................................. 6
    Accounts Receivable, Gross......................................   6

Assets	= Liabilities	+	Shareholders' Equity	(Class.)
−6				
+6				

Writeoff equals €6 (= €35 + €10 − €4 − €35).

7.45 (Pins Company; reconstructing transactions affecting accounts receivable and uncollectible accounts.)

    a. $192,000 Dr. = $700,000 − $500,000 − $8,000.

    b. $6,000 Cr. = (.02 x $700,000) − $8,000.

    c. $21,000 = $10,000 + $11,000.

    d. $16,000 = $6,000 + $10,000.

    e. $676,000 = $192,000 + $800,000 − $16,000 − $300,000.

    f. $289,000 = $300,000 − $11,000.

7.46 (Effect of errors involving accounts receivable on financial statement ratios.)

	Rate of Return on Assets	Accounts Receivable Turnover Ratio	Liabilities to Assets Ratio
a. Bad Debt Expense.................... X Allowance for Uncollectible Accounts	$\dfrac{O/S}{O/S} = O/S$	$\dfrac{NO}{O/S} = U/S$	$\dfrac{NO}{O/S} = U/S$

Assets	=	Liabilities	+	Shareholders' Equity	(Class)
−Amount				−Amount	IncSt → RE

b. Allowance for Uncollectible Accounts......... X Accounts Receivable	$\dfrac{NO}{NO} = NO$	$\dfrac{NO}{NO} = NO$	$\dfrac{NO}{NO} = NO$

Assets	=	Liabilities	+	Shareholders' Equity	(Class)
+Amount					
−Amount					

c. Advances from Customers................ X Accounts Receivable	$\dfrac{NO}{O/S} = U/S$	$\dfrac{NO}{O/S} = U/S$	$\dfrac{O/S}{O/S} = O/S$

Assets	=	Liabilities	+	Shareholders' Equity	(Class)
−Amount		−Amount			

Solutions   7-38

7.46 continued.

d. Sales Revenue X
   Accounts Receivable   X

Assets	=	Liabilities	+	Shareholders' Equity	(Class)
−Amount				−Amount	

$\dfrac{\text{O/S}}{\text{O/S}} = \text{O/S}$ $\dfrac{\text{O/S}}{\text{O/S}} = \text{O/S}$ $\dfrac{\text{NO}}{\text{O/S}} = \text{U/S}$

Inventory X
   Cost of Goods Sold   X

Assets	=	Liabilities	+	Shareholders' Equity	(Class)
+Amount				+Amount	

e. Sales Return X
   Accounts Receivable   X

Assets	=	Liabilities	+	Shareholders' Equity	(Class)
−Amount				−Amount	

$\dfrac{\text{O/S}}{\text{O/S}} = \text{O/S}$ $\dfrac{\text{O/S}}{\text{O/S}} = \text{O/S}$ $\dfrac{\text{NO}}{\text{O/S}} = \text{U/S}$

Inventory X
   Cost of Goods Sold   X

Assets	=	Liabilities	+	Shareholders' Equity	(Class)
+Amount				+Amount	

Note: This problem asks only for the net effect of each error on the three financial ratios. The journal entries and the numerator and denominator effects show the reason for the net effect.

7-39   Solutions

7.47 (Areva Group: income recognition for uranium enrichment plant.) (Amounts in Millions)

a.1. Percentage-of-Completion Method

Year	Incremental Percentage Complete	Revenue Recognized	Expenses Recognized	Income
2008	340/1,700 (.20)	$ 400	$ 340	$ 60
2009	238/1,700 (.14)	280	238	42
2010	238/1,700 (.14)	280	238	42
2011	238/1,700 (.14)	280	238	42
2012	238/1,700 (.14)	280	238	42
2013	238/1,700 (.14)	280	238	42
2014	170/1,700 (.10)	200	170	30
Total.....	120/120 (1.00)	$ 2,000	$ 1,700	$ 300

2. Completed Contract Method

Year	Revenue Recognized	Expenses Recognized	Income
2008	-0-	-0-	-0-
2009	-0-	-0-	-0-
2010	-0-	-0-	-0-
2011	-0-	-0-	-0-
2012	-0-	-0-	-0-
2013	-0-	-0-	-0-
2014	$ 2,000	$ 1,700	$ 300
Total....	$ 2,000	$ 1,700	$ 300

b. **Journal Entries:**

1. Percentage-of-Completion Method

2007
December 20, 2007: At time of contract signing.
Cash.. 20
    Advances from Customer.. 20

Assets	=	Liabilities	+	Shareholders' Equity	(Class.)
+20		+20			

Solutions 7-40

7.47 b. continued.

2008

| Construction in Process | 340 | |
| Cash | | 340 |

Assets	=	Liabilities	+	Shareholders' Equity	(Class.)
+340					
−340					

Cash	100	
Advances from Customer	20	
Receivable from Customer	280	
Sales Revenue		400

Assets	=	Liabilities	+	Shareholders' Equity	(Class.)
+100		−20		+400	IncSt → RE
+280					

| Cost of Sales | 340 | |
| Construction in Process | | 340 |

Assets	=	Liabilities	+	Shareholders' Equity	(Class.)
−340				−340	IncSt → RE

2009–2013

| Construction in Process | 238 | |
| Cash | | 238 |

Assets	=	Liabilities	+	Shareholders' Equity	(Class.)
+238					
−238					

Cash	100	
Receivable from Customer	180	
Sales Revenue		280

Assets	=	Liabilities	+	Shareholders' Equity	(Class.)
+100				+280	IncSt → RE
+180					

7.47 b. continued.

Cost of Sales.. 238
    Construction in Process.. 238

Assets	=	Liabilities	+	Shareholders' Equity	(Class.)
−238				−238	IncSt → RE

2014
Construction in Process.. 170
    Cash... 170

Assets	=	Liabilities	+	Shareholders' Equity	(Class.)
+170					
−170					

Cash.. 1,380
    Receivable from Customer... 1,180
    Sales Revenue... 200

Assets	=	Liabilities	+	Shareholders' Equity	(Class.)
+1,380				+200	IncSt → RE
−1,180					

Cost of Sales.. 170
    Construction in Process.. 170

Assets	=	Liabilities	+	Shareholders' Equity	(Class.)
−170				−170	IncSt → RE

2. **Completed Contract Method**

2007
December 20, 2007: At time of contract signing.
Cash.. 20
    Advances from Customer.. 20

Assets	=	Liabilities	+	Shareholders' Equity	(Class.)
+20		+20			

Solutions

7.47 b. continued.

2008

Construction in Process..	340	
Cash		340

Assets	= Liabilities	+	Shareholders' Equity	(Class.)
+340				
−340				

Cash..	100	
Advances from Customer...		100

Assets	= Liabilities	+	Shareholders' Equity	(Class.)
+100	+100			

2009–2013

Construction in Process..	238	
Cash		238

Assets	= Liabilities	+	Shareholders' Equity	(Class.)
+238				
−238				

Cash..	100	
Advances form Customer...		100

Assets	= Liabilities	+	Shareholders' Equity	(Class.)
+100	+100			

2014

Construction in Process..	170	
Cash		170

Assets	= Liabilities	+	Shareholders' Equity	(Class.)
+170				
−170				

7.47 b. continued.

```
Cash................................................................. 1,380
Advances from Customer..................................... 620
    Sales Revenue..............................................         2,000
```

Assets	=	Liabilities	+	Shareholders' Equity	(Class.)
+1,380		−620		+2,000	IncSt → RE

```
Cost of Sales....................................................... 1,700
    Construction in Process.................................         1,700
```

Assets	=	Liabilities	+	Shareholders' Equity	(Class.)
−1,700				−1,700	IncSt → RE

7.48 (Flanikin Construction Company; income recognition for a contractor.)

a. **Calculation of Revenues, Expenses, and Income**

1. **Percentage-of-Completion Method**

Year	Incremental Percentage Complete	Revenue Recognized	Expenses Recognized	Income
2005	12/120 (.10)	$ 18,000,000	$ 12,000,000	$ 6,000,000
2006	36/120 (.30)	54,000,000	36,000,000	18,000,000
2007	48/120 (.40)	72,000,000	48,000,000	24,000,000
2008	24/120 (.20)	36,000,000	24,000,000	12,000,000
Total.......	120/120 (1.00)	$180,000,000	$120,000,000	$60,000,000

2. **Completed Contract Method**

Year	Revenue Recognized	Expenses Recognized	Income
2005	-0-	-0-	-0-
2006	-0-	-0-	-0-
2007	-0-	-0-	-0-
2008	$180,000,000	$120,000,000	$60,000,000
Total....	$180,000,000	$120,000,000	$60,000,000

7.48 continued.

b. Journal Entries

1. Percentage-of-Completion Method

2005

Construction in Process 12
    Accounts Payable   12

Assets	= Liabilities	+	Shareholders' Equity	(Class.)
+12	+12			

Cash 36
    Advances from Customer   18
    Sales Revenue   18

Assets	= Liabilities	+	Shareholders' Equity	(Class.)
+36	+18		+18	IncSt → RE

Cost of Sales 12
    Construction in Process   12

Assets	= Liabilities	+	Shareholders' Equity	(Class.)
−12			−12	IncSt → RE

2006

Construction in Process 36
    Accounts Payable   36

Assets	= Liabilities	+	Shareholders' Equity	(Class.)
+36	+36			

Cash 45
Advances from Customer 9
    Sales Revenue   54

Assets	= Liabilities	+	Shareholders' Equity	(Class.)
+45	−9		+54	IncSt → RE

7.48 b. continued.

Cost of Sales.. 36
    Construction in Process... 36

Assets	=	Liabilities	+	Shareholders' Equity	(Class.)
−36				−36	IncSt → RE

2007
Construction in Process... 48
    Accounts Payable.. 48

Assets	=	Liabilities	+	Shareholders' Equity	(Class.)
+48		+48			

Cash... 45
Advances from Customer.. 9
Receivable from Customer.. 18
    Sales Revenue... 72

Assets	=	Liabilities	+	Shareholders' Equity	(Class.)
+45		−9		+72	IncSt → RE
+18					

Cost of Sales... 48
    Construction in Process... 48

Assets	=	Liabilities	+	Shareholders' Equity	(Class.)
−48				−48	IncSt → RE

2008
Construction in Process... 24
    Accounts Payable.. 24

Assets	=	Liabilities	+	Shareholders' Equity	(Class.)
+24		+24			

7.48 b. continued.

Cash 54
    Receivable from Customer 18
    Sales Revenue 36

Assets	=	Liabilities	+	Shareholders' Equity	(Class.)
+54				+36	IncSt → RE
−18					

Cost of Sales 24
    Construction in Process 24

Assets	=	Liabilities	+	Shareholders' Equity	(Class.)
−24				−24	IncSt → RE

2. Completed Contract Method

2005
Construction in Process 12
    Accounts Payable 12

Assets	=	Liabilities	+	Shareholders' Equity	(Class.)
+12		+12			

Cash 36
    Advances from Customer 36

Assets	=	Liabilities	+	Shareholders' Equity	(Class.)
+36		+36			

2006
Construction in Process 36
    Accounts Payable 36

Assets	=	Liabilities	+	Shareholders' Equity	(Class.)
+36		+36			

7.48 b. continued.

Cash.. 45
    Advances from Customer...   45

Assets	=	Liabilities	+	Shareholders' Equity	(Class.)
+45		+45			

2007
Construction in Process... 48
    Accounts Payable...   48

Assets	=	Liabilities	+	Shareholders' Equity	(Class.)
+48		+48			

Cash.. 45
    Advances from Customer...   45

Assets	=	Liabilities	+	Shareholders' Equity	(Class.)
+45		+45			

2008
Construction in Process... 24
    Accounts Payable...   24

Assets	=	Liabilities	+	Shareholders' Equity	(Class.)
+24		+24			

Cash.. 54
Advances from Customer... 126
    Sales Revenue..   180

Assets	=	Liabilities	+	Shareholders' Equity	(Class.)
+54		−126		+180	IncSt → RE

Cost of Sales... 120
    Construction in Process...   120

Assets	=	Liabilities	+	Shareholders' Equity	(Class.)
−120				−120	IncSt → RE

7.48 continued.

c. The percentage-of-completion method probably gives the best measure of Flanikin's performance each year under the contract. The original estimates of costs on the contract turned out to be correct. Also, the periodic cash collections suggest that the firm will probably collect cash in the amount of the contract price.

7.49 (Furniture Retailers; revenue recognition when payment is uncertain.)

a. **Installment Method**

(1) **January 2008**

Accounts Receivable	8,400	
Inventory		6,800
Deferred Gross Margin		1,600

Assets	=	Liabilities	+	Shareholders' Equity	(Class.)
+8,400					
−6,800		+1,600			

(2) **When Furniture Retailer Receives Each Payment**

The customer will make 21 payments of $400 each. The gross margin percentage is 19% (= $1,600/$8,400). When each monthly payment is received, Furniture Retailers will recognize $400 of revenues and $76 (= 0.19 x $400) of Deferred Gross Margin.

Cash	400	
Deferred Gross Margin	76	
Cost of Goods Sold (Plug)	324	
Sales Revenue		400
Accounts Receivable		400

Assets	=	Liabilities	+	Shareholders' Equity	(Class.)
+400		−76		−324	IncSt → RE
−400				+400	IncSt → RE

7.49 continued.

b. Cost Recovery Method

(1) January 2008

Accounts Receivable	8,400	
Inventory		6,800
Deferred Gross Margin		1,600

Assets	=	Liabilities	+	Shareholders' Equity	(Class.)
+8,400		+1,600			
–6,800					

(2) When Each Payment is Received

The customer will make 21 payments of $400 each. Furniture Retailers will recover the $6,800 cost of furniture after the customer has made seventeen payments (= $6,800/$400). To record the first seventeen payments, Furniture Retailers makes the following journal entry:

Cash	400	
Cost of Goods Sold	400	
Sales Revenue		400
Accounts Receivable		400

Assets	=	Liabilities	+	Shareholders' Equity	(Class.)
+400				+400	IncSt → RE
–400				–400	IncSt → RE

To record the last four payments, Furniture Retailers makes the following journal entry:

Cash	400	
Deferred Gross Margin	400	
Sales Revenue		400
Accounts Receivable		400

Assets	=	Liabilities	+	Shareholders' Equity	(Class.)
+400		–400		+400	IncSt → RE
–400					

7.50 (Appliance Sales and Service; revenue recognition when payment is uncertain.)

a. Customer makes all 10 payments.

(1) **Installment Method**

July 2008

The customer will make 10 payments of $244 each, so the total amount owed is $2,440. The gross margin percentage of 9% on this sale means that the deferred gross margin is $220 (= 9% x $2,440). The difference between the amount of cash the customer has promised to pay ($2,440) and the deferred gross margin ($220) is credited to inventory.

Accounts Receivable	2,440
Inventory	2,220
Deferred Gross Margin	220

Assets	=	Liabilities	+	Shareholders' Equity	(Class.)
+2,440		+220			
–2,220					

When Each Payment Is Received. When each monthly payment is received, Appliance Sales and Service will recognize $244 revenue and $22 (= 9% x $244) of Deferred Gross Margin.

Cash	244
Deferred Gross Margin	22
Cost of Goods Sold (Plug)	222
Sales Revenue	244
Accounts Receivable	244

Assets	=	Liabilities	+	Shareholders' Equity	(Class.)
+244		–22		+244	IncSt → RE
–244				–222	IncSt → RE

(2) **Cost Recovery Method**

July 2008

The customer will make 10 payments of $244 each. Appliance Sales and Service will not recover the entire $2,220 cost of appliances until after the customer has made all payments. To record the first nine payments of $244, the following journal entry is made:

7.50 a. continued.

Accounts Receivable 2,440
    Inventory...   2,220
    Deferred Gross Margin...   220

Assets	=	Liabilities	+	Shareholders' Equity	(Class.)
+2,440		+220			
−2,220					

To Record the First Nine Payments of $244:

Cash... 244
Cost of Goods Sold... 244
    Sales Revenue..   244
    Accounts Receivable...   244

Assets	=	Liabilities	+	Shareholders' Equity	(Class.)
+244				+244	IncSt → RE
−244				−244	IncSt → RE

To Record the Last Payment of $244. Note that after the ninth payment, Appliance Sales and Service has recognized $2,196 (= 9 × $244) of the total cost of goods sold of $2,220. The remainder, $24, is recognized on receipt of the last payment.

Cash... 244
Cost of Goods Sold... 24
Deferred Gross Margin... 220
    Sales Revenue..   244
    Accounts Receivable...   244

Assets	=	Liabilities	+	Shareholders' Equity	(Class.)
+244		+220		+244	IncSt → RE
−244				−24	IncSt → RE

Solutions

7.50 continued.

b. Customer stops making payments after November 2008.

(1) Installment Method

The customer has made the first five payments (July–November, 2008) so the amount owed is $1,220 [= $2,440 − (5 × $244)].

Deferred Gross Margin...	110	
Loss on Repossessed Appliances..............................	130	
Inventory—Repossessed Appliances........................	980	
Accounts Receivable..		1,220

Assets	=	Liabilities	+	Shareholders' Equity	(Class.)
+980		−110		−130	IncSt → RE
−1,220					

(2) Cost Recovery Method

The customer has made the first five payments (July–November, 2008) so the amount owed is $1,220 [= $2,440 − (5 × $244)].

Deferred Gross Margin...	220	
Loss on Repossession...	20	
Inventory—Repossessed Appliances........................	980	
Accounts Receivable..		1,220

Assets	=	Liabilities	+	Shareholders' Equity	(Class.)
+980		−220		−20	IncSt → RE
−1,220					

7.51 (J. C. Spangle; point-of-sales versus installment method of income recognition.)

a.

	2008	2007
Sales	$300,000	$200,000
Expenses:		
Cost of Goods Sold*	$186,000	$120,000
All Other Expenses	44,000	32,000
Total Expenses	$230,000	$152,000
Net Income	$ 70,000	$ 48,000
*Beginning Inventory	$ 60,000	$ 0
Purchases	240,000	180,000
Goods Available	$300,000	$180,000
Ending Inventory	(114,000)	(60,000)
Cost of Goods Sold	$186,000	$120,000

Cost of Goods Sold/Sales:
   2007 — $120,000/$200,000 = 60%.
   2008 — $186,000/$300,000 = 62%.

b.

	2008	2007
Collections from Customers	$230,000	$ 90,000
Expenses:		
Merchandise Cost of Collections*	$140,400	$ 54,000
All Other Expenses	44,000	32,000
Total Expenses	$184,400	$ 86,000
Net Income	$ 45,600	$ 4,000

*Calculation	2008	2007
Merchandise Cost of Collections:		
Of Goods Sold:		
In 2007, 60% of $90,000		$ 54,000
In 2008, 60% of $110,000	$ 66,000	
Of Goods Sold in 2008:		
62% of $120,000	74,400	
	$140,400	$ 54,000

An Alternative Presentation Would Be:	2008	2007
Realized Gross Margin	$ 89,600	$ 36,000
All Other Expenses	44,000	32,000
Net Income	$ 45,600	$ 4,000

7.52 (Picking Chicken; revenue recognition for a franchise.)

a.
Year	Pickin Chicken, Inc.	Country Delight, Inc.
2006	$400,000 (= $50,000 × 8)	$160,000 (= $20,000 × 8)
2007	250,000 (= $50,000 × 5)	148,000 (= $20,000 × 5 + $6,000 × 8)
2008	0	78,000 (= $6,000 × 13)
2009	0	78,000 (= $6,000 × 13)
2010	0	78,000 (= $6,000 × 13)
2011	0	78,000 (= $6,000 × 13)
2012	0	30,000 (= $6,000 × 5)
Total..	$650,000	$650,000

b. The issue here is whether sufficient uncertainty exists regarding the amount the firm will ultimately collect to justify postponing revenue recognition until the time of collection. The casualty rate among franchisees has been very high and has led some accountants to argue that the installment method is the appropriate basis for revenue recognition.

7.53 (Income recognition for various types of businesses.)

a. **Amgen**—The principal income recognition issue for Amgen is the significant lag between the incurrence of research and development expenditures and the realization of sales from any resulting products. Biotechnology firms are a relatively new industry and, therefore, have few commercially feasible products. Thus, research and development expenditures will likely represent a significant percentage of revenues, as is the case for Amgen. More established technology firms, such as pharmaceuticals, have established products as well as products in the pipeline and, therefore, research and development expenditures represent both a smaller and a more stable percentage of revenues. GAAP requires biotechnology firms to expense research and development expenditures in the year incurred.

Brown Forman—The principal revenue recognition issue for Brown Forman is whether it should recognize the increase in value of hard liquors while they are aging (that is, revalue the liquors to market value each year) or wait until the liquors are sold at the end of the aging process. Most accountants would argue that the market values of aging liquors are too uncertain prior to sale to justify periodic revaluations and revenue recognition. Brown Forman should include in the cost of the liquor inventory not only the initial production costs but also the cost incurred during the aging process. In this way, the firm can match total incurred costs with revenues generated at the time of sale.

7.53 a. continued.

Deere—Deere faces issues of revenue recognition with respect to both the sale of farm equipment to dealers and the provision of financing services. The concern with respect to the sale of farm equipment to dealers is the right of dealers to return any unsold equipment. If dealers have no right of return, then recognition of revenue at the time of sale is appropriate. If dealers can return any equipment discovered to be faulty prior to sale and the amount of such returns is reasonably predictable, then Deere can reduce the amount of revenue recognized each year for estimated returns. If dealers can return any unsold equipment, then delaying recognition of revenue until the dealer sells the equipment is appropriate. Deere should match the cost of manufacturing the equipment against the sales revenue. Deere reports research and development expense in its income statement. Given the farm equipment industry, one wonders about what proportions of these expenditures Deere makes to enhance existing products versus to develop new products. Although contrary to GAAP, one can make the case that Deere should capitalize and amortize expenditures on new products.

Deere should accrue revenue from financing (interest) and insurance (premiums) services over time. To achieve matching, Deere should capitalize and amortize any initial administrative costs to check customer credit quality and prepare legal documents.

Fluor—The appropriate timing of revenue recognition for Fluor depends on the basis for pricing its services. If the fee is fixed for any particular construction project, then Fluor should recognize the fee in relation to the degree of completion of the construction project. If the fee is a percentage of total construction costs incurred on the project, then Fluor should recognize revenue in relation to costs incurred. If the fee is a percentage of the costs incurred by Fluor (salaries of their employees working on the project), then it should recognize revenue in relation to the incurrence of these costs. It seems clear that the percentage-of-completion method of revenue recognition is more appropriate than the completed contract method.

Golden West—Golden West should recognize interest revenue from home mortgage loans as time passes. It should provide for estimated uncollectible accounts each year. The uncollectible amount should reflect the resale value of homes repossessed. The more difficult question relates to recognition of revenue from points. One possibility is to recognize the full amount in the initial year of the loan. The rationale for such a procedure is that the points cover administrative costs of setting up the loan. Both the points and the administrative costs would be recognized in full in the initial year of the loan. An alter-

7.53 a. continued.

native view is that the points effectively reduce the amount lent by the savings and loan company and increase its yield beyond the stated interest rate. This view suggests that Golden West amortize the points over the term of the loan and match against this revenue amortization of the initial administrative costs to set up the loan. Golden West should recognize interest expense on deposits as time passes. There is no direct relation between interest expense on deposits and interest revenue from loans so Golden West matches interest expense to the period it is incurred.

Merrill Lynch—The principal income recognition issue for Merrill Lynch is whether it should report financial instruments held as assets and liabilities at their acquisition cost or their current fair value. These assets and liabilities generally have easily measured fair values. They are typically held for short periods of time (days or weeks). Thus, one can argue that use of current fair values is appropriate. However, we are still left with the question as to whether the unrealized gain or loss should flow through to the income statement immediately or wait until realization at the time of sale. The argument for immediate recognition is that Merrill Lynch takes short-term financing and investing positions for short-term returns. Its income statement should reflect its operating performance during this period. The case for not recognizing the unrealized gains and losses is that they could reverse prior to realization and, in any case, will be realized very soon. Merrill Lynch should recognize revenue from fee-based services as it provides the services.

Rockwell—The absence of research and development expense from the income statement suggests that Rockwell charges all such costs to specific contracts. These costs become expenses as Rockwell recognizes revenue from the contracts. The multi-year nature of its contracts and the credit quality of the U.S. government suggest use of the percentage-of-completion method of income recognition. One difficulty encountered in applying the percentage-of-completion method is that Rockwell's contracts for projects such as the space shuttle get continually renewed. This procedure makes it difficult to identify a single contract price and accumulate costs for a single contract, which the percentage-of-completion method envisions.

b. **Amgen**—Amgen realized the highest profit margin of the seven companies. Its biotechnology products are protected by patents. It therefore maintains a monopoly position. Note that the cost of manufacturing its products is a small percent of revenues. Amgen's major cost is for research and development. Sales of its existing products are not only sufficient to cover its high, on-going research work but to provide a substantial profit margin as well. Its relatively low revenue to assets percentage is somewhat unexpected, given that

7.53 b. continued.

its major "assets" are patents and research scientists. The reason for this low percentage (reason not provided in the case) is that cash and marketable securities comprise approximately 25% of its assets. These assets generated a return of approximately 3% during the year. This rate of return decreased the overall ratio of revenues to assets for Amgen.

Brown Forman—Brown Forman realized the third highest profit margin among the seven companies. If one views the excise taxes as a reduction in revenues rather than as an expense, its profit margin is 10.4% [= 8.8%/(100.0% − 15.4%)]. Concerns about excess alcoholic drinking in recent years have resulted in some exodus of companies from the industry, leaving the remaining companies with a larger share of a smaller market. The products of Brown Forman carry brand name recognition, permitting the firm to obtain attractive prices.

Deere—Deere's relatively low profit margin reflects (1) weaknesses in the farming industry in recent years, which puts downward pressure on margins, and (2) decreased interest rates, which lowers profit margins. The revenue-to-assets percentage of Deere reflects its capital-intensive manufacturing operations and the low interest rate on outstanding loans to dealers and customers.

Fluor—The low profit margin of Fluor reflects the relatively low value added of construction services. It may also reflect recessionary conditions when construction activity is weak and profit margins are thin.

Golden West—The 12% profit margin (ignoring an addback for interest expense, which is common for financial services firms) seems high, relative to interest rates in recent years. Recall though that Golden West pays short-term interest rates on its deposits but obtains long-term interest rates on its loans. An upward-sloping yield curve provides a positive differential. Also, the existence of shareholders' equity funds in the capital structure means that Golden West has assets earning returns for which it recognizes no expense in its income statement (that is, firms do not recognize an expense for the implicit cost of shareholders' funds). Note also that the ratio of revenue to assets is only .1. Thus, the assets of Golden West earned a return of only 1.2% (= 12.0% x .1) during the year.

Merrill Lynch—The lower profit margin for Merrill Lynch relative to Golden West reflects in part the fact that both the investments and financing of Merrill Lynch are short term. Merrill Lynch, however, realizes revenue from fee-based services. Firms like Merrill Lynch can differentiate these services somewhat and realize attractive profit margins. However, such services have been quickly copied by competitors in recent years, reducing the profit margins accordingly.

7.53 b. continued.

        Rockwell—Rockwell's profit margin is in the middle of the seven companies. Factors arguing for a high profit margin include Rockwell's technological know-how and its role in long-term contracts with the U.S. government. Factors arguing for a lower profit margin include cutbacks in defense expenditures and excess capacity in the aerospace industry.

7.54   (Understanding the purpose of the Allowance for Uncollectible Accounts account.)

        This case has the following history. Over the last several years, we have lectured to audit committee, and other board members, about the meaning of the requirement that audit committee members be financially literate, as specified by the New York Stock Exchange and the NASDAQ in its listing requirements. Many experienced members suggest our criteria for literacy are too stringent, because, they say, I do not need to know all that accounting stuff, as I know how to ask the tough questions. We believe that being able to ask tough questions is not enough, if the questioner cannot evaluate the answers, recognizing incorrect answers and being able to ask follow-up questions for correct, but only partial, answers. We devised a Tough Questions Quiz virtually identical to this case. Of the audit committee members who have taken the quiz [as you might imagine, its hard to get them to do so], the median number of correct responses is just under half. Former SEC Commissioner Arthur Levitt contributed to the malaise of the financially illiterate audit committee room by saying in a speech that he wanted board members to be able to ask the tough questions, without adding and be able to evaluate the answers.

    a.   This response does not address the question. Judging the adequacy of the allowance account focuses on estimating the portion of accounts receivable that a firm does not expect to collect. Thus, the question concerns the valuation of accounts receivable net of estimated uncollectibles. The CFO in essence is saying that even if the firm has more uncollectibles than the amount in the allowance account the firm will survive. The CFO's response does not demonstrate an understanding of the purpose of the allowance account.

    b.   This response demonstrates an understanding of the need to match estimated uncollectibles with sales of the period. Although the amount of bad debt expense this period may reflect accurately the expected amount of the current period's sales that a firm does not expect to collect, it does not say anything about the adequacy of prior periods' provisions to cover estimated uncollectibles from those periods' sales account.

7.54 continued.

    c. This response demonstrates an understanding that the allowance account should reflect the estimated amounts of accounts receivable that the firm does not expect to collect. It also shows that the CFO knows to use an aging of accounts receivable to judge the adequacy of the balance in the account. The misunderstanding is that the allowance account reflects the estimated amounts from sales of all periods, not just the current period, that the firm does not expect to collect.

    d. This response demonstrates an accurate understanding of the purpose of the allowance account and the approach a firm should follow to judge the adequacy of the amount in the allowance account.

    e. This response does not address the question. The CFO addresses the appropriateness of writing off accounts that were written off. It does not address the adequacy of the balance in the allowance account to cover accounts not yet written off.

    f. This confirmation of receivables simply evidences that a valid receivable exists. It does not provide evidence about what portion of these receivables the firm does and does not expect to collect, which is the question asked.

    g. This response demonstrates an understanding that the allowance account should carry a sufficient balance to equal amounts from the current and prior period's sales that the firm does not expect to collect. It also shows a need to assess the adequacy of the balance in the allowance account each period. Finally, it shows the use of external benchmarks to assess the adequacy of the amount of bad debt expense. The one remaining response that would have demonstrated even more understanding about the adequacy of the balance in the allowance account was for the CFO to state that the benchmark percentages from the credit reporting agencies have historically matched the firm's credit loss experience.

CHAPTER 8

WORKING CAPITAL

Questions, Exercises, and Problems: Answers and Solutions

8.1 See the text or the glossary at the end of the book.

8.2 Prepayments are future economic benefits that a firm will receive because it has exchanged cash for the right to receive services in the future. Firms charge the asset to expense over the period during which it receives services.

8.3 The underlying principle is that acquisition cost includes all costs required to prepare an asset for its intended use. Assets provide future services. Costs that a firm must incur to obtain those expected services are, therefore, included in the acquisition cost valuation of the asset. In the case of merchandise inventory, this includes the costs associated with obtaining the goods (purchase price, transportation costs, insurance costs). For inventory, which the firm manufactures, acquisition costs include labor, overhead, and materials.

8.4 Depreciation on manufacturing equipment is a product cost and remains in inventory accounts until the firm sells the manufactured goods. Depreciation on selling and administrative equipment is a period expense, because the use of such equipment does not create an asset with future service potential.

8.5 Both the Merchandise Inventory and Finished Goods Inventory accounts include the cost of completed units ready for sale. A merchandising firm acquires the units in finished form and debits Merchandise Inventory for their acquisition cost. A manufacturing firm incurs direct material, direct labor, and manufacturing overhead costs in transforming the units to a finished, salable condition. The Raw Materials Inventory and Work-in-Process Inventory accounts include such costs until the completion of manufacturing operations. Thus, the accountant debits the Finished Goods Inventory account for the cost of producing completed units. The accountant credits both the Merchandise Inventory and Finished Goods Inventory accounts for the cost of units sold and reports the inventory accounts as current assets on the balance sheet.

8.6 Accounting reports cost flows, not flows of physical quantities. Cost flow assumptions trace costs, not physical flows of goods. With specific identification, management can manipulate cost flows by controlling goods physical flow of goods.

8.7 **Rising Purchase Prices**
Higher Inventory Amount: FIFO
Lower Inventory Amount: LIFO
Higher Cost of Goods
  Sold Amount: LIFO.
Lower Cost of Goods
  Sold Amount: FIFO

8.8 Suppliers often grant a discount if customers pay within a certain number of days after the invoice date, in which case this source of funds has an explicit interest cost. Suppliers who do not offer discounts for prompt payment often include an implicit interest change in the selling price of the product. Customers in this second category should delay payment as long as possible because they are paying for the use of the funds. Firms should not delay payment to such an extent that it hurts their credit rating and raises their cost of financing

8.9 The Parker School should accrue the salary in ten monthly installments of $360,000 each at the end of each month, September through June. It will have paid $300,000 at the end of each of these months, so that by the end of the reporting year, it reports a current liability of $600,000 [= $3,600,000 − (10 x $300,000)].

8.10 It is cheaper (and, therefore, more profitable) to repair a few sets than to have such stringent quality control that the manufacturing process produces zero defectives. An allowance is justified when firms expect to have warranty costs. Manufacturers of TV sets for use on space ships or heart pacemakers should strive for zero defects.

8.11 **Similarities:** The accountant makes estimates of future events in both cases. The accountant charges the cost of estimated uncollectibles or warranties to income in the period of sale, not in the later period when specific items become uncollectible or break down. The income statement reports the charge against income as an expense in both cases, although some accountants report the charge for estimated uncollectibles as a revenue contra.

Differences: The balance sheet account showing the expected costs of future uncollectibles reduces an asset account, whereas that for estimated warranties appears as a liability.

8.12 A reversal implies that the previously accrued charge turned out to be too high, in light of the new information (including realized expenditures). Because the reversal lowers the amount of expense reported in the current period, it increases income.

8.13 (Delhaize Group; accounting for prepayments.)

  a. Journal entry to record insurance premium payments in 2007, 2006, and 2005:

  Prepayments... 50.0
    Cash... 50.0

Assets	= Liabilities	+	Shareholders' Equity	(Class.)
+50.0				
−50.0				

  b. Adjusting journal entries required each year.

  2006:
  Insurance Expense.. 66.3
    Prepayments.. 66.3

Assets	= Liabilities	+	Shareholders' Equity	(Class.)
−66.3			−66.3	IncSt → RE

  To adjust Prepayments for the amount consumed during 2006, of €66.3 million (= €42.1 + €50.0 − €25.8).

  2007:
  Insurance Expense.. 45.1
    Prepayments.. 45.1

Assets	= Liabilities	+	Shareholders' Equity	(Class.)
−45.1			−45.1	IncSt → RE

  To adjust Prepayments for the amount consumed during 2007, of €45.1 million (= €25.8 + €50.0 − €30.7).

8.14 (LG Corporation; accounting for prepayments.)

  a. Adjusting journal entry to record portion of prepaid rent consumed during each month, January–March:

  Rent Expense.. 86,775
    Prepaid Rent.. 86,775

Assets	= Liabilities	+	Shareholders' Equity	(Class.)
−86,775			−86,775	IncSt → RE

8.14 a. continued.

Rent expense is KRW86,775 million (= KRW260,324 million/3 months).

b. March 31, 2007: To record prepayment of rent for next 12 months.

Prepaid Rent..1,382,436
   Cash 1,382,436

Assets	=	Liabilities	+	Shareholders' Equity	(Class.)
+1,382,436					
−1,382,436					

To record cash prepayments for 12 months of rent of KRW1,382,436 million. The 2007 ending balance of Prepayments of KRW345,609 million consists of 3 months of prepaid rent. The total amount prepaid as of March 31, 2007 is, therefore, KRW345,609 x €4 = KRW1,382,436.

c. Adjusting journal entry to record portion of prepaid rent consumed during each month, April–December.

Rent Expense.. 115,203
   Prepaid Rent.. 115,203

Assets	=	Liabilities	+	Shareholders' Equity	(Class.)
−115,203				−115,203	IncSt → RE

Rent expense is KRW115,203 million (= KRW1,382,436 million/12 months); alternatively, note that the balance of Prepayments at December 31, 2007 consists of 3 months of prepaid rent (KRW115,203 = KRW345,609/3 months).

8.15 (Harnet Winery; identifying inventory cost inclusions.)

Harnet should include the costs to acquire the grapes, process them into wine, and mature the wine, but not the expenditures on advertising or research and development. Thus, the cost of the wine inventory (prior to its sale) is $3,673,000 (= $2,200,000 + $50,000 + $145,000 + $100,000 + $250,000 + $600,000 + $120,000 + $180,000 + $28,000).

8.16 (Trembly Department Store; identifying inventory cost inclusions.)

a.	Purchase Price	$300,000
b.	Freight Cost	13,800
c.	Salary of Purchasing Manager	3,000
d.	Depreciation, Taxes, Insurance and Utilities on Warehouse	27,300
e.	Salary of Warehouse Manager	2,200
f.	Merchandise Returns	(18,500)
g.	Cash Discounts Taken	(4,900)
	Acquisition Cost	$322,900

The underlying principle is that inventories should include all costs required to get the inventory ready for sale. The purchase of the inventory items (items *a.*, *c.*, *f.*, and *g.*) provides the physical goods to be sold, the freight cost (item *b.*) puts the inventory items in the place most convenient for sale, and the storage costs (items *d.* and *e.*) keep the inventory items until the time of sale. Economists characterize these costs as providing form, place, and time utility, or benefits. Although accounting theory suggests the inclusion of each of these items in the valuation of inventory, some firms might exclude items *c.*, *d.*, *e.*, and *g.* on the basis of lack of materiality.

8.17 (ResellFast; effect of inventory valuation on the balance sheet and net income.) (Amounts in Millions)

	Carrying Value	Effect on Income
Q1	$20.0	$0.0
Q2	16.5	(3.5)
Q3	16.5	0.0
Q4	0.0	11.0

8.18 (Target Corporation; inventory and accounts payable journal entries.)

a. Beginning Balance in Merchandise Inventory + Purchases of Inventory = Amount Sold (Cost of Goods Sold) + Ending Balance in Merchandise Inventory.

$6,254 + Purchases = $41,895 + $6,780 Purchases = $42,421.

b.
Merchandise Inventory	42,421	
Accounts Payable		42,421

Assets	=	Liabilities	+	Shareholders' Equity	(Class.)
+42,421		+42,421			

8.18 continued.

c. Beginning Balance in Accounts Payable + Purchases of Merchandise Inventory = Payments to Venders + Ending Balance in Accounts Payable.

$6,575 + 42,421 = Payments to Vendors + $6,721.
Payments to Vendors = $42,275.

| Accounts Payable | 42,275 | |
| Cash | | 42,275 |

Assets	=	Liabilities	+	Shareholders' Equity	(Class.)
−42,275		−42,275			

8.19 (Tesco Plc.; inventory and accounts payable journal entries.)

a.
| Trade Payables | 43,558 | |
| Cash | | 43,558 |

Assets	=	Liabilities	+	Shareholders' Equity	(Class.)
−43,558		−43,558			

b. Beginning Balance in Trade Payables + Purchases of Merchandise Inventory = Payments to Venders + Ending Balance in Trade Payables.

€3,317 + Purchases of Merchandise Inventory = €43,558 (from Part *a.*) + €3,936.

Purchases of Merchandise Inventory = €44,177.

| Merchandise Inventory | 44,177 | |
| Accounts Payable | | 44,177 |

Assets	=	Liabilities	+	Shareholders' Equity	(Class.)
+44,177		+44,177			IncSt → RE

c. Beginning Balance in Merchandise Inventory + Purchases of Inventory = Amount Sold (Cost of Goods Sold) + Ending Balance in Merchandise Inventory.

€1,911 + €44,177 (from Part *b.*) = Cost of Goods Sold + €2,420.
Cost of Goods Sold = €43,668.

8.19 c. continued.

Cost of Goods Sold.. 43,668
    Merchandise Inventory 43,668

Assets	=	Liabilities	+	Shareholders' Equity	(Class.)
–43,668				–43,668	IncSt → RE

8.20   (Fun-in-the-Sun Tanning Lotion Company; income computation for a manufacturing firm.)

Manufacturing Costs Incurred during the Year:
Raw Materials...	$ 56,300
Direct Labor..	36,100
Manufacturing Overhead...	26,800
Total Manufacturing Costs Incurred	$ 119,200
Less Manufacturing Costs Assigned to Work-in-Process Inventory...	(12,700)
Cost of Units Completed during the Year...........................	$ 106,500
Less Cost of Ending Inventory of Finished Goods.............	(28,500)
Cost of Goods Sold	$ 78,000

8.21   (GenMet; income computation for a manufacturing firm.)

Sales...	$ 6,700.2
Less Cost of Goods Sold...	(2,697.6)
Less Selling and Administrative Expenses	(2,903.7)
Less Interest Expense..	(151.9)
Income before Income Taxes	$ 947.0
Income Tax Expense at 35%..	(331.5)
Net Income	$ 615.5
Work-in-Process Inventory, October 31, 2007..................	$ 100.8
Plus Manufacturing Costs Incurred during Fiscal Year 2008......	2,752.0
Less Work-in-Process Inventory, October 31, 2008..........	(119.1)
Cost of Goods Completed during Fiscal Year 2008...........	$ 2,733.7
Plus Finished Goods Inventory, October 31, 2007............	286.2
Less Finished Goods Inventory, October 31, 2008............	(322.3)
Cost of Goods Sold	$ 2,697.6

8.22 (Crystal Chemical Corporation; income computation for a manufacturing firm.)

Sales	€ 32,632
Less Cost of Goods Sold	(28,177)
Less Marketing and Administrative Expenses	(2,436)
Less Interest Expense	(828)
Income before Income Taxes	€ 1,191
Income Tax Expense at 35%	(417)
Net Income	€ 774
Work-in-Process Inventory, December 31, 2007	€ 843
Plus Manufacturing Costs Incurred during 2008	28,044
Less Work-in-Process Inventory, December 31, 2008	(837)
Cost of Goods Completed during 2008	€ 28,050
Plus Finished Goods Inventory, December 31, 2007	2,523
Less Finished Goods Inventory, December 31, 2008	(2,396)
Cost of Goods Sold	€ 28,177

8.23 (Warren Company; effect of inventory errors.)

a. None.
b. None.
c. Understatement by $1,000.
d. Overstatement by $1,000.
e. Overstatement by $1,000.
f. Understatement by $1,000.
g. Understatement by $1,000.
h. None.
i. None.

8.24 (Cemex; lower of cost or market for inventory.)

a. $20,187 million (= $19,631 + $556).

b. Journal entry to record impairment charge for inventory during 2007:

Impairment Loss on Inventory	131	
Allowance for Impairment		131

Assets	=Liabilities	+	Shareholders' Equity	(Class.)
−131			−131	IncSt → RE

8.25 (Ericsson; lower of cost or market for inventory.)

a. SEK22,475 million (= SEK25,227 − SEK2,752).

b. Journal entry to record impairment charge for inventory during 2007:

Impairment Loss on Inventory	1,276	
Allowance for Impairment		1,276

8.25 b. continued.

Assets	= Liabilities	+	Shareholders' Equity	(Class.)
–1,276			–1,276	IncSt → RE

The carrying value of the inventory is now SEK2,224 (= SEK3,500 – SEK1,276).

c. January 2008: Journal entry to record a reversal of a portion of the impairment charge for inventory taken in 2007:

Allowance for Impairment.. 576
    Reversal of Impairment Loss on Inventory..........   576

Assets	= Liabilities	+	Shareholders' Equity	(Class.)
+576			+576	IncSt → RE

To reverse a portion of the impairment loss; SEK576 = SEK2,800 – SEK2,224.

d. U.S. GAAP would not permit Ericsson to reverse a previous impairment of inventory.

8.26 (Sun Health Foods; computations involving different cost flow assumptions.)

	Units	a. FIFO	b. Weighted Average	c. LIFO
Goods Available for Sale.............	2,500	$10,439	$10,439	$10,439
Less Ending Inventory	(420)	(1,722)a	(1,754)c	(1,806)e
Goods Sold	2,080	$ 8,717b	$ 8,685d	$ 8,633f

a(420 x $4.10) = $1,722.
b(460 x $4.30) + (670 x $4.20) + (500 x $4.16) + (450 x $4.10) = $8,717.
c($10,439/2,500) x 420 = $1,754.
d($10,439/2,500) x 2,080 = $8,685.
e(420 x $4.30) = $1,806.
f(870 x $4.10) + (500 x $4.16) + (670 x $4.20) + (40 x $4.30) = $8,633.

8.27 (Arnold Company; computations involving different cost flow assumptions.)

	Pounds	a. FIFO	b. Weighted Average	c. LIFO
Raw Materials Available for Use	10,700	$24,384	$24,384	$ 24,384
Less Ending Inventory	(3,500)	(8,110)a	(7,976)c	(7,818)e
Raw Materials Issued to Production	7,200	$16,274b	$16,408d	$ 16,566f

a(3,000 x $2.32) + (500 x $2.30) = $8,110.
b(1,200 x $2.20) + (2,200 x $2.25) + (2,800 x $2.28) + (1,000 x $2.30) = $16,274.
c($24,384/10,700) x 3,500 = $7,976.
d($24,384/10,700) x 7,200 = $16,408.
e(1,200 x $2.20) + (2,200 x $2.25) + (100 x $2.28) = $7,818.
f(3,000 x $2.32) + (1,500 x $2.30) + (2,700 x $2.28) = $16,566.

8.28 (Harmon Corporation; effect on LIFO on financial statements over several periods.)

a.
Year	Ending Inventory	
2008	19,000 x $20	$380,000
2009	10,000 x $20	$200,000
2010	(10,000 x $20) + (10,000 x $30)	$500,000

b.
Year	Cost of Goods Sold	
2008	64,000 x $20	$ 1,280,000
2009	(92,000 x $25) + (9,000 x $20)	$ 2,480,000
2010	110,000 x $30	$ 3,300,000

Year	Income	
2008	$2,048,000 − $1,280,000	$ 768,000
2009	$4,040,000 − $2,480,000	$ 1,560,000
2010	$5,280,000 − $3,300,000	$ 1,980,000

8.29 (EKG Company; LIFO provides opportunity for income manipulation.)

a. Largest cost of goods sold results from producing 70,000 (or more) additional units at a cost of $22 each, giving cost of goods sold of $1,540,000.

b. Smallest cost of goods sold results from producing no additional units, giving cost of goods sold of $980,000 [= ($8 x 10,000) + ($15 x 60,000)].

c.
	Income Reported	
	Minimum	Maximum
Revenues ($30 x 70,000)	$2,100,000	$2,100,000
Less Cost of Goods Sold	(1,540,000)	(980,000)
Gross Margin	$ 560,000	$1,120,000

8.30 (Caterpillar Incorporated; conversion from LIFO to FIFO.) (Amounts in Millions)

	LIFO	Difference	FIFO
Beginning Inventory	$ 6,351	$ 2,403	$ 8,754
Production Costs (Plug)	33,479	--	33,479
Goods Available for Sale (Plug)	$ 39,830	$ 2,403	$ 42,233
Less Ending Inventory	(7,204)	(2,617)	(9,821)
Cost of Goods Sold	$ 32,626	$ (214)	$ 32,412

8.31 (Ford Motor Company; analysis of LIFO and FIFO disclosures.)

a. Ford Motor Company uses LIFO, so the carrying value of its inventories would be $10,121 million as of December 31, 2007 and $10,017 as of December 31, 2006.

b.
	LIFO	Difference	FIFO
Beginning Inventory	$ 10,017	$ 1,015	$ 11,032
Production Costs (Plug)	142,691	--	142,691
Goods Available for Sale (Plug)	$152,708	$ 1,015	$153,723
Less Ending Inventory	(10,121)	(1,100)	(11,221)
Cost of Goods Sold	$142,587	$ (85)	$142,502

8.32 (McGee Associates; journal entries for payroll.)

a. Wage and Salary Expense.. 700,000
    Withholding and FICA Taxes Payable 210,000
    Wages and Salaries Payable 490,000

Assets	=	Liabilities	+	Shareholders' Equity	(Class.)
		+210,000		−700,000	IncSt → RE
		+490,000			

Amounts payable to and for employees.

Wage and Salary Expense... 114,800
    Taxes Payable 70,000
    Payable to Profit Sharing Fund 28,000
    Vacation Liability 16,800

Assets	=	Liabilities	+	Shareholders' Equity	(Class.)
		+70,000		−114,800	IncSt → RE
		+28,000			
		+16,800			

Employer's additional wage expense; estimated vacation liability is $16,800 (= 1.20 x $14,000).

b. $814,800 = $700,000 + $114,800.

8.33 (Hurley Corporation; accounting for uncollectible accounts and warranties.)

a. **Allowance for Uncollectible Accounts**
Balance, December 31, 2008... $ 355
Plus Bad Debt Expense for 2009: .02 x $18,000 360
Less Accounts Written Off (Plug)....................................... (310)
Balance, December 31, 2009... $ 405
Plus Bad Debt Expense for 2010: .02 x $16,000 320
Less Accounts Written Off (Plug)....................................... (480)
Balance, December 31, 2010... $ 245

b. **Estimated Warranty Liability**
Balance, December 31, 2008... $ 1,325
Plus Warranty Expense for 2009: .06 x $18,000 1,080
Less Actual Warranty Costs (Plug)..................................... (870)
Balance, December 31, 2009... $ 1,535
Plus Warranty Expense for 2010: .06 x $16,000 960
Less Actual Warranty Costs (Plug)..................................... (775)
Balance, December 31, 2010... $ 1,720

8.34 (Miele Company; journal entries for warranty liabilities and subsequent expenditures.)

a. **2008**

Accounts Receivable 1,200,000
    Sales Revenue 1,200,000

Assets	=	Liabilities	+	Shareholders' Equity	(Class.)
+1,200,000				+1,200,000	IncSt → RE

Warranty Liability 12,000
    Cash 12,000

Assets	=	Liabilities	+	Shareholders' Equity	(Class.)
−12,000		−12,000			

Expenditures actually made.

Warranty Expense 48,000
    Warranty Liability 48,000

Assets	=	Liabilities	+	Shareholders' Equity	(Class.)
		+48,000		−48,000	IncSt → RE

.04 x €1,200,000.

2009

Accounts Receivable 1,500,000
    Sales Revenue 1,500,000

Assets	=	Liabilities	+	Shareholders' Equity	(Class.)
+1,500,000				+1,500,000	IncSt → RE

Warranty Liability 50,000
    Cash 50,000

Assets	=	Liabilities	+	Shareholders' Equity	(Class.)
−50,000		−50,000			

Expenditures actually made.

8.34 a. continued.

Warranty Expense.. 60,000
    Warranty Liability 60,000

Assets	=	Liabilities	+	Shareholders' Equity	(Class.)
		+60,000		−60,000	IncSt → RE

.04 x €1,500,000.

b. €76,000 = €30,000 + €48,000 − €12,000 + €60,000 − €50,000.

8.35 (Kingspeed Bikes; journal entries for estimated warranty liabilities and subsequent expenditures.)

a. **2008**
Cash... 800,000
    Sales Revenue... 800,000

Assets	=	Liabilities	+	Shareholders' Equity	(Class.)
+800,000				+800,000	IncSt → RE

Warranty Liability... 22,000
    Cash 13,200
    Parts Inventory 8,800

Assets	=	Liabilities	+	Shareholders' Equity	(Class.)
−13,200		−22,000			
−8,800					

Warranty Expense... 48,000
    Warranty Liability 48,000

Assets	=	Liabilities	+	Shareholders' Equity	(Class.)
		+48,000		−48,000	IncSt → RE

.06 x $800,000 = $48,000.

Solutions   8-14

8.35 a. continued.

2009
Cash 1,200,000
    Sales Revenue 1,200,000

Assets	=	Liabilities	+	Shareholders' Equity	(Class.)
+1,200,000				+1,200,000	IncSt → RE

Warranty Liability 55,000
    Cash 33,000
    Parts Inventory 22,000

Assets	=	Liabilities	+	Shareholders' Equity	(Class.)
−33,000		−55,000			
−22,000					

Warranty Expense 72,000
    Warranty Liability 72,000

Assets	=	Liabilities	+	Shareholders' Equity	(Class.)
		+72,000		−72,000	IncSt → RE

.06 × $1,200,000 = $72,000.

2010
Cash 900,000
    Sales Revenue 900,000

Assets	=	Liabilities	+	Shareholders' Equity	(Class.)
+900,000				+900,000	IncSt → RE

Warranty Liability 52,000
    Cash 31,200
    Parts Inventory 20,800

Assets	=	Liabilities	+	Shareholders' Equity	(Class.)
−31,200		−52,000			
−20,800					

8.35 a. continued.

   Warranty Expense... 54,000
    Warranty Liability   54,000

Assets	=	Liabilities	+	Shareholders' Equity	(Class.)
		+54,000		−54,000	IncSt → RE

.06 x $900,000 = $54,000.

b. $48,000 − $22,000 + $72,000 − $55,000 + $54,000 − $52,000 = $45,000.

8.36 (Sappi Paper Limited; journal entries for restructuring liabilities and subsequent expenditures.)

2008
Restructuring Provision 32
 Cash..   32

Assets	=	Liabilities	+	Shareholders' Equity	(Class.)
−32		−32			

To record cash expenditures on previously accrued restructuring costs.

Restructuring Expense... 7
 Restructuring Provision..   7

Assets	=	Liabilities	+	Shareholders' Equity	(Class.)
		+7		−7	IncSt → RE

During 2008, Sappi recognized restructuring charges of ZAR7 million [= ZAR41 − (ZAR32 + ZAR16)].

8.37 (Delhaize Group; journal entries for restructuring liabilities and subsequent expenditures.)

a. **Journal entries for 2007**
 Restructuring Expense 14.2
  Restructuring Provision 14.2

8.37 a. continued.

Assets	=	Liabilities	+	Shareholders' Equity	(Class.)
		+14.2		−14.2	IncSt → RE

To record new restructuring charges made during 2007.

Restructuring Provision.. 7.3
    Restructuring Expense... 7.3

Assets	=	Liabilities	+	Shareholders' Equity	(Class.)
		−7.3		+7.3	IncSt → RE

To record the reversal of prior period restructuring charges.

Restructuring Provision.. 40.0
    Cash... 40.0

Assets	=	Liabilities	+	Shareholders' Equity	(Class.)
−40.0		−40.0			

To record cash expenditures to settle restructuring Provisions; 40.0 = [(84.0 + 14.2) − (7.3 + 50.9)].

b. Delhaize will report a total restructuring provision of €50.9, classified as follows on its balance sheet:

Current Portion of Restructuring Provision........................ € 12.5 million

Noncurrent Portion of Restructuring Provision.................. € 38.4 million

c. Delhaize's income in 2007 is lower by €6.9 million (= €14.2 million − €7.3 million). The net change in income of €6.9 million is added to income as a noncash expense to calculate cash flow from operations in the statement of cash flows:

8.38 (Katherine's Outdoor Furniture preparation of journal entries and income statement for a manufacturing firm.)

a. (1) Raw Materials Inventory.. 667,200
　　　　Accounts Payable .... 　　　　　667,200

Assets	=	Liabilities	+	Shareholders' Equity	(Class.)
+667,200		+667,200			

(2) Work-in-Process Inventory 689,100
　　　Raw Materials Inventory .... 　　　　　689,100

Assets	=	Liabilities	+	Shareholders' Equity	(Class.)
+689,100					
−689,100					

(3) Work-in-Process Inventory 432,800
　　　Selling Expenses 89,700
　　　Administrative Expenses.................................... 22,300
　　　　Cash.. 　　　　　544,800

Assets	=	Liabilities	+	Shareholders' Equity	(Class.)
+432,800				−89,700	IncSt → RE
−544,800				−22,300	IncSt → RE

(4) Work-in-Process Inventory 182,900
　　　Selling Expenses 87,400
　　　Administrative Expenses.................................... 12,200
　　　　Accumulated Depreciation............................... 　　　　　282,500

Assets	=	Liabilities	+	Shareholders' Equity	(Class.)
+182,900				−87,400	IncSt → RE
−282,500				−12,200	IncSt → RE

(5) Work-in-Process Inventory 218,500
　　　Selling Expenses 55,100
　　　Administrative Expenses.................................... 34,700
　　　　Cash.. 　　　　　308,300

Assets	=	Liabilities	+	Shareholders' Equity	(Class.)
+218,500				−55,100	IncSt → RE
−308,300				−34,700	IncSt → RE

Solutions

8.38 a. continued.

(6) Finished Goods Inventory 1,564,500
      Work-in-Process Inventory 1,564,500

Assets	=	Liabilities	+	Shareholders' Equity	(Class.)
+1,564,500					
−1,564,500					

(7) Accounts Receivable 2,400,000
      Sales Revenue 2,400,000

Assets	=	Liabilities	+	Shareholders' Equity	(Class.)
+2,400,000				+2,400,000	IncSt → RE

(8) Cost of Goods Sold 1,536,600
      Finished Goods Inventory 1,536,600

Assets	=	Liabilities	+	Shareholders' Equity	(Class.)
−1,536,600				−1,536,600	IncSt → RE

$182,700 + $1,564,500 − $210,600 = $1,536,600.

b.   **KATAHERINE'S OUTDOOR FURNITURE**
                     Income Statement
                 For the Month of January

Sales		$2,400,000
Less Expenses:		
Cost of Goods Sold	$1,536,600	
Selling	232,200	
Administrative	69,200	(1,838,000)
Net Income		$ 562,000

Note: Instead of using a functional classification of expenses (that is, selling, administrative), classification by their nature (salary, depreciation, other operating) is acceptable.

8.39 (Lord Cromptom Plc.; flow of manufacturing costs through the accounts.)

a.
Beginning Raw Materials Inventory	€ 46,900
Raw Materials Purchased	429,000
Raw Materials Available for Use	€ 475,900
Subtract Ending Raw Materials Inventory	(43,600)
Cost of Raw Materials Used	€ 432,300
Beginning Factory Supplies Inventory	€ 7,600
Factory Supplies Purchased	22,300
Factory Supplies Available for Use	€ 29,900
Subtract Ending Factory Supplies Inventory	(7,700)
Cost of Factory Supplies Used	€ 22,200

b.
Beginning Work-in-Process Inventory	€ 110,900
Cost of Raw Materials Used (from Part a.)	432,300
Cost of Factory Supplies Used (from Part a.)	22,200
Direct Labor Costs Incurred	362,100
Heat, Light, and Power Costs	10,300
Insurance	4,200
Depreciation of Factory Equipment	36,900
Prepaid Rent Expired	3,600
Total Beginning Work-in-Process and Manufacturing Costs Incurred	€ 982,500
Subtract Ending Work-in-Process Inventory	(115,200)
Cost of Units Completed and Transferred to Finished Goods Storeroom	€ 867,300

c.
Beginning Finished Goods Inventory	€ 76,700
Cost of Units Completed and Transferred to Finished Goods Storeroom (from Part b.)	867,300
Subtract Ending Finished Goods Inventory	(71,400)
Cost of Goods Sold	€ 872,600

d. Net Income is €110,040 [= (1 − .40)(€1,350,000 − €872,600 − €246,900 − €47,100)].

8.40 (Toyota Corporation; flow of manufacturing costs.)

a. Ending Balance of Total Inventory = Ending Balance of Raw Materials Inventory + Ending Balance of Work-in-Process Inventory + Ending Balance of Finished Goods Inventory.

Ending Balance of Total Inventory = ¥374,210 + ¥239,937 + ¥1,211,569 = ¥1,825,716 million.

8.40 continued.

b. Beginning Finished Goods Inventory + Cost of Units Completed = Cost of Products Sold + Writedowns + Ending Finished Goods Inventory.

¥1,204,521 + Cost of Units Completed = ¥20,452,338 + 0 + ¥1,211,569. Cost of Units Completed = ¥20,459,386 million.

c. Beginning Balance in Work-in-Process Inventory + Direct Materials + Direct Labor + Overhead = Cost of Units Completed + Ending Balance in Work-in-Process Inventory.

¥236,749 + Raw Material and Supplies Costs + ¥12,000,000 = ¥20,459,386 (from Part b.) + ¥236,937.

Raw Material and Supplies Costs = ¥8,462,574 million.

Work-in-Process Inventory 8,462,574
    Raw Materials Inventory   8,462,574

Assets	=	Liabilities	+	Shareholders' Equity	(Class.)
+8,462,574					
−8,462,574					

d. Beginning Balance in Raw Materials Inventory + Raw Materials Purchases = Raw Materials Used in Production + Ending Balance of Raw Materials Inventory.

¥362,686 + Raw Materials and Supplies Purchases = ¥8,462,574 + ¥374,210.

Raw Materials and Supplies Purchases = ¥8,474,098 million.

8.41 (Sandvik Group; flow of manufacturing costs.)

a. Ending Balance of Total Inventory = Ending Balance of Raw Materials Inventory + Ending Balance of Work-in-Process Inventory + Ending Balance of Finished Goods Inventory.

Ending Balance of Total Inventory = SEK6,964 + SEK5,157 + SEK13,180 = SEK25,301 million.

b. Loss on Impairment of Inventory 281
    Finished Goods Inventory   281

Assets	=	Liabilities	+	Shareholders' Equity	(Class.)
−281				−281	IncSt → RE

8-21

8.41 continued.

    c. Cost of Sales, after Writedown = Cost of Sales, before Writedown + Writedown.

       SEK57,222 = (Cost of Sales, before Writedown) + SEK281.
       Cost of Sales, before Writedown = SEK56,941 million.

    d. Beginning Finished Goods Inventory + Cost of Units Completed = Cost of Sales + Writedowns + Ending Finished Goods Inventory.

       SEK8,955 + Cost of Units Completed = SEK56,941 + SEK281 + SEK13,180.

       Cost of Units Completed = SEK61,447 million.

    e. Beginning Balance in Work-in-Process Inventory + Direct Materials + Direct Labor + Overhead = Cost of Units Completed + Ending Balance in Work-in-Process Inventory.

       SEK4,093 + Direct Material Costs + 3 × Direct Material Costs = SEK61,447 (from Part *d*.) + SEK5,157.

       Direct Material Costs = SEK62,511/4 = SEK15,628 million.

       Work-in-Process Inventory... 15,628
         Raw Materials Inventory...   15,628

Assets	=	Liabilities	+	Shareholders' Equity	(Class.)
+15,628					
−15,628					

    f. Beginning Balance in Raw Materials Inventory + Raw Materials Purchases = Raw Materials Used in Production + Ending Balance of Raw Materials Inventory.

       SEK5,690 + Raw Material Purchases = SEK15,628 (from Part *e*.) + SEK6,964.

       Raw Materials Purchases = SEK16,902 million.

8.42   (Fortune Brands; lower of cost or market; U.S. GAAP versus IFRS.)

    a. No journal entry will be recorded because U.S. GAAP does not permit firms to writeup the value of their inventory above its acquisition cost.

8.42 continued.

b. **Journal Entry:**

Impairment Loss on Inventory...................................... 167
    Merchandise Inventory 167

Assets	= Liabilities	+	Shareholders' Equity	(Class.)
−167			−167	IncSt → RE

$167 = $2,047.6 − $1,880.6.

c. No journal entry will be recorded because U.S. GAAP does not permit firms to reverse previous writedowns of inventory.

d. **If IFRS Were Used:**

For Part *a*.: No (same answer), because IFRS does not permit firms to writeup the value of their inventory above its acquisition cost.

For Part *b*.: No (same answer), because IFRS also requires firms to report inventory at the lower of cost or market value.

For Part *c*.: Yes (different answer), because IFRS permits firms to reverse previous writedowns up to the original acquisition cost of the inventory. Had it applied IFRS, Fortune Brands would have recorded the following reversal journal entry:

Merchandise Inventory.. 81.7
    Reversal of Impairment Loss 81.7

Assets	= Liabilities	+	Shareholders' Equity	(Class.)
+81.7			+81.7	IncSt → RE

$81.7 = $1,962.3 − $1,880.6.

8.43 (Burton Corporation; detailed comparison of various choices for inventory accounting.)

	FIFO	LIFO	Weighted Average
Inventory, 1/1/2007	$ 0	$ 0	$ 0
Purchases during 2007	14,400	14,400	14,400
Goods Available for Sale during 2007	$14,400	$14,400	$14,400
Less Inventory, 12/31/2007	(3,000)[1]	(2,000)[2]	(2,400)[3]
Cost of Goods Sold for 2007	$11,400	$12,400	$12,000
Inventory, 1/1/2008	$3,000 [1]	$2,000 [2]	$2,400 [3]
Purchases during 2008	21,000	21,000	21,000
Goods Available for Sale during 2008	$24,000	$23,000	$23,400
Less Inventory, 12/31/2008	(5,000)[4]	(6,200)[5]	(5,850)[6]
Cost of Goods Sold for 2008	$19,000	$16,800	$17,550

[1] 200 x $15 = $3,000.
[2] 200 x $10 = $2,000.
[3] ($14,400/1,200) x 200 = $2,400.
[4] 500 x $10 = $5,000.
[5] (200 x $10) + (300 x $14) = $6,200.
[6] ($23,400/2,000) x 500 = $5,850.

a. $11,400.
b. $12,400.
c. $12,000.
d. $19,000.
e. $16,800.
f. $17,550.

g. FIFO results in higher net income for 2007. Purchase prices for inventory items increased during 2007. FIFO uses older, lower purchase prices to measure cost of goods sold, whereas LIFO uses more recent, higher prices.

h. LIFO results in higher net income for 2008. Purchase prices for inventory items decreased during 2008. LIFO uses more recent, lower prices to measure cost of goods sold, whereas FIFO uses older, higher prices.

8.44 (Hanover Oil Products; effect of FIFO and LIFO on income statement and balance sheet.)

a.

	FIFO	LIFO
Beginning Inventory	$ 0	$ 0
Purchases:		
1/1: 4,000 @ $1.40	$ 5,600	$ 5,600
1/13: 6,000 @ $1.46	8,760	8,760
1/28: 5,000 @ $1.50	7,500	7,500
Total Purchases	$ 21,860	$ 21,860
Available for Sale	$ 21,860	$ 21,860
Less Ending Inventory:		
FIFO: 2,000 x $1.50	(3,000)	
LIFO: 2,000 x $1.40		(2,800)
Cost of Goods Sold	$ 18,860	$ 19,060

b.

	FIFO	LIFO
Beginning Inventory	$ 3,000	$ 2,800
Purchases:		
2/5: 7,000 @ $1.53	$ 10,710	$ 10,710
2/14: 6,000 @ $1.47	8,820	8,820
2/21: 10,000 @ $1.42	14,200	14,200
Total Purchases	$ 33,730	$ 33,730
Available for Sale	$ 36,730	$ 36,530
Less Ending Inventory:		
FIFO: 3,000 x $1.42	(4,260)	
LIFO: (2,000 x $1.40) + (1,000 x $1.53)		(4,330)
Cost of Goods Sold	$ 32,470	$ 32,200

c.

	FIFO	LIFO
Beginning Inventory	$ 4,260	$ 4,330
Purchases:		
3/2: 6,000 @ $1.48	$ 8,880	$ 8,880
3/15: 5,000 @ $1.54	7,700	7,700
3/26: 4,000 @ $1.60	6,400	6,400
Total Purchases	$ 22,980	$ 22,980
Available for Sale	$ 27,240	$ 27,310
Less Ending Inventory:		
FIFO: 1,000 x $1.60	(1,600)	
LIFO: 1,000 x $1.40		(1,400)
Cost of Goods Sold	$ 25,640	$ 25,910

d. Acquisition costs increased during January. During such periods, LIFO generally provides larger cost of goods sold amounts than FIFO because LIFO uses the most recent higher cost. Acquisition costs decreased during February. Under these circumstances, FIFO generally results in higher cost of goods sold because it uses the higher older cost. During March, acquisition costs increased. There was a liquidation of LIFO lay-

8.44 d. continued.

ers, however, which makes it more difficult to generalize about which cost flow assumption results in the higher cost of goods sold. LIFO results in the higher cost of goods sold in this case because the effect of increasing purchase costs dominated the effect of the LIFO liquidation.

e.

	January		February		March	
	FIFO	LIFO	FIFO	LIFO	FIFO	LIFO
(1) Sales	$20,840	$20,840	$35,490	$35,490	$28,648	$28,648
(2) Cost of Goods Sold	18,860	19,060	32,470	32,200	25,640	25,910
(2)/(1)	90.5%	91.5%	91.5%	90.7%	89.5%	90.4%

f. LIFO provides the most stable cost of goods sold to sales percentage because LIFO cost of goods sold amounts reflects current replacement cost more fully than FIFO. The firm prices its gasoline at a 10% markup on current replacement cost, so the cost of goods sold to sales percentage under LIFO will be closer to 90.9% (= 1/1.1) than FIFO.

g.
Available for Sale (from Part c.)	$ 27,240	$ 27,310
Plus Additional Purchases: 2,000 x $1.60	3,200	3,200
Less Ending Inventory:		
FIFO: 3,000 x $1.60	(4,800)	
LIFO: (2,000 x $1.40) + (1,000 x $1.53)		(4,330)
Cost of Goods Sold	$ 25,640	$ 26,180

Costs of goods sold will not change under FIFO because the additional purchases simply increase both the quantity and valuation of the ending inventory. Cost of goods sold increases under LIFO because the additional purchases increase the quantity of ending inventory but the purchase price paid substitutes for the LIFO layers liquidated in measuring cost of goods sold.

8.45 (Burch Corporation; reconstructing underlying events from ending inventory amounts [adapted from CPA examination].)

a. Down. Notice that lower of cost or market is lower than acquisition cost (FIFO); current market price is less than cost.

b. Up. FIFO means last-in, still-here. The last purchases (FIFO = LISH) cost $44,000 and the earlier purchases (LIFO = FISH) cost $41,800. Also, lower-of-cost-or-market basis shows acquisition costs which are greater than or equal to current cost.

8.45 continued.

c. LIFO Cost. Other things being equal, the largest income results from the method that shows the largest *increase* in inventory during the year.

Margin = Revenues − Cost of Goods Sold
= Revenues − Beginning Inventory − Purchases + Ending Inventory
= Revenues − Purchases + Increase in Inventory.

Because the beginning inventory in 2006 is zero, the method with the largest closing inventory amount implies the largest increase and hence the largest income.

d. Lower of Cost or Market. The method with the "largest increase in inventory" during the year in this case is the method with the smallest decrease, because all methods show declines in inventory during 2007. Lower of cost or market shows a decrease in inventory of only $3,000 during 2007—the other methods show larger decreases ($3,800; $4,000).

e. Lower of Cost or Market. The method with the largest increase in inventory: $10,000. LIFO shows a $5,400 increase while FIFO shows $8,000.

f. LIFO Cost. The lower income for all three years results from the method that shows the smallest increase in inventory over the three years. Because all beginning inventories were zero under all methods, we need merely find the method with the smallest ending inventory at 2008 year-end.

g. FIFO lower by $2,000. Under FIFO, inventories increased $8,000 during 2008. Under lower of cost or market, inventories increased $10,000 during 2008. Lower of cost or market has a bigger increase—$2,000—and therefore lower of cost or market shows a $2,000 larger income than FIFO for 2008.

8.46 (Wilson Company; LIFO layers influence purchasing behavior and provide opportunity for income manipulation.)

	Cost per Pound	Layer	Beginning Inventory Cost ($000)	+ Purchases Cost ($000)	− Ending Inventory Pounds	Cost ($000)	= Cost of Goods Sold ($000)
a.	(Controller)	1999	$ 60.0	---	2,000	$ 60.0	---
		2004	9.2	---	200	9.2	---
		2005	19.2	---	400	19.2	---
		2008	72.8	---	1,400	72.8	---
	7,000 @ $62/lb.	2009	---	$ 434.0	---	---	434.0
			$ 161.2	$ 434.0	4,000	$ 161.2	$ 434.0

8.46 continued.

	Cost per Pound	Layer	Beginning Inventory Cost ($000)	+ Purchases Cost ($000)	− Ending Inventory Pounds	Cost ($000)	= Cost of Goods Sold ($000)
b. (Purchasing Agent)		1999	$ 60.0	---	600	$ 18.0	$ 42.0
		2004	9.2	---	---	---	9.2
		2005	19.2	---	---	---	19.2
		2008	72.8	---	---	---	72.8
	3,600 @ $62/lb.	2009	---	$ 223.2	---	---	223.2
			$ 161.2	$ 223.2	600	$ 18.0	$ 366.4

c.
Controller's Policy COGS $62/lb.	$ 434.00
Less Purchasing Agent's COGS	(366.40)
Controller's Extra Deductions	$ 67.60
Tax Rate: 40%	x .40
Controller's Tax Savings	$ 27.04
Controller's Extra Cash Costs for Inventory: 3,400 @ $10/lb.	$ 34.00

d. The economically sound action is to follow the purchasing agent's advice. The controller's policy does save taxes but not as much in taxes as the extra inventory costs. This response presumes that allowing inventory quantities to decrease to 600 pounds does not negatively affect operations prior to replenishing the inventory. A quality of earnings issue arises because the increase in net income that results from the LIFO liquidations is nonrecurring. Except for the older costs in the base layer of 600 units, new LIFO layers will use higher current costs. Liquidating those new layers in later years will not likely increase earnings as much as the current year's liquidations produced. One might argue that following the purchasing agent's advice does not raise an ethical issue because it is the economically sound action. However, management does have some discretion (see question e.) as to whether to deplete inventories to 600 units or to stop short of that amount of depletion. To the extent that management has an earning target in mind and can choose the amount of inventory depletion to achieve that level of earnings, some would argue that ethical issues arise.

8.46 continued.

e. To maximize income for 2009, liquidate all our LIFO inventory layers, 4,000 lbs. with total cost $161,200, and purchase only 3,000 lbs. at $62 each during 2009. To minimize income, acquire 7,000 lbs. at $62 each.

Policy	Cost of Goods Sold for 2009
Minimum Income:	
7,000 lbs. x $62	$ 434,000
Maximum Income:	
4,000 lbs. of Old Layers	(161,200)
3,000 lbs. at $62	(186,000)
Income Spread before Taxes	$ 86,800
Taxes at 40%	(34,720)
Income Spread after Taxes	$ 52,080

By manipulating purchases of expensium, Wilson Company reports aftertax income anywhere in the range from $50,000 (by following the controller's policy) up to $102,080 (= $50,000 + $52,080) by acquiring only 3,000 lbs. and liquidating all LIFO layers.

8.47 (Toyota; interpreting inventory disclosures.)

a. **March 31, 2008:**

If Toyota had used FIFO, inventory values would have been ¥13,780 less than LIFO amounts.

Ending Balance of Total Inventory (FIFO) = (¥374,210 + ¥239,937 + ¥1,211,569) − ¥13,780 = ¥1,825,716 − ¥13,780 = ¥1,811,936 million.

March 31, 2007:

If Toyota had used FIFO, inventory values would have been ¥30,360 less than LIFO amounts.

Ending Balance of Total Inventory (FIFO) = (¥362,686 + ¥236,749 + ¥1,204,521) − ¥30,360 = ¥1,803,956 − ¥30,360 = ¥1,773,596 million.

8.47 continued.

    b. Beginning Balance in Finished Goods (FIFO) + Cost of Units Completed = Cost of Products Sold (FIFO) + Ending Balance in Finished Goods (FIFO).

    Beginning Balance of Finished Goods Inventory (FIFO) = ¥1,204,521 – ¥30,360 = ¥1,174,161 million.

    Ending Balance of Finished Goods Inventory (FIFO) = ¥1,211,569 – ¥13,780 = ¥1,197,789 million.

    ¥1,174,161 + ¥20,459,386 (from Problem 8.40, Part b.) = Cost of Products Sold (FIFO) + ¥1,197,789.

    Cost of Goods Sold (FIFO) = ¥20,435,758 million.

    Also, could calculate as follows:

Cost of Goods Sold (LIFO)	¥ 20,452,338
Change in LIFO reserve (¥30,360 – ¥13,780)	(16,580)
Cost of Goods Sold (FIFO)	¥ 20,435,758

8.48 (Central Appliance; allowance method for warranties; reconstructing transactions.)

    a. $720,000 = $820,000 (Goods Available for Sale) – $100,000 (Beginning Inventory).

    b. $700,000 = $820,000 (Goods Available for Sale) – $120,000 (Ending Inventory).

    c. $21,000 = $6,000 (Cr. Balance) + $15,000 (Dr. Balance).

    d. $20,000 = $5,000 (Required Cr. Balance) + $15,000 (Existing Dr. Balance).

    e. Warranty Liability.. 21,000
        Various Assets Used for Repairs........................   21,000

Assets	=	Liabilities	+	Shareholders' Equity	(Class.)
–21,000		–21,000			

Repairs made during 2008.

8.48 e. continued.

Warranty Expense.. 20,000
    Warranty Liability... 20,000

Assets	=	Liabilities	+	Shareholders' Equity	(Class.)
		+20,000		−20,000	IncSt → RE

Expense recognition for 2008.

Cost of Goods Sold... 700,000
    Merchandise Inventory.. 700,000

Assets	=	Liabilities	+	Shareholders' Equity	(Class.)
−700,000				−700,000	IncSt → RE

Cost of goods sold is goods available for sale less ending inventory.

8.49 (Bayer Group; interpreting restructuring disclosures.)

a. Restructuring Provision... 134
       Cash... 134

Assets	=	Liabilities	+	Shareholders' Equity	(Class.)
−134		−134			

To record utilizations.

Restructuring Provision... 31
    Reversal of Restructuring Expense............................... 31

Assets	=	Liabilities	+	Shareholders' Equity	(Class.)
		−31		+31	IncSt → RE

To record reversal.

8.49 continued.

b. Journal entry to record additions to Restructuring Provision during 2007:

Restructuring Expense 128
    Restructuring Provision   128

Assets	=	Liabilities	+	Shareholders' Equity	(Class.)
		+128		−128	IncSt → RE

To record €128 million of restructuring charges made during 2007.

Beginning Balance of Restructuring Provision + Additions = Utilizations + Net Other Effects + Reversals + Ending Balance of Restructuring Provision €196 + Additions = €134 + €5 + €31 + €154.

Additions = €128 million.

CHAPTER 9

LONG-LIVED TANGIBLE AND INTANGIBLE ASSETS

Questions, Exercises, and Problems: Answers and Solutions

9.1   See the text or the glossary at the end of the book.

9.2   The central concept underlying GAAP for these three items is the ability to identify and reliably measure expected future benefits. The self-constructed building has physical substance and the accountant can observe the effect of an expenditure on the physical structure of the building. The building provides evidence of future benefits. Research and development expenditures may give rise to an intangible, a patent on a new technology. However, the accountant cannot observe the physical creation of an asset with future benefits when a firm makes expenditures. Thus, reliably identifying and measuring future benefits is problematic. GAAP in the United States does not permit recognition of an asset for research and development expenditures. Expenditures on software development present an in-between case. The programming underlying the software is embedded in a computer but the accountant can observe how well the software works. When the software has not yet reached the stage of technological feasibility, future benefits are uncertain. Thus, GAAP treats expenditures up to this point as expenses of the period when incurred. When software reaches the point of technological feasibility, future benefits become more certain. GAAP, therefore, permits firms to capitalize software development expenditures after this point.

9.3   The central concept underlying GAAP for these three items is the ability to identify and reliably measure expected future benefits. Expenditures to research new drugs may give rise to future benefits, but identifying the existence of those future benefits while research progresses is problematic. Thus, GAAP in the United States requires immediate expensing of research and development expenditures. The external market transaction for a patent on a new drug validates both the existence and fair value of the patent. GAAP, therefore, recognizes the patent as an asset. In-process R&D has characteristics of the previous two cases. Whether the in-process project will yield future benefits is uncertain, suggesting that firms should expense such expenditures at the time of acquisition. However, an external market transaction between independent parties suggests the existence of future benefits, supporting recognition of an asset until such time as the status of the research project becomes more certain. FASB *Statement No.*

9.3 continued.

141 (Revised) requires firms to recognize as an asset the fair value of in-process R&D acquired in a corporate acquisition, placing greater weight on the evidence provided by the external market transaction than on the uncertainty of future benefits.

9.4 a. Over the life of the project, income is cash-in less cash-out. Capitalizing and then amortizing interest versus expensing it affects the timing but not the total amount of income. Capitalizing interest defers expense from the construction period to the periods of use, increasing income in the early years of construction and decreasing it in the periods of use, when depreciation charges are larger.

b. The "catch-up" described in the preceding part is indefinitely delayed. Reported income in each year increases by the policy of capitalizing interest. When the self-construction activity declines, then the reported income declines as a result of reduced capitalization of interest, but not before.

9.5 A long-lived asset with a finite life is expected to provide benefits for a limited amount of time. Benefits will eventually decline to zero, either because of physical use, obsolescence, or disposal. Firms depreciate or amortize assets with a finite life. Note that firms must estimate the finite life in most cases (except for benefit periods limited by contract). An asset with an infinite life is one that is expected to last forever. GAAP assumes that all assets eventually wear out, become obsolete, or are sold. Thus, GAAP does not allow firms to assume long-lived assets have an infinite life. GAAP treats assets that have an extended life, but for which the length of that life is highly uncertain, as having an indefinite life. GAAP does not require firms to depreciate or amortize assets with an indefinite life but must test those assets annually for possible asset impairment.

9.6 PepsiCo must demonstrate that the brand names amortized have a finite life and those not amortized have an indefinite life. PepsiCo would examine the age of particular brand names, the pace at which brand names come in and out of favor in a particular industry, and similar factors in deciding the classification of a particular brand name acquired. This process likely involves considerable subjectivity, but is subject to audit by the PepsiCo's independent accountant.

9.7 The treatment of this change in depreciable life would depend on the reason for and the materiality of the change. The change in this case appears prompted by new governmental regulations imposed on the airline industry. If the change in expected life is material, the firm can make a strong case for recognizing an asset impairment loss and revising its depreciation going forward. If the impact is not material, the airline might treat the change in depreciable life as a change in an estimate and spread the effect of the change over the current and future years. The purpose of this question is to demonstrate that judgments are often required in applying GAAP.

9.8 The relevant question to apply generally accepted accounting principles is whether the expenditure maintained the originally expected useful life or extended that useful life. Firms should expense, as maintenance or repairs, expenditures that maintain the originally expected five-year life. In this case, the expenditure both maintains and extends the useful life. A portion of the expenditure should appear as an expense immediately (perhaps two-thirds) and a portion (perhaps one-third) should increase the depreciable base for the asset.

9.9 Generally accepted accounting principles compares the undiscounted cash flows from an asset to its carrying value to determine if an impairment loss has occurred. The rationale is that an impairment loss has not occurred if a firm will receive cash flows in the future at least equal to the carrying value of the asset. Receiving such cash flows will permit the firm to recover the carrying value. This criterion ignores the time value of money. Cash received earlier has more economic value than cash received later, but this criterion ignores such differences.

9.10 The cash recoverability criterion requires firms to estimate the expected undiscounted cash flows. This estimate requires projection of cash flows for a finite period of time. Nonamortized intangibles have an indefinite life and, therefore, no basis for projecting the total undiscounted cash flows.

9.11 An asset impairment loss that arises during a period results from a decline in fair value due to some external event. Using undiscounted, instead of discounted, cash flows to signal an impairment loss ignores the decline in fair value that occurred. Firms will not recognize the asset impairment loss as long as the undiscounted cash flows exceed the carrying value of the asset.

9.12 This statement is not correct. The excess purchase price will affect net income when the firm recognizes an asset impairment loss. Firms must test goodwill annually for possible impairment. However, firms may not end up recognizing an impairment loss on the excess purchase price. The procedure for testing goodwill for impairment is subject to considerable estimation. Management would not want to admit that they overpaid for another firm soon after making an acquisition, so will not likely recognize an asset impairment loss on the goodwill right away. Also, management might operate the acquired entity in such a way that its value increases over time, thereby offsetting the effect of initial overpayment.

9.13 (Outback Steakhouse; calculating acquisition costs of long-lived assets.)

The relative market values of the land and building are 20% (= $52,000/$260,000) for the land and 80% (= $208,000/$260,000) for the building. We use these percentages to allocate joint cost of the land and building.

9.13 continued.

	Land	Building
Purchase Price of Land and Building	$ 52,000	$ 208,000
Legal Costs Split 20% and 80%	2,520	10,080
Renovation Costs	--	35,900
Property and Liability Insurance Costs during Renovation Split 20% and 80%	800	3,200
Property Taxes during Renovation Split 20% and 80%	1,000	4,000
Total	$ 56,320	$ 261,180

Note: One might argue that the split of the insurance and property taxes should recognize the increase in market value of the building as a result of the renovation and use some other percentages besides 20% and 80%. Note also that the insurance and property taxes for the period after opening are expenses of the first year of operation.

9.14 (Classifying expenditure as asset or expense.)

    a. (3) Expense.

    b. (3) Expense.

    c. (3) Expense.

    d. (1) Noncurrent asset (machine).

    e. (3) Expense.

    f. (3) Expense.

    g. (2) Current asset (inventory).

    h. (1) Noncurrent asset (equipment).

    i. (3) Expense.

    j. (1) Noncurrent asset (ore deposit).

    k. (1) Current asset (prepayment).

    l. (1) Current asset (marketable securities).

    m. (2) Current asset product cost (inventories).

    n. (1) Noncurrent asset (trademark).

9.14 continued.

    o. (1) Noncurrent asset (copyright).

    p. (1) Noncurrent asset (computer software).

    q. (3) Expense. The required capitalization of in-process R&D under FASB *Statement No. 141* applies only to business combinations.

9.15 (Bolton Company; cost of self-constructed assets.)

Land: $70,000 + $2,000 (14) = $72,000.

Factory Building: $200,000 (1) + $12,000 (2) + $140,000 (3) + $6,000 (5) – $7,000 (7) + $10,000 (8) + $8,000 (9) + $3,000^a (10) + $8,000 (11) + $4,000 (13) + $1,000^a (15) = $385,000.

Office Building: $20,000 + $13,000 (4) = $33,000.

Site Improvements: $5,000 (12).

    ^{a}The firm might expense these items. It depends on the rationality of the firm's "self-insurance" policy.

    Item (6) is omitted because of *SFAS No. 34*.

    Item (16) is omitted because no arm's length transaction occurred in which the firm earned a profit.

9.16 (Duck Vehicle Manufacturing Company; cost of self-developed product.)

The first four items qualify as research and development costs which the firm must expense in the year incurred. It might appear that the firm should capitalize the cost of the prototype because it acquires the prototype from an external contractor. However, completion of a prototype does not signify a viable product. Purchasing the prototype externally versus constructing it internally does not change the accounting.
    The firm should capitalize the legal fees to register and establish the patent as part of the cost of the patent. The firm might consider this cost as sufficiently immaterial to warrant treatment as an asset and expense it immediately.
    The firm should capitalize the cost of the castings and amortize them over the expected useful life of the vehicle. The cost of the manufacturing permits and the cost of manufacturing the first vehicle are product costs that increase work-in-process inventory.

9.17 (Bulls Eye Stores; calculating interest capitalized during construction.)

Capitalized Interest on Borrowing Directly Related to Construction: .06 x $2,000,000 .... $120,000
Capitalized Interest of Other Borrowing: .07 x $1,400,000 98,000
Total Interest Capitalized $218,000

9.18 (Nexor; amount of interest capitalized during construction.)

a. Average Construction = ($30,000,000 + $60,000,000)/2 = $45,000,000.

Relevant Loans	**Interest Anticipated**
$ 25,000,000 at .08	$2,000,000
20,000,000 at .06	1,200,000
$ 45,000,000	$3,200,000

b. Interest Expense 8,000,000
   Interest Payable 8,000,000

Assets	=	Liabilities	+	Shareholders' Equity	(Class.)
		+8,000,000		−8,000,000	IncSt → RE

($25,000,000 x .08) + ($100,000,000 x .06).

Construction in Process 3,200,000
   Interest Expense 3,200,000

Assets	=	Liabilities	+	Shareholders' Equity	(Class.)
+3,200,000				+3,200,000	IncSt → RE

c. Interest Expense 8,000,000
   Interest Payable 8,000,000

Assets	=	Liabilities	+	Shareholders' Equity	(Class.)
		+8,000,000		−8,000,000	IncSt → RE

($25,000,000 x .08) + ($100,000,000 x .06).

Construction in Process 7,100,000
   Interest Expense 7,100,000

Assets	=	Liabilities	+	Shareholders' Equity	(Class.)
+7,100,000				+7,100,000	IncSt → RE

($25,000,000 x .08) + ($85,000,000 x .06).

9.19 (Alcoa; calculations for various depreciation methods.)

		Year 1	Year 2	Year 3
a.	Straight-Line (Time) Method........	$14,000	$14,000	$14,000

($88,800 − $4,800)/6 = $14,000.

		Year 1	Year 2	Year 3
b.	Straight-Line (Use) Method...........	$12,600	$14,000	$15,400

$84,000/30,000 = $2.80 per hour.

9.20 (Luck Delivery Company; calculations for various depreciation methods.)

a. **Depreciation Charge (Straight-Line)**
2008......................... $ 6,000   ($30,000/5)
2009.........................   6,000
2010.........................   6,000
2011.........................   6,000
2012.........................   6,000
                              $30,000

b. **Depreciation Charge (Declining-Balance)**
2008......................... $12,000   ($30,000 x .40)
2009.........................   7,200   ($18,000 x .40)
2010.........................   4,320   ($10,800 x .40)
2011.........................   3,240   ($6,480/2)
2012.........................   3,240   (balance)
                              $30,000

c. **Depreciation Charge (Sum-of-the-Years'-Digits)**
2008......................... $10,000   ($30,000 x 5/15)
2009.........................   8,000   ($30,000 x 4/15)
2010.........................   6,000   ($30,000 x 3/15)
2011.........................   4,000   ($30,000 x 2/15)
2012.........................   2,000   ($30,000 x 1/15)
                              $30,000

d. **Tax Depreciation**
2008......................... $ 6,000   (= $30,000 x .20)
2009.........................   9,600   (= $30,000 x .32)
2010.........................   5,760   (= $30,000 x .192)
2011.........................   3,450   (= $30,000 x .115)
2012.........................   3,450   (= $30,000 x .115)
2013.........................   1,740   (= $30,000 x .058)
                              $30,000

9.21 (Thompson Financial; change in depreciable life and salvage value.)

Carrying Value on January 1, 2008: $10,000,000 − {2 × [($10,000,000 − $1,000,000)/6]} = $7,000,000. Depreciation expense for 2008 based on the new depreciable life and salvage value is $3,200,000 [= ($7,000,000 − $600,000)/2].

9.22 (Florida Manufacturing Corporation; journal entries for revising estimate of life.)

a. Work-in-Process Inventory.. 2,400
    Accumulated Depreciation.................................... 2,400

Assets	=	Liabilities	+	Shareholders' Equity	(Class.)
+2,400					
−2,400					

($180,000 − $7,200)/144 = $1,200 per month.

b. Work-in-Process Inventory.. 14,400
    Accumulated Depreciation.................................... 14,400

Assets	=	Liabilities	+	Shareholders' Equity	(Class.)
+14,400					
−14,400					

12 × $1,200 = $14,400.

c. Depreciation to 1/1/2014 = 62 months × $1,200 = $74,400.
Remaining depreciation = $180,000 − $74,400 − $3,840 = $101,760.
Remaining life = 168 months − 62 months = 106 months as of 1/1/2014.
Depreciation charge per month = $101,760/106 = $960.

Work-in-Process Inventory.. 11,520
    Accumulated Depreciation.................................... 11,520

Assets	=	Liabilities	+	Shareholders' Equity	(Class.)
+11,520					
−11,520					

12 × $960 = $11,520.

9.22 continued.

    d. By March 31, 2019, the machine has been on the new depreciation schedule for 2014 through 2018 plus 3 months or 63 months altogether. Accumulated depreciation is $74,400 + (63 \times \$960) = \$74,400 + \$60,480 = \$134,880$.

Carrying value is $\$180,000 - \$134,880 = \$45,120$; sale at $40,000 results in a loss of $5,120 (= \$40,000 - \$45,120)$.

Journal entries are as follows:

Work-in-Process Inventory.................................... 2,880
    Accumulated Depreciation................................... 2,880

Assets	=	Liabilities	+	Shareholders' Equity	(Class.)
+2,880					
–2,880					

$3 \times \$960 = \$2,880$; to bring depreciation up to date as of 3/31/2019.

Cash.. 40,000
Accumulated Depreciation..................................... 134,880
Loss on Disposal of Machinery................................. 5,120
    Machinery... 180,000

Assets	=	Liabilities	+	Shareholders' Equity	(Class.)
+40,000				–5,120	IncSt → RE
+134,880					
–180,000					

9.23   (Disney World; distinguishing repairs versus betterments.)

Repair: $(1.00/1.20 \times \$30,200) + \$86,100 + (1.00/1.25 \times \$26,900) + \$12,600 = \$145,387$.

Betterment: $(.20/1.20 \times \$30,200) + (.25/1.25 \times \$26,900) = \$10,413$.

9.24 (Wildwood Properties; computing the amount of an impairment loss on tangible long-lived assets.)

The undiscounted cash flows total $12,400,000 [= ($1,400,000 x 6) + $4,000,000]. The carrying value of the building of $15,000,000 exceeds the undiscounted estimated cash flows, so an impairment loss has occurred. The present value of the expected cash flows when discounted at 10% is $8,355,244 [= ($1,400,000 x 4.35526) + ($4,000,000 x .56447) = $6,097,364 + $2,257,880]. The impairment loss is, therefore, $6,644,756 (= $15,000,000 − $8,355,244) under both U.S. GAAP and IFRS.

9.25 (Kieran Corporation; computing the amount of impairment loss.)

	Carrying Value	Undiscounted Cash Flows	Impairment Loss Recognized	Fair Value	Amount of Loss
Land	$ 550,000	$ 575,000	No	$ 550,000	$ 0
Buildings	580,000	600,000	No	580,000	0
Equipment	1,200,000	950,000	Yes	800,000	400,000
Goodwill	500,000[a]	--	Yes	270,000	230,000
Total	$ 2,830,000			$2,200,000	$ 630,000

[a]$500,000 = $2,400,000 − $400,000 − $600,000 − $900,000.

After recognizing the impairment losses on the property, plant, and equipment, the carrying value of Kieran Corporation is $2,430,000 (= $550,000 for land + $580,000 for buildings + $800,000 for equipment + $500,000 for goodwill). The carrying value of $2,430,000 exceeds the fair value of the entity of $2,200,000, so a goodwill impairment loss may have occurred (Step 1 of goodwill impairment test). The fair value column above shows the allocation of the $2,200,000 fair value to identifiable assets, with the residual of $270,000 attributed to goodwill. The carrying value of the goodwill of $500,000 exceeds its implied fair value of $270,000, so Kieran Corporation recognizes an impairment loss on the goodwill of $230,000 (Step 2 of goodwill impairment test).

9.26 (Fedup Express; computing the gain or loss on sale of equipment.)

Annual depreciation is $7,000 [= ($48,000 − $6,000)/6]. Depreciation expense for the first six months of 2008 is $3,500.

Depreciation Expense.. 3,500
   Accumulated Depreciation...   3,500

Assets	=	Liabilities	+	Shareholders' Equity	(Class.)
−3,500				−3,500	IncSt → RE

The carrying value of the delivery truck after the entry above is $16,500 [= $48,000 − (4.5 × $7,000)]. The accumulated depreciation totals $31,500 (= 4.5 × $7,000). The entry to record the sale is:

Cash.. 14,000
Accumulated Depreciation.. 31,500
Loss on Sale of Delivery Truck.. 2,500
   Delivery Truck..   48,000

Assets	=	Liabilities	+	Shareholders' Equity	(Class.)
+14,000				−2,500	IncSt → RE
+31,500					
−48,000					

9.27 (Wilcox Corporation; working backwards to derive proceeds from disposition of plant assets.)

Cost of Equipment Sold: $400,000 + $230,000 − $550,000 = $80,000.
Accumulated Depreciation
  on Equipment Sold: $180,000 + $50,000 − $160,000 = $70,000.
Carrying Value of Equip-
  ment Sold: $80,000 − $70,000 = $10,000.
Proceeds of Sale: $10,000 + $4,000 = $14,000.

9.28 (Journal entries to correct accounting errors.)

a. Depreciation Expense 375
     Accumulated Depreciation..   375

Assets	=	Liabilities	+	Shareholders' Equity	(Class.)
−375				−375	IncSt → RE

$3,000 × .25 × 6/12 = $375.

9.28 a. continued.

Accumulated Depreciation.. 1,875
Loss on Disposal of Equipment.................................. 325
    Equipment 2,200

Assets	=	Liabilities	+	Shareholders' Equity	(Class.)
+1,875				−325	IncSt → RE
−2,200					

$3,000 x .25 x 2.5 = $1,875. $3,200 + $3,000 − $4,000 = $2,200. $800 selling price − $1,125 carrying value = $325 loss.

b. Accumulated Depreciation.. 5,000
    Truck.. 5,000

Assets	=	Liabilities	+	Shareholders' Equity	(Class.)
+5,000					
−5,000					

c. Depreciation Expense 60
    Accumulated Depreciation.. 60

Assets	=	Liabilities	+	Shareholders' Equity	(Class.)
−60				−60	IncSt → RE

$1,200 x .10 x 6/12 = $60.

Accumulated Depreciation.. 270
    Theft Loss... 270

Assets	=	Liabilities	+	Shareholders' Equity	(Class.)
+270				+270	IncSt → RE

$1,200 x .10 x 27/12 = $270.

9.29 (Moon Macrosystems; recording transactions involving tangible and intangible assets.)

a. Office Equipment 400,000
   Computer Software 40,000
      Cash 440,000

Assets	=	Liabilities	+	Shareholders' Equity	(Class.)
+400,000					
+40,000					
−440,000					

b. Office Equipment 20,000
   Computer Software 10,000
      Cash 30,000

Assets	=	Liabilities	+	Shareholders' Equity	(Class.)
+20,000					
+10,000					
−30,000					

c. **2006 and 2007**
   Depreciation Expense [($400,000 + $20,000 − $40,000)/10] 38,000
   Amortization Expense [($40,000 + $10,000)/4] 12,500
      Accumulated Depreciation 38,000
      Computer Software 12,500

Assets	=	Liabilities	+	Shareholders' Equity	(Class.)
−38,000				−38,000	IncSt → RE
−12,500				−12,500	IncSt → RE

d. Impairment Loss of Computer Software
   ($40,000 + $10,000 − $12,500 − $12,500) 25,000
      Computer Software 25,000

Assets	=	Liabilities	+	Shareholders' Equity	(Class.)
−25,000				−25,000	IncSt → RE

9.29 continued.

e. Depreciation Expense [($400,000 + $20,000 − $38,000 − $38,000 − $56,000)/12]............ 24,000
    Accumulated Depreciation... 24,000

Assets	=	Liabilities	+	Shareholders' Equity	(Class.)
−24,000				−24,000	IncSt → RE

f. Depreciation Expense 24,000
    Accumulated Depreciation... 24,000

Assets	=	Liabilities	+	Shareholders' Equity	(Class.)
−24,000				−24,000	IncSt → RE

Cash.. 260,000
Accumulated Depreciation ($38,000 + $38,000 + $24,000 + $24,000).. 124,000
Loss on Sale of Office Equipment................................ 36,000
    Office Equipment... 420,000

Assets	=	Liabilities	+	Shareholders' Equity	(Class.)
+260,000				−36,000	IncSt → RE
+124,000					
−420,000					

9.30 (American Airlines; effect on net income of changes in estimates for depreciable assets.)

Income has been about $180 million (= .06 × $3 billion) per year.

Reconciliation of Plant Data:
Airplanes Cost .... $ 2,500,000,000
    Less Salvage Value (10%).. 250,000,000
    Depreciable Basis .... $ 2,250,000,000
Divided by 10-Year Life Equals Yearly Depreciation
    Charges.. $ 225,000,000
Times 4 Years Equals Accumulated Depreciation............... $ 900,000,000
Plus Net Carrying Value.. 1,600,000,000
Airplanes Cost .... $ 2,500,000,000

9.30 continued.

New Depreciation Charge:

Net Carrying Value...	$ 1,600,000,000
Less Salvage Value (12% of Cost).................................	300,000,000
Depreciation Basis...	$ 1,300,000,000
Divided by 10 (= 14 – 4) Years Equals Revised Yearly Depreciation Charge...	$ 130,000,000

Increase in Pretax Income:

Old Depreciation Charges..	$ 225,000,000
New Depreciation Charges...	130,000,000
	$ 95,000,000
Multiplied by (1 – tax rate) = 1 – .35 = .65	X .65
Increase in Aftertax Income...	$ 61,750,000

Income will rise by about 34.3% (= $61.75/$180.0).

Note that a modest change in depreciation parameters can significantly affect net income.

9.31 (Recognizing and measuring impairment losses.)

a. The loss occurs because of an adverse action by a governmental entity. The undiscounted cash flows of $50 million are less than the carrying value of the building of $60 million. An impairment loss has therefore occurred. The fair value of the building of $32 million is less than the carrying value of $60 million. Thus, the amount of the impairment loss is $28 million (= $60 million – $32 million). The journal entry to record the impairment loss is (in millions):

Loss from Impairment......................................	28	
Accumulated Depreciation...............................	20	
Building...		48

Assets	= Liabilities	+	Shareholders' Equity	(Class.)
+20			–28	IncSt → RE
–48				

This entry records the impairment loss, eliminates the accumulated depreciation, and writes down the building to its fair value of $32 million (= $80 – $48).

b. The undiscounted cash flows of $70 million exceed the carrying value of the building of $60 million. Thus, no impairment loss occurs according to the definition in FASB *Statement No. 144*. An *economic* loss occurred but U.S. GAAP does not recognize it.

9.31 continued.

c. The loss arises because the accumulated costs significantly exceed the amount originally anticipated. The carrying value of the building of $25 million exceeds the undiscounted future cash flows of $22 million. Thus, an impairment loss has occurred. The impairment loss recognized equals $9 million (= $25 million − $16 million). The journal entry is (in millions):

Loss from Impairment.. 9
    Construction in Process..   9

Assets	=	Liabilities	+	Shareholders' Equity	(Class.)
−9				−9	IncSt → RE

d. The loss occurs because of a significant decline in the fair value of the patent. FASB *Statement No. 142* requires calculation of the impairment loss on the patent before computing the impairment loss on goodwill. The undiscounted future cash flows of $18 million are less than the carrying value of the patent of $20 million. Thus, an impairment loss occurred. The amount of the loss is $8 million (= $20 million − $12 million). The journal entry to record the loss is:

Loss from Impairment.. 8
    Patent..   8

Assets	=	Liabilities	+	Shareholders' Equity	(Class.)
−8				−8	IncSt → RE

The second step is to determine if an impairment loss on the goodwill occurred. The fair value of the entity is $25 million. The carrying value after writing down the patent is $27 million (= $12 million for patent and $15 million for goodwill). Thus, a goodwill impairment loss occurred. If the fair value of the patent is $12 million, the market value of the goodwill is $13 million. The impairment loss on goodwill is therefore $2 million (= $15 million − $13 million). The journal entry is:

Loss from Impairment.. 2
    Goodwill..   2

Assets	=	Liabilities	+	Shareholders' Equity	(Class.)
−2				−2	IncSt → RE

9.31 continued.

e. The loss occurs because of a significant change in the business climate for Chicken Franchisees. One might question whether this loss is temporary or permanent. Evidence from previous similar events (for example, Tylenol) suggests that consumers soon forget or at least forgive the offending company. The FASB reporting standard discusses but rejects the use of a permanency criterion in identifying impairment losses. Thus, an impairment loss occurs in this case because the future undiscounted cash flows of $6 million from the franchise rights are less than the carrying value of the franchise rights of $10 million. The amount of the impairment loss is $7 million (= $10 million – $3 million). The journal entry is (in millions):

Impairment Loss.. 7
    Franchise Rights 7

Assets	=	Liabilities	+	Shareholders' Equity	(Class.)
–7				–7	IncSt → RE

This entry assumes that Chicken Franchisees does not use an Accumulated Amortization account.

9.32 (Pfizer; expensing versus capitalizing research and development costs.) (Amounts in Millions)

	Year 1	Year 2	Year 3	Year 4
a. **Expense Costs as Incurred**				
Other Income	$ 30	$ 30	$ 30	$ 30
Additional Income from R&D:				
First Year's R&D	36	36	36	
Second Year's R&D		36	36	36
Third Year's R&D			36	36
Fourth Year's R&D				36
R&D Expense.......................	(90)	(90)	(90)	(90)
Income (Loss) before Taxes	$ (24)	$ 12	$ 48	$ 48

9.32 continued.

b. **Capitalize and Amortize Over 3 Years (Including Year of Occurrence)**

	Year 1	Year 2	Year 3	Year 4
Other Income	$ 30	$ 30	$ 30	$ 30
Additional Income from R&D:				
First Year's R&D	36	36	36	
Second Year's R&D		36	36	36
Third Year's R&D			36	36
Fourth Year's R&D				36
R&D Amortization Expense:				
First Year's R&D	(30)	(30)	(30)	
Second Year's R&D		(30)	(30)	(30)
Third Year's R&D			(30)	(30)
Fourth Year's R&D				(30)
Income before Taxes	$ 36	$ 42	$ 48	$ 48
Deferred R&D Asset on Balance Sheet:				
First Year's R&D	$ 60	$ 30		
Second Year's R&D		60	$ 30	
Third Year's R&D			60	$ 30
Fourth Year's R&D				60
Total	$ 60	$ 90	$ 90	$ 90

c. The expensing policy leads to higher expenses and lower income before income taxes, in the first two years. After that, the two policies are the same. When the firm ceases to spend on R&D, the policy of expensing will show higher income in the two years when the benefits of prior R&D continue, but there are no matching expenses. There are no expenses under Policy (1), but Policy (2) continues to show amortization expense. Thus, Policy (1) is more conservative in the sense that it results in smaller cumulative income before taxes until the firm ceases to spend on R&D. Policy (1) also results in smaller assets on the balance sheet because, unlike Policy (2), it shows no asset for Deferred R&D Costs.

d. The pre-tax income under the two policies will continue to be the same if there is no growth or change in policy. Policy (2) will show a lower rate of return on total assets and a lower rate of return on stockholders' equity than will Policy (1) because the asset and equity totals are larger under Policy (2) than under Policy (1).

9.33 (General Mills; interpreting disclosures regarding long-lived assets.) (Amounts in Millions)

a. General Mills purchased software for its internal use from a software developer. General Mills expects to receive future benefits from using the software and the acquisition cost provides evidence of the amount of expected future benefits.

b. Yes. The computer software has a finite life because of technological obsolescence and would be depreciated.

c. Average Total Life: .5($5,806 − $54 − $252 + $6,096 − $61 − $276)/$421 = 13.4 years.

Average Age: .5($2,809 + $3,082)/$421 = 7.0 years.

d. Yes. The accumulated depreciation account increased by $273 (= $3,082 − $2,809). Depreciation expense increased accumulated depreciation by $421. Thus, the accumulated depreciation on assets sold or abandoned was $148 (= $273 − $421).

e. General Mills has grown heavily by corporate acquisitions. Intangibles comprise 57.9% (= $10,529/$18,184) of total assets. Because GAAP does not require firms to recognize internally developed intangibles, these intangibles arise from corporate acquisitions.

f. Yes. The amount for brands and goodwill increased. Because firms cannot write up assets for increases in fair value, the increased amounts suggest a small acquisition during the year.

g. Patents have a 20-year legal life and, therefore, have a finite life. Trademarks are subject to renewal at the end of their legal life as long as a firm continues to use them. General Mills must intend not to renew these trademarks.

h. General Mills must expect the brand names to have an indefinite life. The firm would need to provide evidence based on past experience for its brand names and from industry experience to convince its independent accountants that the timing of any cessation of benefits is highly uncertain.

i. General Mills shows amounts in its Construction in Progress account. Thus, General Mills must capitalize a portion of interest expense. The reported amount is the net of total interest cost minus the amount capitalized in Construction in Progress.

9.34 (Amgen, Inc.; interpreting disclosures regarding long-lived assets.) (Amounts in Millions)

a. No. Firms do not commence recognizing depreciation until they put an asset into service. The assets under construction have not yet reached that stage.

b. Average Total Life: .5($7,321 − $294 − $958 + $8,688 − $398 − $1,271)/$593 = 11.0 years.

Average Age: .5($2,283 + $2,767)/$593 = 4.3 years.

c. Yes. Accumulated depreciation experienced a net increase of $484 (= $2,767 − $2,283) during the year. Depreciation increased the Accumulated Depreciation account by $593. Thus, accumulated depreciation on assets sold or abandoned was $109 (= $484 − $593).

d. Amgen is in an industry subject to technological change. Thus, any technology-based intangible likely has a finite life and is, therefore, subject to amortization. The Developed Product Technology likely relates to specific biotechnology products it currently sells. Either Amgen or another company will likely develop new products that will lead to obsolescence in the near future. The Core Technology intangible relates to basic findings and principles that affect the development and sale of biotechnology products in general. One might expect this item to have a longer useful life than Developed Product Technology. However, given the relatively young age of the biotechnology industry, the extent to which core technologies will last is uncertain. Amgen could probably make a stronger case for treating Core Technologies as an intangible with an indefinite life than is the case for Developed Product Technology. It apparently chose to treat it as having a finite life. The Trade Name likely attaches to a particular product and, like Developed Product Technology, is subject to replacement by a more technologically-advanced product. The Acquired Technology Rights arise from contractual arrangements that have prescribed time limits during which Amgen can enjoy the benefits.

e. Average Total Life: .5($4,950 + $5,219)/$370 = 13.7 years.

Average Age: .5($1,208 + $1,472)/$370 = 3.6 years.

f. It appears that Amgen made no corporate acquisition during 2007 because the acquisition cost of Core Technology and Trade Name remained the same. The decrease in the acquisition cost of Developed Product Technology might have occurred because of the discontinuance of a particular product or because of the recognition of an asset impairment loss on that intangible.

9.34 continued.

g. Goodwill likely includes technologies that are not separately identifiable, the value of research scientists, and perhaps some overpayment for acquired companies.

h. Amgen shows amounts in its Construction in Progress account. Thus, Amgen must capitalize a portion of interest expense. The reported amount is the net of total interest cost minus the amount capitalized in Construction in Progress.

9.35 (Hewlett-Packard Company; interpreting disclosures regarding long-lived assets.) (Amounts in Millions)

a. Average Total Life: .5($15,024 − $534 + $16,411 − $464)/$1,922 = 7.9 years.

Average Age: .5($8,161 + $8,613)/$1,922 = 4.4 years.

b. Yes. The Accumulated Depreciation account increased $452 (= $8,613 − $8,161). Depreciation increased the Accumulated Depreciation account by $1,922. Thus, the accumulated depreciation on assets sold or abandoned was $1,470 (= $452 − $1,922).

c. Customer Contracts have a specific term and, therefore, have a finite life. Core Technology likely involves technologies related to the design of computer hardware and software in general and is not product specific. Given the pace of change in the computer industry, even core technologies change over time. HP would likely encounter difficulties in convincing its independent accountants that core technologies do not have a finite, albeit uncertain, life. Patents have a 20-year life, although the technological life in the computer industry is much shorter. Trademarks are renewable as long as a firm continues to use them. HP must expect to discontinue using the trademarks.

d. Average Remaining Total Life: .5($4,612 + $6,122)/$783 = 6.9 years.

Average Age: .5($2,682 + $3,465)/$783 = 3.9 years.

e. At the time of the acquisition, the Compaq name was highly recognizable. HP likely had no difficulty convincing its independent accountants that the brand name had an indefinite life. Given the elapsed time since the acquisition and the merging of Compaq products into HP's line of offerings, one wonders whether HP will write off the brand name at some point.

f. Yes. The amount of each intangible, except the Compaq brand name, increased during 2007. HP allocated a portion of the purchase price to these intangibles, with most of the increase involving goodwill.

9.36 (Ross Laboratories; valuation of brand name.) (Dollar amounts in millions.)

	Part a.	Part b.
(1) Operating Margin	$ 600.0	$ 600.0
Employed Physical Capital $500.0		
Subtract Return Required on Physical Capital Required at .10 (Part *a*.) or .20 (Part *b*.)	(50.0)	(100.0)
(2) Pre-Tax Profit Generated by Brand	$ 550.0	$ 500.0
Subtract Income Taxes at 40%	(220.0)	(200.0)
(3) Net Brand Name Profits	$ 330.0	$ 300.0
Multiply by After-Tax Capitalization Factor	17.0	8.0
(4) Estimate of Brand Value	$5,610.0	$2,400.0

CHAPTER 10

NOTES, BONDS, AND LEASES

Questions, Exercises, and Problems: Answers and Solutions

10.1 See the text or the glossary at the end of the book.

10.2 Generally, accountants initially record assets at acquisition cost and then allocate this amount to future periods as an expense. Changes in the fair value of most assets (except for use of the lower-of-cost-or-market method for inventories; the market value method for marketable securities and investments in securities; and impairments) do not appear in the accounting records. Similarly, using the market interest rate at the time of issue to account for bonds results in an initial liability equal to the amount of cash received and a subsequent liability that reflects amortization of this initial amount. Changes in the market value of bonds do not appear in the accounting records, unless a firm chooses the fair value option.

10.3 Applying the effective interest method using the historical market interest rate gives a constant amount of interest expense only if a firm initially issued bonds at face value. If a firm issued bonds at a discount or a premium to face value, then the amount of interest expense will change each period. A statement that applies to all bonds, whether issued at face value, a discount, or a premium, is that using the historical market interest rate in applying the effective interest method gives a constant rate of interest expense as a percentage of the liability at the beginning of the period. That constant rate is the historical market interest rate.

10.4 Firms repay a portion of the principal on serial bonds each period but repay all of the principal on coupon bonds at maturity. Thus, the amount of unpaid principal on serial bonds at any date prior to maturity is less than on coupon bonds, giving rise to less interest expense for serial bonds.

10.5 The initial issue prices will differ. Although the present value of the $1,000,000 face amount of these bonds will be the same for the two issues, the present value of the coupon payments will differ because the 9% coupon bonds requires larger cash outflows each year than the 7% coupon bonds.

10.6 This statement is correct. Over the life of the bonds, the effect on net income before taxes is the difference between the cash received when the firm issued the bonds and the cash disbursed for interest and repayment of principal at maturity. Using the historical market interest rate or the current market interest rate to account for the bonds simply allocates this total income differently across the periods while the bonds are outstanding.

10.7 The statement is still correct. Instead of repaying the bonds at maturity, the firm repurchases them in the market. The amount paid to repurchase the bonds depends on market interest rates at the time, but that amount is independent of whether the firm used the historical market interest rate or the current market interest rate to account for the bonds while they were outstanding.

10.8 The party with the risks and rewards of ownership effectively owns the asset, whatever the legal niceties. The asset should appear on the balance sheet of the owner. The capital lease criteria attempt to state unambiguously who has economic ownership.

10.9 The minimum contractual lease payments do not include the rental based on sales. If sales are zero, the lease payment will be zero. Thus, the "minimum" payment is zero. The present value of the "small fixed amount" will not likely exceed 90% of the fair market value of the property. The ten-year lease is also likely less than 75% of the useful life of the building.

10.10 The present value of the minimum lease payments includes both the monthly rental and the minimum guaranteed resale. Thus, the lessee bears the risk of technological change, damage, and other factors that affect the value of the vehicle at the end of three years. The lessor bears little risk. Although the three-year lease period is likely less than 75% of the useful life of the vehicle, the lease likely satisfies the fourth criterion for a capital lease.

10.11 The distinction depends upon which criteria of the lease made it a capital lease. The major difference is that at the end of a lease term the asset reverts to the lessor in a capital lease, whereas at the end of the installment payments, the asset belongs to the purchaser. The criteria for capitalizing a lease are such that the expected value of the asset when it reverts to the lessor is small, but misestimates can occur. In most other respects, capital leases and installment purchases are similar in economic substance.

10.12 Disagree. Operating Lease: Rent revenue for the lessor will equal rent expense for the lessee on an operating lease, but lessor also has depreciation expense on leased assets. Capital Lease: Interest revenue for the lessor should equal interest expense for the lessee on a capital lease. The lessor recognizes its cost to acquire or manufacture the leased asset as cost of goods sold under a capital lease. The lessor also recognizes revenue under a capital lease equal to the "selling price" of the lease asset on the date of signing the lease.

10.13 Using the operating lease method for financial reporting permits the lessee to keep the lease liability off the balance sheet and report less cumulative expenses than the capital lease method. The lessee prefers the capital lease for income tax reporting because it reports more cumulative expenses than the operating lease method and therefore minimizes the present value of income tax payments.

10.14 Using the capital lease method for financial reporting permits the lessor to report a gross margin from the "sale" of the leased asset in the year the entities sign the lease and more cumulative revenue for interest than the operating lease method recognizes as rent revenue. The lessor prefers the operating lease method for income tax reporting because it excludes the gross margin from taxable income in the year of signing the lease and delays the recognition of rent revenue relative to the amount of interest revenue recognized under the capital lease method.

10.15 (Hagar Company; amortization schedule for note where stated interest rate differs from historical market rate of interest.)

a. **Amortization Schedule for a Three-Year Note with a Maturity Value of $40,000, Calling for 6% Annual Interest Payments, Yield of 8% per Year**

Year (1)	Carrying Value Start of Year (2)	Interest Expense for Period (3)a	Payment (4)	Interest Added to Carrying Value (5)	Carrying Value End of Year (6)
1	$37,938	$3,035	$2,400	$635	$38,573
2	38,573	3,086	2,400	686	39,259
3	39,259	3,141	2,400	741	40,000

a(3) = (2) X .08.

b. Computer... 37,938
    Note Payable... 37,938

Assets	=	Liabilities	+	Shareholders' Equity	(Class.)
+37,938		+37,938			

To record purchase of computer.

10.15 b. continued.

Annual Journal Entry for Interest and Principal

Interest Expense............. Amount in Col. (3)
   Cash .... Amount in Col. (4)*
   Note Payable............... Amount in Col. (5)*

Assets	=	Liabilities	+	Shareholders' Equity	(Class.)
–Amt (4)		+Amt (5)		–Amt (3)	IncSt → RE

*In third year, the firm also debits Note Payable and credits Cash for $40,000.

10.16 (Computing the issue price of bonds.)

  a. $10,000,000 x .20829[a] .... $ 2,082,900

    [a]Present value of $1 for 40 periods at 4%.

  b. $500,000 x 23.11477[a] .... $ 11,557,385

    [a]Present value of annuity for 40 periods at 3%.

10.17 (Computing the issue price of bonds.)

  a. $1,000,000 x .14205[a] .... $ 142,050

    [a]Present value of $1 for 40 periods at 5%.

  b. $50,000 x 23.11477[a] .... $ 1,155,739

    [a]Present value of annuity for 40 periods at 3%.

  c. $50,000 x 19.79277[a] .... $ 989,639
    $1,000,000 x .20829[b]   208,290
                                                                                                           $ 1,197,929

    [a]Present value of annuity for 40 periods at 4%.
    [b]Present value of $1 for 40 periods at 4%.

10.17 continued.

d. $30,000 x 12.46221[a] .... $ 373,866
    $40,000 x 12.46221[a] x .37689[b]   187,875
    $1,000,000 x .14205[c]   142,050
                                                                                         $ 703,791

[a]Present value of annuity for 20 periods at 5%.
[b]Present value of $1 for 20 periods at 5%.
[c]Present value of $1 for 40 periods at 5%.

10.18 (Womack Company; amortization schedule for bonds.)

a. $100,000 x .67556[a] .... $ 67,556
    $5,000 x 8.11090[b]   40,555
       Issue Price $108,111

[a]Table 2, 4% column and 10-period row.
[b]Table 4, 4% column and 10-period row.

b.

Six-Month Period	Liability at Start of Period	Interest at 4% for Period	Cash Payment	Decrease in Carrying Value of Liability	Liability at End of Period
0					$108,111
1	$108,111	$ 4,324	$ 5,000	$ (676)	107,435
2	107,435	4,297	5,000	(703)	106,732
3	106,732	4,269	5,000	(731)	106,001
4	106,001	4,240	5,000	(760)	105,241
5	105,241	4,210	5,000	(790)	104,451
6	104,451	4,178	5,000	(822)	103,629
7	103,629	4,145	5,000	(855)	102,774
8	102,774	4,111	5,000	(889)	101,885
9	101,885	4,075	5,000	(925)	100,960
10	100,960	4,040[a]	5,000	(960)	100,000
Total		$41,889	$50,000	$(8,111)	

[a]Does not equal .04 x $100,960 due to rounding.

10.18 continued.

c. Carrying Value of Bonds: $10,363.

Bonds Payable 10,363
   Gain on Bond Retirement 63
   Cash 10,300

Assets	=	Liabilities	+	Shareholders' Equity	(Class.)
−10,300		−10,363		+63	IncSt → RE

To record retirement of bonds.

10.19 (Seward Corporation; amortization schedule for bonds.)

a. $100,000 × .74622[a] .... $ 74,622
   $4,000 × 5.07569[b] 20,303
   Issue Price .... $ 94,925

[a]Table 2, 5% column and 6-period row.
[b]Table 4, 5% column and 6-period row.

b.

Six-Month Period	Liability at Start of Period	Interest at 5% for Period	Cash Payment	Increase in Carrying Value of Liability	Liability at End of Period
1	$94,925	$ 4,746	$ 4,000	$ 746	$ 95,671
2	95,671	4,784	4,000	784	96,455
3	96,455	4,823	4,000	823	97,278
4	97,278	4,864	4,000	864	98,142
5	98,142	4,907	4,000	907	99,049
6	99,049	4,951[a]	4,000	951	100,000
Total		$ 29,075	$ 24,000	$ 5,075	

[a]Does not equal .05 × $99,049 due to rounding.

c. **January 2, 2008**
Cash 94,925
   Bonds Payable 94,925

Assets	=	Liabilities	+	Shareholders' Equity	(Class.)
−94,925		+94,925			

To record issue of bonds.

10.19 c. continued.

June 30, 2008
Interest Expense	4,746	
Cash Payable		4,000
Bonds Payable		746

Assets	=	Liabilities	+	Shareholders' Equity	(Class.)
–4,000		+746		–4,746	IncSt → RE

To record interest expense for first six months, the cash payment, and the increase in the liability for the difference.

December 31, 2008
Interest Expense	4,784	
Cash		4,000
Bonds Payable		784

Assets	=	Liabilities	+	Shareholders' Equity	(Class.)
–4,000		+784		–4,784	IncSt → RE

To record interest expense for the second six months, the cash payment, and the increase in the liability for the difference.

d.
Bonds Payable (.20 x $98,142)	19,628	
Loss on Retirement of Bonds	772	
Cash		20,400

Assets	=	Liabilities	+	Shareholders' Equity	(Class.)
–20,400		–19,628		–772	IncSt → RE

10.20 (O'Brien Corporation; accounting for bonds using amortized cost measurement based on the historical market interest rate.)

a.
$8,000,000 x .30656[a]	$ 2,452,480
$320,000 x 23.11477[b]	7,396,726
Issue Price	$ 9,849,206

[a]Table 2, 3% column and 40-period row.
[b]Table 4, 3% column and 40-period row.

b. .03 x $9,849,206 = $295,476.

10.20 continued.

c. .03($9,849,206 + $295,476 − $320,000) = $294,740.

d. Carrying Value: ($9,849,206 + $295,476 − $320,000 + $294,740 − $320,000) .... $ 9,799,422

e. $8,000,000 x .32523[a] .... $ 2,601,840
$320,000 x 22.49246[b] 7,197,587
Present Value.. $ 9,799,427

[a]Table 2, 3% column and 38-period row.
[b]Table 4, 3% column and 38-period row.

The difference between the carrying value in Part *d.* and the present value in Part *e.* results from rounding present value factors.

10.21 (Robinson Company; accounting for bonds using amortized cost measurement based on the historical market interest rate.)

a. $5,000,000 x .37689[a] .... $ 1,884,450
$200,000 x 12.46221[b] 2,492,442
Issue Price .... $ 4,376,892

[a]Table 2, 5% column and 20-period row.
[b]Table 4, 5% column and 20-period row.

b. .05 x $4,376,892 = $218,845.

c. .05($4,376,892 + $218,845 − $200,000) = $219,787.

d. $4,376,892 + $218,845 − $200,000 + $219,787 − $200,000 = $4,415,524.

e. $5,000,000 x .41552[a] .... $ 2,077,600
$200,000 x 11.68959[b] 2,337,918
Present Value... $ 4,415,518

[a]Table 2, 5% column and 18-period row.
[b]Table 4, 5% column and 18-period row.

The difference between the carrying value in Part *d.* and the present value in Part *e.* results from rounding present value factors.

10.22 (Huergo Dooley Corporation; accounting for bonds using amortized cost measurement based on the historical market interest rate.)

a. $2,000,000 x .61391^a .... $ 1,227,820
    $80,000 x 7.72173^b 617,738
    $ 1,845,558

    ^aPresent value of $1 for 10 periods at 5%.
    ^bPresent value of an annuity for 10 periods at 5%.

b. Interest Expense (.05 x $1,845,558) 92,278
       Cash (.04 x $2,000,000).. 80,000
       Bonds Payable (Plug)... 12,278

Assets	=	Liabilities	+	Shareholders' Equity	(Class.)
−80,000		+12,278		−92,278	IncSt → RE

c. Interest Expense [.05 x ($1,845,558 + $12,278)].... 92,892
       Cash (.04 x $2,000,000).. 80,000
       Bonds Payable (Plug)... 12,892

Assets	=	Liabilities	+	Shareholders' Equity	(Class.)
−80,000		+12,892		−92,892	IncSt → RE

d. Bonds Payable [.20 x ($1,845,558 + $12,278 + $12,892)]... 374,146
    Loss on Repurchase of Bonds....................................... 53,933
       Cash... 428,079

Assets	=	Liabilities	+	Shareholders' Equity	(Class.)
−428,079		−374,146		−53,933	IncSt → RE

$2,000,000 x .78941^a .... $ 1,578,820
$80,000 x 7.01969^b 561,575
$ 2,140,395
Total... X .20
Purchase Price.. $ 428,079

^aPresent value of $1 for 8 periods at 3%.
^bPresent value of an annuity for 8 periods at 3%.

10.23 (Stroud Corporation; accounting for bonds using the fair value option based on the current market interest rate.)

a. January 1, 2008: The carrying value of these bonds is $10,000,000, their issue price. The issue price equals the face value because the coupon rate and the required market yield both equal 6%.

June 30, 2008:
$10,000,000 × .5598676[a] .... $ 5,598,676
$300,000 × 14.197818[b] 4,259,346
$ 9,858,022

[a] Present value of $1 for 19 periods at 3.1%.
[b] Present value of an annuity for 19 periods at 3.1%.

December 31, 2008:
$10,000,000 × .557435[a] .... $ 5,574,350
$300,000 × 13.411061[b] 4,023,318
$ 9,597,668

[a] Present value of $1 for 18 periods at 3.3%.
[b] Present value of an annuity for 18 periods at 3.3%.

b. Interest Expense: .03 × $10,000,000 = $300,000.

Unrealized Gain: $141,978 (= $10,000,000 − $9,858,022).

c. Interest Expense: .031 × $9,858,022 = $303,599. The carrying value of the bonds at the end of the second six months before computing the unrealized gain or loss is $9,861,621 (= $9,858,022 + $303,599 − $300,000).

Unrealized Gain: $263,953 (= $9,861,621 − $9,597,668).

d. **January 1, 2008**
Cash 10,000,000
  Bonds Payable 10,000,000

Assets	=	Liabilities	+	Shareholders' Equity	(Class.)
+10,000,000		+10,000,000			

To record issue of $10 million bonds at face value.

10.23 d. continued.

June 30, 2008
Interest Expense 300,000
    Cash 300,000

Assets	=	Liabilities	+	Shareholders' Equity	(Class.)
−300,000				−300,000	IncSt → RE

To record interest expense for the first six months.

June 30, 2008
Bonds Payable.. 141,978
    Unrealized Gain from Revaluation of Bonds......... 141,978

Assets	=	Liabilities	+	Shareholders' Equity	(Class.)
		−141,978		+141,978	IncSt → RE

To revalue bonds to current fair value.

December 31, 2008
Interest Expense 303,599
    Cash 300,000
    Bonds Payable... 3,599

Assets	=	Liabilities	+	Shareholders' Equity	(Class.)
−300,000		+3,599		−303,599	IncSt → RE

To record interest expense for the second six months.

December 31, 2008
Bonds Payable.. 263,953
    Unrealized Gain on Revaluation of Bonds............. 263,953

Assets	=	Liabilities	+	Shareholders' Equity	(Class.)
		−263,953		+263,953	IncSt → RE

To revalue bonds to current fair value.

10.24 (Restin Corporation; accounting for bonds using the fair value option based on the current market interest rate.)

a. **January 1, 2008:**

$20,000,000 x .5025659[a] $10,051,318
$800,000 x 14.212403[b] 11,369,923
$21,421,241

[a]Present value of $1 for 20 periods at 3.5%.
[b]Present value of an annuity for 20 periods at 3.5%.

June 30, 2008:

$20,000,000 x .5297973[a] $10,595,946
$800,000 x 13.82949[b] 11,063,592
$21,659,538

[a]Present value of $1 for 19 periods at 3.4%.
[b]Present value of an annuity for 19 periods at 3.4%.

December 31, 2008:

$20,000,000 x .5672382[a] $11,344,763
$800,000 x 13.523807[b] 10,819,046
$22,163,809

[a]Present value of $1 for 18 periods at 3.2%.
[b]Present value of an annuity for 18 periods at 3.2%.

b. Interest Expense: .035 x $21,421,241 = $749,743. The carrying value before computing the unrealized gain or loss for the first six months is $21,370,984 (= $21,421,241 + $749,743 − $800,000).

Unrealized Loss: $288,554 (= $21,659,538 − $21,370,984).

c. Interest Expense: .034 x $21,659,538 = $736,424. The carrying value of the bonds at the end of the second six months before computing the unrealized gain or loss is $21,595,962 (= $21,659,538 + $736,424 − $800,000).

Unrealized Loss: $567,847 (= $22,163,809 − $21,595,962).

10.24 continued.

d. **January 1, 2008:**
Cash 21,421,241
    Bonds Payable 21,421,241

Assets	=	Liabilities	+	Shareholders' Equity	(Class.)
+21,421,241		+21,421,241			

To record issue of $20 million, 8% semiannual bonds priced to yield 7% compounded semiannually.

June 30, 2008:
Interest Expense 749,743
Bonds Payable 50,257
    Cash 800,000

Assets	=	Liabilities	+	Shareholders' Equity	(Class.)
–800,000		–50,257		–749,743	IncSt → RE

To record interest expense for the first six months, cash payment, and reduction in the liability for the difference.

June 30, 2008:
Unrealized Loss from Revaluation of Bonds 288,554
    Bonds Payable 288,554

Assets	=	Liabilities	+	Shareholders' Equity	(Class.)
		+288,554		–288,554	IncSt → RE

To revalue bonds to current fair value.

December 31, 2008:
Interest Expense 736,424
Bonds Payable 63,576
    Cash 800,000

Assets	=	Liabilities	+	Shareholders' Equity	(Class.)
–800,000		–63,576		–736,424	IncSt → RE

To record interest expense for the second six months, the cash payment, and the reduction in the liability.

10.24 d. continued.

December 31, 2008:
Unrealized Loss on Revaluation of Bonds.................. 567,847
  Bonds Payable   567,847

Assets	=	Liabilities	+	Shareholders' Equity	(Class.)
		+567,847		−567,847	IncSt → RE

To revalue bonds to current fair value.

10.25 (Boeing and American; applying the capital lease criteria.)

  a. This lease is a capital lease because the lease period of 20 years exceeds 75% of the expected life of the aircraft. The lease does not meet any other capital lease criteria. The aircraft reverts to Boeing at the end of 20 years. The present value of the lease payments when discounted at 10% is $51.1 million ($6 million x 8.51356), which is less than $54 million (= 90% of the fair value of $60 million).

  b. This lease is a capital lease because the present value of the lease payments of $54.8 million (= $7.2 million x 7.60608) exceeds 90% of the $60 million fair value of the aircraft.

  c. The lease is not a capital lease. The present value of the required lease payments of $36.9 million (= $5.5 million x 6.71008) is less than $54 million (= 90% of the fair value of the aircraft). The life of the lease is less than 75% of the expected useful life of the aircraft. The purchase option price coupled with the rental payments provides Boeing with a present value of all cash flows exceeding $62.4 million [= ($5.5 million x 6.71008) + ($55 million x .46319)]. This amount exceeds the usual sales price of $60 million, so there does not appear to be a bargain purchase option.

  d. This lease is not a capital lease. The present value of the minimum required lease payments is $50.9 million (= $6.2 million x 8.20141). The fee contingent on usage could be zero, so the calculations exclude it. The life of the lease is less than 75% of the useful life of the aircraft. The aircraft reverts to Boeing at the end of the lease period.

10.26 (FedUp Delivery Services; preparing lessee's journal entries for an operating and a capital lease.)

a. This lease is a capital lease because the present value of the lease payments of $24,653 (= $750 x 32.87102) exceeds 90% of the fair value of the leased asset (.90 x $25,000 = $22,500). The life of the lease is less than 75% of the life of the leased property and the property reverts to GM at the end of the lease period, so the lease fails these criteria for a capital lease.

b. **Time of Signing Lease**
No Entry.

End of Each Month
Rent Expense... 750
   Cash... 750

Assets	=	Liabilities	+	Shareholders' Equity	(Class.)
–750				–750	IncSt → RE

To record monthly rental expense and payment.

c. **Time of Signing Lease**
Leased Asset.. 24,653
   Lease Liability... 24,653

Assets	=	Liabilities	+	Shareholders' Equity	(Class.)
+24,653		+24,653			

To record capital lease.

End of First Month
Interest Expense (= .005 x $24,653).......................... 123.27
Lease Liability... 626.73
   Cash... 750.00

Assets	=	Liabilities	+	Shareholders' Equity	(Class.)
–750.00		–626.73		–123.27	IncSt → RE

To record interest expense and cash payment for first month; the carrying value of the lease liability is now $24,026.27 (= $24,653.00 – $626.73).

10.26 c. continued.

Depreciation Expense			684.80	
Accumulated Depreciation				684.80

Assets	=	Liabilities	+	Shareholders' Equity	(Class.)
−684.80				−684.80	IncSt → RE

To record depreciation expense for the first month of $684.80 (= $24,653/36).

End of Second Month

Interest Expense (= .005 × $24,026.27)	120.13	
Lease Liability	629.87	
Cash		750.00

Assets	=	Liabilities	+	Shareholders' Equity	(Class.)
−750.00		−629.87		−120.13	IncSt → RE

To record interest expense and cash payment for the second month.

Depreciation Expense	684.80	
Accumulated Depreciation		684.80

Assets	=	Liabilities	+	Shareholders' Equity	(Class.)
−684.80				−684.80	IncSt → RE

To record depreciation expense for the second month.

10.27 (Sun Microsystems; preparing lessor's journal entries for an operating lease and a capital lease.)

    a. This lease is a capital lease. The life of the lease equals the expected useful life of the property. The present value of the lease payments of $12,000 [= $4,386.70 + ($4,386.70 × 1.73554)] equals the fair value of the leased asset.

10.27 continued.

b. **Beginning of Each Year**
Cash.. 4,386.70
    Rental Fees Received in Advance...........................   4,386.70

Assets	=	Liabilities	+	Shareholders' Equity	(Class.)
+4,386.70		+4,386.70			

To record cash received in advance from lessee.

End of Each Year
Rental Fees Received in Advance................................ 4,386.70
    Rent Revenue...   4,386.70

Assets	=	Liabilities	+	Shareholders' Equity	(Class.)
		−4,386.70		+4,386.70	IncSt → RE

To record rent revenue for each year.

Depreciation Expense... 2,400.00
    Accumulated Depreciation..   2,400.00

Assets	=	Liabilities	+	Shareholders' Equity	(Class.)
−2,400.00				−2,400.00	IncSt → RE

To record annual depreciation (= $7,200/3).

c. **January 1, 2008**
Cash.. 4,386.70
Lease Receivable (= $4,386.70 x 1.73554)................. 7,613.30
    Sales Revenue...   12,000.00

Assets	=	Liabilities	+	Shareholders' Equity	(Class.)
+4,386.70				+12,000.00	IncSt → RE
+7,613.30					

To record "sale" of workstation.

10.27 c. continued.

Cost of Goods Sold... 7,200.00
    Inventory 7,200.00

Assets	=	Liabilities	+	Shareholders' Equity	(Class.)
−7,200.00				−7,200.00	IncSt → RE

To record cost of workstation "sold".

December 31, 2008
Lease Receivable (= .10 x $7,613.30)......................... 761.33
    Interest Revenue..   761.33

Assets	=	Liabilities	+	Shareholders' Equity	(Class.)
+761.33				+761.33	IncSt → RE

To record interest revenue for 2008.

January 1, 2009
Cash.. 4,386.70
    Lease Receivable...   4,386.70

Assets	=	Liabilities	+	Shareholders' Equity	(Class.)
+4,386.70					
−4,386.70					

To record cash received at the beginning of 2009.
The carrying value of the receivable is now $3,987.93
(= $7,613.30 + $761.33 − $4,386.70).

December 31, 2009
Lease Receivable (= .10 x $3,987.93)......................... 398.77
    Interest Revenue..   398.77

Assets	=	Liabilities	+	Shareholders' Equity	(Class.)
+398.77				+398.77	IncSt → RE

To record interest revenue for 2009. Interest revenue is slightly less than .10 x $3,987.93 due to rounding of present value factors. The carrying value of the receivable is now $4,386.70 (= $3,987.93 + $398.77).

10.27 c. continued.

January 1, 2010
Cash.. 4,386.70
   Lease Receivable.. 4,386.70

Assets	=	Liabilities	+	Shareholders' Equity	(Class.)
+4,386.70					
−4,386.70					

To record cash received for 2010.

10.28 (Baldwin Products; preparing lessee's journal entries for an operating lease and a capital lease.)

a. This lease does not satisfy any of the criteria for a capital lease, so it is an operating lease. The leased asset reverts to the lessor at the end of the lease period. The life of the lease (3 years) is less than 75% of the expected useful life of the leased asset (5 years). The present value of the lease payments of $25,771 (= $10,000 x 2.57710) is less than 90% of the fair value of the leased asset of $30,000.

b. **December 31, of Each Year**
Rent Expense.. 10,000
   Cash... 10,000

Assets	=	Liabilities	+	Shareholders' Equity	(Class.)
−10,000				−10,000	IncSt → RE

To record annual rent expense and cash payment.

c. **January 2, 2008**
Leased Asset.. 25,771
   Lease Liability.. 25,771

Assets	=	Liabilities	+	Shareholders' Equity	(Class.)
+25,771		+25,771			

To record capital lease.

10.28 c. continued.

December 31, 2008

Interest Expense (= .08 x $25,771)...............................	2,062
Lease Liability..	7,938
Cash...	10,000

Assets	=	Liabilities	+	Shareholders' Equity	(Class.)
–10,000		–7,938		–2,062	IncSt → RE

To record interest expense and cash payment for 2008. The carrying value of the lease liability is now $17,833 (= $25,771 – $7,938).

Depreciation Expense or Work-in-Process Inventory ($25,771/3)...	8,590
Accumulated Depreciation.................................	8,590

Assets	=	Liabilities	+	Shareholders' Equity	(Class.)
–8,590				–8,590	IncSt → RE

To record depreciation expense for 2008.

December 31, 2009

Interest Expense (= .08 x $17,833)............................	1,427
Lease Liability..	8,573
Cash...	10,000

Assets	=	Liabilities	+	Shareholders' Equity	(Class.)
–10,000		–8,573		–1,427	IncSt → RE

To record interest expense and cash payment for 2009. The carrying value of the lease liability is now $9,260 (= $17,833 – $8,573).

Depreciation Expense or Work-in-Process Inventory...	8,590
Accumulated Depreciation.................................	8,590

Assets	=	Liabilities	+	Shareholders' Equity	(Class.)
–8,590				–8,590	IncSt → RE

To record depreciation expense for 2009.

10.28 c. continued.

December 31, 2010
Interest Expense (= .08 x $9,260)... 740
Lease Liability.. 9,260
   Cash... 10,000

Assets	=Liabilities	+	Shareholders' Equity	(Class.)
–10,000	–9,260		–740	IncSt → RE

To record interest expense and cash payment for 2010. Interest expense does not precisely equal .08 x $9,260 due to rounding. Carrying value of the liability is now zero.

Depreciation Expense or Work-in-Process
  Inventory 8,591
    Accumulated Depreciation.. 8,591

Assets	=Liabilities	+	Shareholders' Equity	(Class.)
–8,591			–8,591	IncSt → RE

To record depreciation expense for 2010.

  d. Operating Lease Method: Rent Expense (= $10,000 x 3) ..... $ 30,000
     Capital Lease Method: Interest Expense (= $2,062 +
      $1,427 + $740)... $ 4,229
     Depreciation [= ($8,590 x 2) + $8,591]...................................... 25,771
     Total Expenses.. $ 30,000

10.29 (Aggarwal Corporation; accounting for long-term bonds.)

  a. **Interest Expense**
    First Six Months: .05 x $301,512 = $15,076.
    Second Six Months: .05($301,512 + $15,076) = $15,829.
    Carrying value of bonds on December 31, 2008: $301,512 + $15,076 + $15,829 = $332,417.

10.29 continued.

b. **Carrying Value of Bonds on December 31, 2007**
Interest:
$35,000 × 8.11090 = $ 283,882   (Table 4, 10 periods and 4%)
Principal:
$1,000,000 × .67556 = $675,560   (Table 2, 10 periods and 4%)
Total.............................. $ 959,442

Carrying Value of Bonds, December 31, 2007........................	$ 959,442
Add Interest Expense for 2008	x
Subtract Coupon Payments during 2008	(70,000)
Carrying Value of Bonds, December 31, 2008........................	$ 966,336

Interest expense for 2008 is $76,894.

c. **Carrying Value of Bonds on July 1, 2008**

Carrying Value of Bonds, December 31, 2007......................	$ 1,305,832
Plus Interest Expense for First Six Months of 2008: .03 × $1,305,832...	39,175
Subtract Coupon Payment during First Six Months of 2008	(45,000)
Carrying Value of Bonds, July 1, 2008...................................	$ 1,300,007
Carrying Value of One-Half of Bonds.....................................	$ 650,004

July 1, 2008

Bonds Payable..	650,004	
Cash..		526,720
Gain on Bonds Retirement		123,284

Assets	=	Liabilities	+	Shareholders' Equity	(Class.)
–526,720		–650,004		+123,284	IncSt → RE

d. **Interest Expense for Second Six Months**
.03 × $650,004 = $19,500.

10.30 (Time Warner, Inc.; accounting for zero-coupon debt; see *The Wall Street Journal* for December 8, 1992.)

a. $483 million = $1,550 million/3.20714; see table 1, 6% column, 20-period row. Alternatively, $483 million = $1,550 × .31180; see table 2, 6% column, 20-period row.

10.30 continued.

b. $5.82\% = (\$1,550/\$500)^{1/20} - 1 = 3.10^{1/20} - 1$. That is, for each dollar of the initial issue proceeds (of the $500 million), Time Warner must pay $3.10 (= $1,550/$500) at maturity of the notes. You can find the periodic interest rate to make $1.00 grow to $3.10 in 20 periods by trial and error or by using the exponential function on your computer or calculator. Note that you can state an equation to solve, as follows:

$$(1 + r)^{20} = 3.10; \text{ solve for } r.$$

You can see from Table 1 that 5.82% is approximately correct.

c. $28 million = .07 × $400 million.

d. $101.4 million. Ask, first, what must the carrying value of the notes be at the end of 2026. Then, compute interest for the year on that amount. The carrying value of the notes at the end of 2026 must be $1,448.6 (= $1,550/1.07) million. Interest for one year at 7% on $1,448.6 million is $101.4 (= .07 × $1,448.6 = $1,550.0 − $1,448.6) million. You can check this approach to finding the answer by noting that:

$$\$1,448.6 \times 1.07 = \$1,550.0.$$

e. The carrying value of the $700 million face value of zero coupon bonds is $391 million (= $700 × .55839; see table 2, 6% column and 10-period row). The market value of the $700 million face value of zero coupon bonds is $324 million (= $700 × .46319; see table 2, 8% column and 10-period row). The journal entry to record the repurchase and retirement of the bonds is:

December 31, 2017
Bonds Payable.. 391
   Cash... 324
   Gain on Bonds Retirement.. 67

Assets	=	Liabilities	+	Shareholders' Equity	(Class.)
−324		−391		+67	IncSt → RE

To record the repurchase and retirement of $700 million face value bonds.

10.31 (Understanding and using bond tables.)

a. The coupon rate on these bonds of 8% compounded semiannually equals the historical market interest rate of 8% compounded semiannually. The initial issue price therefore equals the face value. The carrying value increases each period for interest expense equal to 4% of the carrying value of the liability at the beginning of the period and decreases for 4% of the face value of the liability. Because the carrying value equals the face value throughout the life of the bonds, the carrying value remains at face value.

b. The coupon rate on these bonds is 8% compounded semiannually. When the historical market interest rate exceeds the coupon rate, the bonds will have a carrying value greater than face value. When the historical market interest rate is less than the coupon rate, the bonds will have a carrying value less than face value.

c. Firms amortize any initial issue premium as a reduction in interest expense and a reduction in the bond liability over the life of the bonds. Firms amortize any initial issue discount as an increase in interest expense and an increase in the bond liability over the life of the bonds.

d. $1,000,000 x 111.7278% = $1,117,278. Note that the rows indicate *years* to maturity, not the total number of periods.

e. $1,000,000 x 110.6775% = $1,106,775.

f.
Cash Payment for Interest...	$ 80,000
Decrease in Carrying Value of Liability during 2013: $1,000,000 x (110.6775% − 110.4205%).............................	(2,570)
Interest Expense...	$ 77,430
Interest Expense, First Six Months: .035 x ($1,000,000 x 110.6775%)...	$ 38,737
Interest Expense, Second Six Months: .035 x ($1,000,000 x 110.5512%)...	38,693
Interest Expense...	$ 77,430

10.31 continued.

g.
Carrying Value of Liability: $1,000,000 × 107.1062%		$ 1,071,062
Market Value of Liability: $1,000,000 × 101.3711%		1,013,711
Unrealized Gain Increasing Retained Earnings		$ 57,351

h. Interest expense for first six months is $39,535 (= .078/2 × $1,013,711). The carrying value of the liability at the end of the first six months before recognizing any unrealized gain or loss is $1,013,246 (= $1,013,711 + $39,535 − $40,000) = $1,000,000 × 101.3246%.

Unrealized Gain:
Carrying Value before Unrealized Gain	$ 1,013,246
Market Value on June 30, 2023: $1,000,000 × 98.0548%	980,548
Unrealized Gain	$ 32,698

i. Interest expense for the second six months is $40,692 (= .083/2 × $980,548). The carrying value of the liability at the end of the second six months before recognizing any unrealized gain or loss is $981,240 (= $980,548 + $40,692 − $40,000) = $1,000,000 × 98.1240%.

Unrealized Gain:
Carrying Value before Unrealized Gain	$ 981,240
Market Value on December 31, 2023: $1,000,000 × 93.920%	939,200
Unrealized Gain	$ 42,040

10.32 (Lowe's; interpreting disclosures of long-term debt.)

a. The likely explanation is that Lowe's issued these notes and bonds at face value and therefore has no discount or premium to amortize. Another possible explanation is that Lowe's issued these bonds for such a small discount or premium that the amount of any discount or premium disappears when rounding to the nearest million.

10.32 continued.

b.

Issue Date	Face Value	Term to Maturity at Issue Date	Issue Price	Coupon Interest Rate	Historical Market Interest Rate
October 2005	$500 Million	10 Years	$496 Million	5%	5.1%[a]
October 2005	$500 Million	30 Years	$492 Million	5.5%	5.61%[b]
October 2006	$550 Million	10 Years	$545.6 Million	5.4%	5.48%[c]
October 2006	$450 Million	30 Years	$445.6 Million	5.8%	5.87%[d]

[a]= PV(.0255,20,12500000, 500000000,0). 5.1% = 2.55% x 2.
[b]= PV(.02805,60,13750000,500000000,0). 5.61% = 2.805% x 2.
[c]= PV(.0274,20,14850000,550000000,0). 5.48% = 2.74% x 2
[d]= PV(.02935,60,13050000,450000000,0). 5.87% = 2.935% x 2.

c. Lowe's has amortized some of the initial issue discount, so that the carrying value on February 2, 2007 exceeds the issue price by the amount of discount amortized. The initial discounts are so small because the historical market interest rates are only slightly higher than the coupon rates.

d. Holders of the convertible notes receive a portion of their return in the value of the option to convert the notes into common stock. Thus, even though they bear more risk than more senior debt and require a higher return to compensate for the higher risk, they do not demand that return to be in the form of periodic cash payments.

e. The weighted average historical market interest rate is higher than the weighted average current market interest rate at each date because the carrying, or book, value is less than the current fair value.

f. Excess of Fair Value over Carrying Value on February 2, 2007:
$4,301 − $4,013.. $ 288
Excess of Fair Value over Carrying Value on February 3, 2006:
$3,578 − $3,107.. 471
Unrealized Loss for Year Ended February 2, 2007....................... $ 183

10.33 (IBM and Adair Corporation; accounting for lease by lessor and lessee.)

a. **January 1, 2008**

Cash.. 10,000
    Note Payable.. 10,000

Assets	=	Liabilities	+	Shareholders' Equity	(Class.)
+10,000		+10,000			

Computer.. 10,000
    Cash... 10,000

Assets	=	Liabilities	+	Shareholders' Equity	(Class.)
+10,000					
–10,000					

December 31, 2008

Depreciation Expense.. 3,333
    Accumulated Depreciation.. 3,333

Assets	=	Liabilities	+	Shareholders' Equity	(Class.)
–3,333				–3,333	IncSt → RE

Interest Expense (.08 x $10,000)....................................... 800
Note Payable (Plug)... 3,080
    Cash ($10,000/2.57710).. 3,880

Assets	=	Liabilities	+	Shareholders' Equity	(Class.)
–3,880		–3,080		–800	IncSt → RE

December 31, 2009

Depreciation Expense.. 3,333
    Accumulated Depreciation.. 3,333

Assets	=	Liabilities	+	Shareholders' Equity	(Class.)
–3,333				–3,333	IncSt → RE

10.33 a. continued.

Interest Expense [.08 × ($10,000 − $3,080)]	554	
Note Payable (Plug)	3,326	
Cash		3,880

Assets	=	Liabilities	+	Shareholders' Equity	(Class.)
−3,880		−3,326		−554	IncSt → RE

b. **January 1, 2008**
No entry.

December 31, 2008

Rent Expense	3,810	
Cash		3,810

Assets	=	Liabilities	+	Shareholders' Equity	(Class.)
−3,810				−3,810	IncSt → RE

December 31, 2009

Rent Expense	3,810	
Cash		3,810

Assets	=	Liabilities	+	Shareholders' Equity	(Class.)
−3,810				−3,810	IncSt → RE

c. **January 1, 2008**

Leased Asset	10,000	
Lease Liability		10,000

Assets	=	Liabilities	+	Shareholders' Equity	(Class.)
+10,000		+10,000			

December 31, 2008

Depreciation Expense	3,333	
Accumulated Depreciation		3,333

Assets	=	Liabilities	+	Shareholders' Equity	(Class.)
−3,333				−3,333	IncSt → RE

Solutions

10.33 c. continued.

Interest Expense (.07 × $10,000) 700
Lease Liability (Plug) 3,110
    Cash ($10,000/2.62432) 3,810

Assets	=	Liabilities	+	Shareholders' Equity	(Class.)
−3,810		−3,110		−700	IncSt → RE

December 31, 2009
Depreciation Expense 3,333
    Accumulated Depreciation 3,333

Assets	=	Liabilities	+	Shareholders' Equity	(Class.)
−3,333				−3,333	IncSt → RE

Interest Expense [.07 × ($10,000 − $3,110)] 482
Lease Liability (Plug) 3,328
    Cash 3,810

Assets	=	Liabilities	+	Shareholders' Equity	(Class.)
−3,810		−3,328		−482	IncSt → RE

d. **January 1, 2008**
Cash 10,000
    Sales Revenue 10,000

Assets	=	Liabilities	+	Shareholders' Equity	(Class.)
+10,000				+10,000	IncSt → RE

Cost of Goods Sold 6,000
    Inventory 6,000

Assets	=	Liabilities	+	Shareholders' Equity	(Class.)
−6,000				−6,000	IncSt → RE

December 31, 2008 and 2009
No entries necessary.

10.33 continued.

e. **January 1, 2008**
Computer Equipment 6,000
  Inventory 6,000

Assets	=	Liabilities	+	Shareholders' Equity	(Class.)
+6,000					
−6,000					

December 31, 2008
Depreciation Expense 2,000
  Accumulated Depreciation 2,000

Assets	=	Liabilities	+	Shareholders' Equity	(Class.)
−2,000				−2,000	IncSt → RE

Cash 3,810
  Rent Revenue 3,810

Assets	=	Liabilities	+	Shareholders' Equity	(Class.)
+3,810				+3,810	IncSt → RE

December 31, 2009
Depreciation Expense 2,000
  Accumulated Depreciation 2,000

Assets	=	Liabilities	+	Shareholders' Equity	(Class.)
−2,000				−2,000	IncSt → RE

Cash 3,810
  Rent Revenue 3,810

Assets	=	Liabilities	+	Shareholders' Equity	(Class.)
+3,810				+3,810	IncSt → RE

10.33 continued.

f. **January 1, 2008**

Lease Receivable 10,000
    Sales Revenue   10,000

Assets	=	Liabilities	+	Shareholders' Equity	(Class.)
+10,000				+10,000	IncSt → RE

Cost of Goods Sold 6,000
    Inventory   6,000

Assets	=	Liabilities	+	Shareholders' Equity	(Class.)
–6,000				–6,000	IncSt → RE

December 31, 2008

Cash 3,810
    Interest Revenue (see Part c.)   700
    Lease Receivable   3,110

Assets	=	Liabilities	+	Shareholders' Equity	(Class.)
+3,810				+700	IncSt → RE
–3,110					

December 31, 2009

Cash 3,810
    Interest Revenue (see Part c.)   482
    Lease Receivable   3,328

Assets	=	Liabilities	+	Shareholders' Equity	(Class.)
+3,810				+482	IncSt → RE
–3,328					

10.33 continued.

	g. Lessee **Borrow and Purchase**	2008	2009	2010	Total
	Depreciation Expense.....	$ 3,333	$ 3,333	$ 3,334	$ 10,000
	Interest Expense.............	800	554	286	1,640
		$ 4,133	$ 3,887	$ 3,620	$ 11,640
	Operating Lease				
	Rent Expense.................	$ 3,810	$ 3,810	$ 3,810	$ 11,430
	Capital Lease				
	Depreciation Expense.....	$ 3,333	$ 3,333	$ 3,334	$ 10,000
	Interest Expense.............	700	482	248	1,430
		$ 4,033	$ 3,815	$ 3,582	$ 11,430

	h. Lessor **Sale**	2008	2009	2010	Total
	Sales Revenue.................	$10,000	$ --	$ --	$ 10,000
	Cost of Goods Sold..........	(6,000)	--	--	(6,000)
		$ 4,000	$ --	$ --	$ 4,000
	Operating Lease				
	Rent Revenue.................	$ 3,810	$ 3,810	$ 3,810	$ 11,430
	Depreciation Expense.....	(2,000)	(2,000)	(2,000)	(6,000)
		$ 1,810	$ 1,810	$ 1,810	$ 5,430
	Capital Lease				
	Sales Revenue.................	$10,000	$ --	$ --	$ 10,000
	Cost of Goods Sold..........	(6,000)	--	--	(6,000)
	Interest Revenue.............	700	482	248	1,430
		$ 4,700	$ 482	$ 248	$ 5,430

10.34 (Carom Sports Collectibles Shop; comparison of borrow/buy with operating and capital leases.)

a. $100,000/3.79079 = $26,379.725 = $26,380.

Carom Sports Collectibles Shop Amortization Schedule

Year	Start of Year Balance	Interest (10%)	Payment	Reduction	End of Year Balance
1	$100,000	$10,000	$26,380	$16,380	$83,620
2	83,620	8,362	26,380	18,018	65,602
3	65,602	6,560	26,380	19,820	45,782
4	45,782	4,578	26,380	21,802	23,980
5	23,980	2,398	26,380	23,982	(2)

10.34 continued.

    b. **Plan (1):**
        Asset—Cash.
        Asset—Computer System.
        Asset Contra—Accumulated Depreciation on Computer System.
        Liability—Bonds Payable and Interest Payable.

       Plan (2): Operating Lease Method: None.

       Plan (2): Capital Lease Method
        Asset—Cash.
        Asset—Leased Computer System.
        Asset Contra—Accumulated Depreciation.
        Liability—Lease Liability.

    c. $150,000 = $100,000 Depreciation + (.10 x $100,000 x 5) Interest.

    d. (1) Operating Lease Method: $131,900 = $26,380 x 5.
       (2) Capital Lease Method: $131,900.

    e. The method of accounting for a lease affects only the timing of expenses, not their total. Expenses under Plan (1) are larger because the firm borrows $100,000 for the entire 5 years, whereas under Plan (2) it pays the loan with part of each lease payment; with smaller average borrowing, interest expense is smaller.

    f. (1) $30,000 = $20,000 depreciation + $10,000 bond interest.
       (2) Operating Lease Method: $26,380 rent.
           Capital Lease Method: $30,000 = $20,000 depreciation +
                                       $10,000 lease interest.

    g. (1) $30,000.
       (2) Operating Lease Method: $26,380 rent.
           Capital Lease Method: $22,400 (or $22,398) = $20,000
                                       depreciation + $2,400 (or $2,398)
                                       interest.

10.34 g. continued.

CAROM SPORTS COLLECTIBLES SHOP SUMMARY
(Not Required)

	2008	2009	2010	2011	2012	Total
Plan 1						
Depreciation Expense	$20,000	$20,000	$20,000	$20,000	$20,000	$100,000
Interest Expense	10,000	10,000	10,000	10,000	10,000	50,000
Total	$30,000	$30,000	$30,000	$30,000	$30,000	$150,000
Plan 2 (Operating)						
Lease Expense	$26,380	$26,380	$26,380	$26,380	$26,380	$131,900
Plan 2 (Financing)						
Depreciation Expense	$20,000	$20,000	$20,000	$20,000	$20,000	$100,000
Interest Expense	10,000	8,362	6,560	4,578	2,400*	31,900
Total	$30,000	$28,362	$26,560	$24,578	$22,400	$131,900

*Plug to correct for rounding. By computation, this number is $2,398 = [$26,380 − ($26,380/1.10)].

10.35 (Northern Airlines; financial statement effects of capital and operating leases.) (Amounts in Millions)

a.
Capital Lease Liability, December 31, 2007	$ 1,088
Plus Interest Expense (Plug)	102
Plus New Capital Leases Signed[a]	0
Less Cash Payment on Capital Leases	(263)
Capital Lease Liability, December 31, 2008	$ 927

[a] A comparison of the commitments under capital leases on December 31, 2007 and December 31, 2008 indicates that Northern Airlines did not sign any new capital leases during 2008.

b. $102/$1,088 = 9.375%.

c.
Capitalized Leased Asset, December 31, 2007	$ 1,019
Plus New Capital Leases Signed[a]	0
Less Depreciation on Capital Leases (Plug)	(154)
Capital Leased Asset, December 31, 2008	$ 865

[a] See Footnote a to Part a. above.

10.35 continued.

d. **December 31, 2008**
Interest Expense... 102
Lease Liability.. 161
    Cash.. 263

Assets	=	Liabilities	+	Shareholders' Equity	(Class.)
−263		−161		−102	IncSt → RE

To record interest expense on capital leases, the cash payment, and decrease in the capital lease liability for the difference.

December 31, 2008
Depreciation Expense 154
    Accumulated Depreciation..................................... 154

Assets	=	Liabilities	+	Shareholders' Equity	(Class.)
−154				−154	IncSt → RE

To recognize depreciation expense on capitalized leased asset for 2008.

e. **December 31, 2008**
Rent Expense.. 1,065
    Cash.. 1,065

Assets	=	Liabilities	+	Shareholders' Equity	(Class.)
−1,065				−1,065	IncSt → RE

To recognize rent expense on operating leases for 2008.

10.35 continued.

f.   **Present Value of Operating Lease Commitment on December 31, 2007**

Year	Payments	Present Value Factor at 10.0%	Present Value
2008	$ 1,065	.90909	$ 968
2009	$ 1,039	.82645	859
2010	$ 973	.75131	731
2011	$ 872	.68301	596
2012	$ 815	.62092	506
After 2012	$ 7,453[a]	5.81723[b] x .62092[c]	2,944
Total			$ 6,604

[a]Assume that the firm pays the $7,453 at the rate of $815 a year for 9.145 (= $7,453/$815) periods at 10%.

[b]Factor for the present value of an annuity of $815 million for 9.145 periods at 10%.

[c]Factor for the present value of $1 for five periods at 10%.

Present Value of Operating Lease Commitment on December 31, 2008

Year	Payments	Present Value Factor at 10.0%	Present Value
2009	$ 1,098	.90909	$ 998
2010	$ 1,032	.82645	853
2011	$ 929	.75131	698
2012	$ 860	.68301	587
2013	$ 855	.62092	531
After 2013	$ 6,710[a]	5.26685[b] x .62092[c]	2,796
Total			$ 6,463

[a]Assume that the firm pays the $6,710 at the rate of $855 a period for 7.848 (= $6,710/$855) periods.

[b]Factor for the present value of an annuity of $855 million for 7.848 periods at 10%.

[c]Factor for the present value of $1 for five periods at 10%.

10.35 continued.

- g. **Long-Term Debt Ratio Based on Reported Amounts:**
  December 31, 2007: $13,456/$29,495 = 45.6%
  December 31, 2008: $12,041/$29,145 = 41.3%

- h. **Long-Term Debt Ratio Including Capitalization of Operating Leases:**
  December 31, 2007: ($13,456 + $6,604 − $968)/($29,495 + $6,604) = 52.9%
  December 31, 2008: ($12,041 + $6,463 − $998)/($29,145 + $6,463) = 49.2%

10.36 (FedUp Corporation; financial statement effects of capital and operating leases.) (Amounts in Millions)

- a.
Capital Lease Liability, May 31, 2007	$ 401
Plus Interest Expense: .05 × $401	20
Plus New Capital Leases Signed (Plug)	10
Less Cash Payment on Capital Leases	(121)
Capital Lease Liability, December 31, 2008	$ 310

- b.
Capital Leased Asset, May 31, 2007	$ 273
Plus New Capital Leases Signed (from Part a. above)	10
Less Depreciation on Capital Leases (Plug)	(133)
Capitalized Leased Asset, December 31, 2008	$ 150

- c. **During Fiscal 2008**

Capitalized Leased Asset	10	
Lease Liability		10

Assets	=	Liabilities	+	Shareholders' Equity	(Class.)
+10		+10			

  To record new capital leases signed.

  May 31, 2008

Interest Expense	20	
Lease Liability	101	
Cash		121

Assets	=	Liabilities	+	Shareholders' Equity	(Class.)
−121		−101		−20	IncSt → RE

  To record interest expense on capital leases, the cash payment, and decrease in the capital lease liability for the difference.

10.36 c. continued.

May 31, 2008
Depreciation Expense 133
    Accumulated Depreciation 133

Assets	=	Liabilities	+	Shareholders' Equity	(Class.)
−133				−133	IncSt → RE

To recognize depreciation expense on capitalized leased asset for 2008.

d. **May 31, 2008**
Rent Expense 1,646
    Cash 1,646

Assets	=	Liabilities	+	Shareholders' Equity	(Class.)
−1,646				−1,646	IncSt → RE

To recognize rent expense on operating leases for 2008.

e. **Present Value of Operating Lease Commitment on May 31, 2007**

Year	Payments	Present Value Factor at 5%	Present Value
2008	$ 1,646	.95238	$ 1,568
2009	$ 1,518	.90703	1,377
2010	$ 1,356	.86384	1,171
2011	$ 1,191	.82270	980
2012	$ 1,045	.78353	819
After 2012	$ 7,249[a]	5.74262[b] x .78353[c]	4,701
Total			$ 10,616

[a]Assume that the firm pays the $7,249 at the rate of $1,045 per period for 6.937 (= $7,249/$1,045) periods.

[b]Factor for the present value of an annuity of $1,045 million for 6.937 periods at 5%.

[c]Factor for the present value of $1 for five periods at 5%.

10.36 e. continued.

Present Value of Operating Lease Commitment on May 31, 2008

Year	Payments	Present Value Factor at 5%	Present Value
2009	$ 1,672	.95238	$ 1,592
2010	$ 1,478	.90703	1,341
2011	$ 1,290	.86384	1,114
2012	$ 1,120	.82270	921
2013	$ 984	.78353	771
After 2013	$ 6,780[a]	5.70988[b] x .78353[bc]	4,402
Total			$ 10,141

[a] Assume that the firm pays the $6,780 at the rate of $984 per period for 6.890 (= $6,780/$984) periods.

[b] Factor for the present value of an annuity of $984 million for 6.890 periods at 5%.

[c] Factor for the present value of $1 for five periods at 5%.

f. **Long-Term Debt Ratio Based on Reported Amounts:**
May 31, 2007: $2,427/$20,404 = 11.9%
May 31, 2008: $1,592/$22,690 = 7.0%

Debt-Equity Ratio:
May 31, 2007: $2,427/$9,588 = 25.3%
May 31, 2008: $1,592/$11,511 = 13.8%

g. **Long-Term Debt Ratio Including Capitalization of Operation Leases:**
May 31, 2007: ($2,427 + $10,616 − $1,568)/($20,404 + $10,616) = 37.0%
May 31, 2008: ($1,592 + $10,141 − $1,592)/($22,690 + $10,141) = 30.9%

10.37 (GSB Corporation; measuring interest expense.)

The Carrying value of a liability changes during a period as follows:

Beginning Balance + Interest Expense − Cash Payment = Ending Balance

Substituting the known information:
  BB + .05BB − $4,400 = $110,000

Solving for BB:
  1.05BB = $114,400
    BB = $108,952

Thus, interest expense for this last six month period equals $5,447.62 (= .05 x $108,952).

CHAPTER 11

LIABILITIES: OFF-BALANCE-SHEET FINANCING, RETIREMENT BENEFITS, AND INCOME TAXES

Questions, Exercises, and Problems: Answers and Solutions

11.1 See the text or the glossary at the end of the book.

11.2 Using an executory contract to achieve off-balance-sheet financing results in the recognition of neither an asset (for example, leased assets) nor a liability (for example, lease liability) on the balance sheet. Using an asset sale with recourse may result in either a sale (an asset such as accounts receivable decreases and cash increases) or a collateralized loan (cash increases and a liability increases), depending on which entity enjoys the benefits and bears the risk of the asset sold.

11.3 The financial components approach records the benefits to each entity as an asset and the obligations of each entity as a liability. Although accountants must make a judgment about whether the seller of an asset retains most of the benefits and risks (the asset and the related financing appear on the balance sheet) or whether the purchaser obtains most of the benefits and risks (the seller removes the asset and does not record a liability on the balance sheet), each entity records assets and liabilities for any benefits obtained and risks incurred. Absent the financial components approach, the recording would reflect an all-or-nothing approach.

11.4 All executory contracts do not carry the same amounts of risk. A firm might back out of a purchase commitment more easily than an employment contract or lease contract. Furthermore, the expected benefits might carry different degrees of risk. An employee might back out of an employment contract more easily than a lessor could demand return of a leased asset prior to the end of the lease. Users of the financial statements might assume that all rights and obligations under executory contracts are equally certain. A contrary view argues that assets and liabilities now recognized on the balance sheet (for example, cash, inventory, equipment, goodwill) carry different degrees of uncertainty with respect to expected benefits and risks. Recognizing the benefits and obligations related to executory contracts provides information that firms now report only in the notes to the financial statements. Recording them in the balance sheet increases their visibility.

11.5 The use of a special purpose entity enhances the ability of a firm to demonstrate that it has transferred control of the receivables to the purchaser. Whether the transferor has in fact transferred control depends on its relation to the special purpose entity and its rights and obligations related to the receivables. The special purpose entity at least permits separation of the receivables from the transferring entity.

11.6 Accrual accounting recognizes a cost as an expense in the period when a firm uses, or consumes, goods and services. Employees provide labor services each period in return for both current compensation (salary, health care benefits) and compensation deferred until retirement (pensions, health care benefits). The absence of deferred compensation arrangements would presumably lead employees to demand higher current compensation to permit them to fund their own retirement plans. Thus, firms must recognize an expense during the current period for both compensation paid and the present value of deferred compensation.

11.7 Laws require firms to contribute funds to an independent trustee to manage on behalf of employees. The employer cannot use these funds for its general corporate purposes.

11.8 The amounts that pension plans pay to retirees derive from the employer's contributions plus earnings from investments. Earnings from pension investments appear on the books of the pension plan and theoretically fund the increase in the pension obligation that results from the passage of time. Although expected earnings from investments and the interest cost on the pension obligation flow through net pension expense on the employer's books, these amounts in theory should perfectly offset and leave pension expense equal to the employer's cash contribution to the pension plan.

11.9 Firms typically have multiple pension plans for their different groups of employees (for example, wage earners versus corporate officers, domestic employees versus non-domestic employees). Some plans have assets that exceed liabilities and other plans have liabilities that exceed assets. Netting all pension plans results in loss of information about the mix of overfunded and underfunded plans.

11.10 GAAP allows firms to defer and amortize changes in prior service costs and actuarial gains and losses that originate during a period. The rationale is that firms should take a long-term view of its pension plan, permitting firms to average out short-term changes in prior service costs and actuarial gains and losses over longer periods. These items affect other comprehensive income in the period when they originate. When firms amortize these items and include the amortization as an element of net pension expense, the firms remove the amount originally recognized in other comprehensive income.

11.11 GAAP requires firms to increase pension expense for the increase in the pension obligation that results from the passage of time (that is, the interest cost). Firms must generate earnings from investments sufficient to fund this increase in present value. Earnings from pension investments offset the interest cost, explaining why GAAP requires a subtraction for earnings from investments.

11.12 Subtracting the expected instead of the actual return on investments smoothes out variations between expected and actual rates of return and enhances a long-term viewpoint appropriate for pension benefits.

11.13 Income tax expense equals income taxes payable currently plus (minus) the income taxes the firm expects to pay (save) in the future when revenues and expenses that appear in book income now appear in tax returns later.

11.14 This statement is incorrect. In order for deferred taxes to be a loan, there must be a receipt of cash or other goods or services at the inception of the loan and a disbursement of cash or other goods or services at the maturity date. The entries for a deferred tax liability are as follows:

When Timing Differences Originate:

Income Tax Expense.. X
    Deferred Tax Liability.. X

Assets	=	Liabilities	+	Shareholders' Equity	(Class.)
		+X		–X	IncSt → RE

When Timing Differences Reverse:

Deferred Tax Liability... X
    Income Tax Expense.. X

Assets	=	Liabilities	+	Shareholders' Equity	(Class.)
		–X		+X	IncSt → RE

There are no cash or other asset flows involved and, therefore, no loan.

    Another approach is to raise the question: How would cash flows have differed if a firm used the same methods of accounting for book as it used for tax? The response is that cash flows would have been the same even though deferred income taxes would have been eliminated. Thus, recognizing or not recognizing deferred taxes has no incremental effect on cash or other asset flows and, therefore, cannot represent a loan.

11.15 Deferred tax assets (liabilities) arise when a firm recognizes revenue (expense) earlier for tax purposes than book purposes or expenses (revenues) later for tax purposes than for book purposes. Deferred tax assets (liabilities) provide for lower (higher) taxable income in the future relative to book income and, therefore, future tax savings (costs).

11.16 When firms choose accounting methods that result in recognizing income earlier for book purposes than for tax purposes, they delay the payment of taxes. Yet, income tax expense does not reflect the benefit of the delayed cash outflow in that period because firms must include the delayed payment amount in both income tax expense and a deferred income tax liability. In the later period when income for tax purposes exceeds income for book purposes, firms reduce income tax expense and the deferred income tax liability for the additional taxes paid, thereby increasing net income. When firms choose accounting methods that result in recognizing income earlier for tax purposes than for book purposes, they accelerate the payment of taxes. Yet, income tax expense does not reflect the cost of the accelerated cash outflow in that period because firms must include the accelerated payment amount as a reduction in income tax expense and a deferred income tax asset. In the later period when income for book purposes exceeds income for tax purposes, firms increase income tax expense and reduce the deferred income tax asset for the taxes paid previously, thereby decreasing net income.

11.17 Analysts often forecast earnings and need to make some assumption about a firm's average, or effective, tax rate in future periods. The information in the tax reconciliation helps the analysts in judging whether reconciling items in recent years will likely continue or not.

11.18 Information on individual deferred tax assets and deferred tax liabilities provide information about a firm's operating, investing, and financing activities related to those individual items. For example, a continual increase in deferred tax liabilities for depreciation timing differences suggests a continuing increase in expenditures on depreciable assets. A decrease in deferred tax assets for warranties might suggest a reduction in sale of warranted products.

11.19 (Cypres Appliance Store; using accounts receivable to achieve off-balance-sheet financing.)

a. (1) **January 2, 2008**
Cash.. 92,593
    Bank Loan Payable... 92,593

Assets	=	Liabilities	+	Shareholders' Equity	(Class.)
+92,593		+92,593			

To record bank loan.

December 31, 2008
Cash.. 100,000
    Accounts Receivable... 100,000

Assets	=	Liabilities	+	Shareholders' Equity	(Class.)
+100,000					
–100,000					

To record collections from customers.

Interest Expense (= .08 x $92,593)............... 7,407
Bank Loan Payable.. 92,593
    Cash.. 100,000

Assets	=	Liabilities	+	Shareholders' Equity	(Class.)
–100,000		–92,593		–7,407	IncSt → RE

To record interest expense on loan for 2008 and repayment of the loan.

(2) Cash.. 92,593
Loss from Sale of Accounts Receivable............. 7,407
    Accounts Receivable... 100,000

Assets	=	Liabilities	+	Shareholders' Equity	(Class.)
+92,593				–7,407	IncSt → RE
–100,000					

To record sale of accounts receivable; an alternative title for the loss account is interest expense.

11.19 continued.

b. Both transactions result in an expense of $7,407 for 2008 for this financing. Both transactions result in an immediate increase in cash. Liabilities increase for the collateralized loan, whereas an asset decreases for the sale.

c. Cypres Appliance Store must attempt to shift credit and interest rate risk to the bank. The bank should have no rights to demand additional receivables if interest rates increase or uncollectible accounts appear. Likewise, Cypres Appliance Store should have no rights to buy back the accounts receivable if interest rates decline. The bank of course will not both lend on the receivables and purchase the receivables at the same price because it incurs different amounts of risk in each case.

11.20 (P. J. Lorimar Company; using inventory to achieve off-balance-sheet financing.)

a. (i) **January 2, 2008**
Cash... 300,000
　Bank Loan Payable.. 300,000

Assets	= Liabilities	+	Shareholders' Equity	(Class.)
+300,000	+300,000			

To record bank loan.

December 31, 2008
Interest Expense (= .1 × $300,000)................... 30,000
　Bank Loan Payable.. 30,000

Assets	= Liabilities	+	Shareholders' Equity	(Class.)
	+30,000		–30,000	IncSt → RE

To record interest expense for 2008.

December 31, 2009
Cash... 363,000
　Sales Revenue... 363,000

Assets	= Liabilities	+	Shareholders' Equity	(Class.)
+363,000			+363,000	IncSt → RE

To record sale of tobacco inventory.

11.20 a. continued.

Cost of Goods Sold.. 200,000
    Inventory.. 200,000

Assets	=	Liabilities	+	Shareholders' Equity	(Class.)
–200,000				–200,000	IncSt → RE

To record cost of tobacco inventory sold.

Interest Expense (= .10 x $330,000)................. 33,000
Bank Loan Payable 330,000
    Cash 363,000

Assets	=	Liabilities	+	Shareholders' Equity	(Class.)
–363,000		–330,000		–33,000	IncSt → RE

To record interest expense for 2009 and repayment of loan.

(ii) **January 2, 2008**
Cash... 300,000
    Sales Revenue 300,000

Assets	=	Liabilities	+	Shareholders' Equity	(Class.)
+300,000				+300,000	IncSt → RE

To record "sale" of tobacco to bank.

Cost of Goods Sold.. 200,000
    Inventory.. 200,000

Assets	=	Liabilities	+	Shareholders' Equity	(Class.)
–200,000				–200,000	IncSt → RE

To record cost of tobacco "sold".

b. Both transactions result in a total of $100,000 income for the two years combined. The collateralized loan shows $163,000 gross profit from the sale in 2009 and interest expense of $30,000 in 2008 and $33,000 in 2009. The "sale" results in $100,000 gross profit in 2008. Cash increases by $300,000 in both transactions. Liabilities increase for the collateralized loan, whereas an asset decreases for the "sale".

11.20 continued.

c. P. J. Lorimar Company must shift the risk of changes in storage costs for 2008 and 2009 and the selling price for the tobacco at the end of 2009 to the bank. The firm should not guarantee a price or agree to cover insurance and other storage costs. Of course, the bank will not both lend on the inventory and "purchase" the inventory for $300,000 because it incurs different amounts of risk in each case.

11.21 (Preparing journal entry for pension plan.) (Amounts in Millions)

2008

Pension Expense	1,050	
Pension Asset ($46,203 – $45,582)	621	
Pension Liability ($45,183 – $43,484)	1,699	
Cash		526
Other Comprehensive Income (Actuarial Gains and Losses: $960 gain + $1,101 amortization)		2,061
Other Comprehensive Income (Excess of Actual Return over Expected Return on Investments: $4,239 – $3,456)		783

Assets	=	Liabilities	+	Shareholders' Equity	(Class.)
+621		–1,699		–1,050	IncSt → RE
–526				+2,061	OCI → AOCI
				+783	OCI → AOCI

To record pension expense and pension funding for 2008, eliminate the net pension liability at the beginning of the year, recognize the net pension asset at the end of the year, and recognize other comprehensive income for the change in actuarial and performance gains and losses.

11.22 (Preparing journal entry for pension plan.) (Amounts in Millions)

2008

Pension Expense	340	
Pension Liability [($5,947 – $5,385) – ($5,771 – $5,086)]	123	
Cash		19
Other Comprehensive Income (Actuarial Gains and Losses: $155 gain + $167 amortization)		322
Other Comprehensive Income (Excess of Actual Return over Expected Return on Investments: $513 – $391)		122

11.22 continued.

Assets	=	Liabilities	+	Shareholders' Equity	(Class.)
–19		–123		–340	IncSt → RE
				+322	OCI → AOCI
				+122	OCI → AOCI

To record pension expense, pension funding, the increase in net pension liabilities, and other comprehensive income related to the change in actuarial and performance gains and losses.

11.23 (Preparing journal entry for health care plan.) (Amounts in Millions)

2008
Health Care Expense..	2,183	
Health Care Liability [($30,863 – $5,460) – ($39,274 – $6,497)]..	7,374	
Other Comprehensive Income (Actuarial Gains and Losses: $9,485 gain + $41 amortization).....		9,526
Other Comprehensive Income (Excess of Actual Return over Expected Return on Investments: $510 – $479)..		31

Assets	=	Liabilities	+	Shareholders' Equity	(Class.)
		–7,374		–2,183	IncSt → RE
				+9,526	OCI → AOCI
				+31	OCI → AOCI

To record health care expense for 2008, the reduction in the health care liability, and other comprehensive income for the change in actuarial and performance gains and losses.

11.24 (Preparing journal entries for income tax expense.) (Amounts in Millions)

a. **2006**
Income Tax Expense	504.4	
Income Tax Payable		495.4
Deferred Tax Liability...		9.0

11.24 a. continued.

Assets	=	Liabilities	+	Shareholders' Equity	(Class.)
		+495.4		–504.4	IncSt → RE
		+9.0			

To record income tax expense, income tax payable, and the change in deferred taxes for 2006.

2007
Income Tax Expense 648.2
   Income Tax Payable 622.8
   Deferred Tax Liability 25.4

Assets	=	Liabilities	+	Shareholders' Equity	(Class.)
		+622.8		–648.2	IncSt → RE
		+25.4			

To record income tax expense, income tax payable, and the change in deferred taxes for 2007.

2008
Income Tax Expense 749.6
Deferred Tax Liability 26.0
   Income Tax Payable 775.6

Assets	=	Liabilities	+	Shareholders' Equity	(Class.)
		–26.0		–749.6	IncSt → RE
		+775.6			

To record income tax expense, income tax payable, and the change in deferred taxes for 2008.

b. The firm has overfunded retirement benefit plans, suggesting that the firm has contributed more cash to the pension plan and, thereby, received a tax deduction that it has expensed for financial reporting. The firm recognized a deferred tax liability for this temporary difference. The deferred tax liability increased in 2007 due to increased overfunding. The deferred tax liability decreased in 2008 due to a decrease in the extent of overfunding.

11.25 (Preparing journal entries for income tax expense.) (Amounts in Millions)

a. **2006**

Income Tax Expense	272	
Income Tax Receivable	96	
Deferred Tax Liability		368

Assets	=	Liabilities	+	Shareholders' Equity	(Class.)
+96		+368		−272	IncSt → RE

To record income tax expense, a claim for a refund in taxes paid previously, and the increase in the deferred tax liability for 2006.

2007

Income Tax Expense	341	
Deferred Tax Liability	74	
Income Tax Payable		415

Assets	=	Liabilities	+	Shareholders' Equity	(Class.)
		−74		−341	IncSt → RE
		+415			

To record income tax expense, income tax payable, and the decrease in the deferred tax liability for 2007.

2008

Income Tax Expense	390	
Income Tax Payable		46
Deferred Tax Liability		344

Assets	=	Liabilities	+	Shareholders' Equity	(Class.)
		+46		−390	IncSt → RE
		+344			

To record income tax expense, income tax payable, and the increase in the deferred tax liability for 2008.

11.25 continued.

b. The firm operated at a net taxable loss for 2006 and likely received a refund of taxes paid in previous years due to net operating loss carryforward provisions in the income tax law. The net taxable loss likely occurred because the firm acquired new equipment for which accelerated depreciation deductions for tax purposes exceeded straight-line depreciation for financial reporting. The increase in the deferred tax liability for 2006 supports this explanation. 2007 was a profitable year for both financial and tax reporting. The decrease in the deferred tax liability for temporary depreciation differences suggests that the firm reduced its capital expenditures sufficiently during 2007 to permit straight-line depreciation for financial reporting to exceed accelerated depreciation for tax reporting. 2008 was similar to 2006 except that accelerated depreciation for tax purposes resulted in low but positive taxable income and again led to an increase in the deferred tax liability. Note that income before taxes for financial reporting increased each year in line with the increase in income tax expense because of the stable effective tax rate.

11.26 (Pownall Company; deriving permanent and temporary differences from financial statement disclosures.)

a. Income Tax Expense = Income Taxes Currently Payable + Change in Deferred Tax Liability

$156,000 = $48,000 + x

x = $108,000

Temporary Differences = Changes in Deferred Tax Liability/.40

= $108,000/.40

= $270,000

Because income tax expense exceeds income taxes payable, book income exceeded taxable income.

b.
Taxable Income: $48,000/.40	$ 120,000
Temporary Differences	270,000
Book Income before Taxes Excluding Permanent Differences	$ 390,000
Permanent Differences (Plug)	72,000
Book Income before Taxes (Given)	$ 318,000

11.27 (Lilly Company; reconstructing information about income taxes.)

LILLY COMPANY
Illustrations of Timing Differences and Permanent Differences

	Financial Statements	Type of Difference	Income Tax Return
Operating Income Except Depreciation	$427,800 (6)	--	$427,800 (4)
Depreciation	(322,800) (g)	Temporary	(358,800) (3)
Municipal Bond Interest	85,800 (5)	Permanent	--
Taxable Income	--		$ 69,000 (2)
Pretax Book Income	$190,800 (g)		
Income Taxes Payable at 40%			$ 27,600 (g)
Income Tax Expense at 40% of $105,000 = $427,800 − $322,800, Which Is Income Excluding Permanent Differences	(42,000) (g)		
Net Income	$148,800 (1)		

Order and derivation of computations:
- (g) Given.
- (1) $148,800 = $190,800 − $42,000.
- (2) $69,000 = $27,600/.40.
- (3) Temporary difference for depreciation is ($42,000 − $27,600)/.40 = $36,000. Because income taxes payable are less than income tax expense, we know that depreciation deducted on tax return exceeds depreciation expense on financial statements. Thus, the depreciation deduction on the tax return is $358,800 = $322,800 + $36,000.
- (4) $427,800 = $358,800 + $69,000.
- (5) Taxable income on financial statements is $105,000 = $42,000/.40. Total financial statement income before taxes, including permanent differences, is $190,800. Hence, permanent differences are $190,800 − $105,000 = $85,800.
- (6) $190,800 + $322,800 − $85,800 = $427,800. See also (4), for check.

11.28 (Woodward Corporation; effect of temporary differences on income taxes.)

a.

	2008	2009	2010	2011
Other Pre-Tax Income	$35,000	$35,000	$35,000	$35,000
Income before Depreciation from Machine	25,000	25,000	25,000	25,000
Depreciation Deduction:				
.33 × $50,000	(16,500)			
.44 × $50,000		(22,000)		
.15 × $50,000			(7,500)	
.08 × $50,000				(4,000)
Taxable Income	$43,500	$38,000	$52,500	$56,000
Tax Rate	.40	.40	.40	.40
Income Taxes Payable	$17,400	$15,200	$21,000	$22,400

b.

Financial Reporting	2008	2009	2010	2011
Carrying Value, January 1	$50,000	$37,500	$25,000	$12,500
Depreciation Expense	(12,500)	(12,500)	(12,500)	(12,500)
Carrying Value, December 31	$37,500	$25,000	$12,500	$ --
Tax Reporting				
Tax Basis, January 1	$50,000	$33,500	$11,500	$ 4,000
Depreciation Deduction	(16,500)	(22,000)	(7,500)	(4,000)
Tax Basis, December 31	$33,500	$11,500	$ 4,000	$ --

c.

Financial Reporting	2008	2009	2010	2011
Income before Depreciation	$60,000	$60,000	$60,000	$60,000
Depreciation Expense ($50,000/4)	(12,500)	(12,500)	(12,500)	(12,500)
Pretax Income	$47,500	$47,500	$47,500	$47,500
Income Tax Expense at .40	$19,000	$19,000	$19,000	$19,000

d.

	2008	2009	2010	2011
Income Tax Payable (from Part a.)—Cr.	$17,400	$15,200	$21,000	$22,400
Change in Deferred Tax Liability (Plug): Cr. if Positive Dr. if Negative	1,600	3,800	(2,000)	(3,400)
Income Tax Expense—Dr.	$19,000	$19,000	$19,000	$19,000

11.28 d. continued.

2008

Income Tax Expense	19,000	
Cash or Income Tax Payable		17,400
Deferred Tax Liability		1,600

Assets	=	Liabilities	+	Shareholders' Equity	(Class.)
−17,400		+1,600		−19,000	IncSt → RE

2009

Income Tax Expense	19,000	
Cash or Income Tax Payable		15,200
Deferred Tax Liability		3,800

Assets	=	Liabilities	+	Shareholders' Equity	(Class.)
−15,200		+3,800		−19,000	IncSt → RE

2010

Income Tax Expense	19,000	
Deferred Tax Liability	2,000	
Cash or Income Tax Payable		21,000

Assets	=	Liabilities	+	Shareholders' Equity	(Class.)
−21,000		−2,000		−19,000	IncSt → RE

2011

Income Tax Expense	19,000	
Deferred Tax Liability	3,400	
Cash or Income Tax Payable		22,400

Assets	=	Liabilities	+	Shareholders' Equity	(Class.)
−22,400		−3,400		−19,000	IncSt → RE

11.29 (Federated Department Stores; interpreting disclosures regarding sales of receivables.)

  a. Exhibit 11.2 in the text contains the GAAP criteria to qualify a transfer of receivables as a sale.

     1. The receivables are isolated from the transferor: the receivables are in the possession and ownership of Citibank.

11.29 a. continued.

    2. The receivables are transferred to an entity that has the right to pledge or exchange the receivables: Federated Department Stores (Federated) has not placed restrictions on the receivables that constrain Citibank from doing what it pleases with the receivables.

    3. The transferor does not maintain control over the receivables: Citibank incurs interest rate, credit, and bankruptcy risk, controls which customers receive credit, and services the credit accounts.

b. Federated benefits from the increased sales revenue that the credit cards provide without incurring interest rate, credit, and bankruptcy risk. Federated also does not incur the administrative cost of the credit card operation. Federated loses control over which of its customers can obtain credit cards, perhaps losing sales it would otherwise obtain if Federated controlled the granting of credit. The disclosures in Exhibit 11.16 in the text do not indicate the nature of any other marketing provisions but perhaps Citibank advertises its association with Federated and, thereby, enhances the Federated brand name.

c. These special purpose entities likely enhanced Federated's ability to isolate the receivables that it sold to GE Capital Consumer Co. and, thereby, qualify the transfers as sales instead of collateralized borrowing. Federated appears to have maintained a closer association with the credit cards under the arrangement with GE Capital Consumer Co. than under the new arrangement with Citibank. The arrangement with GE Capital Consumer Co. appears to primarily involve financing services, whereas the new arrangement involves a shift of the credit card operation to Citibank.

11.30 (Louisiana-Pacific Corporation; interpreting note on off-balance sheet financing.)

Exhibit 11.2 in the text contains the GAAP criteria to qualify a transfer of receivables as a sale.

1. The receivables are isolated from the transferor: the receivables are in the possession and ownership of the qualified special purpose entity (QSPE). Louisiana-Pacific Corporation (LA) appears to own all of the common stock of the QSPE but restrictions in the arrangement do not permit LA to exercise control.

2. The receivables are transferred to an entity that has the right to pledge or exchange the receivables: LA has not placed restrictions on the receivables that constrain the QSPE from doing what it pleases with the receivables.

11.30 continued.

3. The transferor does not maintain control over the receivables: The QSPE incurs most of the interest rate, credit, and bankruptcy risk, although LA's investment in the common stock of the QSPE is at risk to the claims of creditors of the QSPE.

11.31 (Interpreting retirement plans disclosures.) (Amounts in Millions)

a. The firm increased the discount rate it used to compute the pension and health care obligations from 5.7% to 5.8%, thereby reducing the present value of these obligations and resulting in an actuarial gain. Also, the firm reduced the initial health care cost trend rate from 10% to 9%, which reduced the health care obligation and resulted in an actuarial gain. Offsetting these two factors is a change in the assumed rate of compensation increases, which increases the pension obligation and offsets the actuarial gains from the preceding two factors. Note that the firm amortized an actuarial loss from previous years in computing its net pension expense and net health care expense. The question does not address this amortization but only the actuarial gain that arose in 2008.

b. The actual return on investments (disclosed in the change in fair value of plan assets) exceeded the expected return on investments (disclosed in the computation of net pension expense) each year.

c. The firm contributed cash to the health care plan each year equal to the benefits paid. Thus, the health care plan has no assets to invest on which to generate a return. Common terminology refers to such funding arrangements as *pay as you go*.

d.
Prior Service Cost, End of 2007	$ 5
Plus Increase in Prior Service Cost during 2008 from Plan Amendments	11
Less Amortization of Prior Service Cost during 2008	(3)
Prior Service Cost, End of 2008	$ 13

e.
Net Actuarial Loss, End of 2007	$ 2,285
Less Decrease in Actuarial Loss during 2008 from Actuarial Gain in Pension Obligation	(163)
Less Amortization of Actuarial Loss during 2008	(164)
Less Excess of Actual Return over Expected Return on Pension Investments ($513 – $391)	(122)
Prior Service Credit, End of 2008	$ 1,836

f.
Prior Service Credit, End of 2007	$ 114
Less Amortization of Prior Service Cost during 2008	(13)
Prior Service Credit, End of 2008	$ 101

11.31 continued.

g.
Net Actuarial Loss, End of 2007		$419
Less Decrease in Actuarial Loss from Actuarial Gain in Pension Obligation during 2008		(34)
Less Amortization of Actuarial Loss during 2008		(21)
Net Actuarial Loss, End of 2008		$364

h. **2008**

	Dr.	Cr.
Pension Expense	340	
Pension Liability (Noncurrent Liabilities: $2,753 – $729)	2,024	
Other Comprehensive Income (Prior Service Cost: $13 – $5)	8	
Other ($7 – $3)	4	
Cash		19
Pension Asset (Noncurrent Assets: $2,068 – $185)		1,883
Pension Liability (Current Liabilities: $25 – $0)		25
Other Comprehensive Income (Actuarial Loss: $2,285 – $1,836)		449

Assets	=	Liabilities	+	Shareholders' Equity	(Class.)
+4		−2,024		−340	IncSt → RE
−19		+25		−8	OCI → AOCI
−1,883				+449	OCI → AOCI

To record pension expense, pension funding, and the change in balance sheet accounts relating to the pension plan for 2008.

i. **2008**

	Dr.	Cr.
Health Care Expense	126	
Health Care Liability (Noncurrent Liabilities: $1,312 – $1,270)	42	
Other Comprehensive Income (Prior Service Cost: $114 – $101)	13	
Other	49	
Cash		75
Health Care Liability (Current Liabilities: $100 – $0)		100
Other Comprehensive Income (Actuarial Loss: $419 – $364)		55

11.31 i. continued.

Assets	= Liabilities	+	Shareholders' Equity	(Class.)
+49	−42		−126	IncSt → RE
−75	+100		−13	OCI → AOCI
			+55	OCI → AOCI

To record health care expense, health care funding, and the change in balance sheet accounts relating to the health care plan for 2008.

11.32 (Interpreting retirement plan disclosures.) (Amounts in Millions)

a. Pension plans measure the amount of interest cost using the present value of the pension obligation and the related discount rate. Pension plans measure the amount of the expected return on plan assets using the fair value of the pension assets and the assumed rate of return on investments. For the firm, the expected rate of return on investments exceeds the discount rate but the pension obligation exceeds pension assets. Thus, the amounts for interest cost and expected return on investments are a mixture of these four factors. The higher pension obligation exceeds the lower discount rate for 2006 and 2007 and results in interest cost exceeding the expected return on investments. The net effect of these four factors results in equal amounts for interest cost and expected return on investments for 2008, and is simply a coincidence.

b. The decline in net health care expense results from a decline in interest cost, likely the result of decreases in the health care obligation that more than offset the effects of increases in the discount rate.

c. The firm contributes sufficient cash each year to fund current benefits but no excess contributions to invest in assets.

d. The firm increased the discount rate it uses to compute the pension obligation and health care obligation from 5.5% in 2007 to 5.75% in 2008. The increased discount rate reduces the obligations and results in an actuarial gain. In addition, the firm decreased the initial health care cost trend rate from 11.5% in 2007 to 11.2% in 2008, which reduces the health care obligation and results in an actuarial gain.

11.32 continued.

e. Prior Service Cost, End of 2007 .... $ 314
Plus Increase in Prior Service Cost during 2008 from Plan
  Amendments 111
Less Amortization of Prior Service Cost during 2008 .... (59)
Prior Service Cost, End of 2008 .... $ 366

f. Net Actuarial Loss, End of 2007 .... $ 1,646
Less Decrease in Actuarial Loss during 2008 from Actuarial
  Gain in Pension Obligation .... (120)
Less Amortization of Actuarial Loss during 2008 .... (91)
Less Excess of Actual Return over Expected Return on Pen-
  sion Investments ($478 – $295) .... (183)
Net Actuarial Loss, End of 2008 .... $ 1,252

g. Prior Service Cost, End of 2007 .... $ 339
Plus Increase in Prior Service Cost during 2008 from Plan
  Amendments 1
Less Amortization of Prior Service Cost during 2008 .... (41)
Prior Service Cost, End of 2008 .... $ 299

h. Net Actuarial Loss, End of 2007 .... $ 340
Less Decrease in Actuarial Loss during 2008 from Actuarial
  Gain in Health Care Obligation .... (110)
Less Amortization of Actuarial Loss during 2008 .... (9)
Net Actuarial Loss, End of 2008 .... $ 221

i. **2008**

Pension Expense..	253	
Pension Liability (Noncurrent Liabilities: $736 – $19)...	717	
Other Comprehensive Income (Prior Service Cost: $366 – $314)...	52	
Other...	20	
Cash..		567
Pension Liability (Noncurrent Liabilities: $1,348 – $1,267)..		81
Other Comprehensive Income (Actuarial Loss: $1,646 – $1,252)..		394

Solutions 11-20

11.32 i. continued.

Assets	=	Liabilities	+	Shareholders' Equity	(Class.)
+20		−717		−253	IncSt → RE
−567		+81		−52	OCI → AOCI
				+394	OCI → AOCI

To record pension expense, pension funding, and the change in balance sheet accounts relating to the pension plan for 2008.

j. **2008**

Health Care Expense	210	
Health Care Liability (Current Liabilities: $254 − $231)..	23	
Health Care Liability (Noncurrent Liabilities: $2,375 − $2,243)...	132	
Other...	27	
Cash		233
Other Comprehensive Income (Prior Service Cost: $339 − $299)..		40
Other Comprehensive Income (Actuarial Loss: $340 − $221)...		119

Assets	=	Liabilities	+	Shareholders' Equity	(Class.)
+27		−23		−210	IncSt → RE
−233		−132		+40	OCI → AOCI
				+119	OCI → AOCI

To record health care expense, health care funding, and the change in balance sheet accounts relating to the health care plan for 2008.

11.33 (Interpreting income tax disclosures.) (Amounts in Millions)

    a. **2007**

Income Tax Expense..	699	
Deferred Income Taxes...	39	
Income Tax Payable..		738

Assets	=	Liabilities	+	Shareholders' Equity	(Class.)
+39	or	–39		–699	IncSt → RE
		+738			

To record income tax expense, income tax payable, and a debit change in deferred income taxes for 2007.

    b. **2008**

Income Tax Expense..	742	
Income Tax Payable..		736
Deferred Income Taxes...		6

Assets	=	Liabilities	+	Shareholders' Equity	(Class.)
		+736		–742	IncSt → RE
–6	or	+6			

To record income tax expense, income tax payable, and the credit change in deferred income taxes for 2008.

    c. The first line of the tax reconciliation assumes that governmental entities tax income before income taxes at 35%. However, 35% is only the U.S. federal tax rate. State and local taxes (net of any tax savings from subtracting state and local taxes in computing U.S. federal taxable income) increase the effective tax rate above 35%.

    d. Nondeductible items increase the effective tax rate, despite their appearing with other reconciling items with a negative sign in this case. The first line of the tax reconciliation assumes that all costs or expenses save income taxes at a 35% tax rate. If firms cannot deduct a particular cost or expense for tax purposes, the effective tax rate on income before income taxes increases.

11.33 continued.

e. A recognized pension liability or health care liability suggests that a firm has recognized more pension or health care expense than the firm has contributed cash. The contribution of cash gives rise to an income tax deduction. Thus, taxable income exceeds book income, resulting in a deferred tax asset for the higher taxes paid currently. A recognized prepaid pension asset suggests that a firm has contributed more cash to the pension fund than it had recognized as pension expense. Thus, book income exceeds taxable income, resulting in a deferred tax liability for the delayed payment of taxes.

f. GAAP requires firms using the accrual basis of accounting to recognize sales allowances as an expense in the period of sale, whereas firms cannot deduct sales allowances in computing taxable income until making actual expenditures. Thus, a growing firm will likely record higher taxable income than book income and recognize a deferred tax asset for the early payment of taxes.

g. This firm increased the deferred tax asset for expected benefits from tax loss and tax credit carryforwards. If the entity that realized the tax losses is not yet profitable, uncertainty exists as to whether this firm will benefit from the tax losses and tax credit carryforwards, creating the need for a valuation allowance. Some of the other items in deferred tax assets may relate to the unprofitable entity, leading as well to uncertainty about the ability to realize those tax benefits.

h. The decreasing amount of deferred tax liability for temporary depreciation differences suggests that book depreciation exceeds tax depreciation. The likely explanation is that this firm reduced its expenditures on depreciable assets, resulting in more assets in the later years of their lives when straight-line depreciation for book purposes exceeds accelerated depreciation for tax purposes than assets in their early years when accelerated depreciation exceeds straight-line depreciation. Cumulative depreciation for tax purposes still exceeds cumulative depreciation for book purposes because this firm reports a deferred tax liability.

i. This firm is the lessor. The reporting of a deferred tax liability indicates that cumulative book income exceeds cumulative taxable income. This firm likely accounts for these leases as capital leases for financial reporting and operating leases for tax reporting. The capital lease method results in the lessor reporting a gain in the year the parties sign the lease, whereas the operating lease method spreads the income over the term of the lease.

11.34 (Interpreting income tax disclosures.) (Amounts in Millions)

a. **2007**

Income Tax Expense 4,232
    Income Tax Payable 2,047
    Deferred Income Taxes 2,185

Assets	=	Liabilities	+	Shareholders' Equity	(Class.)
		+2,047		–4,232	IncSt → RE
–2,185	or	+2,185			

To record income tax expense, income tax payable, and the change in deferred income taxes for 2007.

b. **2008**

Income Tax Expense 3,901
    Income Tax Payable 2,177
    Deferred Income Taxes 1,724

Assets	=	Liabilities	+	Shareholders' Equity	(Class.)
		+2,177		–3,901	IncSt → RE
–1,724	or	+1,724			

To record income tax expense, income tax payable, and the change in deferred income taxes for 2008.

c. The deferred tax amounts in Exhibit 11.23 in the text relate not only to amounts affecting income tax expense of the current period but also to tax effects of items included in other balance sheet items. For example, when firms debit or credit other comprehensive income when initially recognizing or subsequently amortizing prior service costs and actuarial gains and losses of pension and health care plans, the firms must credit or debit other comprehensive income for the income tax effects of these items. The deferred tax amounts in Exhibit 11.23 in the text include the tax effects of all temporary differences, not just those affecting income tax expense of the current period.

d. The first line of the tax reconciliation assumes that governmental entities tax income before income taxes at 35%. However, 35% is only the U.S. federal tax rate. State and local taxes (net of any tax savings from subtracting state and local taxes in computing U.S. federal taxable income) increase the effective tax rate above 35%.

11.34 continued.

e. This firm recognizes a deferred tax asset for underfunded retirement plans and a deferred tax liability for overfunded retirement plans. GAAP requires firms to report underfunded retirement plans as liabilities and overfunded retirement plans as assets and not to net them. Similarly, GAAP requires firms to report the deferred tax assets and deferred tax liabilities related to these plans separately and not to net them.

f. A deferred tax asset for expenses suggests this firm recognizes expenses earlier for financial reporting than for tax reporting. GAAP requires firms to recognize expenses for bad debts and warranties in the period of sale, whereas the income tax law does not permit a deduction for such items until actual uncollectible accounts receivable materialize and firms make warranty expenditures.

g. This firm is the lessor. The reporting of a deferred tax liability indicates that cumulative book income exceeds cumulative taxable income. This firm likely accounts for these leases as capital leases for financial reporting and operating leases for tax reporting. The capital lease method results in the lessor reporting a gain in the year the parties sign the lease, whereas the operating lease method spreads the income over the term of the lease.

h. A deferred tax liability for software development costs suggests that this firm recognizes expenses earlier for tax reporting than for financial reporting. GAAP requires firms to capitalize as assets and subsequently amortize software development costs incurred after the software reaches the point of technological feasibility. Firms can deduct expenditures on software development costs as incurred and need not capitalize and then amortize such costs for tax purposes, regardless of the stage of technological feasibility.

11.35 (Interpreting income tax disclosures.) (Amounts in Millions)

a. **2006**

Income Tax Expense 1,146
   Income Tax Payable 1,052
   Deferred Income Taxes... 94

Assets	=	Liabilities	+	Shareholders' Equity	(Class.)
		+1,052		–1,146	IncSt → RE
–94	or	+94			

To record income tax expense, income tax payable, and the change in deferred income taxes for 2006.

11.35 continued.

b. **2007**

Income Tax Expense	1,452	
Deferred Income Taxes	122	
Income Tax Payable		1,574

Assets	=	Liabilities	+	Shareholders' Equity	(Class.)
–122	or	–122		–1,452	IncSt → RE
		+1,574			

To record income tax expense, income tax payable, and the change in deferred income taxes for 2007.

c. **2008**

Income Tax Expense	1,710	
Deferred Income Taxes	201	
Income Tax Payable		1,911

Assets	=	Liabilities	+	Shareholders' Equity	(Class.)
–201	or	–201		–1,710	IncSt → RE
		+1,911			

To record income tax expense, income tax payable, and the change in deferred income taxes for 2008.

d. The deferred tax amounts in Exhibit 11.24 in the text relate not only to amounts affecting income tax expense of the current period but also to tax effects of items included in other balance sheet items. For example, when firms debit or credit other comprehensive income when initially recognizing or subsequently amortizing prior service costs and actuarial gains and losses of pension and health care plans, the firms must credit or debit other comprehensive income for the income tax effects of these items. The deferred tax amounts in Exhibit 11.24 in the text include the tax effects of all temporary differences, not just those affecting income tax expense of the current period.

e. The first line of the tax reconciliation assumes that governmental entities tax income before income taxes at 35%. However, 35% is only the U.S. federal tax rate. State and local taxes (net of any tax savings from subtracting state and local taxes in computing U.S. federal taxable income) increase the effective tax rate above 35%.

11.35 continued.

    f. The deferred tax asset for health care benefits suggests that this firm has an underfunded health care plan. This firm has recognized more health care expenses than it has contributed cash to the health care benefits plan. The cash contribution triggers an income tax deduction for computing taxable income. This firm has prepaid income taxes because health care expense for tax is less than book, giving rise to the deferred tax asset. The deferred tax liability for pension care benefits suggests that this firm has an overfunded pension plan. The firm has recognized less pension expenses than it has contributed cash to the pension benefits plan. The cash contribution triggers an income tax deduction for computing taxable income. The firm has delayed paying income taxes because pension expense for tax exceeds pension expense for book, giving rise to the deferred tax liability.

    g. A steady deferred tax liability for temporary depreciation differences suggests that depreciation using the accelerated method for tax purposes approximately equals straight-line depreciation for book purposes. This equality generally occurs around the mid-point of assets' lives. The relatively flat deferred tax amount suggests that this firm replaces depreciable assets at approximately the same rate as they wear out.

    h. This firm is profitable and more likely than not to realize the benefits of deferred tax assets.

11.36 (Equilibrium Company; behavior of deferred income tax account when a firm acquires new assets every year.)

Year	Units Acquired
1	1
2	1
3	1
4	1
5	1
6	1
7	1

TAX DEPRECIATION (MACRS)

	Year 1	Year 2	Year 3	Year 4	Year 5	Year 6	Year 7
	$2,400	$3,840	$2,280	$1,440	$1,320	$ 720	$ 0
		2,400	3,840	2,280	1,440	1,320	720
			2,400	3,840	2,280	1,440	1,320
				2,400	3,840	2,280	1,440
					2,400	3,840	2,280
						2,400	3,840
							2,400
a. Annual Depreciation	$2,400	$6,240	$8,520	$9,960	$11,280	$12,000	$12,000
b. Straight Line Depreciation = $2,000 per Machine per Year	2,000	4,000	6,000	8,000	10,000	12,000	12,000
c. Difference	$ 400	$2,240	$2,520	$1,960	$ 1,280	$ 0	$ 0
d. Increase in Deferred Tax (40%)	$ 160	$ 896	$1,008	$ 784	$ 512	$ 0	$ 0
e. Balance of Deferred Income Taxes	$ 160	$1,056	$2,064	$2,848	$ 3,360	$ 3,360	$ 3,360

f. The Deferred Income Taxes account balance will remain constant at $3,360 so long as the firm continues this replacement policy. If asset prices increase or physical assets increase, or both, the Deferred Tax Liability will continue to grow.

11.37 (Shiraz Company; attempts to achieve off-balance-sheet financing.)

[The chapter does not give sufficient information for the student to know the GAAP answers. The six items are designed to generate a lively discussion.]

Transfer of Receivables with Recourse *SFAS No. 140* sets out the following criteria to treat a transfer of receivables with recourse as a sale: (1) the arrangement separates the receivables from the seller (Shiraz), (2) the purchaser of the receivables (Credit Company) is free to sell or exchange the receivables without undue restrictions placed by the seller, and (3) the seller does not maintain effective control over the receivables.

Shiraz Company retains control of the future economic benefits. If interest rates decrease, Shiraz can borrow funds at the lower interest rate and repurchase the receivables. Because the receivables carry a fixed interest return, Shiraz enjoys the benefit of the difference between the fixed interest return on the receivables and the lower borrowing cost. If interest rates increase, Shiraz will not repurchase the receivables. Credit Company bears the risk of interest rate increases because of the fixed interest return on the receivables. The right of Shiraz to repurchase the receivables restricts the ability of Credit Company to sell or exchange the receivables. The control of who benefits from interest rate changes and who bears the risk resides with Shiraz. Shiraz, therefore, maintains effective control of the receivables. Shiraz Company also bears credit risk in excess of the allowance. Thus, this transaction does not meet the last two criteria as a sale. Shiraz Company should report the transaction as a collateralized loan.

Product Financing Arrangement *SFAS No. 49* (1981) provides that firms recognize product financing arrangements as liabilities if (1) the arrangement requires the sponsoring firm (Shiraz) to purchase the inventory at specified prices and (2) the payments made to the other entity (Credit Company) cover all acquisition, holding, and financing costs.

Shiraz Company agrees to repurchase the inventory at a fixed price, thereby incurring the risk of changing prices. The purchase price formula includes a fixed interest rate, so Shiraz enjoys the benefits or incurs the risk of interest rate changes. Shiraz also controls the benefits and risk of changes in storage costs. Thus, Shiraz treats this product financing arrangement as a collateralized loan.

Throughput Contract *SFAS Statement No. 49* (1981) treats throughput contracts as executory contracts and does not require their recognition as a liability. Note, however, the similarity between a product financing arrangement (involving inventory) and a throughput contract (involving a service). Shiraz Company must pay specified amounts each period regardless of whether it uses the shipping services. The wording of the problem makes it unclear as to whether the initial contract specifies a selling price (railroad bears risk of operating cost increases) or whether the selling price is the railroad's current charges for shipping services each period (Shiraz bears risk of operating cost increases). It seems unlikely that the railroad would accept a fixed price for all ten years. Thus, it appears that Shiraz incurs a commitment to make highly probable future cash pay-

11.37 continued.

ments in amounts that cover the railroad's operating and financing costs. This transaction has the economic characteristics of a collateralized loan, even though GAAP permits treatment as an executory contract.

Construction Joint Venture The construction loan will appear as a liability on the books of Chemical, the joint entity. Shiraz will recognize the fair value of its loan guarantee as a liability. Shiraz and Mission each own 50% but Shiraz appears to have the residual owners' equity because in return for guaranteeing the debt of Chemical, it can buy out Mission for a fixed cost-based price if the venture turns out well. (Chapter 13 discusses consolidated financial statements and variable interest entities.)

GAAP treats the commitment to pay one-half of the operating and debt service costs as an executory contract, similar to the throughput contract. Even though the probability of making future cash payments is high, GAAP concludes that a liability does not arise until the firm receives future benefits from Chemical.

Research and Development Partnership *SFAS No. 68* (1982) requires firms to recognize financings related to research and development (R & D) as liabilities if (1) the sponsoring firm (Shiraz) must repay the financing regardless of the outcome of the R & D work, or (2) the sponsoring firm, even in the absence of a loan guarantee, bears the risk of failure of the R & D effort.

Shiraz guarantees the bank loan in this case regardless of the outcome of the R & D effort and therefore must recognize a liability (satisfies first criterion above). It does not matter whether Shiraz has an option or an obligation to purchase the results of the R & D effort.

If Shiraz did not guarantee the bank loan, then the second criterion above determines whether Shiraz recognizes a liability. If Shiraz has the option to purchase the results of the R & D work, it does not bear the risk of failure and need not recognize a liability. If Shiraz has the obligation to purchase the results, it recognizes a liability for the probable amount payable. The problem does not make it clear whether the amount payable includes the unpaid balance of the loan or merely the value of the R & D work (which could be zero). It seems unlikely that the bank would lend funds for the R & D work without some commitment or obligation by Shiraz to repay the loan.

11.37 continued.

Hotel Financing Shiraz Company will recognize a liability for the fair value of its guarantee, which is likely to be less than the amount of the loan. It appears in this case that the probability of Shiraz having to make payments under the loan guarantee is low. The hotel is profitable and probably generating cash flows. In addition, the bank can sell the hotel in the event of loan default to satisfy the unpaid balance of the loan. Thus, Shiraz's loan guarantee is a third level of defense against loan default. If default does occur and the first two lines of defense prove inadequate to repay the loan in full, then Shiraz would recognize a liability for the unpaid portion.

This page is intentionally left blank

CHAPTER 12

MARKETABLE SECURITIES AND DERIVATIVES

Questions, Exercises, and Problems: Answers and Solutions

12.1 See the text or the glossary at the end of the book.

12.2 a. Debt securities that a firm intends to hold to maturity (for example, to lock in the yield at acquisition for the full period to maturity) and has the ability to hold to maturity (for example, the firm has adequate liquid assets and borrowing capacity such that it need not sell the debt securities prior to maturity to obtain cash) appear as "debt held to maturity." All other debt securities appear in the "available for sale" category. The latter includes short-term investments in government debt securities that serve as a liquid investment of excess cash and short-and long-term investments in government and corporate debt securities that serve either as hedges of interest rate, exchange rate, or similar risks or as sources of cash at a later date to pay debt coming due.

b. The classification as "trading securities" implies a firm's active involvement in buying and selling securities for profit. The holding period of trading securities is typically measured in minutes or hours instead of days. The classification as "available for sale" implies less frequent trading and usually relates to an operating purpose other than profit alone (for example, to generate income while a firm has temporarily excess cash, to invest in a firm with potential new technologies). The holding period of securities available for sale is typically measured in days, months, or years.

c. Amortized acquisition cost equals the purchase price of debt securities plus or minus amortization of any difference between acquisition cost and maturity value. Amortized acquisition cost bears no necessary relation to the fair value of the debt security during the periods subsequent to acquisition. The fair value of a debt security depends on the risk characteristics of the issuer, the provisions of the debt security with respect to interest rate, term to maturity, and similar factors, and the general level of interest rates in the economy.

12.2 continued.

    d. Unrealized holding gains and losses occur when the fair value of a security changes while the firm holds the security. The unrealized holding gain or loss on trading securities appears in the income statement each period, whereas it appears in Accumulated Other Comprehensive Income, a separate shareholders' equity account, each period for securities available for sale.

    e. Realized gains and losses appear in the income statement when a firm sells a security. The realized gain or loss on trading securities equals the selling price minus the fair value of the security on the most recent balance sheet. The realized gain or loss on securities available for sale equals the selling price minus the acquisition cost of the security.

12.3 Firms acquire trading securities primarily for their short-term profit potential. Including the unrealized holding gain or loss in income provides the financial statement user with relevant information for assessing the performance of the trading activity. Firms acquire securities available for sale to support an operating activity (for example, investment of temporarily excess cash) instead of primarily for their profit potential. Deferring recognition of any gain or loss until sale treats securities available for sale the same as inventories, equipment and other assets. Excluding the unrealized gain or loss from earnings also reduces earnings volatility.

12.4 The required accounting does appear to contain a degree of inconsistency. One might explain this seeming inconsistency by arguing that the balance sheet and income statement serve different purposes. The balance sheet attempts to portray the resources of a firm and the claims on those users by creditors and owners. Fair values for securities are more relevant than acquisition cost or lower-of-cost-or-market for assessing the adequacy of resources to satisfy claims. The income statement reports the results of operating performance. One might argue that operating performance from investing in marketable securities available for sale is not complete until the firm sells the securities. Another argument for excluding at least unrealized gains on marketable securities from earnings is that it achieves consistency with the delayed recognition of unrealized gains on inventories, equipment, and other assets.

    As for earnings quality issues, the unrealized holding gains can be realized at management whim, which means management can bring the gains from accumulated other comprehensive income into net income. Management cannot manipulate other comprehensive income, only net income. When analysts become accustomed to analyzing other comprehensive income, the manipulation of net income will be less of an earnings quality issue.

12.5 A derivative is a hedge when the firm bears a risk such that the change in the value of the derivative attempts to offset the change in the value of the firm as time passes. We distinguish an attempt at hedging from an effective hedge or even from a partially effective hedge. A firm attempting to hedge by holding a derivative has a hedge, even though that hedge may be only partially effective. When the firm acquires a derivative that is completely ineffective, that is, zero correlated with the hedged item, then we would say the firm does not hold a hedge, even though the firm says it attempts to reduce risk.

Under this interpretation, a derivative is not a hedge when changes in the fair value of the derivative do not at least partially offset other changes in firm value occurring at the same time.

If the firm chooses not to use hedge accounting when it could, the fluctuations in the fair value of the derivative appear in income, not offset by the changes in fair value of the hedged item. We would say that choosing not to use hedge accounting reduces opportunity for manipulation rather than that it increases it because firms cannot offset gains and losses on the derivative against losses and gains on the hedged item.

12.6 A *fair-value hedge* is a hedge of an exposure to changes in the fair value of a recognized asset or liability or of an unrecognized firm commitment. A *cash-flow hedge* is a hedge of an exposure to variability in the cash flows of a recognized asset or liability, such as variable interest rates, or of a forecasted transaction, such as expected future foreign sales.

12.7 Firms do not recognize the fair value of the commitment except to the extent that firms recognize the fair value of the derivative that is hedging that commitment. Thus, firms recognize a portion of the commitment relating to the hedging activity but not the full fair value of that commitment. Firms also do not recognize the asset that the firm will receive when it satisfies the commitment.

12.8 The rationale relates to matching. Under a fair value hedge, firms report recognized assets and liabilities at fair value and include unrealized gains and losses in net income. Firms also report associated derivatives at fair value and include unrealized gains and losses in net income. Thus, the treatment of the hedged asset or liabilities parallels the treatment of the derivative. Under a cash flow hedge, firms do not necessarily report the hedged asset or liability at fair value. Including unrealized gains and losses on the derivative in net income but not including the unrealized gains and losses on the hedged item in net income is inconsistent. The gains or loss on the hedged item usually affects net income when the firm receives or disburses cash. At that time, the firm transfers gains and losses on the associated derivative out of accumulated other comprehensive income and recognizes those gains and losses in net income.

12.9   To qualify for hedge accounting, there must be an expectation that the derivative will be effective in hedging a particular risk. Obtaining a derivative that will be highly effective in hedging a particular risk may be costly. A firm might be satisfied with obtaining a derivative that will hedge a significant portion of the risk, accepting the likelihood that the derivative will not be fully effective. Because firms must report gains and losses when derivatives are not highly effective, they may not wish to classify a derivative as a hedge and have to report such information. Another explanation is that the firm wishes to speculate on movements in interest rates, foreign exchange rates, or commodity prices. That is, firms acquire certain derivatives for trading gains and not to hedge a business risk.

12.10 This statement is correct. Firms would report all financial assets and financial liabilities at fair value and include unrealized gains and losses in net income.

12.11 (Classifying securities.)

   a. Securities available for sale; current asset.

   b. Debt securities held to maturity; noncurrent asset.

   c. Securities available for sale; current asset.

   d. Securities available for sale; noncurrent asset.

   e. Trading securities; current asset.

   f. Securities available for sale; noncurrent asset (although a portion of these bonds might appear as a current asset).

12.12 (Accounting principles for marketable securities and derivatives).

   a. (4) The firm has option to use hedge accounting, deferring income effects until realization and reporting changes in fair value in periodic other comprehensive income, or to not use hedge accounting and reporting holding gains and losses, like trading securities gains and losses, in current period income.

   b. (1) This derivative is not an accounting hedge, so gains and losses appear in current income.

   c. (1) Because not both ability and intent to hold to maturity are present, it will appear at fair value. Because the firm trades securities such as this, the classification is as a trading security. If the firm were not a trader, then Treatment (3) would apply.

   d. (3) Standard treatment for securities available for sale.

12.13 (Murray Company; accounting for bonds held to maturity.)

a. Present Value of Periodic Payments: $3,000 × 6.73274[a] = $ 20,198
Present Value of Maturity Amount: $100,000 × .73069[b] = 73,069
Total .... $ 93,267

[a]Present value of an annuity for 8 periods at 4%.
[b]Present value of $1 for 8 periods at 4%.

b. See Schedule 12.1 below.

Schedule 12.1
Amortization Table for $100,000 Bonds with Interest Paid Semiannually at 6% and Priced to Yield 8% Compounded Semiannually
(Exercise 13)

Period	Balance at Beginning of Period	Interest Revenue for Period	Cash Received	Portion of Payment Increasing Carrying Value	Balance at End of Period
1	$93,267	$3,731	$3,000	$731	$ 93,998
2	$93,998	$3,760	$3,000	$760	$ 94,758
3	$94,758	$3,790	$3,000	$790	$ 95,548
4	$95,548	$3,822	$3,000	$822	$ 96,370
5	$96,370	$3,855	$3,000	$855	$ 97,225
6	$97,225	$3,889	$3,000	$889	$ 98,114
7	$98,114	$3,925	$3,000	$925	$ 99,038
8	$99,038	$3,962	$3,000	$962	$100,000

c. January 1, 2008
Marketable Debt Securities 93,267
Cash 93,267

Assets	= Liabilities	+	Shareholders' Equity	(Class.)
−93,267				
+93,267				

12.13 c. continued.

June 30, 2008

Cash	3,000	
Marketable Debt Securities	731	
Interest Revenue		3,731

Assets	= Liabilities	+ Shareholders' Equity	(Class.)
+3,000		+3,731	IncSt → RE
+731			

December 31, 2008

Cash	3,000	
Marketable Debt Securities	760	
Interest Revenue		3,760

Assets	= Liabilities	+ Shareholders' Equity	(Class.)
+3,000		+3,760	IncSt → RE
+760			

d. **December 31, 2011**

Cash	3,000	
Marketable Debt Securities	962	
Interest Revenue		3,962

Assets	= Liabilities	+ Shareholders' Equity	(Class.)
+3,000		+3,962	IncSt → RE
+962			

December 31, 2011

Cash	100,000	
Marketable Debt Securities		100,000

Assets	= Liabilities	+ Shareholders' Equity	(Class.)
+100,000			
−100,000			

12.14 (Kelly Company, accounting for bonds held to maturity.)

a. Present Value of Periodic Payments: $17,500 × 5.41719[a] = $ 94,801
Present Value of Maturity Amount: $500,000 × .83748[b] = 418,740
Total .... $ 513,541

[a]Present value of an annuity for 6 periods at 3%.
[b]Present value of $1 for 6 periods at 3%.

b. See Schedule 12.2 below.

Schedule 12.2
Amortization Table for $500,000 Bonds with Interest
Paid Semiannually at 7% and Priced to Yield 6%
Compounded Semiannually
(Exercise 14)

Period (1)	Balance at Beginning of Period (2)	Interest Revenue for Period (3)	Cash Received (4)	Portion of Payment Reducing Carrying Value (5)	Balance at End of Period (6)
1	$513,541	$15,406	$17,500	$(2,094)	$511,447
2	$511,447	$15,343	$17,500	$(2,157)	$509,291
3	$509,291	$15,279	$17,500	$(2,221)	$507,069
4	$507,069	$15,212	$17,500	$(2,288)	$504,781
5	$504,781	$15,143	$17,500	$(2,357)	$502,425
6	$502,225	$15,075[a]	$17,500	$(2,425)	$500,000

[a]Amount does not equal 3% of balance at the beginning of the period due to rounding.

c. **January 1, 2008**
Marketable Debt Securities 513,341
    Cash 513,341

Assets	= Liabilities	+	Shareholders' Equity	(Class.)
–513,341				
+513,341				

12.14 c. continued.

June 30, 2008

Cash	17,500	
Interest Revenue		15,406
Marketable Debt Securities		2,094

Assets	=	Liabilities	+	Shareholders' Equity	(Class.)
+17,500				+15,406	IncSt → RE
–2,094					

December 31, 2008

Cash	17,500	
Interest Revenue		15,343
Marketable Debt Securities		2,157

Assets	=	Liabilities	+	Shareholders' Equity	(Class.)
+17,500				+15,343	IncSt → RE
–2,157					

d. **December 31, 2010**

Cash	17,500	
Interest Revenue		15,075
Marketable Debt Securities		2,425

Assets	=	Liabilities	+	Shareholders' Equity	(Class.)
+17,500				+15,075	IncSt → RE
–2,425					

December 31, 2011

Cash	500,000	
Marketable Debt Securities		500,000

Assets	=	Liabilities	+	Shareholders' Equity	(Class.)
+500,000					
–500,000					

12.15 (Elston Corporation; accounting for securities available for sale.)

10/15/2008
Marketable Securities (Security A).................................. 28,000
    Cash   28,000

Assets	=	Liabilities	+	Shareholders' Equity	(Class.)
+28,000					
−28,000					

To record acquisition of shares of Security A.

11/02/2008
Marketable Securities (Security B).................................. 49,000
    Cash   49,000

Assets	=	Liabilities	+	Shareholders' Equity	(Class.)
+49,000					
−49,000					

To record acquisition of shares of Security B.

12/31/2008
Cash 1,000
    Dividend Revenue   1,000

Assets	=	Liabilities	+	Shareholders' Equity	(Class.)
+1,000				+1,000	IncSt → RE

To record dividend received from Security B.

12/31/2008
Unrealized Holding Loss on Security A Available for
    Sale (Other Comprehensive Income) 3,000
        Marketable Securities (Security A)........................   3,000

Assets	=	Liabilities	+	Shareholders' Equity	(Class.)
−3,000				−3,000	OCInc → AOCInc

To record unrealized holding loss on Security A.

12.15 continued.

12/31/2008

Marketable Securities (Security B)..	6,000	
Unrealized Holding Gain on Security B Available		
for Sale (Other Comprehensive Income)		6,000

Assets	=	Liabilities	+	Shareholders' Equity	(Class.)
+6,000				+6,000	OCInc → AOCInc

To record unrealized holding gain on Security B.

2/10/2009

Cash	24,000	
Realized Loss on Sale of Securities Available for Sale		
(= $24,000 − $28,000)..	4,000	
Marketable Securities (Security A)........................		25,000
Unrealized Holding Loss on Security A		
Available for Sale (Other Comprehensive		
Income)..		3,000

Assets	=	Liabilities	+	Shareholders' Equity	(Class.)
+24,000				−4,000	IncSt → RE
−25,000				+3,000	OCInc → AOCInc

To record sale of Security A.

12/31/2009

Cash	1,200	
Dividend Revenue		1,200

Assets	=	Liabilities	+	Shareholders' Equity	(Class.)
+1,200				+1,200	IncSt → RE

To record dividend received from Security B.

12.15 continued.

12/31/2009

Unrealized Holding Gain on Security B Available for
  Sale (Other Comprehensive Income).......................... 2,000
    Marketable Securities (Security B) (= $53,000
      – $55,000).. 2,000

Assets	=	Liabilities	+	Shareholders' Equity	(Class.)
–2,000				–2,000	OCInc → AOCInc

To revalue Security B to market value.

7/15/2010

Cash... 57,000
Unrealized Holding Gain on Security B Available for
  Sale (= $6,000 – $2,000) (Other Comprehensive
  Income).. 4,000
    Marketable Securities (Security B)........................ 53,000
    Realized Gain on Sale of Securities Available for
      Sale (= $57,000 – $49,000)................................... 8,000

Assets	=	Liabilities	+	Shareholders' Equity	(Class.)
+57,000				+8,000	IncSt → RE
–53,000				–4,000	OCInc → AOCInc

To record sale of Security B.

12.16 (Simmons Corporation; accounting for securities available for sale.)

6/13/2008

Marketable Securities (Security S).................................. 12,000
Marketable Securities (Security T).................................. 29,000
Marketable Securities (Security U)................................. 43,000
  Cash 84,000

12.16 continued.

Assets	=	Liabilities	+	Shareholders' Equity	(Class.)
+12,000					
+29,000					
+43,000					
–84,000					

To record acquisition of marketable equity securities as a temporary investment.

10/11/2008
Cash 39,000
Realized Loss on Sale of Security U Available for
 Sale 4,000
  Marketable Securities (Security U)....................... 43,000

Assets	=	Liabilities	+	Shareholders' Equity	(Class.)
+39,000				–4,000	IncSt → RE
–43,000					

To record sale of Security U.

12/31/2008
Marketable Securities (Security S) (= $13,500 –
 $12,000)... 1,500
  Unrealized Holding Gain on Security S Available for Sale (Other Comprehensive
   Income)... 1,500

Assets	=	Liabilities	+	Shareholders' Equity	(Class.)
+1,500				+1,500	OCInc → AOCInc

To revalue Security S to market value.

Solutions 12-12

12.16 continued.

12/31/2008

Unrealized Holding Loss on Security T Available for Sale (Other Comprehensive Income)..........................	2,800	
Marketable Securities (Security T) (= $26,200 − $29,000)...		2,800

Assets	=	Liabilities	+	Shareholders' Equity	(Class.)
−2,800				−2,800	OCInc → AOCInc

To revalue Security T to market value.

12/31/2009

Marketable Securities (Security S) (= $15,200 − $13,500)..	1,700	
Unrealized Holding Gain on Security S Available for Sale (Other Comprehensive Income)..		1,700

Assets	=	Liabilities	+	Shareholders' Equity	(Class.)
+1,700				+1,700	OCInc → AOCInc

To revalue Security S to market value.

12/31/2009

Marketable Securities (Security T) (= $31,700 − $26,200)..	5,500	
Unrealized Holding Loss on Security T Available for Sale (from 12/31/2008 Entry) (Other Comprehensive Income).........................		2,800
Unrealized Holding Gain on Security T Available for Sale (Other Comprehensive Income)..		2,700

Assets	=	Liabilities	+	Shareholders' Equity	(Class.)
+5,500				+2,800	OCInc → AOCInc
				+2,700	OCInc → AOCInc

To revalue Security T to market value.

12.16 continued.

2/15/2010

Cash 14,900	
Unrealized Holding Gain on Security S Available for Sale (= $1,500 + $1,700) (Other Comprehensive Income)... 3,200	
Marketable Securities (Security S)	15,200
Realized Gain on Sale of Security S Available for Sale (= $14,900 – $12,000)	2,900

Assets	=	Liabilities	+	Shareholders' Equity	(Class.)
+14,900				+2,900	IncSt → RE
–15,200				–3,200	OCInc → AOCInc

To record sale of Security S.

8/22/2010

Cash 28,500	
Unrealized Holding Gain on Security T Available for Sale (Other Comprehensive Income) 2,700	
Realized Loss on Sale of Securities Available for Sale (Security T) (= $28,500 – $29,000) 500	
Marketable Securities (Security T)	31,700

Assets	=	Liabilities	+	Shareholders' Equity	(Class.)
+28,500				–500	IncSt → RE
–31,700				–2,700	OCInc → AOCInc

To record sale of Security T.

12.17 (Fischer/Black Co.; working backwards from data on marketable securities transaction.)

a. $21,000 = $18,000 + $3,000.

b. $18,000, the amount credited to Marketable Securities in the journal entry which the student might think of as $21,000 acquisition cost, derived above, less $3,000 of Unrealized Holding Loss.

c. $5,000 loss from the debit for Realized Loss.

12.18 (Canning/Werther; working backwards from data on marketable securities transaction.)

a. $15,000 = $18,000 proceeds − $4,000 realized gain + $1,000 loss previously recognized because they are trading securities.

b. $14,000 = $18,000 proceeds − $4,000 realized gain which is selling price less acquisition cost because they are securities available for sale.

12.19 (Reconstructing events from journal entries.)

a. The fair value of a marketable security classified as available for sale is $4,000 less than its carrying value and the firm increases the Unrealized Holding Loss account on the balance sheet.

b. A firm sells marketable securities classified as either trading securities or as securities available for sale in the same period as it purchased the securities for an amount that is $200 (= $1,100 − $1,300) less than was originally paid for them.

c. The fair value of marketable securities classified as available for sale is $750 more than its carrying value and the firm increases the Unrealized Holding Gain account on the balance sheet.

d. A firm sells marketable securities classified as either trading securities or as securities available for sale in the same period that it purchased the securities for an amount that is $100 (= $1,800 − $1,700) more than was originally paid for them.

12.20 (Zeff Corporation; reconstructing transactions involving short-term securities available for sale.)

a. Sale of marketable securities during 2008: Proceeds of $14,000; gain on sale is $4,000 = $14,000 − $10,000, so acquisition cost was $10,000.

b. Carrying value at time of sale was $13,000, so unrealized holding gain at time of sale was $3,000 = $13,000 − $10,000.

c. The ending balance of Net Unrealized holding Gains was $2,000 less at the end of 2008 than at the beginning, while the unrealized holding gain on the securities sold was $3,000. The sale reduced the balance by $3,000. Since the ending balance declined by only $2,000, the securities on hand must have increased during the year by $1,000, so the net decline is $2,000 = $3,000 − $1,000.

12.20 continued.

d. The Marketable Securities account increased by $8,000 = $195,000 − $187,000 during 2008. The sale reduced the account by $13,000 and the unrealized holding gain on the securities held at the end of the year increased the balance by $1,000; see Part *c.* above. A net increase of $9,000 after a reduction of $12,000 means the cost of new securities is $20,000 = $8,000 + $12,000.

12.21 (Turner Corporation; accounting for forward foreign exchange contract as a fair value hedge.)

a. The amount that Turner Corporation would receive if the contract were settled on December 31, 2008 is $1,020 (= $52,000 − $50,980). The present value of $1,020 discounted back six months at 8% per year is $981 (= $1,020 x .96154). Turner Corporation would report this amount as an asset.

b. Turner Corporation would also report a commitment to purchase the equipment for $981. The firm would not report a liability for the full purchase price; the commitment is an executory contract. It recognizes the commitment only to the extent of the derivative on the asset side of the balance sheet.

c. The fair value of the foreign exchange contract on June 30, 2009 just before settlement is the amount of cash Turner Corporation will receive from the counterparty, which is $3,757 (= $54,737 − $50,980).

d. **June 30, 2009**
Equipment 50,980
Commitment to Purchase Equipment........................ 3,757
   Cash 54,737

Assets	=	Liabilities	+	Shareholders' Equity	(Class.)
+50,980		−3,757			
−54,737					

e. **June 30, 2009**
Cash... 3,757
   Forward Foreign Exchange Contract 3,757

Assets	=	Liabilities	+	Shareholders' Equity	(Class.)
+3,757					
−3,757					

12.22 (Biddle Corporation; accounting for forward foreign exchange contract as a cash flow hedge.)

a. The amount that Biddle Corporation would receive if the contract were settled on December 31, 2008 is $1,200 (= $54,000 − $52,800). Biddle Corporation would report this amount as an asset.

b. Biddle Corporation would report a payable to the supplier of $54,000 (= €40,000 × $1.35).

c. The fair value of the foreign exchange contract on March 31, 2009 just before settlement is the amount of cash Biddle Corporation will receive from the counterparty, which is $3,200 (= $56,000 − $52,800).

d. **March 31, 2009**

Note Payable 56,000	
Cash	56,000

Assets	= Liabilities	+	Shareholders' Equity	(Class.)
−56,000	−56,000			

e. **March 31, 2009**

Cash 3,200	
Forward Foreign Exchange Contract	3,200

Assets	= Liabilities	+	Shareholders' Equity	(Class.)
+3,200				
−3,200				

The carrying value of the equipment before recognizing any depreciation is $52,800. The net cash outflow is $52,800 (= $56,000 − $3,200). The gains in Accumulated Other Comprehensive Income from revaluing the forward foreign exchange contract of $3,200 exactly offset the losses from revaluing the Note Payable of $3,200. Thus, Biddle Corporation could make an entry clearing these amounts from Accumulated Other Comprehensive Income.

12.23 (Dostal Corporation; journal entries and financial statement presentation of short-term securities available for sale.)

a. **2/05/2008**
Marketable Securities (Security A).............................. 60,000
   Cash 60,000

Assets	=	Liabilities	+	Shareholders' Equity	(Class.)
+60,000					
−60,000					

8/12/2008
Marketable Securities (Security B).............................. 25,000
   Cash 25,000

Assets	=	Liabilities	+	Shareholders' Equity	(Class.)
+25,000					
−25,000					

12/31/2008
Marketable Securities (Security A) (= $66,000 − $60,000).. 6,000
   Unrealized Holding Gain on Security A Available for Sale (Other Comprehensive Income).. 6,000

Assets	=	Liabilities	+	Shareholders' Equity	(Class.)
+6,000				+6,000	OCInc → AOCInc

Unrealized Holding Loss on Security B Available for Sale (Other Comprehensive Income) 5,000
   Marketable Securities (Security B) (= $20,000 − $25,000)... 5,000

Assets	=	Liabilities	+	Shareholders' Equity	(Class.)
−5,000				−5,000	OCInc → AOCInc

12.23 a. continued.

1/22/2009

Marketable Securities (Security C)............................	82,000	
Cash		82,000

Assets	=	Liabilities	+	Shareholders' Equity	(Class.)
+82,000					
−82,000					

2/25/2009

Marketable Securities (Security D)............................	42,000	
Cash		42,000

Assets	=	Liabilities	+	Shareholders' Equity	(Class.)
+42,000					
−42,000					

3/25/2009

Marketable Securities (Security E).............................	75,000	
Cash		75,000

Assets	=	Liabilities	+	Shareholders' Equity	(Class.)
+75,000					
−75,000					

6/05/2009

Cash..	72,000	
Unrealized Holding Gain on Security A Available for Sale (Other Comprehensive Income)	6,000	
Marketable Securities (Security A)....................		66,000
Realized Gain on Sale of Securities Available for Sale		12,000

Assets	=	Liabilities	+	Shareholders' Equity	(Class.)
+72,000				+12,000	IncSt → RE
−66,000				−6,000	OCInc → AOCInc

12.23 a. continued.

6/05/2009

Cash..	39,000
Realized Loss on Sale of Securities Available for Sale...	3,000
Marketable Securities (Security D).....................	42,000

Assets	=	Liabilities	+	Shareholders' Equity	(Class.)
+39,000				–3,000	IncSt → RE
–42,000					

12/31/2009

Unrealized Holding Loss on Security C Available for Sale (Other Comprehensive Income)................	3,000
Marketable Securities (Security C) (= $79,000 – $82,000)...	3,000

Assets	=	Liabilities	+	Shareholders' Equity	(Class.)
–3,000				–3,000	OCInc → AOCInc

12/31/2009

Marketable Securities (Security E) (= $80,000 – $75,000)...	5,000
Unrealized Holding Gain on Security E Available for Sale (Other Comprehensive Income)...	5,000

Assets	=	Liabilities	+	Shareholders' Equity	(Class.)
+5,000				+5,000	OCInc → AOCInc

b. **Balance Sheet on December 31, 2008**

Marketable Securities at Fair Value..	$ 86,000
Net Unrealized Holding Gain on Securities Available for Sale ($6,000 – $5,000)..	$ 1,000

Note
Marketable Securities on December 31, 2008 had an acquisition cost of $85,000 and a fair value of $86,000. Gross unrealized gains total $6,000 and gross unrealized losses total $5,000.

12.23 continued.

c. **Balance Sheet on December 31, 2009**
Marketable Securities at Fair Value.. $ 179,000
Net Unrealized Holding Loss on Securities Available for
  Sale.. $ (3,000)

Note
Marketable Securities on December 31, 2009 had an acquisition cost of $182,000 and a fair value of $179,000. Gross unrealized gains total $5,000 and gross unrealized losses total $8,000. Proceeds from sales of marketable securities totaled $111,000 during 2009. These sales resulted in gross realized gains of $12,000 and gross realized losses of $3,000. The net unrealized holding loss on securities available for sale changed as follows during 2009:

Balance, December 31, 2008 .... $ 1,000 Cr.
Accumulated Other Comprehensive Income (Unre-
  alized Holding Gain on Securities Sold)............................ (6,000) Dr.
Change in Net Unrealized Loss on Securities Held at
  Year End ($5,000 – $3,000).. 2,000 Cr.
Balance, December 31, 2009.. $ (3,000) Dr.

12.24 (Rice Corporation; journal entries and financial statement presentation of long-term securities available for sale.)

a. **3/05/2008**
Investments in Securities (Security A)...................... 40,000
  Cash 40,000

Assets	=	Liabilities	+	Shareholders' Equity	(Class.)
+40,000					
–40,000					

5/12/2008
Investments in Securities (Security B)...................... 80,000
  Cash 80,000

Assets	=	Liabilities	+	Shareholders' Equity	(Class.)
+80,000					
–80,000					

12.24 a. continued.

12/31/2008
Investments in Securities (Security A) (= $45,000 − $40,000)... 5,000
    Unrealized Holding Gain on Security A Available for Sale (Other Comprehensive Income).. 5,000

Assets	=	Liabilities	+	Shareholders' Equity	(Class.)
+5,000				+5,000	OCInc → AOCInc

12/31/2008
Unrealized Holding Loss on Security B Available for Sale (Other Comprehensive Income)................ 10,000
    Investments in Securities (Security B) (= $70,000 − $80,000)... 10,000

Assets	=	Liabilities	+	Shareholders' Equity	(Class.)
−10,000				−10,000	OCInc → AOCInc

3/22/2009
Investments in Securities (Security C)...................... 32,000
    Cash... 32,000

Assets	=	Liabilities	+	Shareholders' Equity	(Class.)
+32,000					
−32,000					

5/25/2009
Investments in Securities (Security D)...................... 17,000
    Cash... 17,000

Assets	=	Liabilities	+	Shareholders' Equity	(Class.)
+17,000					
−17,000					

12.24 a. continued.

5/25/2009
Investments in Securities (Security E) 63,000
    Cash 63,000

Assets	=	Liabilities	+	Shareholders' Equity	(Class.)
+63,000					
−63,000					

10/05/2009
Cash 52,000
Unrealized Holding Gain on Security A Available
  for Sale (Other Comprehensive Income) 5,000
    Investments in Securities (Security A) 45,000
    Realized Gain on Sale of Securities Available
      for Sale 12,000

Assets	=	Liabilities	+	Shareholders' Equity	(Class.)
+52,000				+12,000	IncSt → RE
−45,000				−5,000	OCInc → AOCInc

10/05/2009
Cash 16,000
Realized Loss on Sale of Securities Available for
  Sale 1,000
    Investments in Securities (Security D) 17,000

Assets	=	Liabilities	+	Shareholders' Equity	(Class.)
+16,000				−1,000	IncSt → RE
−17,000					

12.24 a. continued.

12/31/2009
Investments in Securities (Security B) (= $83,000 − $70,000) 13,000
    Unrealized Holding Loss on Security B Available for Sale (Other Comprehensive Income) 10,000
    Unrealized Holding Gain on Security B Available for Sale (Other Comprehensive Income) 3,000

Assets	=	Liabilities	+	Shareholders' Equity	(Class.)
+13,000				+10,000	OCInc → AOCInc
				+3,000	OCInc → AOCInc

12/31/2009
Unrealized Holding Loss on Security C Available for Sale (Other Comprehensive Income) (= $27,000 − $32,000) 5,000
    Investments in Securities (Security C) 5,000

Assets	=	Liabilities	+	Shareholders' Equity	(Class.)
−5,000				−5,000	OCInc → AOCInc

12/31/2009
Investments in Securities (Security E) (= $67,000 − $63,000) 4,000
    Unrealized Holding Gain on Security E Available for Sale (Other Comprehensive Income) 4,000

Assets	=	Liabilities	+	Shareholders' Equity	(Class.)
+4,000				+4,000	OCInc → AOCInc

b. **Balance Sheet on December 31, 2008**
Investments in Securities at Fair Value .... $ 115,000
Net Unrealized Holding Loss on Securities Available for Sale ($5,000 − $10,000) .... $ (5,000)

12.24 b. continued.

> *Note*
> Investments in Securities on December 31, 2008 had an acquisition cost of $120,000 and a fair value of $115,000. Gross unrealized gains total $5,000 and gross unrealized losses total $10,000.

c. **Balance Sheet on December 31, 2009**

Investments in Securities at Fair Value	$ 177,000
Net Unrealized Holding Gain on Securities Available for Sale	$ 2,000

> *Note*
> Investments in Securities on December 31, 2009 had an acquisition cost of $175,000 and a fair value of $177,000. Gross unrealized gains total $7,000 (= $3,000 + $4,000) and gross unrealized losses total $5,000. Proceeds from sales of investments in securities totaled $68,000 during 2009. These sales resulted in gross realized gains of $12,000 and gross realized losses of $1,000. The net unrealized holding loss on securities available for sale changed as follows during 2009:

Balance, December 31, 2008	$ (5,000)	Dr.
Unrealized Holding Gain on Securities Sold	(5,000)	Dr.
Change in Net Unrealized Loss on Securities Held at Year End ($13,000 – $5,000 + $4,000)	12,000	Cr.
Balance, December 31, 2009	$ 2,000	Cr.

12.25 (Moonshine Mining Company; analysis of financial statement disclosures for securities available for sale.) (Amounts in Thousands)

a. $10,267 loss = $11,418 – $21,685.

b. $2,649 gain = $8,807 – $6,158.

c. $12,459 = $21,685 – $6,158 – $3,068.

d. None. The unrealized holding loss on current marketable securities of $2,466 (= $4,601 – $7,067) and the unrealized holding gain on noncurrent marketable securities of $2,649 (= $8,807 – $6,158) appear in the shareholders' equity section of the balance sheet.

12.26 (Callahan Corporation; effect of various methods of accounting for marketable equity securities.)

a. **Trading Securities**

	2008	2009
Income Statement:		
Dividend Revenue	$ 3,300	$ 2,200
Unrealized Holding Gain (Loss):		
($54,000 – $55,000)	(1,000)	--
($17,000 – $14,000)	--	3,000
Realized Holding Gain (Loss) ($14,500 + $26,000) – ($16,000 + $24,000)	--	500
Total	$ 2,300	$ 5,700
Balance Sheet:		
Current Assets:		
Marketable Securities at Fair Value	$54,000	$ 17,000

b. **Securities Available for Sale (Current Asset)**

	2008	2009
Income Statement:		
Dividend Revenue	$ 3,300	$ 2,200
Realized Holding Gain (Loss): [= $40,500 – ($18,000 + $25,000)]	--	(2,500)
Total	$ 3,300	$ (300)
Balance Sheet:		
Current Assets:		
Marketable Securities at Fair Value	$54,000	$ 17,000
Shareholders' Equity:		
Net Unrealized Holding Gain (Loss) on Securities Available for Sale (Part of Accumulated Other Comprehensive Income):		
($54,000 – $55,000)	(1,000)	--
($17,000 – $12,000)	--	5,000

c. Same as Part b. except that the securities appear as Investments in Securities in the noncurrent assets section of the balance sheet.

d.

	Trading Securities	Securities Available for Sale Current Assets	Securities Available for Sale Noncurrent Assets
2008	$ 2,300	$ 3,300	$ 3,300
2009	5,700	(300)	(300)
Total	$ 8,000	$ 3,000	$ 3,000

The unrealized gain on Security I of $5,000 (= $17,000 – $12,000) at the end of 2009 appears in income if these securities are trading securities but in a separate shareholders' equity account if these securities are se-

12.26 d. continued.

curities available for sale (either a current asset or a noncurrent asset). Total shareholders' equity is the same. Retained earnings (pre-tax) are $5,000 larger if these securities are trading securities and the unrealized holding gain account is $5,000 larger if these securities are classified as securities available for sale.

12.27 (Analysis of financial statement disclosures related to marketable securities and quality of earnings.) (Amounts in Millions)

a.
Cash	37,600	
Realized Loss on Sale of Securities Available for Sale	113	
Realized Gain on Securities Available for Sale		443
Marketable Securities		37,270[a]

Assets	=	Liabilities	+	Shareholders' Equity	(Class.)
+37,600				–113	IncSt → RE
–37,270[a]				+443	IncSt → RE

[a]$14,075 + $37,163 – $13,968 = $37,270.

Marketable Securities	262	
Unrealized Holding Loss on Securities Available for Sale (= $37,270 – $37,008) (Other Comprehensive Income)		262

Assets	=	Liabilities	+	Shareholders' Equity	(Class.)
+262				+262	OCInc → AOCInc

b.
Balance, December 31, 2008 (= $957 – $510)	$ 447 Cr.
Net Unrealized Holding Loss on Securities Sold (from Part a.)	262 Cr.
Increase in Net Unrealized Holding Gain on Securities Held on December 31, 2009 (Plug)	518 Cr.
Balance, December 31, 2009 (= $1,445 – $218)	$ 1,227 Cr.

c.
Interest and Dividend Revenue	$ 1,081
Net Realized Gain on Securities Sold from Market Price Changes Occurring during 2009: (= $37,600 – $37,008)	592
Net Unrealized Holding Gain on Securities Held on December 31, 2009 (from Part b.)	518
Total Income	$ 2,191

12.27 continued.

d. The bank sold marketable securities during 2009, which had net unrealized holding losses of $262 million as of December 31, 2009. The sale of these securities at a gain suggests that fair prices increased substantially ($592 million) during 2009. The substantial increase in the net unrealized holding gain of $518 lends support to this conclusion about market price increases. The bank could have increased its income still further by selecting securities for sale that had unrealized holding *gains* as of December 31, 2008. If prices continued to increase on such securities during 2009 prior to sale, the realized gain would have been even larger than the reported net realized gain of $330 million (= $443 – $113). Firms with securities available for sale with unrealized holding gains can manage income by choosing which items to sell. This will not affect comprehensive income, but until analysts focus on comprehensive income, rather than net income, managements will be tempted to manage the net income figure.

12.28 (Accounting for forward commodity price contract as a cash flow hedge.)

a. Firm D does not make an entry on October 31, 2008, because the forward commodity price contract is a mutually unexecuted contract and requires no initial investment.

b. The fair value of the forward contract increases $100,000 [= 10,000 x ($320 – $310)].

December 31, 2008
Forward Commodity Contract 100,000
    Other Comprehensive Income 100,000

Assets	=	Liabilities	+	Shareholders' Equity	(Class.)
+100,000				+100,000	OCInc → AOCInc

The forward contract is an asset because the firm has the right to receive cash from the counterparty equal to the decline in the fair value of the inventory; $100,000 = [10,000 x ($320 – $310)].

c. The fair value of the inventory of approximately $310 per gallon exceeds its acquisition cost of $225 per gallon, so Firm D would not write down its inventory.

12.28 continued.

d. **March 31, 2009**
Forward Commodity Contract 400,000
  Other Comprehensive Income 400,000

Assets	=	Liabilities	+	Shareholders' Equity	(Class.)
+400,000				+400,000	OCInc → AOCInc

$400,000 = [10,000 gallons x ($310 − $270)].

e. **March 31, 2009**
Other Comprehensive Income 400,000
  Inventory 400,000

Assets	=	Liabilities	+	Shareholders' Equity	(Class.)
−400,000				−400,000	OCInc → AOCInc

f. **March 31, 2009**
Cash 500,000
  Forward Commodity Contract 500,000

Assets	=	Liabilities	+	Shareholders' Equity	(Class.)
+500,000					
−500,000					

$500,000 = [10,000 gallons x ($320 − $270)].

g. **March 31, 2009**
Cash 2,700,000
  Sales Revenue 2,700,000

Assets	=	Liabilities	+	Shareholders' Equity	(Class.)
+2,700,000				+2,700,000	IncSt → RE

$2,700,000 = 10,000 gallons x $270.

12.28 g. continued.

March 31, 2009

Other Comprehensive Income................................	500,000	
Cost of Goods Sold..	1,750,000	
Inventory...		2,250,000

Assets	= Liabilities	+	Shareholders' Equity	(Class.)
			-500,000	OCInc → AOCInc
-2,250,000			-1,750,000	IncSt → RE

The net balance in Other Comprehensive Income before the entry above related to the forward contract is a credit of $500,000 (= $100,000 + $400,000). The gross margin on the sale is $950,000 (= $2,700,000 − $1,750,000). This is the same gross margin that Firm D would have reported if it had not obtained the forward contract and the market price for whiskey on March 31, 2009 had been Firm D's anticipated amount of $320 per gallon ($950,000 = $3,200,000 − $2,250,000). The forward contract shifted the risk of changes in the selling price to the counterparty.

  h. Firm D would recognize changes in the fair value of both the inventory and the forward commodity contract and include the unrealized gains and losses in net income.

  i. A justification for treating the forward commodity price contract as a fair value hedge is that the firm wanted to protect the gross margin on the sale of $950,000 against commodity price changes. A justification for treating the contract as a cash flow hedge is that it wanted to ensure that it received a net cash inflow of $3,200,000 on the sale of the whiskey.

12.29 (Owens Corporation; accounting for forward foreign exchange contract as a fair value hedge and a cash flow hedge.)

  a. **October 1, 2008:** The purchase commitment and the forward foreign exchange contract are mutually unexecuted contracts as of October 1, 2008. GAAP provisions do not require firms to recognize mutually unexecuted contracts in the accounts.

December 31, 2008: The change in the value of the undiscounted cash flows related to the purchase commitment and the forward foreign exchange contract is $1,800 [= (60,000 x $1.35) − (60,000 x $1.32)]. The present value of $1,800 discounted at 8% for six months is $1,731 (= $1,800 x .96154).

12.29 a. continued.

December 31, 2008
Loss on Firm Commitment 1,731
    Commitment to Purchase Equipment 1,731

Assets	=	Liabilities	+	Shareholders' Equity	(Class.)
		+1,731		−1,731	IncSt → RE

To record a loss in net income on a previously unrecognized firm commitment because the U.S. dollar decreased in value relative to the euro.

December 31, 2008
Forward Foreign Exchange Contract 1,731
    Gain on Forward Foreign Exchange Contract 1,731

Assets	=	Liabilities	+	Shareholders' Equity	(Class.)
+1,731				+1,731	IncSt → RE

To measure the foreign exchange contract at fair value and recognize a gain in net income.

June 30, 2009
Interest Expense 69
    Commitment to Purchase Equipment 69

Assets	=	Liabilities	+	Shareholders' Equity	(Class.)
		+69		−69	IncSt → RE

To recognize interest on the commitment because of the passage of time: $69 = .04 \times \$1,731$.

June 30, 2009
Forward Foreign Exchange Contract 69
    Interest Revenue 69

Assets	=	Liabilities	+	Shareholders' Equity	(Class.)
+69				+69	IncSt → RE

To record interest on the foreign contract because of the passage of time: $69 = .04 \times \$1,731$.

12.29 a. continued.

The change in the value of the purchase commitment and the forward foreign exchange contract due to exchange rate changes between December 31, 2008 and June 30, 2009 is $3,000 [= (60,000 x $1.40) − (60,000 x $1.35)].

June 30, 2009
Loss on Firm Commitment.. 3,000
    Commitment to Purchase Equipment................... 3,000

Assets	=	Liabilities	+	Shareholders' Equity	(Class.)
		+3,000		−3,000	IncSt → RE

To record a loss on the purchase commitment because the value of the U.S. dollar declined relative to the euro.

June 30, 2009
Forward Foreign Exchange Contract........................... 3,000
    Gain on Forward Foreign Exchange Contract 3,000

Assets	=	Liabilities	+	Shareholders' Equity	(Class.)
+3,000				+3,000	IncSt → RE

To record the increase in the fair value of the forward foreign exchange contract because the U.S. dollar declined in value relative to the euro.

June 30, 2009
Equipment 79,200
Commitment to Purchase Equipment......................... 4,800
    Cash 84,000

Assets	=	Liabilities	+	Shareholders' Equity	(Class.)
+79,200		−4,800			
−84,000					

To record the amount paid in U.S. dollars to acquire €60,000 [$84,000 = (€60,000 x $1.4)], to eliminate the balance in the Commitment to Purchase Equipment account of $4,800 (= $1,731 + $69 + $3,000), and to record the acquisition cost of the equipment for $79,200.

12.29 a. continued.

June 30, 2009

Cash.. 4,800
    Forward Foreign Exchange Contract...................... 4,800

Assets	= Liabilities	+	Shareholders' Equity	(Class.)
+4,800				
–4,800				

To record cash received from the counterparty and eliminate the balance in the Forward Foreign Exchange account of $4,800 (= $1,731 + $69 + $3,000).

b. Owens Corporation would not recognize changes in the value of the purchase commitment. The entries for changes in the fair value of the forward foreign exchange contract would affect other comprehensive income each period instead of net income. On June 30, 2009, Accumulated Other Comprehensive Income would have a balance of $4,800 (= $1,731 + $69 + $3,000). The entry on this date to purchase the equipment would involve a debit to Other Comprehensive Income instead of the Commitment to Purchase Equipment account as shown in Part *a.* above.

c. To treat this hedge as a fair value hedge, Owens Corporation must desire to protect the value of the equipment. Perhaps Owens Corporation has committed to resell the equipment to a customer on June 30, 2009 for a fixed price in U.S. dollars and wants to protect its expected profit margin from the sale. To treat this hedge as a cash flow hedge, Owens Corporation must desire to protect the amount of cash it pays to the European supplier.

12.30 (Sandretto Corporation; accounting for interest rate swap as a fair value hedge.)

a. **January 1, 2008**

Equipment	50,000	
Note Payable		50,000

Assets	=	Liabilities	+	Shareholders' Equity	(Class.)
+50,000		+50,000			

To record the acquisition of equipment by giving a $50,000 note payable with a fixed interest rate of 6%.

December 31, 2008

Interest Expense	3,000	
Cash		3,000

Assets	=	Liabilities	+	Shareholders' Equity	(Class.)
–3,000				–3,000	IncSt → RE

To recognize interest expense and cash payment at the fixed interest rate of 6%: $3,000 = .06 x $50,000.

Interest rates increased during 2008. On December 31, the counterparty with whom Sandretto Corporation entered into the swap contract resets the interest rate for 2009 to 8%. Sandretto Corporation must restate the note payable to fair value and record the change in the fair value of the swap contract caused by the increase in the interest rate. The present value of the remaining cash flows on the note payable when discounted at 8% is:

Present Value of Interest Payments: $3,000 x 1.78326 = ... $ 5,350
Present Value of Principal: $50,000 x .85734 = ... 42,867
    Total Present Value .... $ 48,217

Sandretto Corporation makes the following entry to record the change in fair value:

12.30 a. continued.

December 31, 2008
Note Payable... 1,783
   Gain on Revaluation of Note Payable 1,783

Assets	=	Liabilities	+	Shareholders' Equity	(Class.)
		−1,783		+1,783	IncSt → RE

To measure the note payable at fair value with cash flows discounted at 8%: $1,783 = $50,000 − $48,217.

The increase in interest rate to 8% means that Sandretto Corporation must pay an additional $1,000 [= (.08 − .06) x $50,000] each year in interest payments. The present value of a $1,000 annuity for two periods at 8% is $1,783 (= $1,000 x 1.78326). Thus, the fair value of the swap contract increased from zero at the beginning of 2008 to $1,783 at the end of 2008. Sandretto Corporation makes the following entry:

December 31, 2008
Loss on Revaluation of Swap Contract...................... 1,783
   Swap Contract... 1,783

Assets	=	Liabilities	+	Shareholders' Equity	(Class.)
		+1,783		−1,783	IncSt → RE

To measure the swap contract at fair value and recognize a liability on the balance sheet and a loss in net income.

December 31, 2009
Interest Expense... 3,857
   Note Payable.. 857
   Cash 3,000

Assets	=	Liabilities	+	Shareholders' Equity	(Class.)
−3,000		+857		−3,857	IncSt → RE

To record interest expense at 8% of the carrying value of the note payable at the beginning of the year ($3,857 = .08 x $48,217), the cash payment at the contractual interest rate of 6% on the face amount of the note ($3,000 = .06 x $50,000), and the increase in the carrying value of the note payable for the difference.

12.30 a. continued.

December 31, 2009
Interest Expense.. 143
   Swap Contract.. 143

Assets	=	Liabilities	+	Shareholders' Equity	(Class.)
+143				+143	IncSt → RE

To record interest expense for the increase in the carrying value of the swap contract for the passage of time: $143 = .08 \times \$1,783$.

December 31, 2009
Swap Contract... 1,000
   Cash 1,000

Assets	=	Liabilities	+	Shareholders' Equity	(Class.)
−1,000		−1,000			

To record cash paid to the counterparty because the interest rate increased from 6% to 8%.

Firm B must revalue the note payable and the swap contract for changes in fair value. The bank resets the interest rate in the swap agreement to 4% for 2010. The present value of the remaining payments on the note at 4% is:

Present Value of Interest Payments: $3,000 \times .96154 = $......... $ 2,885
Present Value of Principal: $50,000 \times .96154 = $..................... <u>48,077</u>
   Total Present Value .... <u>$ 50,962</u>

The carrying value of the note payable before revaluation is $49,074 (= $48,217 + $857). The entry to measure the note payable at fair value is:

December 31, 2009
Loss on Revaluation of Note Payable.................. 1,888
   Note Payable... 1,888

Assets	=	Liabilities	+	Shareholders' Equity	(Class.)
		+1,888		−1,888	IncSt → RE

To measure the note payable at fair value using an interest rate of 4% to discount the remaining cash flows to a present value: $1,888 = $50,962 − $49,074.

12.30 a. continued.

The fair value of the swap contract increases. Sandretto Corporation will receive $1,000 at the end of 2010 because of the swap contract. Thus, the swap contract becomes an asset instead of a liability. The present value of $1,000 when discounted at 4% is $962 (= $1,000 × .96154). The carrying value of the swap contract before revaluation is a liability of $926 (= $1,783 + $143 – $1,000). The entry to revalue the swap contract is:

December 31, 2009
Swap Contract (Liability).. 926
Swap Contract (Asset).. 962
   Gain on Revaluation of Swap Contract..................   1,888

Assets	=	Liabilities	+	Shareholders' Equity	(Class.)
+962		–926		–1,888	IncSt → RE

To measure the swap contract at fair value using a discount rate of 4% and recognize a gain from the increase in fair value.

At the end of 2009, the Note Payable account has a balance of $50,962 and the Swap Contract account has a debit balance of $962.

b. **January 1, 2010**
Note Payable... 50,962
   Cash..   50,000
   Swap Contract (Asset)...   962

Assets	=	Liabilities	+	Shareholders' Equity	(Class.)
–50,000		–50,962			
–962					

To repay note payable prior to maturity and close out the swap contract.

c. The entries would be identical if Sandretto Corporation chose the fair value option because the note payable and swap agreement would be measured at fair value and changes in fair value included in net income under both the accounting for the derivative as a fair value hedge and the accounting under the fair value option.

12.31 (Avery Corporation; accounting for an interest rate swap as a cash flow hedge.)

January 1, 2008

Equipment	50,000	
Note Payable		50,000

Assets	=	Liabilities	+	Shareholders' Equity	(Class.)
+50,000		+50,000			

To record the acquisition of equipment by giving a $50,000 note payable with a variable interest rate of 6%.

December 31, 2008

Interest Expense	3,000	
Cash		3,000

Assets	=	Liabilities	+	Shareholders' Equity	(Class.)
–3,000				–3,000	IncSt → RE

To recognize interest expense and cash payment at the variable interest rate of 6%: $3,000 = .06 x $50,000.

The fair value of the swap agreement on December 31, 2008 after the counterparty resets the interest rate to 8% is $1,783 (= $1,000 x 1.78326). This amount is the present value of the $1,000 that the counterparty will pay Avery Corporation on December 31 of 2009 and December 31 of 2010 if the interest rate remains at 8%.

December 31, 2008

Swap Contract	1,783	
Gain on Revaluation of Swap Contract		1,783

Assets	=	Liabilities	+	Shareholders' Equity	(Class.)
+1,783				+1,783	OCInc → AOCInc

To measure the swap contract at fair value and recognize an asset on the balance sheet and a gain in other comprehensive income.

12.31 continued.

December 31, 2009
Interest Expense 4,000
   Cash 4,000

Assets	=	Liabilities	+	Shareholders' Equity	(Class.)
–4,000				–4,000	IncSt → RE

To recognize interest expense and cash payment at the variable interest rate: $4,000 = .08 \times $50,000.

Avery Corporation must also recognize interest on the swap contract because of the passage of time.

December 31, 2009
Swap Contract 143
   Interest on Swap Contract... 143

Assets	=	Liabilities	+	Shareholders' Equity	(Class.)
+143				+143	OCInc → AOCInc

To record interest for the increase in the carrying value of the swap contract for the passage of time: $143 = .08 \times $1,783.

Avery Corporation receives from the counterparty the $1,000 [= $50,000 × (.08 – .06)] required by the swap contract. The entry is:

December 31, 2009
Cash 1,000
   Swap Contract 1,000

Assets	=	Liabilities	+	Shareholders' Equity	(Class.)
+1,000					
–1,000					

To record cash received from the counterparty because the interest rate increased from 6% to 8%.

12.31 continued.

December 31, 2009

Other Comprehensive Income	1,000	
Interest Expense		1,000

Assets	=	Liabilities	+	Shareholders' Equity	(Class.)
				–1,000	OCInc → AOCInc
				+1,000	IncSt → RE

To reclassify a portion of other comprehensive income to net income for the hedged portion of interest expense on the note payable.

At this point the swap contract account has a debit balance of $926 (= $1,783 + $143 − $1,000). Other comprehensive income related to this transaction, likewise, has a credit balance of $926.
    Resetting the interest rate on December 31, 2009 to 4% changes the fair value of the swap contract from an asset to a liability. The present value of the $1,000 that Avery Corporation will pay to the counterparty at the end of 2010 when discounted at 4% is $962 (= $1,000 × .96154). The entry to revalue to swap contract is:

December 31, 2009

Loss on Revaluation of Swap Contract	1,888	
Swap Contract (Asset)		926
Swap Contract (Liability)		962

Assets	=	Liabilities	+	Shareholders' Equity	(Class.)
–926		+962		–1,888	OCInc → AOCInc

To measure the swap contract at fair value and recognize a liability on the balance sheet and a loss in other comprehensive income.

December 31, 2010

Interest Expense	2,000	
Cash		2,000

Assets	=	Liabilities	+	Shareholders' Equity	(Class.)
–2,000				–2,000	IncSt → RE

To recognize interest expense and cash payment at the variable interest rate of 4%: $2,000 = .04 × $50,000.

12.31 continued.

December 31, 2010
Interest on Swap Contract.. 38
    Swap Contract..   38

Assets	=	Liabilities	+	Shareholders' Equity	(Class.)
		+38		−38	OCInc → AOCInc

To record interest for the increase in the carrying value of the swap contract for the passage of time: $38 = .04 \times \$962$.

December 31, 2010
Swap Contract.. 1,000
    Cash..   1,000

Assets	=	Liabilities	+	Shareholders' Equity	(Class.)
−1,000		−1,000			

To record cash paid to the counterparty because the interest rate decreased from 10% to 4%.

December 31, 2010
Interest Expense... 1,000
    Other Comprehensive Income.................................   1,000

Assets	=	Liabilities	+	Shareholders' Equity	(Class.)
				−1,000	IncSt → RE
				+1,000	OCInc → AOCInc

To reclassify a portion of other comprehensive income to net income for the hedged portion of interest expense on the note payable.

December 31, 2010
Note Payable.. 50,000
    Cash..   50,000

Assets	=	Liabilities	+	Shareholders' Equity	(Class.)
−50,000		−50,000			

To record repayment of note payable at maturity.

12.31 continued.

The Swap Contract account has a balance of zero on December 31, 2010 (= $962 + $38 − $1,000). Thus, Avery Corporation need make no entry to close out the swap contract account.

CHAPTER 13

INTERCORPORATE INVESTMENTS IN COMMON STOCK

Questions, Exercises, and Problems: Answers and Solutions

13.1 See the text or the glossary at the end of the book.

13.2 Control is present when one entity has sufficient ownership interest or contractual rights to make both strategic and operating decisions for another entity. Significant influence is present when one entity has sufficient ownership interest or contractual rights to influence those decisions but cannot unilaterally make those decisions. Ownership of more than 50% of the voting stock of another entity usually implies an ability to control that entity and the preparation of consolidated financial statements. Authoritative guidance specifies that ownership of 20% to 50% of the voting stock implies an ability to exert significant influence over another entity and the use of the equity method. Ownership of less than 20% may permit significant influence and ownership of greater than 20% may not permit significant influence, so firms must apply judgment in deciding on the appropriate accounting method.

13.3 Dividends represent revenues under the fair-value method, or a return of capital under the equity method, or eliminated under the consolidation method.

13.4 Firms use over time the service potential of assets with a limited life. The depreciation and amortization allocate the acquisition cost of this service potential to the periods of benefit, whether the amount is in the Investments, Property, Plant, and Equipment, or some other account.

13.5 When control is present, a parent and a subsidiary operate as a single economic entity. Eliminating intercompany profit and loss in these cases reflects transactions of the economic entity with all other entities. When significant influence is present, the investor and investee operate as economic entity to a lesser extent than when control is present. Thus, the concept of operating as an economic entity, in part, justifies eliminating intercompany profit and loss on equity method investments. Also, the ability to exert significant influence places the firms in a related party arrangement where prices set on intercompany transactions may not reflect arms-length dealings.

13.6   The Investment account changes under the equity method with all changes in the shareholders' equity of the investee, whether those changes are from additional stock issues, treasury stock transactions, net income, other comprehensive income, or dividends.

13.7   Under the equity method, the change each period in the net assets, or shareholders' equity, of the subsidiary appears on the one line, Investment in Subsidiary, on the balance sheet. When the parent consolidates the subsidiary, changes in the individual assets and liabilities that comprise the net asset change appear in the individual consolidated assets and liabilities. Likewise, under the equity method, the investor's interest in the investee's earnings appears in one line on the income statement, Equity in Earnings of Unconsolidated Subsidiary. When the parent consolidates the subsidiary, the individual revenues and expenses of the subsidiary appear in consolidated revenues and expenses.

13.8   When the investor uses the equity method, total assets include the Investment in Subsidiary account. The investment account reflects the parent's interest in the *net* assets (assets minus liabilities) of the subsidiary. When the investor consolidates the subsidiary, total consolidated assets include all of the subsidiary's assets. Consolidated liabilities include the liabilities of the subsidiary. Thus, total assets on a consolidated basis exceed total assets when the investor uses the equity method.

13.9   If Company A owns less than, or equal to, 50% of Company B's voting stock, it is a minority investor in Company B. If Company A owns more than 50% of Company C, it is a majority investor in Company C. The entities holding the remainder of the voting stock of Company C are minority investors. Their minority, or noncontrolling, interest appears on the consolidated balance sheet of Company A and Company C.

13.10   An economic entity is a group of companies that operates under the control of a parent company instead of as separate companies. The parent company makes strategic and operating decisions with the interest of the group of companies, instead of the separate companies, foremost in mind. Thus, the economic entity operates as if it were a single company. Consolidated financial statements reflect the financial position and results of operations of the economic entity with all other entities and not the results of any one company within the consolidated group.

13.11   Failing to eliminate the Investment in Subsidiary account will result in double counting the net assets of the subsidiary in the consolidated balance sheet, once as the Investment account on the parent's books and once as the individual net assets on the subsidiary's books.

13.12 The noncontrolling interest in net income is an income statement account that shows the claim of the noncontrolling shareholders on the net income of the consolidated group of companies. The noncontrolling interest in net assets is a balance sheet account that shows the claim of the noncontrolling shareholders on the net assets of the consolidated group of companies. Technically, the noncontrolling shareholders' claim is only on the net income and net assets of the particular subsidiary in which they have an ownership interest. Because the net income and net assets of the subsidiary merge with those of the parent and other subsidiaries in consolidated financial statements, the noncontrolling interest appears as a claim against consolidated net income and consolidated net assets.

13.13 One can envision scenarios where the equity method or proportionate consolidation better reflects the relation between the joint owners and the joint venture. For example, assume a joint venture in which one of the joint owners manages day-to-day operations and the other joint owner(s) simply takes part in making strategic decisions. In this case, the equity method may better reflect the relation for the less active owner(s). As another example assume one joint owner manages operations in the United States and another joint owner manages operations in Europe. In this case, the assets, markets, pricing, and other factors are separate. Proportionate consolidation may better reflect the relation for the joint owners.

13.14 Contracts or other agreements might shift control of the entity from its owners to some other entity. For example, a court might control a subsidiary in bankruptcy even though a parent company owns 100% of the common stock. As another example, one entity might agree to cover all losses of another entity even though it owns none of the other entity's common stock.

13.15 (Hanna Company; equity method entries.)

Investment in Stock of Denver Company.......................... 550,000
    Cash 550,000

Assets	=	Liabilities	+	Shareholders' Equity	(Class.)
+550,000					
−550,000					

To record acquisition of common stock.

Investment in Stock of Denver Company.......................... 120,000
    Equity in Earnings of Denver Company..................... 120,000

Assets	=	Liabilities	+	Shareholders' Equity	(Class.)
+120,000				+120,000	IncSt → RE

To accrue 100% share of Denver Company's earnings.

13.15 continued.

Cash or Dividends Receivable... 30,000
    Investment in Stock of Denver Company................. 30,000

Assets	=	Liabilities	+	Shareholders' Equity	(Class.)
+30,000					
−30,000					

To accrue dividends received or receivable.

13.16 (Weber Corporation; equity method entries.) (Amounts in Millions)

Investment in Stock of Albee Computer........................ 100
    Cash 100

Assets	=	Liabilities	+	Shareholders' Equity	(Class.)
+100					
−100					

To record acquisition of shares of common stock.

Investment in Stock of Weber Computer 20
    Equity in Earnings of Weber Computer..................... 20

Assets	=	Liabilities	+	Shareholders' Equity	(Class.)
+20				+20	IncSt → RE

To accrue Weber Computer's earnings for the year.

Cash (or Dividends Receivable) 6
    Investment in Stock of Weber Computer 6

Assets	=	Liabilities	+	Shareholders' Equity	(Class.)
+6					
−6					

To record dividends received or receivable.

13.16 continued.

    Amortization Expense 1.6
        Investment in Stock of Weber Computer 1.6

Assets	=	Liabilities	+	Shareholders' Equity	(Class.)
+1.6				−1.6	IncSt → RE

To amortize patent; $1.6 = [.20 \times (\$500 − \$420)10]$.
Investment is now $112.4 = \$100 + \$20 − \$6 − \$1.6$.

13.17 (Wood Corporation; journal entries to apply the equity method of accounting for investments in securities.)

January 2
Investment in Securities (Knox) 350,000
Investment in Securities (Vachi) 196,000
Investment in Securities (Snow) 100,000
    Cash 646,000

Assets	=	Liabilities	+	Shareholders' Equity	(Class.)
+350,000					
+196,000					
+100,000					
−646,000					

December 31
Investment in Securities (Knox) 35,000
Investment in Securities (Vachi) 12,000
    Investment in Securities (Snow) 4,800
    Equity in Earnings of Affiliates 42,200

Assets	=	Liabilities	+	Shareholders' Equity	(Class.)
+35,000				+42,200	IncSt → RE
+12,000					
−4,800					

$(.50 \times \$70,000) + (.30 \times \$40,000) − (.20 \times \$24,000) = \$42,200$.

13.17 continued.

December 31
Cash	19,500	
Investment in Securities (Knox)		15,000
Investment in Securities (Vachi)		4,500

Assets	=	Liabilities	+	Shareholders' Equity	(Class.)
+19,500					
−15,000					
−4,500					

(.50 × $30,000) + (.30 × $15,000) = $19,500.

13.18 (Stebbins Corporation; journal entries to apply the equity method of accounting for investments in securities.)

a. **January 1, 2008**

Investment in Securities (R)	250,000	
Investment in Securities (S)	325,000	
Investment in Securities (T)	475,000	
Cash		1,050,000

Assets	=	Liabilities	+	Shareholders' Equity	(Class.)
+250,000					
+325,000					
+475,000					
−1,050,000					

December 31, 2008

Investment in Securities (R)	50,000	
Investment in Securities (S)	48,000	
Investment in Securities (T)		75,000
Equity in Earnings of Affiliates		23,000

Assets	=	Liabilities	+	Shareholders' Equity	(Class.)
+50,000				+23,000	IncSt → RE
+48,000					
−75,000					

(.25 × $200,000) + (.40 × $120,000) − (.50 × $150,000) = $23,000.

Solutions

13.18 a. continued.

December 31, 2008
Cash.. 63,250
    Investment in Securities (R).. 31,250
    Investment in Securities (S)... 32,000

Assets	= Liabilities	+	Shareholders' Equity	(Class.)
+63,250				
−31,250				
−32,000				

(.25 x $125,000) + (.40 x $80,000) = $63,250.

December 31, 2008
Depreciation Expense.. 4,000
    Investment in Securities (R).. 4,000

Assets	= Liabilities	+	Shareholders' Equity	(Class.)
−4,000			−4,000	IncSt → RE

The cost of the investment in Company R exceeds the carrying value of the net assets acquired by $50,000 [= $250,000 − (.25 x $800,000)]. Stebbins Corporation attributes $40,000 of the excess to buildings and must depreciate $4,000 (= $40,000/10) each year. The firm attributes the remaining excess to goodwill, which it need not depreciate.

The cost of the investment in Company S exceeds its carrying value by $25,000 [= $325,000 − (.40 x $750,000)]. Stebbins Corporation attributes this excess to goodwill. The acquisition cost of the investment in Security T equals the carrying value of the net assets acquired.

December 31, 2009
Investment in Securities (R).. 56,250
Investment in Securities (S).. 30,000
Investment in Securities (T).. 25,000
    Equity in Earnings of Affiliates...................................... 111,250

Assets	= Liabilities	+	Shareholders' Equity	(Class.)
+56,250			+111,250	IncSt → RE
+30,000				
+25,000				

(.25 x $225,000) + (.40 x $75,000) + (.50 x $50,000) = $111,250.

13.18 a. continued.

December 31, 2009
Cash 64,500
    Investment in Securities (R) 32,500
    Investment in Securities (S) 32,000

Assets	=	Liabilities	+	Shareholders' Equity	(Class.)
+64,500					
−32,500					
−32,000					

(.25 × $130,000) + (.40 × $80,000).

December 31, 2009
Depreciation Expense 4,000
    Investment in Securities (R) 4,000

Assets	=	Liabilities	+	Shareholders' Equity	(Class.)
−4,000				−4,000	IncSt → RE

b. **January 1, 2010**
Cash 275,000
Loss on Sale of Investments 9,500
    Investment in Securities (R) 284,500

Assets	=	Liabilities	+	Shareholders' Equity	(Class.)
+275,000				−9,500	IncSt → RE
−284,500					

$250,000 + $50,000 − $31,250 − $4,000 + $56,250 − $32,500 − $4,000 = $284,500.

13.19 (Laesch Company; working backwards to consolidation relations.)

    a. $70,000 = ($156,000 − $100,000)/.80.

    b. 72.7 percent = ($156,000 − $100,000)/$77,000.

    c. $56,000 = ($156,000 − $100,000).

13.20 Dealco Corporation; working backwards from consolidated income statements.) (Amounts in Millions)

a. $56/$140 = 40\%$.

b. $[.40 \times (1 - .25) \times \$140] = \$42$.

c. $[1 - (\$42/\$280)] = 1 - .15 = 85\%$.

13.21 (CAR Corporation; consolidation policy and principal consolidation concepts.)

a. CAR Corporation should consolidate Alexandre du France Software Systems and R Credit Corporation or, under exceptional circumstances, use the fair value method.

b.
Charles Electronics	$(.75 \times \$120,000) =$	$\$\ 90,000$
Alexandre du France Software Systems	$(.80 \times 60,000) =$	$48,000$
R Credit Corporation	$(.90 \times 144,000) =$	$\underline{129,600}$
Total Income from Subsidiaries		$\underline{\$267,600}$

c. Noncontrolling Interest shown under accounting assumed in problem:

Charles Electronics	$(.25 \times \$120,000) =$	$\$30,000$
Alexandre du France Software Systems	(None) =	--
R Credit Corporation	(None) =	$\underline{}$
		$\underline{\$30,000}$

CAR Corporation subtracts the noncontrolling interest in computing net income.

d. Charles Electronics, no increase because already consolidated.

Alexandre du France Software Systems increase by 80% of net income less dividends:

$.80 \times (\$96,000 - \$60,000) = \$28,800$.

R Credit Corporation, no increase because equity method results in the same income statement effects as do consolidated statements. Net income of CAR Corporation would be:

$\$1,228,800 = \$1,200,000$ (as reported) $+ \$28,800$ (increase).

e. Noncontrolling Interest shown if CAR Corporation consolidated all companies:

Charles Electronics	$(.25 \times \$120,000) =$	$\$\ 30,000$
Alexandre du France Software Systems	$(.20 \times 96,000) =$	$19,200$
R Credit Corporation	$(.10 \times 144,000) =$	$\underline{14,400}$
		$\underline{\$\ 63,600}$

13.22 (Joyce Company and Vogel Company; equity method entries.)

Joyce Company's Books

(1) Investment in Stock of Vogel Company 420,000
    Cash 420,000

Assets	=	Liabilities	+	Shareholders' Equity	(Class.)
+420,000					
−420,000					

To record acquisition of common stock.

(2) Accounts Receivable 29,000
    Sales Revenue 29,000

Assets	=	Liabilities	+	Shareholders' Equity	(Class.)
+29,000				+29,000	IncSt → RE

To record intercompany sales on account.

(2) Cost of Goods Sold 29,000
    Inventories 29,000

Assets	=	Liabilities	+	Shareholders' Equity	(Class.)
−29,000				−29,000	IncSt → RE

To record cost of intercompany sales.

(3) Advance to Vogel Company 6,000
    Cash 6,000

Assets	=	Liabilities	+	Shareholders' Equity	(Class.)
+6,000					
−6,000					

To record advance to Vogel Company.

13.22 continued.

(4) Cash 16,000
   Accounts Receivable 16,000

Assets	= Liabilities	+	Shareholders' Equity	(Class.)
+16,000				
−16,000				

To record collections on account from Vogel Company.

(5) Cash 4,000
   Advance to Vogel Company 4,000

Assets	= Liabilities	+	Shareholders' Equity	(Class.)
+4,000				
−4,000				

To record collection of advance from Vogel Company.

(6) Cash 20,000
   Investment in Stock of Vogel Company 20,000

Assets	= Liabilities	+	Shareholders' Equity	(Class.)
+20,000				
−20,000				

To record dividend from Vogel Company.

(7) Investment in Stock of Vogel Company 30,000
   Equity in Earnings of Vogel Company 30,000

Assets	= Liabilities	+	Shareholders' Equity	(Class.)
+30,000			+30,000	IncSt → RE

To accrue 100% share of Vogel Company's net income.

13.22 continued.

(8) Amortization Expense.. 4,000
      Investment in Stock of Vogel Company............... 4,000

Assets	= Liabilities	+	Shareholders' Equity	(Class.)
−4,000			−4,000	IncSt → RE

To record amortization of patent; $4,000 = ($20,000 − $380,000)/10.

Vogel Company's Books

(1) No entry.

(2) Inventories... 29,000
      Accounts Payable.. 29,000

Assets	= Liabilities	+	Shareholders' Equity	(Class.)
+29,000	+29,000			

To record intercompany purchase of materials on account.

(3) Cash.. 6,000
      Advance from Joyce Company............................ 6,000

Assets	= Liabilities	+	Shareholders' Equity	(Class.)
+6,000	+6,000			

To record advance from Joyce Company.

(4) Accounts Payable... 16,000
      Cash.. 16,000

Assets	= Liabilities	+	Shareholders' Equity	(Class.)
−16,000	−16,000			

To record payment for purchases on account.

13.22 continued.

(5) Advance from Joyce Company 4,000
    Cash 4,000

Assets	= Liabilities	+	Shareholders' Equity	(Class.)
–4,000	–4,000			

To record repayment of advance.

(6) Retained Earnings 20,000
    Cash 20,000

Assets	= Liabilities	+	Shareholders' Equity	(Class.)
–20,000			–20,000	RE

To record declaration and payment of dividend.

13.23 (Alpha/Omega; working backwards from data which has eliminated intercompany transactions.)

a. $80,000 = $450,000 + $250,000 – $620,000.

b. $30,000 is Omega's cost; $20,000 is Alpha's cost; $20,000 original cost to Alpha.

Markup on the goods sold from Alpha to Omega, which remain in Omega's inventory, is $10,000 (= $60,000 + $50,000 – $100,000).
Because Alpha priced the goods with markup 50% over its costs, the cost to Alpha to produce goods with markup of $10,000 is $20,000 and the total sales price from Alpha to Omega is $30,000 (= $10,000 + $20,000).

13.24 (Homer/Tonga; working backwards from purchase data.)

a. $1,060,000 = $80,000 + $980,000.

b.
Carrying Value of Total Assets (from Part *a*.)	$1,060,000
Less Carrying Value of Current Assets	(210,000)
Less Carrying Value of Goodwill	0
Carrying Value of Depreciable Assets	$ 850,000

13.25 (Effect of equity method versus consolidation.)

    a. (1) When Parent uses the equity method, it recognizes 80% of the net income of Sub. When Parent prepares consolidated financial statements with Sub, it recognizes 100% of the revenues, expenses, and net income of Sub and then subtracts the 20% noncontrolling interest share of net income. Thus, net income is the same whether Parent uses the equity method or consolidates Sub.

       (2) Liabilities in the numerator increase by the amount of the liabilities of Sub. Assets in the denominator decrease by the amount in the investment account and increase by the amount of Sub's assets. In this case where there is no excess purchase price, the denominator increases by the liabilities (= assets of Sub minus shareholders' equity) of Sub. Equal increases in the numerator and denominator of a ratio that is initially less than 1.0 result in an increase in the ratio.

    b. (1) The Parent or investor's share of Sub's net income declines, regardless of whether the amount appears on the single line, Equity in Earnings of Sub, or on multiple revenue and expense lines.

       (2) Total assets decrease when using the equity method because the investor invests less. Total assets do not decrease when preparing consolidated financial statements because Parent eliminates its Investment in Sub account and consolidates 100% of Sub's assets, regardless of its ownership percentage.

       (3) The liabilities of Sub do not appear on Parent's balance sheet when it uses the equity method, regardless of the ownership percentage.

       (4) Total liabilities do not change when preparing consolidated financial statements because Parent consolidates 100% of Sub's liabilities, regardless of its ownership percentage.

       (5) Shareholders' equity decreases when using the equity method because Parent owns less of the net income, dividends, and shareholders' equity of Sub. The shareholders' equity on the consolidated balance sheet is the shareholders' equity of Parent only. Parent eliminates the shareholders' equity of Sub when preparing consolidated financial statements in its entry to eliminate the Investment in Sub account and recognize the noncontrolling interest.

       (6) Assets and liabilities do not change with the decrease in ownership percentage, because consolidated financial statements reflect 100% of Sub's assets and liabilities. The change in the ownership percentage affects the amount of the noncontrolling interest in Sub's net assets.

13.26 (Effect of errors on financial statements.)

	Assets	Liabilities	Shareholders' Equity	Net Income
a.	O/S	No	O/S	O/S
b.	O/S	No	O/S	O/S
c.	No	No	No	No
d.	O/S	O/S	No	No
e.	No	U/S	O/S	O/S

13.27 (Parrot Corporation; accounting for a joint venture.)

a.

	Equity Method	Proportionate Consolidation
Current Assets	$ 300	$ 400
Property, Plant and Equipment (Net)	500	800
Investment in Joint Venture (Equity Method)	200	--
Total Assets	$ 1,000	$ 1,200
Current Liabilities	$ 250	$ 325
Long-Term Debt	450	575
Total Liabilities	$ 700	$ 900
Shareholders' Equity	$ 300	$ 300
Total Liabilities and Shareholders' Equity	$ 1,000	$ 1,200

b. (1) **Equity Method**
Liabilities to Assets Ratio: $700/$1,000 = 70%.
Debt-Equity Ratio: $450/$300 = 150%.

(2) **Consolidation**
Liabilities to Assets Ratio: $900/$1,200 = 75%.
Debt-Equity Ratio: $575/$300 = 191.7%.

c. The liabilities to asset ratio is larger with proportionate consolidation, because the joint venture has a higher proportion of liabilities in its capital structure than does Parrot Corporation. Although the joint venture has a lower debt-equity ratio than Parrot Corporation, consolidation results in an increase in the numerator of the debt-equity ratio with no change in the denominator, so the ratio increases.

13.28 (Ely Company and Sims Company; preparing a consolidated balance sheet.)

	Ely Company	Sims Company	Consolidated
Assets			
Cash	$ 12,000	$ 5,000	$ 17,000
Receivables	25,000	15,000	32,500
Investment in Sims Company	78,000	--	--
Other Assets	85,000	80,000	183,000
Total Assets	$ 200,000	$ 100,000	$ 232,500
Liabilities and Shareholders' Equity			
Current Liabilities	$ 45,000	$ 40,000	$ 77,500
Common Stock	50,000	10,000	50,000
Retained Earnings	105,000	50,000	105,000
Total Liabilities and Shareholders' Equity	$ 200,000	$ 100,000	$ 232,500

The elimination entries (not required) are as follows:

Common Stock	10,000	
Retained Earnings	50,000	
Other Assets (Goodwill)	18,000	
Investment in Sims Company		78,000

Assets	=	Liabilities	+	Shareholders' Equity	(Class.)
+18,000				−10,000	ContriCap
−78,000				−50,000	ContriCap

To eliminate investment account, the shareholders' equity of Sims Company, and recognize the excess price as an asset.

Current Liabilities	7,500	
Receivables		7,500

Assets	=	Liabilities	+	Shareholders' Equity	(Class.)
−7,500		−7,500			IncSt → RE

To eliminate intercompany advances.

13.29 (Company P and Company S; preparing a consolidated balance sheet.)

a.

	Company P	Company S	Consolidated
Assets			
Cash	$ 36,000	$ 26,000	$ 62,000
Accounts and Notes Receivable	180,000	50,000	213,600
Inventories	440,000	250,000	690,000
Investment in Company S (Using the Equity Method)	726,000	--	--
Property, Plant and Equipment (Net)	600,000	424,000	1,080,000
Total Assets	$ 1,982,000	$ 750,000	$ 2,045,600
Liabilities and Shareholders' Equity			
Accounts and Notes Payable	$ 110,000	$ 59,000	$ 152,600
Other Liabilities	286,000	21,000	307,000
Common Stock	1,200,000	500,000	1,200,000
Additional Paid-In Capital	--	100,000	--
Retained Earnings	386,000	70,000	386,000
Total Liabilities and Shareholders' Equity	$ 1,982,000	$ 750,000	$ 2,045,600

The elimination entries (not required) are as follows:

Common Stock	500,000
Additional Paid-In Capital	100,000
Retained Earnings	70,000
Property, Plant and Equipment	56,000
Investment in Company S	726,000

Assets	= Liabilities	+	Shareholders' Equity	(Class.)
+56,000			−500,000	ContriCap
−726,000			−100,000	ContriCap
			−70,000	RE

To eliminate the investment account, the shareholders' equity accounts of Company S, and recognize the unamortized excess acquisition cost.

13.29 a. continued.

      Accounts and Notes Payable.. 16,400
          Accounts and Notes Receivable.. 16,400

Assets	=	Liabilities	+	Shareholders' Equity	(Class.)
−16,400		−16,400			IncSt → RE

To eliminate intercompany note.

b. The unamortized excess acquisition cost on December 31, 2009 is $56,000. With eight years remaining on the building's useful life, the annual depreciation is $7,000 (= $56,000/8). Thus, the excess acquisition on January 1, 2008 was $70,000 [= $56,000 + (2 × $7,000)]. The computation of the acquisition cost on January 1, 2008 is as follows:

Common Stock of Company S	$ 500,000
Additional Paid-In Capital of Company S	100,000
Retained Earnings of Company S	40,000
Excess Acquisition Cost	70,000
Acquisition Cost	$ 710,000

c.
Acquisition Cost on January 1, 2008	$ 710,000
Company P's Share of the Increase in Retained Earnings of Company S for 2008 and 2009; ($70,000 − $40,000)....	30,000
Less Amortization of Excess Acquisition Cost for 2008 and 2009	(14,000)
Carrying Value on December 31, 2009	$ 726,000

13.30 (Peak Company and Valley Company; equity method and consolidated financial statements.)

  a. **January 1**
     Investment in Valley Company.................................... 50,000
        Cash 50,000

Assets	=	Liabilities	+	Shareholders' Equity	(Class.)
+50,000					
−50,000					

To record acquisition of 100% of Valley Company.

13.30 a. continued.

December 31
Investment in Valley Company.................................... 10,000
   Equity in Earnings of Valley Company.................. 10,000

Assets	=	Liabilities	+	Shareholders' Equity	(Class.)
+10,000				+10,000	IncSt → RE

To recognize share of Valley Company's earnings.

December 31
Cash.. 4,000
   Investment in Valley Company............................. 4,000

Assets	=	Liabilities	+	Shareholders' Equity	(Class.)
+4,000					
−4,000					

To recognize dividend received from Valley Company.

b.

	Peak Company	Valley Company	Consolidated
Assets			
Cash..	$ 33,000	$ 6,000	$ 39,000
Accounts Receivable...........	42,000	20,000	54,000
Investment in Valley Company (Using the Equity Method)................	56,000	--	--
Other Assets........................	123,000	85,000	208,000
Total Assets....................	$254,000	$111,000	$ 301,000
Liabilities and Shareholders' Equity			
Accounts Payable...............	$ 80,000	$ 25,000	$ 97,000
Bonds Payable.....................	50,000	30,000	80,000
Common Stock....................	10,000	5,000	10,000
Retained Earnings...............	114,000	51,000	114,000
Total Liabilities and Shareholders' Equity.........................	$254,000	$111,000	$ 301,000

13.30 b. continued.

Sales Revenue	$400,000	$125,000	$525,000
Equity in Earnings of Valley Company	10,000	--	--
Cost of Goods Sold	(320,000)	(90,000)	(410,000)
Selling and Administrative Expense	(44,000)	(20,000)	(64,000)
Income Tax Expense	(12,000)	(5,000)	(17,000)
Net Income	$ 34,000	$ 10,000	$ 34,000

The elimination entries (not required) are as follows:

Common Stock	5,000	
Retained Earnings	51,000	
Investment in Valley Company		56,000

Assets	= Liabilities	+ Shareholders' Equity	(Class.)
–56,000		–5,000	ContriCap
		–51,000	RE

To eliminate the investment account and the shareholders' equity accounts of Valley Company.

An alternative elimination entry using amounts before closing entries is as follows:

Common Stock	5,000	
Retained Earnings	45,000	
Equity in Earnings of Valley Company	10,000	
Dividends Declared		4,000
Investment in Valley Company		56,000

Assets	= Liabilities	+ Shareholders' Equity	(Class.)
–56,000		–5,000	ContriCap
		–45,000	RE
		–10,000	IncSt → RE
		+4,000	RE

To eliminate the investment account and the shareholders' equity accounts of Valley Company.

13.30 continued.

c. **January 1**
Investment in Valley Company.................................. 70,000
  Cash.. 70,000

Assets	=Liabilities	+	Shareholders' Equity	(Class.)
+70,000				
−70,000				

To record acquisition of 100% of Valley Company.

December 31
Investment in Valley Company.................................. 10,000
  Equity in Earnings of Valley Company.................. 10,000

Assets	=Liabilities	+	Shareholders' Equity	(Class.)
+10,000			+10,000	IncSt → RE

To recognize share of Valley Company's earnings.

December 31
Cash.. 4,000
  Investment in Valley Company 4,000

Assets	=Liabilities	+	Shareholders' Equity	(Class.)
+4,000				
−4,000				

To recognize dividend received from Valley Company.

December 31
Selling and Administrative Expenses........................ 2,000
  Investment in Valley Company 2,000

Assets	=Liabilities	+	Shareholders' Equity	(Class.)
−2,000			−2,000	

To recognize acquisition of excess cost: $2,000 = $20,000/10.

13.30 continued.

d. and e.

	Peak Company	Valley Company	Consolidated
Assets			
Cash	$ 13,000	$ 6,000	$ 19,000
Accounts Receivable	42,000	20,000	54,000
Investment in Valley Company (Using the Equity Method)	74,000[a]	--	--
Other Assets	123,000	85,000	226,000
Total Assets	$252,000	$111,000	$299,000
Liabilities and Shareholders' Equity			
Accounts Payable	$ 80,000	$ 25,000	$ 97,000
Bonds Payable	50,000	30,000	80,000
Common Stock	10,000	5,000	10,000
Retained Earnings	112,000[b]	51,000	112,000
Total Liabilities and Shareholders' Equity	$252,000	$111,000	$299,000
Sales Revenue	$400,000	$125,000	$525,000
Equity in Earnings of Valley Company	10,000	--	--
Cost of Goods Sold	(320,000)	(90,000)	(410,000)
Selling and Administrative Expense	(46,000)[c]	(20,000)	(66,000)
Income Tax Expense	(12,000)	(5,000)	(17,000)
Net Income	$ 32,000	$ 10,000	$ 32,000

[a]$74,000 = $70,000 + $10,000 − $4,000 − $2,000.

[b]$112,000 = $114,000 − $2,000 amortization.

[c]$46,000 = $44,000 + $2,000 amortization.

The elimination entry (not required) is as follows:

Common Stock	5,000	
Retained Earnings	51,000	
Other Assets	18,000	
Investment in Valley Company		74,000

13.30 d. and e. continued.

Assets	= Liabilities	+	Shareholders' Equity	(Class.)
+18,000			−5,000	ContriCap
−74,000			−51,000	RE

To eliminate the investment account and the shareholders' equity accounts of Valley Company.

Alternative elimination entries using amounts before closing entries are as follows:

Common Stock	5,000	
Retained Earnings..	45,000	
Equity in Earnings of Valley Company	10,000	
Other Assets	18,000	
Dividends Declared		4,000
Investment in Valley Company		74,000

Assets	= Liabilities	+	Shareholders' Equity	(Class.)
+18,000			−5,000	ContriCap
−74,000			−45,000	RE
			−10,000	IncSt → RE
			+4,000	RE

To eliminate the investment account and the shareholders' equity accounts of Valley Company.

Accounts Payable	8,000	
Accounts and Notes Receivable		8,000

Assets	= Liabilities	+	Shareholders' Equity	(Class.)
−8,000	−8,000			

To eliminate intercompany advance.

13.31 (Parent Company and Sub Company; equity method and consolidated financial statements with noncontrolling interest.)

	Parent Company	Sub Company	Consolidated
Assets			
Cash	$ 38,000	$ 12,000	$ 50,000
Accounts Receivable	63,000	32,000	95,000
Investment in Sub Company (Using Equity Method)	105,600	--	--
Other Assets	296,400	160,000	456,400
Total Assets	$503,000	$204,000	$601,400
Liabilities and Shareholders' Equity			
Accounts Payable	$ 85,000	$ 32,000	$117,000
Bonds Payable	150,000	40,000	190,000
Total Liabilities	$235,000	$ 72,000	$307,000
Noncontrolling Interest in Net Assets of Sub Company	$ --	$ --	$ 26,400
Common Stock	20,000	50,000	20,000
Retained Earnings	248,000	82,000	248,000
Total Shareholders' Equity	$268,000	$132,000	$294,400
Total Liabilities and Shareholders' Equity	$503,000	$204,000	$601,400
Sales Revenue	$800,000	$145,000	$945,000
Equity in Earnings of Sub Company	16,000	--	--
Cost of Goods Sold	(620,000)	(85,000)	(705,000)
Selling and Administrative Expense	(135,000)	(30,000)	(165,000)
Income Tax Expense	(24,000)	(10,000)	(34,000)
Net Income of Consolidated Entity	$ 37,000	$ 20,000	$ 41,000
Noncontrolling Interest in Net Income of Sub Company	--	--	(4,000)
Net Income	$ 37,000	$ 20,000	$ 37,000

The elimination and reclassification entry (not required) is as follows:

Common Stock	40,000	
Retained Earnings	65,600	
Investment in Sub Company		105,600

Solutions

13.31 continued.

Assets	=	Liabilities	+	Shareholders' Equity	(Class.)
−105,600				−40,000	ContriCap
				−65,600	RE

To eliminate investment account and Parent Company's share of the shareholders' equity of Sub Company.

Alternative elimination entries using amounts before closing entries are as follows:

Common Stock...	40,000	
Retained Earnings...	56,000	
Equity in Earnings of Sub Company...........................	16,000	
Dividend Declared..		6,400
Investment in Sub Company.................................		105,600

Assets	=	Liabilities	+	Shareholders' Equity	(Class.)
−105,600				−40,000	ContriCap
				−56,000	RE
				−16,000	IncSt → RE
				+6,400	RE

To eliminate investment account and Parent Company's share of the shareholders' equity of Sub Company.

Common Stock...	10,000	
Retained Earnings...	16,400	
Noncontrolling Interest in Net Assets of Sub Company..		26,400

Assets	=	Liabilities	+	Shareholders' Equity	(Class.)
				−10,000	ContriCap
				−16,400	RE
				+26,400	MinInt

To recognize the noncontrolling interest in Sub Company.

13.31 continued.

An alternative elimination entry using amounts before closing entries is as follows:

Common Stock..	10,000	
Retained Earnings...	14,000	
Noncontrolling Interest in Net Income of Sub Company...	4,000	
Dividend Declared...		1,600
Noncontrolling Interest in Net Assets of Sub Company..		26,400

Assets	=	Liabilities	+	Shareholders' Equity	(Class.)
				−10,000	ContriCap
				−14,000	RE
				−4,000	IncSt → RE
				+1,600	RE
				+26,400	MinInt

To recognize the noncontrolling interest in Sub Company.

13.32 (The Coca-Cola Company; effect of intercorporate investment policies on financial statements.)

    a. Coke's acquisition cost of its investments in the bottlers exceeds the carrying value of the net assets of the bottlers. Coke attributes the excess cost to long-term tangible or intangible assets. Note that consolidated Other Noncurrent Assets of $71,116 million exceeds the sum of the amounts on Coke's books of $23,875 and the bottlers' books of $44,636 by $2,605 million. The portion attributable to Coke's acquisition of bottlers is $785 million. The remainder of $1,820 (= $2,605 − $785) relates to the amount for the external interest in the bottlers. Thus, Coke owns 30.134% (= $785/$2,605) of the bottlers and the external interest owns 69.9%. The amount for the noncontrolling interest in the net assets of the bottlers of $16,899 million comprises the following:

Noncontrolling Interest in Carrying Value of Bottlers Net Assets: .69866 × $21,583	$ 15,079
Excess of Fair Value over Carrying Value of Net Assets Attributed to the Noncontrolling Interest	1,820
Total Noncontrolling Interest	$ 16,899

    b. (1) **Equity Method**
            Liabilities to Assets Ratio: $21,525/$43,269 = 49.7%
            Debt-Equity Ratio: $8,300/$21,744 = 38.2%

13.32 b. continued.

    (2) **Consolidation**
        Liabilities to Assets Ratio: $58,829/$97,472 = 60.4%.
        Debt-Equity Ratio: $31,674/$38,643 = 82.0%

c. The bottlers have a heavier proportion of noncurrent assets and noncurrent liabilities than does Coke. By owning less that 50% of the bottlers, Coke does not have to consolidate them, resulting in lower debt ratios.

13.33 (Smithfield Foods; accounting for joint ventures.)

a.

	Equity Method	Proportionate Consolidation	Full Consolidation
Assets			
Current Assets	$ 2,733.7	$ 3,417.6	$ 4,101.6
Investments in Joint Ventures	420.8	--	--
Other Noncurrent Assets	3,814.1	4,471.6	5,129.1
Total Assets	$ 6,968.6	$ 7,889.2	$ 9,230.7
Liabilities and Shareholders' Equity			
Current Liabilities	$ 1,361.2	$ 1,834.9	$ 2,308.7
Noncurrent Liabilities	3,352.7	3,799.6	4,246.5
Total Liabilities	$ 4,713.9	$ 5,634.5	$ 6,555.2
Joint Owners' Interest in Net Assets of Joint Ventures	$ --	$ --	$ 420.8
Shareholders' Equity	2,254.7	2,254.7	2,254.7
Total Shareholders' Equity	$ 2,254.7	$ 2,254.7	$ 2,675.5
Total Liabilities and Shareholders' Equity	$ 6,968.6	$ 7,889.2	$ 9,230.7
Income Statement			
Sales	$ 11,911.1	$ 13,367.5	$ 14,823.9
Equity in Earnings of Joint Ventures	10.9	--	--
Expenses	(11,733.6)	(13,179.1)	(14,624.6)
Net Income of Consolidated Entity	$ 188.4	$ 188.4	$ 199.3
Joint Owner's Interest in Net Income of Joint Ventures	--	--	(10.9)
Net Income	$ 188.4	$ 188.4	$ 188.4

13.33 a. continued.

The work sheet entries for proportionate consolidation and full consolidation (not required) are as follows:

Proportionate Consolidation
Using Post-Closing Amounts:
Shareholders' Equity... 115.0
Other Noncurrent Assets.. 305.8
    Investment in Joint Ventures................................... 420.8

Assets	=	Liabilities	+	Shareholders' Equity	(Class.)
+305.8				–115.0	ContriCap and RE
–420.8					

To eliminate the investment account, the shareholders' equity account of the joint ventures, and recognize the excess of acquisition cost over carrying value of net assets of joint ventures.

Using Pre-Closing Amounts:
Shareholders' Equity... 104.1
Equity in Earnings of Joint Ventures............................ 10.9
Other Noncurrent Assets.. 305.8
    Investment in Joint Ventures................................... 420.8

Assets	=	Liabilities	+	Shareholders' Equity	(Class.)
+305.8				–104.1	ContriCap and RE
–420.8				–10.9	IncSt → RE

To eliminate the investment account, the shareholders' equity account of the joint ventures, and recognize the excess of acquisition cost over carrying value of net assets of joint ventures.

Full Consolidation
In addition to the entries above to eliminate the investment account, the following entries recognize the interest of the other joint owners.

Using Post-Closing Amounts:
Shareholders' Equity... 115.0
Other Noncurrent Assets.. 305.8
    Joint Owners' Interest in Net Assets of Joint
        Ventures.. 420.8

13.33 a. continued.

Assets	= Liabilities	+	Shareholders' Equity	(Class.)
+305.8			−115.0	ContriCap and RE
			+420.8	Jt.Int.

To recognize the joint owners' interest in the joint ventures and recognize the excess carrying value of net assets of joint ventures.

Using Pre-Closing Amounts:

Shareholders' Equity...	104.1	
Joint Owners' Interest in Earnings of Joint Ventures	10.9	
Other Noncurrent Assets..	305.8	
Joint Owners' Interest in Net Asset of Joint Ventures..		420.8

Assets	= Liabilities	+	Shareholders' Equity	(Class.)
+305.8			−104.1	ContriCap and RE
			−10.9	IncSt → RE
			+420.8	Jt.Int.

To recognize the joint owners' interest in the joint ventures and recognize the excess carrying value of net assets of joint ventures.

b. **Equity Method**
   (1) Liabilities to Assets Ratio: $4,713.9/$7,268.6 = 64.9%.
   (2) Debt-Equity Ratio: $3,352.7/$2,254.7 = 148.7%.
   (3) Net Income to Sales Percentage: $188.4/$11,911.1 = 1.6%.

   Proportionate Consolidation
   (1) Liabilities to Assets Ratio: $5,634.5/$7,889.2 = 71.4%.
   (2) Debt-Equity Ratio: $3,799.6/$2,254.7 = 148.7%.
   (3) Net Income to Sales Percentage: $188.4/$13,367.5 = 1.4%.

   Full Consolidation
   (1) Liabilities to Assets Ratio: $6,555.2/$9,230.7 = 71.0%.
   (2) Debt-Equity Ratio: $4,246.5/$2,675.5 = 158.7%.
   (3) Net Income to Sales Percentage: $188.4/$14,823.9 = 1.3%.

13.33 continued.

    c. Full consolidation is inappropriate, because Smithfield Foods does not control the joint ventures. Whether the equity method or proportionate consolidation better reflects the operating relations between Smithfield Foods and the joint ventures depends on the involvement and responsibilities of each joint owner. If the other joint owners manage day-to-day operations and Smithfield Foods provides only strategic oversight, then the equity method seems more appropriate. If Smithfield Foods operates the joint ventures, or at least approximately 50 percent of the assets of the joint ventures, then proportionate consolidation seems more appropriate.

13.34 (Papa John's International; accounting for variable interest entity.)

Papa John's International appears to be the primary beneficiary of the VIE, even though it has no equity ownership, and should consolidate it. Papa John's International absorbed profits and losses in each of the three years because their amounts exceeded the thresholds on shareholders' equity. This would imply a relatively low shareholders' equity. Papa John's has also lent funds to the VIE, again suggesting an inability of the VIE to operate without additional financing. Given the dispersion of Papa John's franchised restaurants, it seems unlikely that the franchisee owners are in a position to make significant decisions about the operations of the VIE. Papa John's International, instead of the franchisee owners, absorbs losses and has the right to receive returns.

CHAPTER 14

SHAREHOLDERS' EQUITY: CAPITAL CONTRIBUTIONS, DISTRIBUTIONS, AND EARNINGS

Questions, Exercises, and Problems: Answers and Solutions

14.1 See the text or the glossary at the end of the book.

14.2 The three provisions provide different benefits and risks to the issuing firm and the investor and should sell at different prices. Callable preferred stock should sell for less than convertible preferred stock. The issuing firm gains benefits with an option to call, or repurchase, the preferred stock and must thereby accept a lower issue price. The investor gains benefits with an option to convert into common stock and must pay a higher price. The mandatory redemption requirement makes the preferred stock more like debt than shareholders' equity. Its market price depends on market interest rates for similar maturity debt (versus the 4% yield on the preferred stock) and the rank-ordering priority of the preferred stock in bankruptcy.

14.3 Redeemable preferred stock will appear as a liability if it is subject to mandatory redemption on a particular date or upon occurrence of a specified event certain to occur. Redeemable preferred stock will appear in shareholders' equity if it is subject to redemption fully at the option of the issuing firm. Redeemable preferred stock will appear between liabilities and shareholders' equity if redemption is dependent on an event not certain to occur. The latter classification is appropriate if either the issuing firm or the shareholders' have a redemption option.

14.4 All three items permit their holder to acquire shares of common stock at a set price. Their values depend on the difference between the market price and the exercise price on the exercise date and the length of the exercise period. Firms grant stock options to employees, grant stock rights to current shareholders and either sell stock warrants on the open market or attach them to a debt or preferred stock issue. The issuance of stock options and stock rights does not result in an immediate cash inflow, whereas the issuance of a stock warrant usually does. Accountants amortize the cost of stock options to expense over the expected period of benefit. Accountants credit the Additional Paid-in Capital (Stock Warrant) account if the value of the stock warrant is objectively measurable. At the time of exercise of all these items, the accountant records the cash proceeds as a capital contribution.

14.5   The greater the volatility of the stock price, the larger is the potential excess of the market price over the exercise price on the exercise date and the greater the benefit to the employee. The longer the time between the grant date and the exercise date, the more time that elapses for the market price to increase. Offsetting the value of this increased benefit element is the longer time to realize the benefit, which reduces the present value of the option. Stock option valuation models discount the expected benefit element in a stock option to a present value. The larger the discount rate, the smaller is the present value of the benefit.

14.6   The theoretical rationale is allocating the cost of employee compensation to the periods when the firm receives the benefits of employees' services.

14.7   The accounting for each of these transactions potentially involves transfers between contributed capital and retained earnings accounts and clouds the distinction between capital transactions and income transactions. The accounting for stock options results in a reduction in net income and retained earnings and an increase in contributed capital. The accounting for stock dividends results in a reduction in retained earnings and an increase in contributed capital. The purchase of treasury stock represents a reduction in both contributed capital and accumulated earnings. The reissuance of treasury stock at a "loss" may result in a debit to both contributed capital and retained earnings. Thus, the Common Stock and Additional Paid-in Capital accounts do not reflect just capital transactions and Retained Earnings does not reflect just income transactions.

14.8   In the case of a cash dividend, the shareholder now holds the investment in two parts—cash and stock certificates. The sum of the cash and the book value of the stock after the dividend declaration equals the book value of the stock before the firm declared the dividend. It is common to speak of a cash dividend as income, but it is merely the conversion of a portion of the shareholder's investment into a different form. In a sense, the shareholder earns income on the investment when the corporation earns its income. Because of the realization test for income recognition in accounting, however, the shareholders do not recognize income (except under the equity method discussed in Chapter 13) until the firm distributes cash. These comments for a cash dividend apply to a property dividend as well except that the shareholder holds a portion of the investment in a form less liquid than cash. A stock dividend does not even improve the marketability of the investment, although when a firm issues preferred shares to common shareholders or vice versa, shareholders may view the situation as similar to a cash dividend. The stock dividend capitalizes a portion of retained earnings.

14.9 The managers of a firm have knowledge of the plans and risks of the firm that external investors may not possess. Although laws prevent firms from taking advantage of this "inside information," inclusion of gains from treasury stock transactions in net income might motivate firms to buy and sell treasury stock to improve reported earnings. Excluding these gains from net income removes this incentive. Also, the accounting for the acquisition of treasury stock (that is, a reduction from total shareholders' equity) has the same effect on shareholders' equity as a retirement of the capital stock. The reissue of the treasury stock for more than its acquisition cost does not result in a gain any more than the issue of common stock for more than par value represents a gain.

14.10 There are at least two issues here. First, the proposal gives management an opportunity to decide which income items are and are not likely to recur. Firms can manage earnings with their choice. Second, the proposal presumes that an analyst will not overlook certain income items that appear only in the statement of retained earnings. It also presumes that the firm will provide sufficient information about income items for the analyst to judge if it should be in earnings.

14.11 The FASB suggests that the distinction between performance-related (subject to significant influence by management) and non-performance-related (subject to external influences not controllable by management) items drives the exclusion. The real reason, however, we suspect, has to do with the volatility of some of the items of other comprehensive income. Including all unrealized gains and losses on securities held in net income will cause reported earnings to fluctuate (in response to fluctuations in market prices) more than it would otherwise. Many, probably most, managers prefer to report stable net income in contrast to fluctuating net income. All else equal, the less risky the net income stream—that is, the less volatile is reported net income—the higher will be the market price of the firm's shares.

14.12 An error in previously-issued financial statements results from oversights or errors which the firm should not have made given reasonable diligence in accessing available information at the time. Accountants restate the previously-issued financial statements to correct the error. A change in accounting principles results either from a firm's choice to change accounting principles or from a mandated change by a standard-setting body. Firms retroactively restate previously-issued financial statements for the accounting change. A change in an accounting estimate results from *new* information that suggests that the original estimate was inaccurate as judged *ex post*. Accountants adjust for changes in estimates during the current and future periods instead of restating previously-issued financial statements.

14.13 (The Washington Post Company; classification of redeemable preferred stock.)

This redeemable preferred stock will appear between liabilities and shareholders' equity on the balance sheet because its redemption is subject to an event not certain to occur. Neither the company nor the preferred shareholder might initiate redemption.

14.14 (Bank of America; classification of redeemable preferred stock.)

This redeemable preferred stock will appear in shareholders' equity because the redemption right is wholly under the control of Bank of America.

14.15 (Intel; accounting for stock options.)

The value of the stock options on December 31, 2007, is $142.434 (= 24.6 x $5.79) million. Intel amortizes this value as an expense of $47.478 (= $142.434/3) million for 2008, 2009, and 2010. Intel recognizes no additional expense when employees exercise their options in 2012.

14.16 (Morrissey Corporation; journal entries for employee stock options.)

December 31, 2008
No entry.

December 31, 2009 and December 31, 2010
Compensation Expense (= $400,000/2).......................... 200,000
    Additional Paid-in Capital (Stock Options)................   200,000

Assets	=	Liabilities	+	Shareholders' Equity	(Class.)
				−200,000	IncSt → RE
				+200,000	ContriCap

June 30, 2011
Cash (= 30,000 x $60)... 1,800,000
Additional Paid-in Capital (Stock Options) [=
    (30,000/50,000) x $400,000]....................................... 240,000
    Common Stock (= 30,000 x $1)................................   30,000
    Additional Paid-in Capital [= $240,000 +
      (30,000 x $59)]..   2,010,000

Assets	=	Liabilities	+	Shareholders' Equity	(Class.)
+1,800,000				−240,000	ContriCap
				+30,000	ContriCap
				+2,010,000	ContriCap

14.16 continued.

November 15, 2011

Cash (= 20,000 x $60)	1,200,000
Additional Paid-in Capital (Stock Options) [= (20,000/50,000) x $400,000]	160,000
Common Stock (= 20,000 x $1)	20,000
Additional Paid-in Capital [= $160,000 + (20,000 x $59)]	1,340,000

Assets	=	Liabilities	+	Shareholders' Equity	(Class.)
+1,200,000				–160,000	ContriCap
				+20,000	ContriCap
				+1,340,000	ContriCap

14.17 (Watson Corporation; journal entries for employee stock options.)

December 31, 2009, 2010, and 2011

Compensation Expense (= $75,000/3)	25,000
Additional Paid-in Capital (Stock Options)	25,000

Assets	=	Liabilities	+	Shareholders' Equity	(Class.)
				–25,000	IncSt → RE
				+25,000	ContriCap

April 30, 2012

Cash (= 15,000 x $25)	375,000
Additional Paid-in Capital (Stock Options) [= (15,000/20,000) x $75,000]	56,250
Common Stock (= 15,000 x $10)	150,000
Additional Paid-in Capital [= $56,250 + (15,000 x $15)]	281,250

Assets	=	Liabilities	+	Shareholders' Equity	(Class.)
+375,000				–56,250	ContriCap
				+150,000	ContriCap
				+281,250	ContriCap

14.17 continued.

September 15, 2013

Cash (= 5,000 x $25)... 125,000	
Additional Paid-in Capital (Stock Options) [= (5,000/	
20,000) x $75,000].. 18,750	
Common Stock (= 5,000 x $10)..............................	50,000
Additional Paid-in Capital [= $18,750 +	
(5,000 x $15)]..	93,750

Assets	=	Liabilities	+	Shareholders' Equity	(Class.)
+125,000				–18,750	ContriCap
				+50,000	ContriCap
				+93,750	ContriCap

14.18 (Higgins Corporation; journal entries for convertible bonds.)

  a. **1/02/2008**

Cash.. 1,000,000	
Convertible Bonds Payable......................................	1,000,000

Assets	=	Liabilities	+	Shareholders' Equity	(Class.)
+1,0000,000		+1,000,000			

To record the issue of convertible bonds.

1/02/2012

Convertible Bonds Payable... 1,000,000	
Common Stock—$1 Par...	40,000
Additional Paid-in Capital...	960,000

Assets	=	Liabilities	+	Shareholders' Equity	(Class.)
		–1,000,000		+40,000	ContriCap
				+960,000	ContriCap

To record conversion using carrying value of bonds.

14.18 continued.

b. **1/02/2008**
Cash 1,000,000
    Convertible Bonds Payable 685,140.50
    Additional Paid-in Capital 314,859.50

Assets	=	Liabilities	+	Shareholders' Equity	(Class.)
+1,000,000		+685,140.50		+314,859.50	ContriCap

Issue of 10% semiannual coupon convertible bonds at a time when the firm could issue ordinary 10% bonds for $685,140.50 when the market interest rate is 15% compounded semiannually.

Supporting Computations
$50,000 x 12.59441 .... $ 629,720.50
$1,000,000 x .05542 .... 55,420.00
Issue Price .... $ 685,140.50

14.19 (Symantec; accounting for conversion of bonds.)

Carrying Value Method
Convertible Bonds Payable 10,255,000
    Common Stock (= 100,000 x $10) 1,000,000
    Additional Paid-in Capital (Plug) 9,255,000

Assets	=	Liabilities	+	Shareholders' Equity	(Class.)
		−10,225,000		+1,000,000	ContriCap
				+9,255,000	ContriCap

Fair Value Method
Convertible Bonds Payable 10,255,000
Loss on Conversion of Bonds (Plug) 245,000
    Common Stock (= 100,000 x $10) 1,000,000
    Additional Paid-in Capital (= 100,000 x $95) 9,500,000

Assets	=	Liabilities	+	Shareholders' Equity	(Class.)
		−10,255,000		−245,000	IncSt → RE
				+1,000,000	ContriCap
				+9,500,000	ContriCap

14.20 (Kiersten Corporation; journal entries for stock warrants.)

February 26, 2008
Cash 240,000
    Additional Paid-in Capital (Common Stock
        Warrants) (= 60,000 × $4)..................................... 240,000

Assets	=	Liabilities	+	Shareholders' Equity	(Class.)
+240,000				+240,000	ContriCap

June 6, 2010
Cash (= 40,000 × $30).. 1,200,000
Additional Paid-in Capital (Common Stock Warrants)
   (= 40,000 × $4) 160,000
    Common Stock (= 40,000 × $10)............................ 400,000
    Additional Paid-in Capital 960,000

Assets	=	Liabilities	+	Shareholders' Equity	(Class.)
+1,200,000				−160,000	ContriCap
				+400,000	ContriCap
				+960,000	ContriCap

February 26, 2012
Additional Paid-in Capital (Common Stock Warrants)
   (= 20,000 × $4) 80,000
    Additional Paid-in Capital 80,000

Assets	=	Liabilities	+	Shareholders' Equity	(Class.)
				−80,000	ContriCap
				+80,000	ContriCap

14.21 (Altus Pharmaceuticals; journal entries for stock warrants.)

December 7, 2002
Cash 46,180,000
    Convertible Preferred Stock 43,450,000
    Additional Paid-in Capital (Stock Warrants)...... 2,730,000

Assets	=	Liabilities	+	Shareholders' Equity	(Class.)
+46,180,000				+43,450,000	ContriCap
				+2,730,000	ContriCap

To record issuance of convertible preferred stock with stock warrants.

14.21 continued.

January 15, 2007

Convertible Preferred Stock	62,533,000	
Common Stock (5,269,705 x $.01)		52,697
Additional Paid-in Capital		62,480,303

Assets	=	Liabilities	+	Shareholders' Equity	(Class.)
				–62,533,000	ContriCap
				+52,697	ContriCap
				+62,480,303	ContriCap

To record conversion of preferred stock with accumulated dividends into common stock. $62,533,000 = $43,450,000 + $19,083,000.

14.22 (Journal entries for dividends.)

a.
Retained Earnings (Dividends Declared)	19,500	
Dividends Payable—Preferred Stock		19,500

Assets	=	Liabilities	+	Shareholders' Equity	(Class.)
		+19,500		–19,500	RE

Dividend of $1.50 per share on 13,000 shares.

b.
Dividends Payable—Preferred Stock	19,500	
Cash		19,500

Assets	=	Liabilities	+	Shareholders' Equity	(Class.)
–19,500		–19,500			

c.
Retained Earnings (Dividends Declared)	300,000	
Common Stock		300,000

Assets	=	Liabilities	+	Shareholders' Equity	(Class.)
				–300,000	RE
				+300,000	ContriCap

d. No entry.

14.23 (Watt Corporation; journal entries for dividends.)

a. **March 31, 2008**
Retained Earnings (Dividends Declared) 10,000
    Dividends Payable 10,000

Assets	= Liabilities	+	Shareholders' Equity	(Class.)
	+10,000		−10,000	RE

$10,000 = 20,000 x $.50.

b. **April 15, 2008**
Dividends Payable 10,000
    Cash 10,000

Assets	= Liabilities	+	Shareholders' Equity	(Class.)
−10,000	−10,000			

c. **June 30, 2008**
Retained Earnings (Dividends Declared) (= 2,000 x $20) 40,000
    Common Stock (= 2,000 x $15) 30,000
    Additional Paid-in Capital 10,000

Assets	= Liabilities	+	Shareholders' Equity	(Class.)
			−40,000	RE
			+30,000	ContriCap
			+10,000	ContriCap

d. **September 30, 2008**
Retained Earnings (Dividends Declared) 11,000
    Dividends Payable 11,000

Assets	= Liabilities	+	Shareholders' Equity	(Class.)
	+11,000		−11,000	RE

$11,000 = 22,000 x $.50.

14.23 continued.

e. **October 15, 2008**
Dividends Payable.. 11,000
  Cash.. 11,000

Assets	=	Liabilities	+	Shareholders' Equity	(Class.)
−11,000		−11,000			

f. **December 31, 2008**
Additional Paid-in Capital.. 165,000
  Common Stock (= 11,000 x $15).. 165,000

Assets	=	Liabilities	+	Shareholders' Equity	(Class.)
				−165,000	ContriCap
				+165,000	ContriCap

14.24 (Danos Corporation; journal entries for treasury stock transactions.)

a. Treasury Stock—Common 300,000
   Cash (= 10,000 x $30)... 300,000

Assets	=	Liabilities	+	Shareholders' Equity	(Class.)
−300,000				−300,000	ContriCap

b. Cash (= 6,000 x $32)... 192,000
   Additional Paid-in Capital (Common Stock
     Options) (= 6,000 x $6).. 36,000
       Treasury Stock—Common (= 6,000 x $30) 180,000
       Additional Paid-in Capital 48,000

Assets	=	Liabilities	+	Shareholders' Equity	(Class.)
+192,000				−36,000	ContriCap
				+180,000	ContriCap
				+48,000	ContriCap

c. Treasury Stock—Common 266,000
   Cash (= 7,000 x $38)... 266,000

Assets	=	Liabilities	+	Shareholders' Equity	(Class.)
−266,000				−266,000	ContriCap

14.24 continued.

d. Land 300,000
    Treasury Stock—Common [= (4,000 x $30) +
      (4,000 x $38)].. 272,000
    Additional Paid-in Capital 28,000

Assets	=	Liabilities	+	Shareholders' Equity	(Class.)
+300,000				+272,000	ContriCap
				+28,000	ContriCap

e. Cash (= 3,000 x $36) 108,000
   Additional Paid-in Capital... 6,000
    Treasury Stock—Common (= 3,000 x $38).......... 114,000

Assets	=	Liabilities	+	Shareholders' Equity	(Class.)
+108,000				−6,000	ContriCap
				+114,000	ContriCap

14.25 (Melissa Corporation; journal entries for treasury stock transactions.)

a. Treasury Stock—Common 120,000
    Cash (= 10,000 x $12)... 120,000

Assets	=	Liabilities	+	Shareholders' Equity	(Class.)
−120,000				−120,000	ContriCap

b. Bonds Payable 72,000
    Treasury Stock—Common (= 6,000 x $12)........... 72,000

Assets	=	Liabilities	+	Shareholders' Equity	(Class.)
		−72,000		+72,000	ContriCap

c. Treasury Stock—Common 300,000
    Cash (= 20,000 x $15)... 300,000

Assets	=	Liabilities	+	Shareholders' Equity	(Class.)
−300,000				−300,000	ContriCap

14.25 continued.

d.
Land..	540,000	
Treasury Stock—Common [= (4,000 × $12) + (20,000 × $15)]...		348,000
Common Stock (= 6,000 × $5)...............................		30,000
Additional Paid-in Capital...		162,000

Assets	= Liabilities	+	Shareholders' Equity	(Class.)
+540,000			+348,000	ContriCap
			+30,000	ContriCap
			+162,000	ContriCap

14.26 (Treatment of accounting errors, changes in accounting principles, and changes in accounting estimates.)

   (1) Accounting Error:
      2008: $1,100 (= $1,500 − $400)
      2009: $1,800

   (2) Change in Accounting Principle:
      2008: $1,100 (= $1,500 − $400)
      2009: $1,800

   (3) Change in Accounting Estimate:
      2008: $1,500
      2009: $1,800

14.27 (Uncertainty Corporation; journal entries to correct errors and adjust for changes in estimates.)

a.
Retained Earnings..	12,000	
Patent (or Accumulated Amortization).................		12,000

Assets	= Liabilities	+	Shareholders' Equity	(Class.)
−12,000			−12,000	RE

To correct error from neglecting to amortize patent during previous year.

14.27 continued.

    b. Accumulated Depreciation... 7,000
           Retained Earnings.. 4,000
           Retained Earnings.. 3,000

Assets	= Liabilities	+	Shareholders' Equity	(Class.)
+7,000			+4,000	RE
			+3,000	RE

To correct error in recording the sale of a machine by eliminating the balance in accumulated depreciation relating to the machine sold and converting a $4,000 loss on the sale to a $3,000 gain.

    c. Depreciation Expense... 50,000
           Accumulated Depreciation..................................... 50,000

Assets	= Liabilities	+	Shareholders' Equity	(Class.)
–50,000			–50,000	IncSt → RE

To record depreciation expense for 2008. Carrying value on January 1, 2008 is $1,600,00 [= $2,400,000 – ($80,000 x 10)]. The revised annual depreciation is $50,000 (= $1,600,000/32).

    d. Bad Debt Expense... 10,000
           Allowance for Uncollectible Accounts................... 10,000

Assets	= Liabilities	+	Shareholders' Equity	(Class.)
–10,000			–10,000	IncSt → RE

To adjust the balance in the allowance account to the amount needed to cover estimated uncollectibles.

14.28   (Journal entries to record the issuance of capital stock.)

    a. Cash (= 50,000 x $30)... 1,500,000
           Common Stock (= 50,000 x $5)............................... 250,000
           Additional Paid-in Capital (= 50,000 x $25).......... 1,250,000

Assets	= Liabilities	+	Shareholders' Equity	(Class.)
+1,500,000			+250,000	ContriCap
			+1,250,000	ContriCap

14.28 continued.

b. Cash (= 20,000 x $100).. 2,000,000
    Preferred Stock 2,000,000

Assets	= Liabilities	+	Shareholders' Equity	(Class.)
+2,000,000			+2,000,000	ContriCap

c. Patent (= 16,000 x $15)... 240,000
    Common Stock (= 16,000 x $10) 160,000
    Additional Paid-in Capital (= 16,000 x $5)............. 80,000

Assets	= Liabilities	+	Shareholders' Equity	(Class.)
+240,000			+160,000	ContriCap
			+80,000	ContriCap

d. Convertible Preferred Stock... 400,000
    Common Stock (= 25,000 x $1)................................. 25,000
    Additional Paid-in Capital (= $400,000 –
    $25,000) 375,000

Assets	= Liabilities	+	Shareholders' Equity	(Class.)
			–400,000	ContriCap
			+25,000	ContriCap
			+375,000	ContriCap

e. Compensation Expense (= 5,000 x $12)....................... 60,000
    Common Stock (= 5,000 x $10)................................ 50,000
    Additional Paid-in Capital (= 5,000 x $2)............... 10,000

Assets	= Liabilities	+	Shareholders' Equity	(Class.)
			–60,000	IncSt → RE
			+50,000	ContriCap
			+10,000	ContriCap

14.29 (Journal entries for the issuance of common stock.)

a.
Inventory	175,000	
Land	220,000	
Building	1,400,000	
Equipment	405,000	
Common Stock (= 20,000 x $10)		200,000
Additional Paid-in Capital		2,000,000

Assets	= Liabilities	+ Shareholders' Equity	(Class.)
+175,000		+200,000	ContriCap
+220,000		+2,000,000	ContriCap
+1,400,000			
+405,000			

b.
Cash (= 10,000 x $100)	1,000,000	
Redeemable Preferred Stock		1,000,000

Assets	= Liabilities	+ Shareholders' Equity	(Class.)
+1,000,000	+1,000,000		

c.
Cash (= 5,000 x $24)	120,000	
Additional Paid-in Capital (Common Stock Warrants) (= 5,000 x $8)	40,000	
Common Stock (= 5,000 x $1)		5,000
Additional Paid-in Capital		155,000

Assets	= Liabilities	+ Shareholders' Equity	(Class.)
+120,000		–40,000	ContriCap
		+5,000	ContriCap
		+155,000	ContriCap

d.
Preferred Stock (= 10,000 x $50)	500,000	
Common Stock (= 20,000 x $10)		200,000
Additional Paid-in Capital		300,000

Assets	= Liabilities	+ Shareholders' Equity	(Class.)
		–500,000	ContriCap
		+200,000	ContriCap
		+300,000	ContriCap

14.30 (Wilson Supply Company; transactions to incorporate and run a business.)

a. **1/02**
Cash.. 9,000
    Common Stock—$30 Stated Value........................ 9,000

Assets	=	Liabilities	+	Shareholders' Equity	(Class.)
+9,000				+9,000	ContriCap

300 shares x $30 = $9,000.

b. **1/06**
Cash.. 60,000
    Common Stock—$30 Stated Value........................ 60,000

Assets	=	Liabilities	+	Shareholders' Equity	(Class.)
+60,000				+60,000	ContriCap

2,000 shares x $30 = $60,000.

c. **1/08**
Cash.. 400,000
    Preferred Stock—$100 Par Value............................ 400,000

Assets	=	Liabilities	+	Shareholders' Equity	(Class.)
+400,000				+400,000	ContriCap

4,000 shares x $100 = $400,000.

d. **1/09**
No entry.

14.30 continued.

e. **1/12**

Inventories...	50,000	
Land..	80,000	
Building...	210,000	
Equipment...	120,000	
Preferred Stock—$100 Par Value...................		100,000
Common Stock—$30 Stated Value..................		360,000

Assets	=	Liabilities	+	Shareholders' Equity	(Class.)
+50,000				+100,000	ContriCap
+80,000				+360,000	ContriCap
+210,000					
+120,000					

f. **7/03**

Retained Earnings (Dividends Declared).................	20,000	
Dividends Payable on Preferred Stock..............		20,000

Assets	=	Liabilities	+	Shareholders' Equity	(Class.)
		+20,000		−20,000	RE

$100 x (.08/2) x (4,000 + 1,000) shares = $20,000.

g. **7/05**

Cash..	825,000	
Common Stock—$30 Stated Value..................		750,000
Additional Paid-in Capital................................		75,000

Assets	=	Liabilities	+	Shareholders' Equity	(Class.)
+825,000				+750,000	ContriCap
				+75,000	ContriCap

25,000 shares x $33 = $825,000.

h. **7/25**

Dividends Payable on Preferred Stock.....................	20,000	
Cash...		20,000

Assets	=	Liabilities	+	Shareholders' Equity	(Class.)
−20,000		−20,000			

14.30 continued.

i. **10/02**
Retained Earnings (Dividends Declared) 39,300
    Dividends Payable on Common Stock 39,300

Assets	= Liabilities	+	Shareholders' Equity	(Class.)
	+39,300		−39,300	RE

$1 × (300 + 2,000 + 12,000 + 25,000) shares = $39,300.

j. **10/25**
Dividends Payable on Common Stock 39,300
    Cash 39,300

Assets	= Liabilities	+	Shareholders' Equity	(Class.)
−39,300	−39,300			

14.31 (Fisher Company; reconstructing transactions involving shareholders' equity.)

a. $60,000 par value/$10 per share = 6,000 shares.

b. $7,200/360 = $20 per share.

c. 600 − 360 = 240 shares.

d. If the Additional Paid-in Capital is $31,440, then $30,000 [= 6,000 × ($15 − $10)] represents contributions in excess of par value on original issue of 6,000 shares. Then, $1,440 (= $31,440 − $30,000) represents the credit to Additional Paid-in Capital when it reissued the treasury shares.

The $1,440 represents 240 shares reissued times the excess of reissue price over acquisition price:

$$240(\$X - \$20) = \$1,440, \text{ or } X = \$26.$$

The shares were reissued for $26 each.

14.31 continued.

e. (1) Cash (= 6,000 x $15).. 90,000
      Common Stock ($10 Par Value)..................... 60,000
      Additional Paid-in Capital 30,000

Assets	=	Liabilities	+	Shareholders' Equity	(Class.)
+90,000				+60,000	ContriCap
				+30,000	ContriCap

(2) Treasury Stock—Common 12,000
      Cash (= 600 x $20)... 12,000

Assets	=	Liabilities	+	Shareholders' Equity	(Class.)
−12,000				−12,000	ContriCap

(3) Cash (= 240 x $26)... 6,240
      Treasury Stock—Common (= 240 x $20).... 4,800
      Additional Paid-in Capital 1,440

Assets	=	Liabilities	+	Shareholders' Equity	(Class.)
+6,240				+4,800	ContriCap
				+1,440	ContriCap

(4a) Cash... 10,000
      Securities Available for Sale 6,000
      Realized Gain on Sale of Securities Available for Sale... 4,000

Assets	=	Liabilities	+	Shareholders' Equity	(Class.)
+10,000				+4,000	IncSt → RE
−6,000					

(4b) Securities Available for Sale............................... 2,000
      Unrealized Holding Gain on Securities Available for Sale (Accumulated Other Comprehensive Income)............................... 2,000

Assets	=	Liabilities	+	Shareholders' Equity	(Class.)
+2,000				+2,000	OCInc → AOCInc

14.31 continued.

f. The realized gain appears in the income statement and the unrealized gain appears in a statement of other comprehensive income or in reconciliation of accumulated other comprehensive income.

14.32 (Shea Company; reconstructing transactions involving shareholders' equity.)

a. $100,000 par value/$5 per share = 20,000 shares.

b. $33,600/1,200 = $28 per share.

c. 2,000 – 1,200 = 800 shares.

d. If the Additional Paid-in Capital is $509,600, then $500,000 [= 20,000 x ($30 – $5)] represents contributions in excess of par value on original issue of 20,000 shares. Then, $9,600 (= $509,600 – $500,000) represents the credit to Additional Paid-in Capital when it reissued the treasury shares.
The $9,600 represents 800 shares reissued times the excess of reissue price over acquisition price:

$$800(\$X - \$28) = \$9,600, \text{ or } X = \$40.$$

The shares were reissued for $40 each.

e. (1) Cash.. 600,000
      Common Stock ($5 Par Value)...................... 100,000
      Additional Paid-in Capital............................ 500,000

Assets	= Liabilities	+	Shareholders' Equity	(Class.)
+600,000			+100,000	ContriCap
			+500,000	ContriCap

(2) Treasury Shares.. 56,000
      Cash... 56,000

Assets	= Liabilities	+	Shareholders' Equity	(Class.)
–56,000			–56,000	ContriCap

2,000 x $28 = $56,000.

14.32 e. continued.

(3) Cash.. 32,000
    Treasury Shares... 22,400
    Additional Paid-in Capital.. 9,600

Assets	= Liabilities	+	Shareholders' Equity	(Class.)
+32,000			+22,400	ContriCap
			+9,600	ContriCap

800 x $40 = $32,000.
800 x $28 = $22,400.

(4a) Cash.. 12,000
    Realized Loss on Sale of Securities Available
        for Sale... 2,000
        Securities Available for Sale...................... 14,000

Assets	= Liabilities	+	Shareholders' Equity	(Class.)
+12,000			−2,000	IncSt → RE
−14,000				

(4b) Unrealized Holding Loss on Securities Available for Sale (Other Comprehensive Income).. 7,000
    Securities Available for Sale...................... 7,000

Assets	= Liabilities	+	Shareholders' Equity	(Class.)
−7,000			−7,000	OCInc → AOCInc

Write down securities from $25,000 to $18,000.

  f. The realized loss appears in the income statement and the unrealized loss appears in a statement of other comprehensive income or in reconciliation of accumulated other comprehensive income.

14.33 (Lowe Corporation; accounting for stock options.)

Compensation expense reduces net income each year as follows:

2008: zero compensation because all benefits occur after the granting of the stock option.

2009:	.5(5,000 x $2.40)..	$ 6,000
2010:	[.5(5,000 x $2.40) + .5(6,000 x $3.00)]............................	15,000
2011:	[.5(6,000 x $3.00) + .5(7,000 x $3.14)]............................	19,990
2012:	[.5(7,000 x $3.14) + .5(8,000 x $3.25)]............................	23,990
	Total Compensation Expense..	$ 64,980

14.34 (Procter & Gamble Company; accounting for stock options.)

Compensation expense reduces net income each year as follows:

2004: [.5(35,759 x $10.99) + .5(40,866 x $12.50)] = $451,908.21
2005: [.5(40,866 x $12.50) + .5(29,100 x $14.34)] = $464,059.50
2006: [.5(29,100 x $14.34) + .5(33,904 x $16.30)] = $484,964.60
2007: [.5(33,904 x $16.30) + .5(33,091 x $17.29)] = $562,389.30

14.35 (Microsoft Corporation; reconstructing transactions affecting shareholders' equity.) (Amounts in Millions)

(1) Cash.. 6,763
      Common Stock and Additional Paid-in
        Capital... 6,763

Assets	=	Liabilities	+	Shareholders' Equity	(Class.)
+6,763				+6,763	ContriCap

To issue common stock for cash.

(2) Common Stock and Additional Paid-in Capital....... 6,162
    Retained Earnings... 21,212
      Cash... 27,374

Assets	=	Liabilities	+	Shareholders' Equity	(Class.)
−27,374				−6,162	ContriCap
				−21,212	RE

To repurchase common stock for more than its initial issue price.

14.35 continued.

(3) Compensation Expense 889
    Additional Paid-in Capital 889

Assets	=	Liabilities	+	Shareholders' Equity	(Class.)
				−889	IncSt → RE
				+889	ContriCap

(4) Revenues and Gains Net of Expenses and Losses. 14,065
    Retained Earnings 14,065

Assets	=	Liabilities	+	Shareholders' Equity	(Class.)
				−14,065	IncSt → RE
				+14,065	RE

To close revenues, gain, expense, and loss accounts to retained earnings.

(5) Retained Earnings... 3,837
    Cash 3,837

Assets	=	Liabilities	+	Shareholders' Equity	(Class.)
−3,837				−3,837	RE

To declare and pay cash dividends.

(6) Marketable Securities.. 326
    Net Unrealized Gains and Losses on Marketable Securities... 326

Assets	=	Liabilities	+	Shareholders' Equity	(Class.)
+326				+326	OCInc → AOCInc

To record net unrealized gains and losses for changes in fair value of marketable securities.

14.35 continued.

(7) Derivative Securities 14
    Net Unrealized Gains and Losses on
      Derivatives 14

Assets	=	Liabilities	+	Shareholders' Equity	(Class.)
+14	or	–14		+14	OCInc → AOCInc

14.36 (Sirius Satellite Radio, Inc.; journal entries for changes in shareholders' equity.) (Amounts in Thousands)

(1) Cash 82,941
    Common Stock—Par Value 22
    Additional Paid-in Capital 82,919

Assets	=	Liabilities	+	Shareholders' Equity	(Class.)
+82,941				+22	ContriCap
				+82,919	ContriCap

To record the issuance of common stock to third parties for more than par value.

(2) Cash 19,246
    Common Stock—Par Value 4
    Additional Paid-in Capital 19,242

Assets	=	Liabilities	+	Shareholders' Equity	(Class.)
+19,246				+4	ContriCap
				+19,242	ContriCap

To record the issuance of common stock to employees for more than par value.

(3) Compensation Expense 52,683
    Additional Paid-in Capital 52,683

Assets	=	Liabilities	+	Shareholders' Equity	(Class.)
				–52,683	IncSt → RE
				+52,683	ContriCap

To record the amortized cost of employee stock options.

14.36 continued.

(4) Cash 3,532
      Common Stock—Par Value   3
      Additional Paid-in Capital   3,529

Assets	=	Liabilities	+	Shareholders' Equity	(Class.)
+3,532				+3	ContriCap
				+3,529	ContriCap

To record the sale of common stock associated with stock options.

(5) Additional Paid-in Capital 5
      Common Stock—Par Value   5

Assets	=	Liabilities	+	Shareholders' Equity	(Class.)
				−5	ContriCap
				+5	ContriCap

To record exercise of common stock warrants and issuance of shares.

(6) Convertible Notes 3,184
      Common Stock—Par Value   2
      Additional Paid-in Capital   3,182

Assets	=	Liabilities	+	Shareholders' Equity	(Class.)
		−3,184		+2	ContriCap
				+3,182	ContriCap

To record conversion of notes into common stock.

14.37 (Anheuser-Busch Companies; journal entries for changes in shareholders' equity.) (Amounts in Millions)

(1) Cash 292.3
      Common Stock 8.8
      Additional Paid-in Capital 283.5

14.37 continued.

Assets	=	Liabilities	+	Shareholders' Equity	(Class.)
+292.3				+8.8	ContriCap
				+283.5	ContriCap

To record the issuance of common stock to employees under stock option plans.

(2) Compensation Expense 136.3
      Additional Paid-in Capital 136.1
      Treasury Stock—Common....................................... .2

Assets	=	Liabilities	+	Shareholders' Equity	(Class.)
				−136.2	IncSt → RE
				+136.1	ContriCap
				+.2	ContriCap

To record the amortized cost of *employees stock* options. The reason for the *credit* to *Treasury Stock is not explained* by Anheuser-Busch.

(3) Revenues, Gains, Expenses, and Losses 2,115.3
      Retained Earnings... 2,115.3

Assets	=	Liabilities	+	Shareholders' Equity	(Class.)
				−2,115.3	IncSt → RE
				+2,115.3	RE

(4) Retained Earnings... 932.4
      Cash 932.4

Assets	=	Liabilities	+	Shareholders' Equity	(Class.)
−932.4				−932.4	RE

To record the declaration and payment of cash dividends.

14.37 continued.

(5) Treasury Stock—Common 2,707.2
        Cash 2,707.2

Assets	=	Liabilities	+	Shareholders' Equity	(Class.)
−2,707.2				−2,707.2	ContriCap

To record repurchase of common stock held as treasury stock.

(6) Net Unrealized Gains and Losses on Marketable
        Securities.. .3
            Marketable Securities 3

Assets	=	Liabilities	+	Shareholders' Equity	(Class.)
−.3				−.3	OCInc → AOCInc

To record net unrealized loss on marketable securities.

(7) Net Unrealized Gains and Losses on Cash Flow
        Hedges 2.0
            Derivative Securities 2.0

Assets	=	Liabilities	+	Shareholders' Equity	(Class.)
−2.0	or	+2.0		−2.0	OCInc → AOCInc

To record net unrealized loss on cash flow hedges.

(8) Pension Liability 205.2
        Pension Liability Adjustment 205.2

Assets	=	Liabilities	+	Shareholders' Equity	(Class.)
		+205.2		+205.2	OCInc → AOCInc

To reduce pension liability for a reduction in the minimum pension liability or for changes in actuarial assumptions, actuarial performance, or prior cost and increase in other comprehensive income.

Solutions

14.38 (Monk Corporation; treasury shares and their effects on performance ratios.)

a. (1) Cash 714.1
        Treasury Stock—Common 427.6
        Common Stock/Additional Paid-in Capital........ 286.5

Assets	=	Liabilities	+	Shareholders' Equity	(Class.)
+714.1				+427.6	ContriCap
				+286.5	ContriCap

The common shares were issued at an option price of $49.28 per share [= $714.1/(.307 + 14.183)]. The treasury shares issued were purchased for $30.15 per share (= $427.6/14.183). The difference of $19.13 per share (= $49.28 − $30.15) was credited to Additional Paid-in Capital. This amount includes a debit to Additional Paid-in Capital for the cost of stock options previously amortized and a credit for the difference between the cash proceeds plus the cost of the stock options over the par value of the shares issued. The remaining credits to Common Stock and Additional Paid-in Capital were for the amounts received for the .307 common shares issued net of any amounts debited and credited to Additional Paid-in Capital as a result of recognizing the cost of the options in the accounts.

(2) Treasury Stock—Common....................................... 2,572.8
      Cash.. 2,572.8

Assets	=	Liabilities	+	Shareholders' Equity	(Class.)
−2,572.8				−2,572.8	ContriCap

These treasury shares were purchased for an average price of $93.75 per share (= $2,572.8/27.444).

b.

	2006/2007	2007/2008
Net Income:		
[($3,870.5/$3,376.6) − 1].................	+14.6%	
[($4,596.5/$3,870.5) − 1].................		+18.8%
Earnings per Common Share:		
[($3.20/$2.70) − 1]...........................	+18.5%	
[($3.83/$3.20) − 1]...........................		+19.7%

Earnings per share increases faster than net income because Monk reduces the number of shares outstanding each year by repurchasing shares of treasury stock.

14.38 continued.

c.

	2006	2007	2008
Book Value per Share:			
$11,735.7/(1,483.463 − 254.615)$	$9.55		
$11,970.5/(1,483.619 − 277.017)$		$9.92	
$12,613.5/(1,483.926 − 290.278)$			$10.57
Percentage Change:			
$[(\$9.92/\$9.55) − 1]$		+3.9%	
$[(\$10.57/\$9.92) − 1]$			+6.6%

There are several reasons why book value per share increases more slowly than net income and earnings per share. First, dividends reduce shareholders' equity but not net income. Second, the repurchases of treasury shares reduce the numerator proportionally more than they reduce the denominator. The average repurchase price during 2008 of $93.75 per share (see the answer to Part a.) had the effect of reducing book value per share. Book value per share increased overall in 2008 because of net income.

d.

	2006	2007	2008
$[\$3,376.6/.5(\$11,139.0 + \$11,735.7)]$..	29.5%		
$[\$3,870.5/.5(\$11,735.7 + \$11,970.5)]$..		32.7%	
$[\$4,596.5/.5(\$11,970.5 + \$12,613.5)]$..			37.4%

e. No. Monk has purchased considerably more treasury shares than are needed for its stock option plans. Treasury shares do not receive dividends, so Monk does conserve cash. However, dividends have grown at approximately the same growth rate as net income. One purpose might have been to increase the return on common shareholders' equity. Cash generally earns a return of approximately 4% each year after taxes. By eliminating this low-yielding asset from the balance sheet, Monk's overall rate of return on common shareholders' equity increases. The market often interprets stock repurchases as a positive signal that management has inside information and thinks that the stock is undervalued. The positive signal results in an increase in the stock price. One can estimate the increase in market price by observing the average price at which Monk repurchased its shares each year:

2006: $1,570.9/33.377 = $47.07
2007: $2,493.3/38.384 = $64.96
2008: $2,572.8/27.444 = $93.75

Thus, the stock price doubled during the three-year period, whereas earnings increased by approximately 36% [= ($4,596.5/$3,376.6) − 1].

14.39 (Layton Ball Corporation; case introducing earnings-per-share calculations for a complex capital structure.)

a. $\dfrac{\$9,500}{2,500} = \$3.80$ per share.

b. 1,000 options × $15 = $15,000 cash raised.

$\dfrac{\$15,000 \text{ new cash}}{\$25 \text{ per share}} = 600$ shares assumed purchased.

Total number of shares increases by 400 (= 1,000 − 600).

$\dfrac{\$9,500}{2,500 + 400} = \$3.276$ per share.

c. 2,000 warrants × $30 = $60,000 cash raised.

$\dfrac{\$60,000 \text{ new cash}}{\$25 \text{ per share}} = 2,400$ shares purchased.

Total number of shares decreases by 400 (= 2,000 − 2,400).

$\dfrac{\$9,500}{2,500 - 400} = \$4.524$ per share.

d. Before taxes, each converted bond saves $40 in annual interest expense. After taxes, the savings in expense and increase in income is only $24 [= (1 − .40) × $40].

There are 100 bonds outstanding; each is convertible into 10 shares. Thus, the new earnings per share figure is:

$\dfrac{\$9,500 + \$24 \text{ savings per bond} \times 100 \text{ bonds}}{2,500 + 10 \text{ shares per bond} \times 100 \text{ bonds}} = \dfrac{\$11,900}{3,500 \text{ shares}} =$

$3.40 per share.

e. The warrants are antidilutive and should be ignored if we seek the maximum possible dilution of earnings per share.

$\dfrac{\$9,500 + \$2,400 \text{ (Increase from interest savings)}}{2,500 + 1,000 \text{ (bond conversion)} + 400 \text{ (option exercise)}} = \dfrac{\$11,900}{3,900} =$

$3.05 per share.

14.39 continued.

    f.   Probably the *Wall Street Journal* should use the earnings per share that results in the maximum possible dilution. It should clearly ignore antidilutive securities. Do not conclude from the presentation in this problem that one can check the dilution characteristics of potentially dilutive securities one by one and know for sure which combination of assumed exercise and conversions leads to the minimum earnings per share figure.

14.40   (Case for discussion: value of stock options.)

The answer must be either *a.* or *b.* The cost per option cannot exceed one penny per share, for otherwise StartUp would merely buy the shares on the open market, rather than pay Goldman Sachs to relieve StartUp of the burden. The total cost of the options awarded to Bithead, then, cannot exceed $100 (= 10,000 shares x $.01 per share). We think the answer is likely to be in the range of $15–$40 for those shares, so we would answer *b.*

Within the last two decades, no subject has caused more controversy in accounting than the accounting for the cost of employee stock options. When it issued *SFAS No. 119* in 1995, FASB said that this issue threatened to end standard setting in the private sector and that the debate had ceased to be rational.

Some firms, such as GE, grant to employees the right to buy a specified number of shares of the firm's stock at a fixed price, called the *exercise price*, usually the price on the day the firm awards the options to the employee, say $10 per share. The employee, typically, has several years to decide whether to exercise the option—that is, give up the option and cash in return for the shares. If the stock price rises above the exercise price, say to $18 per share, then the employee can give up the option and $10 in return for a share with current market value of $18.

Such options have value to employees who receive them and many companies, particularly the high-tech Silicon Valley companies, award such options as part of their compensation in hopes that the employer's shares will skyrocket in value, enriching the employee.

The accounting issue has been: how much should the employer firm, such as GE, charge to expense in the period when it awards an option to its employees. The FASB's Exposure Draft outlines an approach for computing such amounts of expense and requiring that firms report such amounts as expense.

William H. Scott, Jr. of Scientific Applications International Corporation of San Diego, has studied the costs to the issuing firm. He found that under a wide variety of conditions, the cost to the firm issuing an option exercisable at the market price on the date of grant is, for most firms, about 10%–20% of the market value of the shares on the date of the grant. The cost to the firm of awarding the option can never exceed the market value of the share itself on the date of the award. This is true because the firm can always, on that day, go out into the market to buy a share for the current market price, building that share until the employee exercises the option.

14.40 continued.

At the height of the debate, chief financial officers (CFOs) from Silicon Valley lobbied against the FASB proposal. We believed that many of those CFOs did not understand the FASB proposal, nor its consequences. Consequently, at a private seminar on the subject at which one of us taught, we administered the question in the text to the Silicon Valley CFOs.

The Silicon Valley CFOs answered as follows: $a. = 3$, $b. = 3$, $c. = 6$, $d. = 8$, $e. = 5$, and $f. = 1$. That is, only six of the 26 participating got the answer right, which means that 20 of the 26 got it wrong. In the discussion following, we pointed out that these officers should probably understand the cost of options better than they did before arguing so hard against the proposed accounting. It's no wonder that a CFO would dislike the proposed accounting for options which the CFO thinks cost $10,000 when they actually cost no more than $100. About 25% of the Silicon Valley CFOs had beliefs that much in error.

CHAPTER 15

STATEMENT OF CASH FLOWS: ANOTHER LOOK

Problems and Cases: Answers and Solutions

15.1 (Effects of transactions on statement of cash flows.)

a. The journal entry to record this transaction is:

Retained Earnings	15,000	
Dividends Payable		3,000
Cash		12,000

	ΔCash	=	ΔL	+	ΔSE	−	ΔN$A
Financing	−$12,000	=	$3,000	+	−$15,000	−	$0

The credit to the Cash account reduces Line (11) by $12,000. Paying dividends is a financing activity, so Line (10) increases by $12,000.

b. The journal entry to record this transaction is:

Cash	75,000	
Bank Loan Payable		75,000

	ΔCash	=	ΔL	+	ΔSE	−	ΔN$A
Financing	+$75,000	=	$75,000	+	$0	−	$0

The debit to the Cash account increases Line (11) by $75,000. Borrowing is a financing activity so Line (8) increases by $75,000.

15-1

15.1 continued.

c. The journal entry to record this transaction is:

Cash.. 20,000
Accumulated Depreciation.. 35,000
    Machinery... 40,000
    Gain on Sale of Machinery.. 15,000

	ΔCash	=	ΔL	+	ΔSE	−	ΔN$A
Investing	$20,000	=	$0	+	$15,000	−	−$5,000

The debit to the Cash account results in an increase in Line (11) of $20,000. Selling machinery is an investing activity so Line (6) increases by $20,000. The gain on the sale increases net income on Line (3) by $15,000. Because the full cash proceeds is an investing activity, Line (5) increases by $15,000 to subtract from net income a revenue that did not provide an operating source of cash.

d. The journal entry for this transaction is:

Rent Expense... 28,000
    Cash 28,000

	ΔCash	=	ΔL	+	ΔSE	−	ΔN$A
Operations	−$28,000	=	$0	+	−$28,000	−	$0

The credit to the Cash account reduces Line (11) by $28,000. The recognition of rent expense reduces net income on Line (3) by $28,000. Expenditure matched the expense, so Line (2) shows an increase in the amount subtracted of $28,000.

e. The journal entry to record this transaction is:

Marketable Securities... 39,000
    Cash 39,000

	ΔCash	=	ΔL	+	ΔSE	−	ΔN$A
Investing	−$39,000	=	$0	+	$0	−	$39,000

The credit to the Cash account reduces Line (11) by $39,000. Purchasing marketable securities is an investing transaction so Line (7) increases by $39,000.

15.1 continued.

f. The journal entry to record this transaction is:

Accumulated Depreciation.. 14,000
   Truck.. 14,000

	ΔCash	=	ΔL	+	ΔSE	−	ΔN$A
	$0	=	$0	+	$0	−	$0

Because this transaction affects neither the Cash account nor net income, it does not appear on the statement of cash flows.

g. The journal entry to record this event is:

Unrealized Holding Loss of Marketable Securities (Other Comprehensive Income).................... 8,000
   Marketable Securities... 8,000

	ΔCash	=	ΔL	+	ΔSE	−	ΔN$A
	$0	=	$0	+	−$8,000	−	−$8,000

Because this entry does not affect either the Cash account or net income, it does not appear on the statement of cash flows. The firm discloses in a supplementary schedule or note the write down of marketable equity securities totaling $8,000.

h. The journal entry to record this transaction is:

Interest Expense.. 15,000
   Bonds Payable.. 500
   Cash.. 14,500

	ΔCash	=	ΔL	+	ΔSE	−	ΔN$A
Operations	−$14,500	=	$500	+	−$15,000	−	$0

The credit to the Cash account results in a decrease in Line (11) of $14,500. The recognition of interest expense reduces net income on Line (3) by $15,000. Because the firm used only $14,500 of cash for this expense, Line (4) increases by $500 for the portion of the expense that did not use cash. Line (2) increased the amount to be subtracted by the amount of the expense paid in cash, $14,500.

15.1 continued.

   i. The journal entry for this event is:

   Goodwill Impairment Loss.................................. 22,000
      Goodwill.. 22,000

ΔCash	=	ΔL	+	ΔSE	–	ΔN$A
$0	=	$0	+	–$22,000	–	–$22,000

   This entry does not involve the Cash account so Line (11) does not change. The recognition of the impairment loss reduces net income on Line (3) by $22,000. Because this loss requires no cash outflow, Line (4) increases by $22,000 to convert net income to cash flow from operations.

15.2 (Effects of transactions on statement of cash flows.)

   a. The journal entry to record this transaction is:

   Building.. 400,000
      Note Payable.. 360,000
      Cash.. 40,000

	ΔCash	=	ΔL	+	ΔSE	–	ΔN$A
Investing	–$40,000	=	$360,000	+	$0	–	$400,000

   The credit to the Cash account reduces Line (11) by $40,000. Acquiring a building is an investing transaction so Line (7) increases by $40,000. The firm discloses in a supplementary schedule or note the acquisition of a building costing $400,000, by paying cash and assuming a mortgage for $360,000.

   b. The journal entry for this event is:

   Bad Debt Expense.. 32,000
      Allowance for Uncollectible Accounts 32,000

ΔCash	=	ΔL	+	ΔSE	–	ΔN$A
$0	=	$0	+	–$32,000	–	–$32,000

Solutions

15.2 b. continued.

This entry does not involve the Cash account so Line (11) does not change. The recognition of bad debt expense reduces net income on Line (3) by $32,000. Because this expense does not use cash, Line (4) increases by $32,000 to convert net income to cash flow from operations.

c. The journal entry for this event is:

Allowance for Uncollectible Accounts......................... 28,000
    Accounts Receivable.. 28,000

$$\Delta\text{Cash} = \Delta L + \Delta SE - \Delta N\$A$$
$$\$0 = \$0 + \$0 - \$0$$

This event does not affect the Cash account so Line (11) does not change. The event also does not affect net income so Line (3) does not change. Thus, the event would not normally appear in the statement of cash flows. An alternative acceptable answer is Line (4) increases by $28,000 and Line (5) increases by $28,000.

d. The journal entry to record this transaction is:

Cash... 15,000
    Equity in Earnings of Affiliate............................. 12,000
    Investment in Securities....................................... 3,000

	ΔCash	=	ΔL	+	ΔSE	–	ΔN$A
Investing	$15,000	=	$0	+	$12,000	–	–$3,000

The debit to the Cash account results in an increase in Line (11) of $15,000. Line (1) increases by $15,000 for the dividend received. The caption "Cash Receipt from Customers" needs expanding to include "and from Investments". The recognition of equity in earnings increases net income on Line (3) by $12,000. Because the firm received $3,000 more cash than its equity in earnings, Line (4) increases by $3,000 when converting net income to cash flow from operations. An alternative acceptable answer for the increase in Line (4) of $3,000 is that Line (4) increases by $15,000 for the dividend received and Line (5) increases by $12,000 to subtract the equity in earnings.

15.2 continued.

e. The journal entries to record this transaction are:

Cash...	22,000	
Realized Loss on Sale of Marketable Securities	3,000	
Marketable Securities		25,000

Marketable Securities..	2,000	
Unrealized Holding Loss on Marketable		
Securities		2,000

	ΔCash	=	ΔL	+	ΔSE	−	ΔN$A
Investing	+$22,000	=	$0	+	−$1,000	−	−$23,000

The debit to the Cash account results in an increase in Line (11) of $22,000. Selling marketable securities is an investing transaction so Line (6) increases by $22,000. The recognition of a realized loss on the sale reduces net income on Line (3) by $3,000. Because the loss does not use cash, Line (4) increases by $3,000 to add back the loss to net income when converting net income to cash flow from operations.

f. The journal entry to record this transaction is:

Preferred Stock..	10,000	
Common Stock...		2,000
Additional Paid-in Capital		8,000

ΔCash	=	ΔL	+	ΔSE	−	ΔN$A
$0	=	$0	+	$0	−	$0

This transaction affects neither the Cash account [Line (11)] nor net income [Line (3)]. Thus, it would not appear on the statement of cash flows. The firm discloses in a supplementary schedule or note the conversion of preferred stock into common stock totaling $10,000.

15.2 continued.

g. The journal entry to record this transaction is:

Legal Expense 5,000
   Land 5,000

$$\Delta\text{Cash} = \Delta L + \Delta SE - \Delta N\$A$$
$$\$0 = \$0 + -\$5{,}000 - -\$5{,}000$$

The transaction does not affect the Cash account so Line (11) does not change. The recognition of legal expense reduces net income on Line (3) by $5,000. Because this expense does not use cash, Line (4) increases by $5,000 to convert net income to cash flow from operations.

h. The journal entry for this transaction is:

Rental Fees Received in Advance 8,000
   Rent Revenue 8,000

$$\Delta\text{Cash} = \Delta L + \Delta SE - \Delta N\$A$$
$$\$0 = -\$8{,}000 + \$8{,}000 - \$0$$

This entry does not affect the Cash account so Line (11) does not change. The recognition of rent revenue increases net income on Line (3) by $8,000. Because this revenue does not increase cash during the current period, Line (5) increases by $8,000 to convert net income to cash flow from operations.

i. The journal entry to record this event is:

Long-Term Debt 30,000
   Current Portion of Long-Term Debt 30,000

$$\Delta\text{Cash} = \Delta L + \Delta SE - \Delta N\$A$$
$$\$0 = \$0 + \$0 - \$0$$

This entry affects neither the Cash account [Line (11)] nor net income [Line (3)] and would, therefore, not appear on the statement of cash flows.

15.3 (Effects of transactions on statement of cash flows.)

a. The journal entry to record this event is:

Contracts in Process 15,000
    Contract Revenue 15,000

ΔCash	=	ΔL	+	ΔSE	−	ΔN$A
$0	=	$0	+	$15,000	−	$15,000

This entry does not affect the Cash account so Line (11) does not change. The recognition of contract revenue increases net income on Line (3) by $15,000. Because this revenue does not result in a change in cash, Line (5) increases by $15,000 to convert net income to cash flow from operations.

b. The journal entry to record this transaction is:

Land 50,000
    Donated Capital 50,000

ΔCash	=	ΔL	+	ΔSE	−	ΔN$A
$0	=	$0	+	$50,000	−	$50,000

This transaction affects neither the Cash account [Line (11)] nor net income [Line (3)] and, therefore, does not appear on the statement of cash flows. The firm discloses in a supplementary schedule or note the donation of land by a governmental agency totaling $50,000.

c. The journal entry to record this event is:

Unrealized Holding Loss on Investments in
    Securities (Other Comprehensive Income) 8,000
        Investments in Securities 8,000

ΔCash	=	ΔL	+	ΔSE	−	ΔN$A
$0	=	$0	+	−$8,000	−	−$8,000

This transaction affects neither the Cash account [Line (11)] nor net income [Line (3)] so would not appear on the statement of cash flows. The firm discloses in a supplementary schedule or note the write down of marketable equity investments totaling $8,000.

Solutions

15.3 continued.

d. The journal entry to record the recognition of depreciation is:

Inventories.. 60,000
    Accumulated Depreciation...................................   60,000

The journal entry to record the sale of the inventory items is:

Cost of Goods Sold.. 60,000
    Inventories..   60,000

$$\Delta Cash \;\;=\;\; \Delta L \;\;+\;\; \Delta SE \;\;-\;\; \Delta N\$A$$
$$\$0 \;\;=\;\; \$0 \;\;+\;\; -\$60{,}000 \;\;-\;\; -\$60{,}000$$

These entries do not affect the Cash account so Line (11) does not change. The recognition of cost of goods sold containing depreciation reduces net income on Line (3) by $60,000. Because this expense does not use cash, Line (4) increases by $60,000 to convert net income to cash flow from operations.

e. The journal entry to record this transaction is:

Warranty Expense.. 35,000
    Estimated Warranty Liability..............................   35,000

$$\Delta Cash \;\;=\;\; \Delta L \;\;+\;\; \Delta SE \;\;-\;\; \Delta N\$A$$
$$\$0 \;\;=\;\; \$35{,}000 \;\;+\;\; -\$35{,}000 \;\;-\;\; \$0$$

This entry does not affect the Cash account so Line (11) does not change. The recognition of warranty expense reduces net income on Line (3) by $35,000. Because this expense does not use cash, Line (4) increases by $35,000 to convert net income to cash flow from operations.

f. The journal entry to record this transaction is:

Estimated Warranty Liability....................................... 28,000
    Cash...   28,000

$$\;\;\Delta Cash \;\;=\;\; \Delta L \;\;+\;\; \Delta SE \;\;-\;\; \Delta N\$A$$
$$\text{Operations}\;\; -\$28{,}000 \;\;=\;\; -\$28{,}000 \;\;+\;\; \$0 \;\;-\;\; \$0$$

15.3 f. continued.

The credit to the Cash account reduces Line (11) by $28,000. Honoring warranties is an operating item so Line (2) increases the amount to be subtracted. This entry does not affect net income on Line (3) this period. Thus, Line (5) increases by $28,000 to convert net income to cash flow from operations.

g. The journal entry to record this event is:

Income Tax Expense 80,000
Deferred Tax Liability... 20,000
   Cash 100,000

	ΔCash	=	ΔL	+	ΔSE	−	ΔN$A
Operations	−$100,000	=	−$20,000	+	−$80,000	−	$0

The credit to the Cash account results in a reduction in Line (11) of $100,000. Line (2) increases the amount to be subtracted by $100,000. The recognition of income tax expense reduces net income on Line (3) by $80,000. Because the firm used more cash this period than the amount of income tax expense, Line (5) increases by $20,000 when converting net income to cash flow from operations.

h. The journal entry to record this event is:

Loss from Writedown of Inventories 18,000
   Inventories... 18,000

	ΔCash	=	ΔL	+	ΔSE	−	ΔN$A
	$0	=	$0	+	−$18,000	−	−$18,000

This entry does not affect the Cash account so Line (11) does not change. The recognition of the writedown reduces net income on Line (3) by $18,000. Because the writedown did not use cash, Line (4) increases by $18,000 to convert net income to cash flow from operations.

15.4 (Metals Company; working backwards from statement of cash flows.) (Based on financial statements of Alcoa.)

(2) Cash (Operations—Depreciation Expense Addback) 664.0
  Accumulated Depreciation 664.0

(3) Cash (Operations—Deferred Tax Addback) 82.0
  Deferred Income Tax Liability 82.0

(4) Investment in Affiliates 47.1
  Cash (Operations—Equity in Undistributed Earnings Subtraction) 47.1

(5) Cash (Investing—Sale of Marketable Securities) 49.8
&
(11) Cash (Operations—Gain on Sale of Marketable Securities Subtraction) 20.8
  Marketable Securities 29.0

(6) Cash (Operations—Decrease in Accounts Receivable) 74.6
  Accounts Receivable 74.6

(7) Inventories 198.9
  Cash (Operations—Increase in Inventories) 198.9

(8) Prepayments 40.3
  Cash (Operations—Increase in Prepayments) .. 40.3

(9) Cash (Operations—Increase in Accounts Payable) 33.9
  Accounts Payable 33.9

(10) Other Current Liabilities 110.8
  Cash (Operations—Decrease in Other Current Liabilities) 110.8

(12) Marketable Securities 73.2
  Cash (Investing—Acquisition of Marketable Securities) 73.2

(13) Property, Plant and Equipment 875.7
  Cash (Investing—Acquisition of Property, Plant and Equipment) 875.7

(14) Investments in Securities 44.5
  Cash (Investing—Acquisition of Subsidiaries) ... 44.5

15.4 continued.

(15)	Cash (Financing—Common Stock Issued to Employees)..	34.4	
	Common Stock..		34.4
(16)	Treasury Stock	100.9	
	Cash (Financing—Repurchase of Common Stock)		100.9
(17)	Retained Earnings..	242.9	
	Cash (Financing—Dividends Paid to Shareholders)..		242.9
(18)	Cash (Financing—Additions to Short-Term Borrowing)..	127.6	
	Notes Payable...		127.6
(19)	Cash (Financing—Additions to Long-Term Borrowing)..	121.6	
	Bonds Payable		121.6
(20)	Bonds Payable	476.4	
	Cash (Financing—Payments to Long-Term Borrowing)..		476.4
(21)	Property, Plant and Equipment	76.9	
	Mortgage Payable...		76.9
(22)	Property, Plant and Equipment	98.2	
	Capitalized Lease Obligation............................		98.2
(23)	Convertible Bonds Payable..	47.8	
	Common Stock..		47.8

15.5 (Metals Company deriving direct method cash flow from operations using data from T-account work sheet.) (Based on financial statements of Alcoa.)

a. (The letters here correspond to the column header letters in the exhibit below.) Copy Income Statement and Cash Flow from Operations
b. Copy Information from T-Account Work Sheet Next to Related Income Statement Item
c.–d. Sum Across Rows to Derive Direct Receipts and Expenditures

Operations	(a)	Indirect Method (b)	Changes in Related Balance Sheet Accounts from T-Account Work Sheet (c)	Direct Method (d)	From Operations: Receipts Less Expenditures
Sales Revenues	$20,465.0	$74.6	= Accounts Receivable Decrease	20,539.6	Receipts from Customers
Gain on Sale of Marketable Equity Securities	20.8	(20.8)	Gain Produces No Operating Cash	—	
Equity in Earnings of Affiliates	214.0	(47.1)	Alcoa's Share of Earnings Retained by Affiliates	166.9	Receipts for Equity Method Investments
Cost of Goods Sold	(9,963.3)	664.0	Depreciation on Manufacturing Facilities	(9,464.3)	Payments for Inventory
		33.9	= Accounts Payable Increase		
		(198.9)	= Increase in Inventories		
General and Administrative Expenses	(5,570.2)	(40.3)	= Prepayments Increase	(5,721.3)	Payments for General and Administrative Services
		(110.8)	= Decrease in Other Current Liabilities		
Interest Expense	(2,887.3)	—		(2,887.3)	Payments for Interest
Income Tax Expense	(911.6)	82.0	Deferred Income Taxes Uses no Cash this Period	(829.6)	Payment for Income Taxes
Net Income	= $1,367.4	= 1,367.4	Totals	$1,804.0	= Cash Flow from Operations Derived via Direct Method
		$1,804.0	= Cash Flow from Operations Derived via Indirect Method		

15-13 Solutions

15.6 (Ingers Company; working backwards from statement of cash flows.)

(2) Cash (Operations—Depreciation Expense Addback)..	179.4	
Accumulated Depreciation...............................		179.4
(3) Cash (Investing—Sale of Property, Plant, and Equipment)..	26.5	
(12) Property, Plant and Equipment (Net)..............		22.9
Cash (Operations—Gain on Sale Subtraction)..		3.6
(4) Investment in Securities	41.5	
Cash (Operations—Equity in Earnings Subtraction)..		41.5
(5) Cash (Operations—Deferred Taxes Addback)........	15.1	
Deferred Income Taxes....................................		15.1
(6) Cash (Operations—Decrease in Accounts Receivable)...	50.9	
Accounts Receivable		50.9
(7) Inventories	15.2	
Cash (Operations—Increase in Inventories)......		15.2
(8) Other Current Assets..	33.1	
Cash (Operations—Increase in Other Current Assets)..		33.1
(9) Accounts Payable	37.9	
Cash (Operations—Decrease in Accounts Payable)...		37.9
(10) Cash (Operations—Increase in Other Current Liabilities)...	19.2	
Other Current Liabilities		19.2
(11) Property, Plant and Equipment	211.7	
Cash (Investing—Acquisition of Property, Plant and Equipment)..		211.7

15.6 continued.

(13)	Marketable Securities...	4.6	
	Cash (Investing—Acquisition of Marketable Securities)...		4.6
(14)	Cash (Investing—Advances from Equity Companies)..	18.4	
	Investment in Equity Companies........................		18.4
(15)	Short-Term Debt...	81.5	
	Cash (Financing—Repayment of Short-Term Debt)...		81.5
(16)	Cash (Financing—Issue of Long-Term Debt)..........	147.6	
	Long-Term Debt Payable.......................................		147.6
(17)	Long-Term Debt Payable	129.7	
	Cash (Financing—Repayment of Long-Term Debt)...		129.7
(18)	Cash (Financing—Issue of Common Stock under Option Plan).......................................	47.9	
	Common Stock, Additional Paid-in Capital.....		47.9
(19)	Cash (Financing—Sale of Treasury Stock)	59.3	
	Treasury Stock, Additional Paid-in Capital.........		59.3
(20)	Retained Earnings...	78.5	
	Cash (Financing—Dividends Paid).......................		78.5
(21)	Leasehold Asset...	147.9	
	Capitalized Lease Obligation................................		147.9
(22)	Preferred Stock..	62.0	
	Common Stock, Additional Paid-in Capital.........		62.0
(23)	Investments in Securities	94.3	
	Common Stock, Additional Paid-in Capital.........		94.3

15.7 (Warren Corporation; preparing a statement of cash flows.)

a.

Cash					
√ 223,200					
Operations					
Net Income	(5)	234,000			
Loss on Sale of Machinery	(1b)	15,600			
Amortize Patent	(2b)	5,040			
Decrease in Accounts Receivable	(7)	18,000			
Bad Debt Expense	(8)	2,400			
Decrease in Inventories	(9)	66,000			
Depreciation Expense	(11)	106,800			
Amortize Leasehold Improvements	(12)	10,800			
Increase in Accounts Payable	(13)	153,360			
Investing					
Sale of Machinery	(1b)	57,600	463,200	(1a)	Acquisition of Machinery
			2,400	(2a)	Payment for Patent Defense
			180,000	(10)	Acquisition of Securities
Financing					
			13,200	(3)	Retirement of Preferred Stock
			60,000	(15)	Provision for Current Portion of Serial Bonds
√ 174,000					

15.7 a. continued.

Accounts Receivable		Allowance for Un-collectible Accounts		Inventory	
√ 327,600			20,400 √	√ 645,600	
	3,600 (6)	(6) 3,600	2,400 (8)		66,000 (9)
	18,000 (7)				
√ 306,000			19,200 √	√ 579,600	

Securities Held for Plant Expansion		Machinery and Equipment (Cost)		Accumulated Depreciation	
√ -0-		√ 776,400			446,400 √
(10) 180,000		(1a) 463,200	127,200 (1b)	(1b) 54,000	106,800 (11)
√ 180,000		√ 1,112,400			499,200 √

Leasehold Improvements		Allowance for Amortization		Patents	
√ 104,400			58,800 √	√ 36,000	
		(2a)	10,800 (12)	2,400	5,040 (2b)
√ 104,400			69,600 √	√ 33,360	

Accounts Payable		Dividends Payable		Bonds Payable (Current)	
	126,000 √		-- √		60,000 √
	153,360 (13)		48,000 (4)	(15) 60,000	60,000 (14)
	279,360 √		48,000 √		60,000 √

6-Percent Serial Bonds Payable		Preferred Stock		Common Stock	
	360,000 √		120,000 √		600,000 √
(14) 60,000		(3) 12,000			
	300,000 √		108,000 √		600,000 √

Retained Earnings	
	321,600 √
(4) 48,000	234,000 (5)
(3) 1,200	
	506,400 √

15.7 continued.

b.

WARREN CORPORATION
Statement of Cash Flows
For the Year Ending June 30, 2009

Operations:		
Net Income	$234,000	
Loss on Sale of Machinery	15,600	
Depreciation	106,800	
Amortization of Leasehold Improvements	10,800	
Amortization of Patents	5,040	
Bad Debt Expense	2,400	
Decrease in Accounts Receivable	18,000	
Decrease in Inventories	66,000	
Increase in Accounts Payable	153,360	
Cash Flow from Operations		$612,000
Investing:		
Sale of Machinery	$57,600	
Payment of Legal Fee for Patent Defense	(2,400)	
Acquisition of Securities for Plant Expansion	(180,000)	
Acquisition of Machinery	(463,200)	
Cash Flow from Investing		(588,000)
Financing:		
Retirement of Serial Bonds	$(60,000)	
Retirement of Preferred Stock	(13,200)	
Cash Flow from Financing		(73,200)
Net Change in Cash		$(49,200)
Cash, January 1, 2009		223,200
Cash, June 30, 2009		$174,000

15.8 (Roth Company; preparing a statement of cash flows.)

a.

Cash				
√ 37,950				
Operations				
Net Income	(1) 95,847	3,600	(2)	Gain on Sale of Marketable Securities
Bond Discount Amortization	(6) 225			
Depreciation	(10) 1,875	16,050	(4)	Gain on Condemnation of Land
Increase in Income Taxes Payable	(14) 51,924	37,500	(8)	Increase in Accounts Receivable
Deferred Taxes	(15) 504			
		26,250	(9)	Increase in Inventories
		8,640	(11)	Equity in Earnings
		5,835	(12)	Decrease in Accounts Payable
Investing				
Sale of Marketable Securities	(2) 17,400	122,250	(5)	Acquisition of Equipment
Proceeds from Condemnation of Land	(4) 48,000			
Financing				
Issuance of Bonds	(7) 97,500			
√ 131,100				

Marketable Securities		Accounts Receivable		Inventory	
√ 24,000		√ 36,480		√ 46,635	
	13,800 (2)	(8) 37,500		(9) 26,250	
√ 10,200		√ 73,980		√ 72,885	

Land		Building		Equipment	
√ 60,000		√ 375,000		√ -0-	
	31,950 (4)			(5) 122,250	
√ 28,050		√ 375,000		√ 122,250	

15-19

Solutions

15.8 a. continued.

Accumulated Depreciation		Investment in 30%-Owned Company		Other Assets	
	22,500 √	√ 91,830		√ 22,650	
	1,875 (10)	(11) 8,640			
	24,375 √	√ 100,470		√ 22,650	

Accounts Payable		Dividends Payable		Income Taxes Payable	
	31,830 √		-0- √		-0- √
(12) 5,835			12,000 (13)		51,924 (14)
	25,995 √		12,000 √		51,924 √

Other Liabilities		Bonds Payable		Deferred Income Taxes	
	279,000 √		71,550 √		765 √
			225 (6)		504 (15)
			97,500 (7)		
	279,000 √		169,275 √		1,269 √

Preferred Stock		Common Stock		Unrealized Holding Loss on Marketable Securities	
	45,000 √		120,000 √	√ 750	
(3) 45,000			45,000 (3)		
	-0- √		165,000 √	√ 750	

Retained Earnings	
	124,650 √
(13) 12,000	95,847 (1)
	208,497 √

Solutions 15-20

15.8 continued.

b.
ROTH COMPANY
Statement of Cash Flows
For the Three Months Ended March 31, 2009

Operations:		
Net Income	$ 95,847	
Bond Discount Amortization	225	
Depreciation	1,875	
Deferred Income Taxes	504	
Increase in Income Taxes Payable	51,924	
Gain on Sale of Marketable Securities	(3,600)	
Gain on Condemnation of Land	(16,050)	
Equity in Earnings	(8,640)	
Increase in Accounts Receivable	(37,500)	
Increase in Inventories	(26,250)	
Decrease in Accounts Payable	(5,835)	
Cash Flow from Operations		$ 52,500
Investing:		
Proceeds from Sale of Marketable Securities	$ 17,400	
Proceeds from Condemnation of Land	48,000	
Acquisition of Equipment	(122,250)	
Cash Flow from Investing		(56,850)
Financing:		
Issue of Bonds	$ 97,500	
Cash Flow from Financing		97,500
Net Change in Cash		$ 93,150
Cash, January 1 2009		37,950
Cash, March 31, 2009		$131,100

Supplementary Information

Holders of the firm's preferred stock converted shares with a carrying value of $45,000 into shares of common stock.

15.8 continued.

c. Roth deriving direct method cash flow from operations using data from T-account work sheet.
   (a) (The letters correspond to the column headers in the exhibit below.) Copy Income Statement and Cash Flow from Operations
   (b) Copy Information from T-Account Work Sheet Next to Related Income Statement Item
   (c) – (d) Sum Across Rows to Derive Direct Receipts and Expenditures

Operations	(a)	Indirect Method (b)	Changes in Related Balance Sheet Accounts from T-Account Work Sheet (c)	Direct Method (d)	From Operations: Receipts Less Expenditures
Sales	$364,212	$(37,500)	= Accounts Receivable Increase	326,712	Receipts from Customers
Gain on Sale of Marketable Equity Securities	3,600	(3,600)	Gain Produces No Operating Cash	–	
Equity in Earnings of 30%-Owned Company	8,640	(8,640)	Roth's Share of Earnings Retained by Affiliates	–	Receipts for Equity Method Investments
Gain on Condemnation of Land	16,050	(16,050)		–	Proceeds of Land Condemnation
Cost of Sales	(207,612)	(5,835)	Depreciation on Manufacturing Facilities = Accounts Payable Increase	(239,697)	Payments for Inventory
		(26,250)	= Increase in Inventories		
General and Administrative Expenses	(33,015)		= Prepayments Increase	(33,015)	Payments for Selling and Administrative Services
Depreciation	(1,875)	1,875	= Decrease in Other Current Liabilities		
Interest Expense	(1,725)	225	Bond Discount Amortization Uses No Cash this Period	(1,500)	Payments for Interest
Income Tax Expense	(52,428)	504	Deferred Income Taxes Uses no Cash this Period	–	Payment for Income Taxes
		51,924	= Increase in Income Taxes Payable		
Net Income	$95,847	95,847	Totals	$52,500	= Cash Flow from Operations Derived via Direct Method
		$52,500	= Cash Flow from Operations Derived via Indirect Method		

Solutions
15-22

15.9 (Biddle Corporation; preparing a statement of cash flows.)

a.

Cash				
√ 45,000				

Operations

Income from Continuing Operations	(14)	60,500	6,000 (3)	Gain on Retirement of Bonds Net of Income Taxes
Loss on Sale of Equipment	(4)	2,000	35,000 (7)	Increase in Accounts Receivable
Depreciation	(9)	10,000		
Amortization	(10)	1,500	20,000 (8)	Increase in Inventories
Increase in Accounts Payable	(11)	30,000		
Deferred Income Taxes	(13)	20,000	5,000 (12)	Decrease in Accrued Liabilities

Investing

Sale of Equipment	(4)	9,500	42,500 (6)	Acquisition of Land

Financing

		19,000 (3)	Retirement of Bonds, Including Income Taxes
		1,000 (5)	Dividends

√ 50,000

Accounts Receivable—Net		Inventories		Land	
√ 70,000		√ 110,000		√ 100,000	
(7) 35,000		(8) 20,000		(2) 20,000	
				(6) 42,500	
√ 105,000		√ 130,000		√ 162,500	

15.9 a. continued.

Plant and Equipment		Accumulated Depreciation		Patents	
√ 316,500			50,000 √	√ 16,500	
	26,500 (4)	(4) 15,000	10,000 (9)		1,500 (10)
√ 290,000			45,000 √	√ 15,000	

Accounts Payable		Accrued Liabilities		Deferred Income Taxes	
	100,000 √		105,000 √		50,000 √
	30,000 (11)	(12) 5,000			20,000 (13)
	130,000 √		100,000 √		70,000 √

Long-term Bonds		Common Stock		Additional Paid-in Capital	
	90,000 √		105,000 √		85,000 √
(3) 25,000			10,500 (1)		21,000 (1)
			9,500 (2)		10,500 (2)
	65,000 √		125,000 √		116,500 √

Retained Earnings	
	73,000 √
(1) 31,500	60,500 (14)
(5) 1,000	
	101,000 √

Solutions   15-24

15.9 continued.

b.

BIDDLE CORPORATION
Statement of Cash Flows
For the Year Ended December, 2009

Operations:		
Income from Continuing Operations	$ 54,500	
Loss on Sale of Equipment	2,000	
Depreciation	10,000	
Amortization	1,500	
Deferred Income Taxes	20,000	
Increase in Accounts Payable	30,000	
Increase in Accounts Receivable	(35,000)	
Increase in Inventories	(20,000)	
Decrease in Accrued Liabilities	(5,000)	
Cash Flow from Operations		$ 58,000
Investing:		
Sale of Equipment	$ 9,500	
Acquisition of Land	(42,500)	
Cash Flow from Investing		(33,000)
Financing:		
Retirement of Bonds	$ (19,000)	
Dividends	(1,000)	
Cash Flow from Financing		(20,000)
Net Change in Cash		$ 5,000
Cash, January 1, 2009		45,000
Cash, December 31, 2009		$ 50,000

Supplementary Information

During 2009, Biddle Corporation issued common stock with a market value of $20,000 in the acquisition of land.

15.10 (Plainview Corporation; preparing a statement of cash flows.)

a.

Cash	
√ 165,300	

Operations

Net Income	(1) 236,580	17,000 (5)	Gain on Sale of Marketable Securities
Loss from Fire	(6) 35,000		
Equity in Loss	(9) 17,920		
Decrease in Accounts Receivable—Net	(11) 59,000	131,100 (12)	Increase in Inventories
Depreciation	(15) 79,900	1,400 (13)	Increase in Prepayments
Increase in Accounts Payable	(16) 24,800	1,500 (18)	Decrease in Accrued Payables
Increase in Income Taxes Payable	(19) 66,500	500 (20)	Deferred Taxes
Loss on Retirement of Bonds	(21) 5,000		

Investing

Sale of Marketable Securities	(5) 127,000	28,000 (8)	Acquisition of Machinery
Building Sold	(7) 4,000	103,400 (10)	Acquisition of Marketable Securities
Bond Sinking Funds Used	(14) 63,000		

Financing

Re-issue of Treasury Stock	(3) 6,000	130,000 (2)	Dividends
Issuance of Debentures	(22) 125,000	145,000 (17)	Payment of Note Payable—Current
		315,000 (21)	Retirement of Bonds

√ 142,100

15.10 a. continued.

Marketable Securities		Accounts Receivable—Net		Inventories	
√ 129,200		√ 371,200		√ 124,100	
(10) 103,400	110,000 (5)		59,000 (11)	(12) 131,100	
√ 122,600		√ 312,200		√ 255,200	

Prepayments		Bond Sinking Fund		Investment in Subsidiary	
√ 22,000		√ 63,000		√ 152,000	
(13) 1,400			63,000 (14)		17,920 (9)
√ 23,400		√ -0-		√ 134,080	

Plant and Equipment—Net		Accounts Payable		Notes Payable—Current	
√ 1,534,600			213,300 √		145,000 √
(6) 65,000	100,000 (6)		24,800 (16)	(17) 145,000	
(8) 28,000	4,000 (7)				
	79,900 (15)				
√ 1,443,700			238,100 √		-0- √

Accrued Payables		Income Taxes Payable		Deferred Income Taxes	
	18,000 √		31,000 √		128,400 √
(18) 1,500			66,500 (19)	(20) 500	
	16,500 √		97,500 √		127,900 √

6-Percent Mortgage Bonds		8-Percent Debentures		Common Stock	
	310,000 √		-0- √		950,000 √
(21) 310,000			125,000 (22)		83,500 (4)
	-0- √		125,000 √		1,033,500 √

Additional Paid-in Capital		Unrealized Holding Gain on Marketable Securities		Retained Earnings	
	51,000 √		2,500 √		755,700 √
	16,700 (4)			(2) 130,000	236,580 (1)
				(3) 3,000	
				(4) 100,200	
	67,700 √		2,500 √		759,080 √

Treasury Stock	
√ 43,500	
	9,000 (3)
√ 34,500	

15.10 continued.

b.

PLAINVIEW CORPORATION
Statement of Cash Flows
For the Year Ended December, 2009

Operations:		
Net Income	$236,580	
Loss from Fire	35,000	
Equity in Loss of Subsidiary	17,920	
Loss on Retirement of Bonds	5,000	
Depreciation	79,900	
Gain on Sale of Marketable Securities	(17,000)	
Deferred Income Taxes	(500)	
Decrease in Accounts Receivable—Net	59,000	
Increase in Accounts Payable	24,800	
Increase in Income Taxes Payable	66,500	
Increase in Inventories	(131,100)	
Increase in Prepayments	(1,400)	
Decrease in Accrued Payables	(1,500)	
Cash Flow from Operations		$373,200
Investing:		
Marketable Securities Sold	$127,000	
Building Sold	4,000	
Bond Sinking Funds Used	63,000	
Acquisition of Marketable Securities	(103,400)	
Acquisition of Machinery	(28,000)	
Cash Flow from Investing		62,600
Financing:		
Re-issue of Treasury Stock	$6,000	
Issue of Debentures	125,000	
Dividends	(130,000)	
Retirement of Bonds	(315,000)	
Payment of Short-Term Note	(145,000)	
Cash Flow from Financing		(459,000)
Net Change in Cash		$(23,200)
Cash, January 1, 2009		165,300
Cash, December 31, 2009		$142,100

15.11 (Airlines Corporation; preparing and interpreting the statement of cash flows.) (Based on financial statements of UAL.)

a. T-account work sheet for 2008.

```
                        Cash
              √   1,087

                      Operations
        (1)    324  |  106  (4)
        (3)    517  |  147  (7)
       (11)     56  |   39  (8)
       (15)     42  |   67  (9)
       (17)     12  |   49  (16)

                      Investing
        (4)  1,199  | 1,568  (2)
       (10)     40  |   957  (6)

                      Financing
       (12)    325  |   110  (13)
       (18)      4  |    98  (19)
              √   465
```

```
    Marketable Securities      Accounts Receivable           Inventories
    √     --                   √    741                      √    210
(5)      85                (7)     147                   (8)      39
(6)     957                
    √  1,042                   √    888                      √    249
```

```
                              Property, Plant and           Accumulated
        Prepayments              Equipment                  Depreciation
    √    112                  √   7,710                                 3,769 √
(9)       67              (2)   1,568   1,574 (4)    (4)    481          517 (3)
    √    179                  √   7,704                                 3,805 √
```

```
                                                           Short-Term
        Other Assets             Accounts Payable           Borrowing
    √    610                              540  √                       121  √
                40 (10)                    56 (11)                     325 (12)
    √    570                              596  √                       446  √
```

15-29 Solutions

15.11 a. continued.

Current Portion Long-Term Debt				Advances from Customers			Other Current Liabilities		
		110	√		619	√		1,485	√
(13)	110	84	(14)		42	(15)	(16) 49		
		84	√		661	√		1,436	√

Long-Term Debt				Deferred Tax Liability			Other Noncurrent Liabilities		
		1,418	√		352	√		715	√
(14)	84				12	(17)		4	(18)
		1,334	√		364	√		719	√

Common Stock		Unrealized Holding Gain on Marketable Securities			Retained Earnings	
	119 √		--	√		1,188 √
			85	(5)		324 (1)
	119 √		85	√		1,512 √

Additional Paid-in Capital		Treasury Stock		
	48 √	√	14	
		(19)	98	
	48 √	√	112	

Solutions 15-30

15.11 a. continued.

a. T-account work sheet for 2009.

	Cash		
√	465		

	Operations		
(1)	101	286	(4)
(3)	560	25	(7)
(15)	182	74	(8)
(16)	390	30	(9)
(18)	4	44	(11)

	Investing		
(4)	1,697	2,821	(2)
		17	(6)
		35	(10)

	Financing		
(12)	1	84	(13)
(17)	230		
(19)	2		
(20)	5		
√	221		

Marketable Securities		Accounts Receivable		Inventories	
√ 1,042		√ 888		√ 249	
(5) 7		(7) 25		(8) 74	
(6) 17					
√ 1,066		√ 913		√ 323	

Prepayments		Property, Plant and Equipment		Accumulated Depreciation	
√ 179		√ 7,704			3,805 √
(9) 30		(2) 2,821	1,938 (4)	(4) 527	560 (3)
√ 209		√ 8,587			3,838 √

15.11 a. continued.

Other Assets		Accounts Payable		Short-Term Borrowing	
√ 570			596 √		446 √
(10) 35		(11) 44			1(12)
√ 605			552 √		447 √

Current Portion Long-Term Debt		Advances from Customers		Other Current Liabilities	
	84 √		661 √		1,436 √
(13) 84	89(14)		182(15)		390(16)
	89 √		843 √		1,826 √

Long-Term Debt		Deferred Tax Liability		Other Noncurrent Liabilities	
	1,334 √		364 √		719 √
(14) 89	230(17)		4(18)		2(19)
	1,475 √		368 √		721 √

Common Stock		Additional Paid-in Capital		Unrealized Holding Gain on Marketable Securities	
	119 √		48 √		85 √
	1(20)		4(20)		7 (5)
	120 √		52 √		92 √

Retained Earnings		Treasury Stock	
	1,512 √	√ 112	
	101 (1)		
	1,613 √	√ 112	

15.11 continued.

b. **Comparative Statement of Cash Flows for Airlines Corporation**
(Amounts in Millions)

	2009	2008
Operations:		
Net Income	$ 101	$ 324
Depreciation Expense	560	517
Deferred Income Taxes	4	12
Gain on Sale of Property, Plant and Equipment	(286)	(106)
(Increase) Decrease in Accounts Receivable	(25)	(147)
(Increase) Decrease in Inventories	(74)	(39)
(Increase) Decrease in Prepayments	(30)	(67)
Increase (Decrease) in Accounts Payable	(44)	56
Increase (Decrease) in Advances from Customers	182	42
Increase (Decrease) in Other Current Liabilities	390	(49)
Cash Flow from Operations	$ 778	$ 543
Investing:		
Sale of Property, Plant and Equipment	$ 1,697	$ 1,199
Acquisition of Property, Plant and Equipment	(2,821)	(1,568)
Acquisition of Marketable Securities	(17)	(957)
(Increase) Decrease in Other Noncurrent Assets	(35)	40
Cash Flow from Investing	$(1,176)	$(1,286)
Financing:		
Increase in Short-Term Borrowing	$ 1	$ 325
Increase in Long-Term Borrowing	230	--
Increase in Common Stock	5	--
Decrease in Long-Term Borrowing	(84)	(110)
Acquisition of Treasury Stock	--	(98)
Increase in Other Noncurrent Liabilities	2	4
Cash Flow from Financing	$ 154	$ 121
Net Change in Cash	$ (244)	$ (622)
Cash, January 1	465	1,087
Cash, December 31	$ 221	$ 465

15.11 continued.

    c. During 2008, cash flow from operations exceeded net income primarily because of the noncash expense for depreciation. Cash flows from operations and from the sale of property, plant and equipment were sufficient to finance capital expenditures. Airlines Corporation used the excess cash flow as well as cash from additional short-term borrowing to repay long-term debt and reacquire treasury stock. It invested the remaining excess cash flow in short-term marketable securities. Although the balance in the cash account declined during 2008, the combined balance in cash and marketable securities actually increased.

        Net income declined in 2009 relative to 2008 but cash flow from operations increased. The increase occurred because Airlines Corporation received increased cash advances from customers and stretched its other current liabilities. Cash flow from operations and from the sale of property, plant and equipment were insufficient to finance capital expenditures. Airlines Corporation increased long-term borrowing and decreased the balance in its cash account to finance these capital expenditures.

        One additional item to note for Airlines Corporation is the significant turnover of aircraft each year. The airline sold older aircraft at a gain and replaced them with newer aircraft.

15.12 (Irish Paper Company; preparing and interpreting the statement of cash flows.)

a. T-account work sheet for 2007.

	Cash		
√	374		

Operations			
(1)	376	221	(7)
(6)	306	31	(8)
(9)[1]	2	112	(10)
(12)	54	59	(11)
(14)	72	5	(17)
(18)	87		

Investing			
(7)	5	92	(3)
(13)	8	775	(4)

Financing			
(5)	449	59	(2)
		129	(16)
		201	(19)

| √ | 49 | | |

[1]OK to classify this as (Dis-)Investing source of cash.

15.12 a. continued.

Accounts Receivable		Inventories		Prepayments	
√ 611		√ 522		√ 108	
(10) 112		(11) 59			54 (12)
√ 723		√ 581		√ 54	

Investments in Affiliates		Property, Plant and Equipment		Accumulated Depreciation	
√ 254		√ 5,272			2,160 √
(3) 92	2 (9p)	(4) 775	78 (7)	(7) 74	306 (6)
(8) 31					
√ 375		√ 5,969			2,392 √

Other Assets		Accounts Payable		Current Portion Long-Term Debt	
√ 175			920 √		129 √
(7) 220	8 (13)		72 (14)	(16) 129	221 (15)
√ 387			992 √		221 √

Other Current Liabilities		Long-Term Debt		Deferred Income Taxes	
	98 √		1,450 √		607 √
(17) 5		(15) 221	449 (5)		87 (18)
	93 √		1,678 √		694 √

Common Stock		Retained Earnings		Treasury Stock	
	629 √		1,331 √	√ 15	
(19) 201		(2) 59	376 (1)		
	428 √		1,648 √	√ 15	

15.12 a. continued.

a. T-account work sheet for 2008.

```
                        Cash
              √     49
                     Operations
          (1)    169        19   (8)
          (7)    346        38   (9)
         (10)¹     5       106  (11)
         (14)   186        154  (12)
                            10  (17)
                            26  (18)

                     Investing
          (3)     86       931   (4)
          (8)     21        78  (13)

                     Financing
          (5)    890        59   (2)
         (19)      4       221  (16)
              √    114
```

¹OK to classify this as (Dis-)Investing source of cash.

Accounts Receivable		Inventories		Prepayments	
√ 723		√ 581		√ 54	
(11) 106		(12) 154			
√ 829		√ 735		√ 54	

Investments in Affiliates		Property, Plant and Equipment		Accumulated Depreciation	
√ 375		√ 5,969			2,392 √
(9) 38	86 (3)	(4) 931	42 (8)	(8) 40	346 (7)
	5 (10p)	(6) 221			
√ 322		√ 7,079			2,698 √

Other Assets		Accounts Payable		Current Portion Long-Term Debt	
√ 387			992 √		221 √
(13) 78			186 (14)	(16) 221	334 (15)
√ 465			1,178 √		334 √

15.12 a. continued.

Other Current Liabilities		Long-Term Debt		Deferred Income Taxes	
	93 √		1,678 √		694 √
(17) 10		(15) 334	890 (5)	(18) 26	
			221 (6)		
	83 √		2,455 √		668 √

Common Stock		Retained Earnings		Treasury Stock	
	428 √		1,648 √	√ 15	
	4 (19)	(2) 59	169 (1)		
	432 √		1,758 √	√ 15	

a. T-account work sheet for 2009.

Cash

√ 114	

Operations

(6)	353	142	(1)
(7)	34	30	(8)
(9)	32	2	(12)
(10)	159	45	(17)
(11)	164	7	(18)
(14)	136		

Investing

(7)	114	13	(3)
		315	(4)
		19	(13)

Financing

(5)	36	59	(2)
(19)	8	334	(16)
√	184		

Solutions

15.12 a. continued.

Accounts Receivable		Inventories		Prepayments	
√ 829		√ 735		√ 54	
	159 (10)		164 (11)	(12) 2	
√ 670		√ 571		√ 56	

Investments in Affiliates		Property, Plant and Equipment		Accumulated Depreciation	
√ 322		√ 7,079			2,698 √
(3) 13	32 (9)	(4) 315	222 (7)	(7) 74	353 (6)
(8) 30					
√ 333		√ 7,172			2,977 √

Other Assets		Accounts Payable		Current Portion Long-Term Debt	
√ 465			1,178 √		334 √
(13) 19			136 (14)	(16) 334	158 (15)
√ 484			1,314 √		158 √

Other Current Liabilities		Long-Term Debt		Deferred Income Taxes	
	83 √		2,455 √		668 √
(17) 45		(15) 158	36 (5)	(18) 7	
	38 √		2,333 √		661 √

Common Stock		Retained Earnings		Treasury Stock	
	432 √		1,758 √	√ 15	
	7 (19)	(1) 142			1 (19)
		(2) 59			
	439 √		1,557 √	√ 14	

15.12 continued.

b.

IRISH PAPER COMPANY
Statement of Cash Flows
(Amounts in Millions)

	2007	2008	2009
Operations:			
Net Income (Loss)	$ 376	$ 169	$ (142)
Depreciation Expense	306	346	353
Loss (Gain) on Sale of Property, Plant and Equipment	(221)	(19)	34
Equity in Undistributed Earnings of Affiliates	(29)	(33)	2
Increase (Decrease) in Deferred Income Taxes	87	(26)	(7)
(Increase) Decrease in Accounts Receivable	(112)	(106)	159
(Increase) Decrease in Inventories	(59)	(154)	164
(Increase) Decrease in Prepayments	54	--	(2)
Increase (Decrease) in Accounts Payable	72	186	136
Increase (Decrease) in Other Current Liabilities	(5)	(10)	(45)
Cash Flow from Operations	$ 469	$ 353	$ 652
Investing:			
Sale of Property, Plant and Equipment	$ 5	$ 21	$ 114
Acquisition of Property, Plant and Equipment	(775)	(931)	(315)
(Increase) Decrease in Investments in Affiliates	(92)	86	(13)
(Increase) Decrease in Other Assets	8	(78)	(19)
Cash Flow from Investing	$(854)	$(902)	$ (233)
Financing:			
Issue of Long-Term Debt	$ 449	$ 890	$ 36
Issue of Common Stock or Treasury Stock	--	4	8
Redemption of Long-Term Debt	(129)	(221)	(334)
Redemption of Common Stock Warrants	(201)	--	--
Dividends	(59)	(59)	(59)
Cash Flow from Financing	$ 60	$ 614	$ (349)
Net Change in Cash	$(325)	$ 65	$ 70
Cash, January 1	374	49	114
Cash, December 31	$ 49	$ 114	$ 184

15.12 b. continued.

Supplementary Information

During 2008, Irish Paper Company assumed a mortgage payable of $221 million in the acquisition of property, plant and equipment.

c. The pattern of cash flows for 2007 is typical of a growing, capital-intensive firm. Cash flow from operations exceeds net income because of the addback of depreciation expense. Book income before taxes exceeds taxable income, resulting in a deferral of taxes payable. Accounts receivable and inventories increased to support the growth, while accounts payable increased to finance the increased inventories. Irish made significant capital expenditures during the year for which it had to rely in part on external debt financing.

The pattern of cash flows for 2008 is similar to that for 2007, again typical of a growing firm. In this case, however, cash flow from operations declines relative to 2007 because of reduced net income. The reduced net income occurs in part because of a smaller gain on sale of property, plant and equipment and in part because of larger depreciation and administrative expenses. Irish financed its increased capital expenditures with additional long-term borrowing.

The pattern of cash flows for 2009 is typical of a firm that stopped growing. Sales and net income declined, the result of under-utilizing manufacturing capacity. Cash flow from operations increased, however, because Irish collected receivables and decreased its investment in inventories. It also stretched its accounts payable. Cash flow from operations was more than sufficient to finance a reduced level of capital expenditures and repay long-term debt.

15.13 (Breda Enterprises, Inc.; preparing a statement of cash flows.)

BREDA ENTERPRISES, INC.
Statement of Cash Flows
For the Year Ended December 31, 2009

Operations:		
Net Income (1)	$ 90,000	
Adjustments for Noncash Transactions:		
Decrease in Merchandise Inventory (3)	4,000	
Increase in Accounts Payable (3)	12,000	
Loss on Sale of Equipment (4)	13,000	
Depreciation Expense (4)	42,000	
Amortization of Leasehold Asset (5)	5,000	
Loss on Conversion of Bonds (8)	15,000	
Increase in Accounts Receivable (Net) (2)	(10,600)	
Increase in Notes Receivable (2)	(15,000)	
Increase in Interest Receivable (2) [(.08 x $15,000) x (1/6)]	(200)	
Decrease in Advances from Customers (2)	(2,700)	
Realized Gain on Marketable Securities (7)	(4,600)	
Interest Expense Greater than Cash Paid for Interest = Amortization of Bond Premium (8)	(1,500)	
Cash Flow from Operations		$ 146,400
Investing:		
Sale of Equipment (4)	$ 25,000	
Sale of Marketable Securities (7)	9,100	
Purchase of Equipment (4) ($31,000 + $38,000 − $26,000)	(43,000)	
Cash Flow from Investing		(8,900)
Financing:		
Reduction of Lease Liability (5)	$ (2,400)	
Dividends (6)	(24,000)	
Cash Flow from Financing		(26,400)
Change in Cash		$ 111,100

Solutions

15.14 (Gear Locker; interpreting the statement of cash flows.)

a. The rate of increase in net income suggests that Gear Locker grew rapidly during the three-year period. Increased investments in accounts receivable and inventories used operating cash flow. Increases in supplier credit did not fully finance the increased working capital investments, resulting in negative cash flow from operations.

b. During 2007, Gear Locker sold marketable securities and borrowed short term to finance the negative cash flow from operations. Accounts receivable and inventories convert into cash within one year, so short-term financing is appropriate. Selling marketable securities to help finance these working capital investments suggests that the revenue from these securities was less than the cost of additional short-term borrowing.
   During 2008, Gear Locker relied on short-term borrowing to finance its working capital needs, matching the term structure of its financing with the term structure of its assets.
   During 2009, Gear Locker issued additional common stock to finance its working capital needs. Several explanations for this switch in financing are possible. First, the proportion of debt in the capital structure may have reached a point after the borrowing in 2008 that lenders considered the firm unduly risky, thereby raising the cost of additional borrowing. Second, Gear Locker may have expected continuing rapid growth and wished to infuse a more permanent form of capital than short-term debt into the capital structure. Third, short-term borrowing rates might have increased significantly relative to long-term rates and Gear Locker chose to access longer term sources of capital.

c. Gear Locker is growing rapidly, so that new capacity additions exceed depreciation recognized on existing capacity.

d. Gear Locker is not capital intensive. The firm uses independent manufacturers in East Asia and markets its products through independent retailers. Thus, its property, plant and equipment serves primarily its administrative needs.

e. Gear Locker has few fixed assets that might serve as collateral for such borrowing. The principal collateral is short-term, so lenders likely prefer to extend short-term financing.

15.15 (Canned Soup Company; interpreting the statement of cash flows.) (Based on financial statements of Campbell Soup Company.)

    a. Canned uses suppliers and other creditors to finance its working capital needs. Consumer foods is a mature industry in the United States, so Canned's modest growth rate does not require large incremental investments in accounts receivable and inventories.

    b. (1) Capital expenditures have declined slightly each year, suggesting little need to add productive capacity.

        (2) Depreciation expense is a growing percentage of acquisitions of property, plant and equipment, suggesting slower growth in manufacturing capacity.

        (3) Substantial trading in marketable securities each year. Mature, profitable firms tend to accumulate cash beyond their operating needs and invest in marketable securities until they need cash.

        (4) Acquisition of another business in Year 8. Firms in mature industries grow by acquiring other firms. Canned financed this acquisition in part by selling marketable securities.

    c. (1) Increases in long-term debt approximately equal repayments of long-term debt, particularly for Year 7 and Year 8. Mature firms tend to roll over debt as long as they remain in the no-growth phase.

        (2) Canned repurchased a portion of its common stock with excess cash.

        (3) Dividends have grown in line with increases in net income and represent approximately a 37% payout rate relative to net income.

15.16 (Prime Contracting Services; interpreting the statement of cash flows.)

    a. The firm reduced expenditures on fixed assets beginning in 2007. It sold fixed assets in 2009 and 2010. The firm repaid debt under equipment loans and capital leases, probably because the firm sold or returned fixed assets that served as collateral for this debt. The increase in Other Current Liabilities indicates the heavier use of employees in providing services.

    b. Net income declined between 2006 and 2008 as the firm attempted to build its new people-based service business. It collected accounts receivable from the previous asset-based service contracts. The continually increasing sales suggest that the firm collects receivables from its new people-based services more quickly than on its previous asset-based services contracts. Thus, the increase in accounts receiv-

15.16 b. continued.

able declined each year. The firm also stretched payments to employees, providing cash. Note that the increase in depreciation did not provide cash. The increased depreciation charge reduced net income and the addback merely offsets the reduction. The increased depreciation charge results from expenditures made on fixed assets in 2006 and 2007.

c. The people-based service business began to grow, leading to increasing net income. The firm also sold off fixed assets at a gain, increasing net income. The cash proceeds from sale of the fixed assets appear in the Investing section, not cash flow from operations. The firm experienced increased accounts receivable from this growing business in 2009, which required cash. Additional increases in net income in 2010 coupled with decreases in accounts receivable helped cash flow from operations in that year.

d. Net income has increased and long-term borrowing has decreased, reducing the firm's risk. Offsetting these changes, however, is a significant increase in short-term borrowing in 2010.

15.17 (Cypress Corporation; interpreting the statement of cash flows.)

a. Although net income increased between 2011 and 2013, the firm increased accounts receivable and inventories to support this growth. It stretched its creditors somewhat to finance the buildup of accounts receivable and inventories, but not sufficiently to keep cash from operations from decreasing.

b. The principal factors causing cash flow from operations to increase in 2014 is an increase in net income. Inventories decreased and the firm stretched its payable somewhat as well. The principal factors causing the increased cash flow from operations in 2015 are increased and decreased accounts receivable and decreased inventories, partially offset by decreases in accounts payable and other liabilities.

c. The firm has repaid both short- and long-term debt, likely reducing its debt service payments. It invested excess cash in marketable securities. It also substantially increased its dividend. Even with these actions, cash on the balance sheet increased significantly, particularly in 2015.

5.18 (Deriving cash flows from financial statement data; comprehensive review, including other comprehensive income.)

Cash Flow from Operations.................	$ 181,500	[9]	Plug $181,500
Investing/Disinvesting:			
Purchase of Securities Available for Sale..	(9,000)	[8]	
Proceeds of Sale of Securities Available for Sale........................	7,300	[7]	
Purchase of Land..............................	(11,000)	[6]	
Sale of Old Buildings and Equipment..	53,000	[5]	See below
Purchase of New Buildings and Equipment.......................................	(108,000)	[4]	Increase in B&E (Cost) + Cost of B&E Sold
Financing:			
Increase (Decrease) in Long-Term Debt...	(2,000)	[3]	
Increase (Decrease) in Common Shares...	7,000	[2]	
Cash Dividends.................................	(105,800)	[1]	= Income − Increase in Retained Earnings
Net Change in Cash.............................	$ 13,000	[0]	$13,000

Depreciation Charge...........................	$ 54,000
Less Increase in Accumulated Depreciation......................................	(44,000)
Accumulated Depreciation on Asset Sold..	$ 10,000
Cost of Asset Sold..............................	$ 40,000
Less Accumulated Depreciation on Asset Sold.......................................	(10,000)
Basis of Asset Sold.............................	$ 30,000
Gain on Sale......................................	23,000
Sale Proceeds.....................................	$ 53,000

a. $53,000; see above.

b. $7,300 = $4,000 [cost] + $3,300 [gain].

c. $9,000 = $80,000 [EB] − $68,000 [BB] − $7,000 [OCI] + $4,000 [cost].

d. $10,300 increase = $7,000 [OCI] + $3,300 [gain].

15.18 continued.

e. $900 = $1,600 [Inc St] − ($13,700 [EB] − $13,000 [BB]).

f. $11,000 = $1,100 [Min Int Inc St]/.10($1.00 − Ownership %].

g. $34,000 [Warranty Expense, as BS liability did not change].

h. $123,000 = $125,000 − ($43,000 − $41,000) (2nd term is also $800/.40] [Bad Debt expense less increase in Allowance].

i. $60,000 = $54,000 [expense] + [($34,400 − $32,000)/.40]. Second term in the parentheses is increase in Deferred Tax Liability.

j. $105,800 = $141,000 − ($236,000 − $200,000) [Income less increase in Retained Earnings].

k. $−100,800 = $−105,800 [dividends, see above] − $2,000 [debt payoff] + $7,000 [stock issue].

l. $−67,000 = $−9,000 + $7,300 + $53,000 − $108,000 − $11,000.

m. $181,500 = $13,000 + $100,800 + $67,700 = increase in cash plus outflows for financing + outflows for investing. [derived as plug].

n. $1,356,000 = $1,500,000 − ($154,000 − $143,000) + ($6,000 − $14,000) − $125,000 = Sales less increase in Accounts Receivable, net plus increase in Advance from Customers less Bad Debt Expense.

o. Expenditure of $794,000 = ($212,000 − $58,000) − ($192,000 − $50,000) + $788,000 − ($5,000 − $4,000) − ($141,000 − $136,000) = increase in Inventory plus Cost of Goods Sold − increase in Advances to Suppliers of Inventory.

p. $−53,400 = expenditures of $53,400 = $90,400 − $18,000 − $19,000 Income Tax Expense (Current) less decrease in Prepaid Income Taxes less increase in Income Taxes Payable.

q. LIFO [see balance sheet subtraction for adjustment from FIFO to LIFO].

r. $8,000 larger = $58,000 − $50,000 increase in Allowance to Reduce LIFO Valuation for the year.

15.18 continued.

    s. $58,000 [EB of Allowance].

    t. [e], but holding gains on inventory will become part of net income when US GAAP and IFRS allow or require fair value to be the balance sheet basis for inventory.

CHAPTER 16

SYNTHESIS OF FINANCIAL REPORTING

Exercises and Problems: Answers and Solutions

16.1 (Identifying accounting principles.)

a. FIFO cost flow assumption.

b. Allowance method.

c. Equity method.

d. Capital or financing lease method.

e. Weighted-average cost flow assumption.

f. Effective interest method.

g. Cash flow hedge.

h. Market value method.

i. Percentage-of-completion method.

j. Allowance method.

k. Fair value hedge.

l. Operating lease method.

m. FIFO cost flow assumption.

n. Market value method for securities available for sale.

o. Straight line method.

p. FIFO cost flow assumption.

q. Operating lease method.

r. LIFO cost flow assumption.

16.1 continued.

    s. Capital or financing lease method.

    t. LIFO cost flow assumption.

16.2 (Identifying generally accepted accounting principles.)

    a. Market value method of accounting for either marketable securities or long-term investments in securities classified as available for sale.

       Receipt of a dividend in cash.

    b. Market value method for marketable securities classified as available for sale.

       Writedown of marketable securities to market value.

    c. Equity method of accounting for long-term investments.

       Receipt of dividend from an investee.

    d. Allowance method of accounting for uncollectible accounts.

       Recognition of expected loss from uncollectible accounts.

    e. Operating method of accounting for leases by lessee.

       Payment of rent for rental services received this period.

    f. Equity method of accounting for long-term investments.

       Accrual of investor's share of investee's earnings.

    g. Allowance method of accounting for uncollectible accounts.

       Write off of an uncollectible account.

    h. Lower-of-cost-or-market valuation basis for inventories. In most cases, the debit entry is made to cost of goods sold.

       Write down of inventories to market value.

    i. Capital lease method of accounting for long-term leases by lessee.

       Payment of cash for interest and for reduction in principal of lease liability.

    j. Cost method of accounting for treasury stock.

       Purchase of treasury stock for cash.

16.2 continued.

    k. Fair value method for derivative accounted for as a fair value hedge.

       Remeasurement of swap contract to fair value.

16.3 (Chicago Corporation; comprehensive review problem.)

    a.
Balance, December 31, 2008.	$100,000
Provision for 2009.	120,000
Less Balance, December 31, 2009.	(160,000)
Write-offs during 2009	$ 60,000

    b.

	LIFO	FIFO
Beginning Inventory	$ 1,500,000	$ 1,800,000
Purchases	5,300,000	5,300,000
Available for Sale	$ 6,800,000	$ 7,100,000
Less Ending Inventory	(1,800,000)	(1,700,000)
Cost of Goods Sold	$ 5,000,000	$ 5,400,000
Net Sales	$13,920,000	$13,920,000
Less Cost of Goods Sold	(5,000,000)	(5,400,000)
Gross Profit	$ 8,920,000	$ 8,520,000

    c. The quantity of inventory increased because the LIFO ending inventory is larger than the LIFO beginning inventory. The acquisition costs of the inventory items decreased because the FIFO ending inventory is less than the FIFO beginning inventory despite an increase in quantity during the year.

    d. None of the companies declared dividends during 2009 because the changes (increases) in the investment accounts equal the amounts recognized as Chicago Corporation's equity in the earnings of these companies.

    e.
Investment in Chicago Finance Corporation	1,800,000	
Investment in Rosenwald Company	125,000	
Investment in Hutchinson Company	75,000	
Equity in Earnings of Chicago Finance Corporation		1,800,000
Equity in Earnings of Rosenwald Company		125,000
Equity in Earnings of Hutchinson Company		75,000

Assets	= Liabilities	+	Shareholders' Equity	(Class.)
+1,800,000			+1,800,000	IncSt → RE
+125,000			+125,000	IncSt → RE
+75,000			+75,000	IncSt → RE

    f. $4,000,000/40 = $100,000.

16.3 continued.

g. Cash 400,000
    Accumulated Depreciation 800,000
        Machinery and Equipment 1,000,000
        Gain on Sale of Machinery and Equipment 200,000

Assets	= Liabilities	+	Shareholders' Equity	(Class.)
+400,000			+200,000	IncSt → RE
+800,000				
–1,000,000				

h. Interest Expense 288,000
    Bonds Payable (= $3,648,000 – $3,600,000) 48,000
    Cash (= .06 × $4,000,000) 240,000

Assets	= Liabilities	+	Shareholders' Equity	(Class.)
–240,000	+48,000		–288,000	IncSt → RE

i. Effective interest rate × $3,600,000 = $288,000. The effective interest rate = 8%. Chicago Corporation issued these bonds for less than their face value because the coupon rate of 6% is less than the market interest rate at the time of issue of 8%.

j. Difference between book and taxable depreciation = $150,000/.30 = $500,000.

Because the Deferred Tax Liability account increased, tax depreciation must be $500,000 larger than depreciation for financial reporting.

k. Cash 1,000,000
    Treasury Shares 400,000
    Additional Paid-in Capital 600,000

Assets	= Liabilities	+	Shareholders' Equity	(Class.)
+1,000,000			+400,000	ContriCap
			+600,000	ContriCap

l. Acquisition Cost $1,250,000
    Less Carrying Value .... (750,000)
    Accumulated Amortization .... $ 500,000

Because the patent is being amortized at the rate of $125,000 per year, the patent was acquired four years before the balance sheet date (= $500,000/$125,000).

16.3 continued.

m. If Chicago Corporation owns less than 20% of the common stock of Hutchinson Company, it must use the market-value method. Chicago Corporation would show the Investment in Hutchinson account at its market value of $125,000 (= $100,000 + $25,000) and show a $25,000 amount in the Unrealized Holding Gain on Investment in Securities account in Accumulated Other Comprehensive Income in the shareholders' equity section of the balance sheet. Hutchinson Company did not declare dividends during the year. Thus, net income of Chicago Corporation would decrease by the $75,000 equity in Hutchinson Company's earnings during 2009 recognized under the equity method. Consolidated retained earnings would, therefore, be $75,000 less than as now stated. In the statement of cash flows, there would be $75,000 smaller net income and no subtraction of $75,000 for the equity in earnings of Hutchinson Company.

n. Capitalized Lease Obligation ($1,100,000 – $1,020,000) 80,000
    Interest Expense 90,000
        Cash 170,000

Assets	= Liabilities	+	Shareholders' Equity	(Class.)
–170,000	–80,000		–90,000	IncSt → RE

Amortization of Leased Property Rights 150,000
    Accumulated Amortization 150,000

Assets	= Liabilities	+	Shareholders' Equity	(Class.)
–150,000			–150,000	IncSt → RE

Total expense would be $240,000 (= $90,000 + $150,000).

o. The income statement would show a $200,000 loss from the price decline, and retained earnings would be $200,000 less than as shown. The Inventories account would be shown at $1,600,000 instead of $1,800,000. There would be an addback for the loss on the statement of cash flows because the loss did not use cash.

p. Basic earnings per share = ($4,400,000 – $120,000)/1,600,000 = $2.675.

Fully diluted earnings per share = $4,400,000/(1,600,000 + ?) = $2.20.

The number of common shares that would be issued is 400,000.

16.3 continued.

q.

Cash
√	200,000			

Operations
(1)	4,400,000	100,000	(3)
(11)	1,000,000	300,000	(4)
(12)	125,000	1,800,000	(5)
(13)	150,000	125,000	(6)
(15)	60,000	75,000	(7)
(16)	130,000	200,000	(9)
(17)	50,000	20,000	(14)
(18)	260,000		
(19)	48,000		
(22)	170,000		

Investing
(9)	400,000	100,000	(8)
		1,700,000	(10)

Financing
(23)	1,000,000	2,200,000	(2)
		968,000	(20)
		80,000	(21)
√	325,000		

Accounts Payable
	√	500,000
(3)	100,000	
	√	600,000

Merchandise Inventory
√	1,500,000	
(4)	300,000	
√	1,800,000	

Prepayments
√	200,000	
√	200,000	

Investments in Chicago Finance Corporation
√	2,200,000	
(5)	1,800,000	
√	4,000,000	

Solutions

16.3 q. continued.

Investment in Rosenwald Corporation			Investment in Hutchinson Corporation		
√	900,000		√	100,000	
(6)	125,000		(7)	75,000	
√	1,025,000		√	175,000	

Land			Building		
√	400,000		√	4,000,000	
(8)	100,000				
√	500,000		√	4,000,000	

Merchandise and Equipment			Property Rights under Lease		
√	7,300,000		√	1,500,000	
(10)	1,700,000	1,000,000 (9)			
√	8,000,000		√	1,500,000	

Accumulated Depreciation and Amortization			Patent		
		3,800,000 √	√	875,000	
(9)	800,000	1,000,000 (11)			125,000 (12)
		4,000,000 √	√	750,000	

Goodwill			Accounts Payable		
√	1,125,000				400,000 √
					150,000 (13)
√	1,125,000				550,000 √

Advances from Customers			Salaries Payable		
		660,000 √			240,000 √
(14)	20,000				60,000 (15)
		640,000 √			300,000 √

Income Taxes Payable			Rent Received in Advance		
		300,000 √			0 √
		130,000 (16)			50,000 (17)
		430,000 √			50,000 √

Other Current Liabilities			Bonds Payable		
		200,000 √			3,600,000 √
		260,000 (18)			48,000 (19)
		460,000 √			3,648,000 √

16.3 q. continued.

Equipment Mortgage Payable		
	1,300,000	√
(20) 968,000		
	332,000	√

Capitalized Lease Obligation		
	1,100,000	√
(21) 80,000		
	1,020,000	√

Deferred Tax Liability		
	1,400,000	√
	170,000	(22)
	1,570,000	√

Convertible Preferred Stock		
	2,000,000	√
	2,000,000	√

Common Stock		
	2,000,000	√
	2,000,000	√

Additional Paid-in Capital		
	2,400,000	√
	600,000	(23)
	3,000,000	√

Retained Earnings		
	2,800,000	√
(2) 2,200,000	4,400,000	(1)
	5,000,000	√

Treasury Stock		
√ 1,400,000		
	400,000	(23)
√ 1,000,000		

16.4 (Tuck Corporation; comprehensive review problem.)

a. Balance in Marketable Equity Securities on December 31, 2008 .... $125,000
Less Cost of Marketable Equity Securities Sold .... (35,000)
Plus Decrease in Unrealized Holding Loss on Marketable Securities 4,000
Plus Cost of Marketable Equity Securities Purchased .... ?
Balance in Marketable Equity Securities on December 31, 2009 .... $141,000

The cost of marketable equity securities purchased is $47,000.

b. Cost of Marketable Equity Securities Sold $35,000
Less Loss on Sale of Marketable Equity Securities .... (8,000)
Sales Proceeds $27,000

c. Balance in Allowance Account on December 31, 2008 .... $128,800
Plus Provision for Estimated Uncollectible Accounts .... ?
Less Write-offs of Specific Customers' Accounts .... (63,000)
Balance in Allowance Account on December 31, 2009 .... $210,400

The provision for estimated uncollectibles is $144,600.

Solutions

16.4 continued.

d.

	LIFO	Difference	FIFO
Beginning Inventory	$1,257,261	$ 430,000	$1,687,261
Purchases	2,848,054	--	2,848,054
Available	$4,105,315	$ 430,000	$4,535,315
Less Ending Inventory	(1,525,315)	(410,000)	(1,935,315)
Cost of Goods Sold	$2,580,000	$ 20,000	$2,600,000

e. Unrealized Holding Loss on Investments in
    Securities.. 5,000
       Investments in Securities................................. 5,000

Assets	=	Liabilities	+	Shareholders' Equity	(Class.)
–5,000				–5,000	OCI → AOCI

To recognize unrealized holding loss on investments in securities.

f. Dividend revenue of $8,000. The unrealized loss of $5,000 (see Part e.) is not included in the calculation of net income for 2009.

g. Investment in Davis Corporation 87,000
       Equity in Earnings of Unconsolidated
         Affiliates... 87,000

Assets	=	Liabilities	+	Shareholders' Equity	(Class.)
+87,000				+87,000	IncSt → RE

To recognize share of Davis Corporation's earnings in 2009; .40 × $217,500 = $87,000.

Cash 24,000
   Investment in Davis Corporation 24,000

Assets	=	Liabilities	+	Shareholders' Equity	(Class.)
+24,000					
–24,000					

To recognize dividend received from Davis Corporation; .40 × $60,000 = $24,000.

16.4 g. continued.

Investment in Davis Corporation 20,000
    Cash   20,000

Assets	= Liabilities	+	Shareholders' Equity	(Class.)
+20,000				
−20,000				

To record additional investment in Davis Corporation.

h. Cash 7,000
   Accumulated Depreciation 19,000
    Equipment...   23,000
    Gain on Sale of Equipment   3,000

Assets	= Liabilities	+	Shareholders' Equity	(Class.)
+7,000			+3,000	IncSt → RE
+19,000				
−23,000				

i. Present Value of Lease Payment Due at Signing at January 2, 1997 .... $ 10,000
Present Value of Nineteen Lease Payments Due on January 2 of Each Subsequent Year at 8%; $10,000 x 9.6036   96,036
Total $106,036

j. Balance in Rental Fees Received in Advance on December 31, 2008 .... $ 46,000
Plus Cash Received for Rentals during 2009 .... ?
Less Rental Fees Earned during 2009 .... (240,000)
Balance in Rental Fees Received in Advance on December 31, 2009 .... $ 58,000

Cash received during 2009 totaled $252,000.

k. Balance in Estimated Warranty Liability on December 31, 2008 .... $75,200
Plus Estimated Warranty Cost Provision for 2009 46,800
Less Cost of Actual Warranty Services............................... (?)
Balance in Estimated Warranty Liability on December 31, 2009 .... $78,600

Warranty costs incurred during 2009 totaled $43,400.

16.4 continued.

l. First 6 Months: .025 x $1,104,650.00 .... $27,616.25
    Second 6 Months: .025 x $1,102,266.25a 27,556.66
        Total Interest Expense... $55,172.91

a$1,104,650.00 – ($30,000.00 – $27,616.25) = $1,102,266.25.

m. Interest Expense 20,996
    Mortgage Payable... 19,004
        Cash 40,000

Assets	=	Liabilities	+	Shareholders' Equity	(Class.)
–40,000		–19,004		–20,996	IncSt → RE

To record mortgage interest and principal payment; $20,996 = .07 x ($262,564 + $37,383).

n. Present Value of Payment on January 1, 2009 .... $10,000
    Present Value of Seven Remaining Lease Payments
        ($10,000 x 5.20637) 52,064
            Total $62,064

o. Capitalized Lease Obligation, December 31, 2008 .... $62,064
    Lease Payment on January 1, 2009 .... (10,000)
    Interest Expense for 2009 (.08 x $52,064) 4,165
        Total ($10,000 + $46,229) $56,229

p. Income Tax Expense... 150,000
        Income Tax Payable 135,000
        Deferred Tax Liability ($145,000 – $130,000) ... 15,000

Assets	=	Liabilities	+	Shareholders' Equity	(Class.)
		+135,000		–150,000	IncSt → RE
		+15,000			

q. Income Tax Payable—Current, December 31, 2008 .... $140,000
    Provision for Current Taxes Payable (See Part p.) 135,000
    Less Cash Payments Made during 2009 .... (?)
    Income Tax Payable—Current, December 31, 2009 .... $160,000

Cash payments for income taxes during 2009 were $115,000.

r. $\dfrac{\text{Deferred Tax Expense Relating to Depreciation}}{\text{Income Tax Rate}} = \dfrac{\$12,000}{.30} = \$40,000.$

16.4 continued.

s. Convertible Preferred Stock (5,000 x $100) 500,000
    Common Stock (25,000 x $10) 250,000
    Additional Paid-in Capital 250,000

Assets	= Liabilities	+	Shareholders' Equity	(Class.)
			−500,000	ContriCap
			+250,000	ContriCap
			+250,000	ContriCap

To record conversion of preferred into common stock.

t. Treasury Stock 8,800
    Cash 8,800

Assets	= Liabilities	+	Shareholders' Equity	(Class.)
−8,800			−8,800	ContriCap

To record purchases of treasury stock.

Cash 25,200
    Treasury Stock .... 21,600[a]
    Additional Paid-in Capital .... 3,600[b]

Assets	= Liabilities	+	Shareholders' Equity	(Class.)
+25,200			+21,600	ContriCap
			+3,600	ContriCap

To record the sale of treasury stock.

[a]1,800 shares x $12 = $21,600.

[b]Additional Paid-in Capital on December 31, 2008 .... $130,000
Plus Amount Arising from Conversion of Preferred
   Stock 250,000
Plus Amount Arising from Issue of Common Stock 200,000
Plus Amount Arising from Sale of Treasury Stock .... ?
Additional Paid-in Capital on December 31, 2009 .... $583,600

The additional paid-in capital arising from the treasury stock sales is $3,600.

16.5 (Scania, Inc.; recasting financial statements to proposed reporting format.)

a.
Schedule 16.1
SCANIA, INC.
Recast Statement of Financial Position
(Amounts in Millions)

	December 31, 2006	December 31, 2005
Business Assets and Liabilities		
Short-Term Operating Assets:		
Cash	SEK 1,126	SEK 1,106
Short-Term Investments Comprising Cash and Cash Equivalents	8,808	493
Accounts Receivable, Net	SEK 19,025	SEK 18,377
Inventories	10,100	9,949
Total Short-Term Operating Assets	SEK 39,059	SEK 29,925
Short-Term Operating Liabilities:		
Current Interest-Bearing Liabilities	SEK (16,350)	SEK (9,351)
Current Provisions	(1,125)	(962)
Accrued Expenses and Deferred Income	(7,283)	(6,836)
Advance Payments from Customers	(449)	(593)
Trade Payables	(6,011)	(4,901)
Other Current Liabilities	(1,939)	(2,021)
Total Short-Term Operating Liabilities	SEK (33,157)	SEK (24,664)
Net Short-Term Operating Assets	SEK 5,902	SEK 5,261
Long-Term Operating Assets:		
Intangible Noncurrent Assets	SEK 2,464	SEK 2,698
Tangible Noncurrent Assets	17,130	16,715
Lease Assets	9,666	9,883
Holdings in Associated Companies and Joint Ventures	173	96
Long-Term Interest-Bearing Receivables	16,599	15,543
Other Long-Term Receivables	1,023	1,393
Total Long-Term Operating Assets	SEK 47,055	SEK 46,328
Long-Term Operating Liabilities:		
Provisions for Pensions	SEK (3,605)	SEK (3,458)
Other Noncurrent Provisions	(1,473)	(1,310)
Accrued Expenses and Deferred Income	(1,861)	(2,126)
Other Noncurrent Liabilities	(536)	(621)
Total Long-Term Operating Liabilities	SEK (7,475)	SEK (7,515)
Net Long-Term Operating Liabilities	SEK 39,580	SEK 38,813

16.5 a. continued.

Net Short-Term and Long-Term Operating Assets	SEK 45,482	SEK 44,074
Short-Term Investing Assets:		
Short-Term Investments	SEK 911	SEK 1,194
Net Business Assets and Liabilities	SEK 46,393	SEK 45,268
Financing		
Noncurrent Interest-Bearing Liabilities	SEK (17,918)	SEK (19,323)
Income Taxes		
Short-Term Tax Assets	SEK 370	SEK 206
Short-Term Tax Liabilities	(946)	(645)
Long-Term Deferred Tax Assets	649	565
Long-Term Tax Assets	34	0
Long-Term Deferred Tax Liabilities	(2,278)	(2,140)
Long-Term Other Tax Liabilities	(170)	(195)
Total Income Tax Assets, Net	SEK (2,341)	SEK (2,209)
Net Assets and Liabilities	SEK 26,134	SEK 23,736
Equity		
Share Capital	SEK 2,000	SEK 2,263
Contributed Capital	1,120	1,120
Hedge Reserve	87	(83)
Accumulated Exchange Rate Differences	243	903
Retained Earnings	22,679	19,524
Minority (Noncontrolling) Interest	5	9
Total Shareholders' Equity	SEK 26,134	SEK 23,736

16.5 continued.

b.
Schedule 16.2
SCANIA, INC.
Recast Statement of Comprehensive Income
(Amounts in Millions)

Year Ended December 31:	2006	2005	2004
Business Income			
Net Sales	SEK 70,738	SEK 63,328	SEK 56,788
Cost of Goods Sold	(52,255)	(47,835)	(42,528)
Research and Development	(3,023)	(2,484)	(1,987)
Expenses:			
Selling Expenses	(6,016)	(5,829)	(5,343)
Administrative Expenses	(1,189)	(858)	(789)
Share of Income of Associated Companies and Joint Ventures	5	8	8
Operating Income:			
Vehicles and Service	SEK 8,260	SEK 6,330	SEK 6,149
Interest and Lease Income	SEK 3,527	SEK 3,518	SEK 3,427
Interest and Depreciation Expense	(2,608)	(2,575)	(2,572)
Other Income	232	178	134
Other Expenses	(179)	(138)	(132)
Selling and Administrative Expenses	(416)	(374)	(318)
Bad Debt Expenses	(63)	(80)	(89)
Operating Income:			
Customer Finance	SEK 493	SEK 529	SEK 450
Other Operating Interest Income	SEK 632	SEK 679	SEK 346
Net Operating Income	SEK 9,385	SEK 7,538	SEK 6,945
Other Financial Income	SEK 142	SEK 299	SEK 96
Other Financial Expense	(81)	(206)	(127)
Net Investing Income	SEK 61	SEK 93	SEK (31)
Net Business Income	SEK 9,446	SEK 7,631	SEK 6,914
Financing			
Interest Expense	SEK (863)	SEK (866)	SEK (638)
Income Taxes			
Income Tax Expense	SEK (2,644)	SEK (2,100)	SEK (1,960)
Net Income Consolidated Group	SEK 5,939	SEK 4,665	SEK 4,316
Minority (Noncontrolling) Interest	0	0	(2)
Scania Shareholders' Interest	SEK 5,939	SEK 4,665	SEK 4,314

16.5 b. continued.

Other Comprehensive Income:			
Hedge Reserve	SEK 170	SEK (83)	SEK 0
Exchange Rate Differences	(660)	1,303	(250)
Total Other Comprehensive Income	SEK (490)	SEK 1,220	SEK (250)
Comprehensive Income	SEK 4,959	SEK 5,885	SEK 4,064

c.

Schedule 16.3
SCANIA, INC.
Recast Statement of Cash Flows
(Amounts in Millions)

Year Ended December 31:	2006	2005	2004
Business Cash Flows			
Operating Cash Flows			
Cash Collected from Revenues:			
Net Sales	SEK 70,738	SEK 63,328	SEK 56,788
Interest and Lease Income	3,527	3,518	3,427
Other Income	232	178	134
Interest Income	632	679	346
Share of Income in Associated Companies and Joint Ventures	5	8	8
Plus Decrease (Less Increase) in Receivables	8	439	(1,664)
Less Increase in Net Investments in Credit Portfolio	(3,514)	(1,410)	(478)
Cash Received from Revenues	SEK 71,628	SEK 66,740	SEK 58,561
Cash Disbursed for Manufacturing Costs:			
Cost of Goods Sold	SEK(52,255)	SEK(47,835)	SEK(42,528)
Less Increase (Plus Decrease) in Inventories	(627)	284	(959)
Plus Increase in Taxes Payable	1,276	646	864
Cash Disbursed for Manufacturing Costs	SEK(51,606)	SEK(46,905)	SEK(42,623)

Solutions

16.5 c. continued.

Cash Disbursed for Other Operating Expenses:			
Research and Development Expenses	SEK (3,023)	SEK (2,484)	SEK (1,987)
Selling Expenses: Vehicles and Service	(6,016)	(5,829)	(5,343)
Administrative Expenses: Vehicles and Service	(1,189)	(858)	(789)
Interest and Depreciation Expense: Customer Finance	(2,608)	(2,575)	(2,572)
Selling and Administrative Expenses: Customer Finance	(416)	(374)	(318)
Bad Debt Expense	(63)	(80)	(89)
Other Expenses	(179)	(138)	(132)
Plus Items Not Affecting Cash Flow	3,236	2,953	2,386
Plus Increase in Pensions	96	124	250
Plus Increase (Less Decrease) in Other Liabilities and Provisions	1,126	(731)	356
Cash Disbursed for Other Operating Expenses	SEK (9,036)	SEK (9,992)	SEK (8,238)
Cash Received (Repaid) from Current Operating Borrowing	SEK 8,827	SEK 912	SEK (207)
Cash Disbursed for Acquisitions/Divestments of Businesses	SEK 0	SEK (205)	SEK (49)
Cash Disbursed for Net Investments in Noncurrent Assets	SEK (3,810)	SEK (3,597)	SEK (2,798)
Total Operating Cash Flows	SEK 16,003	SEK 6,953	SEK 4,646

Investing Cash Flows

Cash Received from Investments (Net):			
Other Financial Income	SEK 142	SEK 299	SEK 96
Other Financial Expense	(81)	(206)	(127)
Cash Disbursed for Short-Term Investments Comprising Cash and Cash Equivalents	(8,315)	(23)	(50)
Cash Disbursed for Investments	SEK (8,254)	SEK 70	SEK (81)
Total Business Cash Flows	SEK 7,749	SEK 7,023	SEK 4,565

16.5 c. continued.

Financing Cash Flows

Cash Disbursed for Interest Expense	SEK	(863)	SEK	(866)	SEK	(638)
Change in Debt Financing		7,591		62		(1,264)
Less Change in Current Operating Borrowing		(8,827)		(912)		207
Total Financing Cash Flows	SEK	(2,099)	SEK	(1,716)	SEK	(1,695)

Income Tax Cash Flows

Cash Disbursed for Income Taxes	SEK	(2,552)	SEK	(2,450)	SEK	(1,784)

Equity Cash Flows

Cash Disbursed for Dividends	SEK	(3,000)	SEK	(3,000)	SEK	(1,200)
Effect of Exchange Rate Changes	SEK	(78)	SEK	130	SEK	(10)
Net Change in Cash	SEK	20	SEK	(13)	SEK	(124)
Cash, Beginning of Year		1,106		1,119		1,243
Cash, End of Year	SEK	1,126	SEK	1,106	SEK	1,119

16.6 (Wal-Mart Stores; recasting financial statements to proposed reporting format.)

a.

Schedule 16.4
WAL-MART STORES
Statement of Financial Position under the
Proposed Statement Format
(Amounts in Millions)

Fiscal Year Ended January 31:	2008	2007
Business Assets and Liabilities		
Short-Term Operating Assets:		
Cash	$ 5,569	$ 7,373
Accounts Receivable	3,654	2,840
Inventories	35,180	33,685
Prepayments	3,182	2,690
Total Short-Term Operating Assets	$ 47,585	$ 46,588
Short-Term Operating Liabilities:		
Accounts Payable	$ (30,370)	$ (28,090)
Other Current Liabilities	(15,799)	(14,675)
Total Short-Term Operating Liabilities	$ (46,169)	$ (42,765)
Net Short-Term Operating Assets	$ 1,416	$ 3,823

16.6 a. continued.

Long-Term Operating Assets:		
Property, Plant and Equipment (Net)	$ 105,903	$ 94,512
Other Long-Term Operating Assets	16,188	13,228
Total Long-Term Operating Assets	$ 122,091	$ 107,740
Long-Term Operating Liabilities:		
Other Long-Term Operating Liabilities	(3,564)	(3,096)
Net Long-Term Operating Assets	$ 118,527	$ 104,644
Net Short-Term and Long-Term Operating Assets	$ 119,943	$ 108,467
Short-Term Investing Assets:		
Short-Term Investments	$ 0	$ 0
Net Business Assets and Liabilities	$ 119,943	$ 108,467
Financing		
Short-Term Financing Liabilities:		
Notes Payable	$ (5,040)	$ (2,570)
Current Portion of Long-Term Debt	(6,229)	(5,713)
Long-Term Financing Liabilities:		
Long-Term Debt	(42,288)	(36,807)
Total Financing Liabilities	$ (53,557)	(45,090)
Income Taxes		
Long-Term Deferred Tax Assets	$ 2,724	$ 2,937
Short-Term Income Taxes Payable	(1,016)	(706)
Long-Term Deferred Tax Liabilities	(3,486)	(4,035)
Total Income Tax Assets, Net	$ (1,778)	$ (1,804)
Net Assets and Liabilities	$ 64,608	$ 61,573
Equity		
Common Stock	$ 397	$ 413
Additional Paid-in Capital	3,028	2,834
Retained Earnings	57,319	55,818
Accumulated Other Comprehensive Income	3,864	2,508
Total Shareholders' Equity	$ 64,608	$ 61,573

16.6 continued.

b.

Schedule 16.5
WAL-MART STORES
Statement of Comprehensive Income under the Proposed Reporting Format
(Amounts in Millions)

Fiscal Year Ended January 31:	2008	2007	2006
Business Income			
Sales Revenue	$ 374,526	$ 344,992	$ 308,945
Other Revenues	4,578	3,938	3,398
Cost of Goods Sold	(286,515)	(264,152)	(237,649)
Selling, General and Administrative Expenses	(70,694)	(64,426)	(56,063)
Operating Income	$ 21,895	$ 20,352	$ 18,631
Interest Revenue on Investments in Securities	0	0	0
Total Business Income	$ 21,895	$ 20,352	$ 18,631
Financing			
Interest Expense	(2,103)	(1,809)	(1,420)
Income Taxes			
Income Tax Expense	(6,908)	(6,365)	(5,803)
Net Income	$ 12,884	$ 12,178	$ 11,408
Other Comprehensive Income			
Foreign Currency Translation Adjustment	$ 1,218	$ 1,584	$ (1,691)
Pension Liability	138	(15)	(1)
Derivatives	0	6	51
Adoption of FASB *Statement No. 158*	0	(120)	0
Total Other Comprehensive Income	$ 1,356	$ 1,455	$ (1,641)
Comprehensive Income	$ 14,240	$ 13,633	$ 9,767

16.6 continued.

c.

Schedule 16.6
WAL-MART STORES
Statement of Cash Flows under the Proposed Reporting Format
(Amounts in Millions)

Fiscal Year Ended January 31:	2008	2007	2006
Business Cash Flows			
Operating Cash Flows:			
Cash Receipts from Customers	$ 373,962	$ 344,778	$ 308,489
Cash Received from Other Revenues	4,578	3,938	3,398
Cash Disbursed for Merchandise	(286,425)	(263,082)	(236,992)
Cash Disbursed for Selling and Administrative Expenses	(63,840)	(57,252)	(49,910)
Cash Disbursed to Acquire Property, Plant and Equipment	(14,937)	(15,666)	(14,563)
Cash Disbursed for Other Operating Cash Flows	(733)	1,203	380
Total Operating Cash Flows	$ 12,605	$ 13,919	$ 10,802
Investing Cash Flows:			
Total Investing Cash Flows	0	0	0
Total Business Cash Flows	$ 12,605	$ 13,919	$ 10,802

16.6 c. continued.

Financing Cash Flows			
Cash Disbursed for Interest Expense	$ (1,622)	$ (1,553)	$ (1,390)
Cash Received (Disbursed) for Short-Term Debt	2,376	(1,193)	(704)
Cash Received from Long-Term Debt	11,167	7,199	7,691
Cash Disbursed to Repay Long-Term Debt	(9,066)	(6,098)	(2,969)
Other Financing Cash Flows	312	(130)	(451)
Total Financing Cash Flows	$ 3,167	$ (1,775)	$ 2,177
Income Tax Cash Flows			
Cash Disbursed for Income Tax Expense	$ (6,299)	$ (6,665)	$ (5,962)
Equity Cash Flows			
Cash Disbursed for Dividends	$ (3,586)	$ (2,802)	$ (2,511)
Cash Disbursed to Repurchase Common Stock	(7,691)	(1,718)	(3,580)
Total Equity Cash Flows	$ (11,277)	$ (4,520)	$ (6,091)
Net (Decrease) Increase in Cash	$ (1,804)	$ 959	$ 926
Cash at Beginning of Year	7,373	6,414	5,488
Cash at End of Year	$ 5,569	$ 7,373	$ 6,414

APPENDIX

TIME VALUE OF CASH FLOWS

Questions, Exercises, and Problems: Answers and Solutions

A.1 See the text or the glossary at the end of the book.

A.2 The value of cash flows differs over time because cash can earn interest. Extracting, or discounting, the interest element in a future cash flow permits expressing that future cash flow in terms of an equivalent present cash flow.

A.3 In simple interest, only the principal sum earns interest. In compound interest, interest is earned on the principal plus amounts of interest not paid or withdrawn.

A.4 There is no difference; these items refer to the same thing.

A.5 The timing of the first payment for an annuity due is *now* (at the beginning of the first period) while that for an ordinary annuity is at the *end* of the first period. The future value of an annuity due is computed as of one year after the final payment, but for an ordinary annuity is computed as of the time of the last payment.

A.6 The discount rate that sets the net present value of a stream of payments equal to zero is the implicit rate for that stream. Excel® provides a procedure to solve for the implicit interest rate. One can also solve for implicit interest rate by trial and error.

(1) Guess a rate.

(2) Compute the net present values of the cash flows using the current guess.

(3) If the net present value in (2) is less than zero, then increase the rate guessed and go to Step (2).

(4) If the net present value in (2) is greater than zero, then reduce the rate guessed and go to Step (2).

(5) Otherwise, the current guess is the implicit rate of return.

The process will converge to the right answer only if one is systematic with the guesses, narrowing the range successively.

A.7 Present values increase when interest rates decrease and present values decrease when interest rates increase, regardless of the time period.

A.8 6%. The present value will be larger the smaller the discount rate.

A.9 The formula assumes that the growth [represented by the parameter g in the formula $1/(r-g)$] continues forever. That is a long time. The formula assumes also that the discount and growth rates remain constant. In our experience, more harm results from assuming the growth persists forever than from the other assumptions.

A.10 a. $5,000 × 3.20714 × 1.06 = $16,998.

b. $5,000 × 10.06266 × 1.25971 = $63,380.

A.11 a. $150,000 × .62741 = $94,112.

b. $150,000 × .54027 = $81,041.

A.12 a. $4,000 × 6.97532 = $27,901.

b. $4,000 × 7.33593 = $29,344.

A.13 a. ¥45,000,000/10.63663 = ¥4.23 million.

b. ¥45,000,000/12.29969 = ¥3.66 million.

A.14 a. €90,000 × 14.20679 × 1.05 = €90,000 × (15.91713 − 1.0) = €1,342,542.

b. €90,000 × 18.53117 × 1.10 = €90,000 × (21.38428 − 1.0) = €1,834,585.

A.15 a. £145,000/4.62288 = £31,366.

b. £145,000/4.11141 = £35,268.

A.16 a. (10) $5,000 × T(1, 21, 6).

(11) $150,000 × T(2, 8, 6).

(12) $4,000 × T(3, 6, 6).

(13) ¥45,000,000/T(3, 8, 8).

(14) €90,000 × T(3, 11, 5) × 1.05 = €90,000 × [T(3, 12, 5) − 1.0].

(15) £145,000/T(4, 6, 8).

A.16 continued.

    b. Asking questions about compound interest calculations on examinations presents a difficult logistical problem to teachers. They may want the students to use compound interest tables, but not wish to incur the costs of reproducing them in sufficient numbers for each student to have a copy. They may not wish to give an open book test. This device is useful for posing test questions about compound interest.

    The device is based on the fact that teachers of accounting are not particularly interested in testing their students' ability to do arithmetic. Teachers want to be sure that students know how to use the tables and calculating devices efficiently in combination. Such a combination suggests that the humans do the thinking and the calculators do the multiplications and divisions.

A.17 (Effective interest rates.)

    a. 12% per period; 5 periods.

    b. 6% per period; 10 periods.

    c. 3% per period; 20 periods.

    d. 1% per period; 60 periods.

A.18   a. $100 x 1.21665 = $121.67.

    b. $500 x 1.34587 = $672.94.

    c. $200 x 1.26899 = $253.80.

    d. $2,500 x (1.74102 x 1.74102) = $7,577.88

        $(1.02)^{56} = (1.02)^{28} \times (1.02)^{28}$.

    e. $600 x 1.43077 = $858.46.

A.19   a. $100 x .30832 = $30.83.

    b. $250 x .53063 = $132.66.

    c. $1,000 x .78757 = $787.57.

A.20   a. $100 x 14.23683 = $1,423.68.

    b. $850 x 9.89747 = $8,412.85.

    c. $400 x 49.96758 = $19,987.03.

A.21 a. $1,000(1.00 + .94340) + $2,000(4.21236 − .94340) + $2,500(6.80169 − 4.21236) = $14,955.

b. $1,000(1.00 + .92593) + $2,000(3.99271 − .92593) + $2,500(6.24689 − 3.99271) = $13,695.

c. $1,000(1.00 + .90909) + $2,000(3.79079 − .90909) + $2,500(5.75902 − 3.79079) = $12,593.

A.22 a. $3,000 + ($3,000/.06) = $53,000.

b. $3,000 + ($3,000/.08) = $40,500.

A.23 a. $3,000/(.06 − .02) = $75,000.

b. $3,000/(.08 − .02) = $50,000.

c. [$3,000/(.06 − .02)] x .79209 = $59,406.75.

d. [$3,000/(.08 − .02)] x .73503 = $36,751.50.

A.24 a. $60,000 + ($60,000/.1664) = $420,577. $(1.08)^2 − 1 = .1664$.

b. $60,000 + ($60,000/.2544) = $295,850. $(1.12)^2 − 1 = .2544$.

A.25 7.00%. Note that $100,000/$55,307 = 1.80809. See Table 4, 2-period row and observe 1.80809 in the 7% column.

A.26 $12\% = (\$140,493/\$100,000)^{1/3} − 1$.

A.27 a. $16\% = (\$67,280/\$50,000)^{1/2} − 1$.

b.

Year (1)	Carrying Value Start of Year (2)	Interest for Year = (2) x .16 (3)	Amount (Reducing) Increasing Carrying Value (4)	Carrying Value End of Year = (2) + (3) + (4) (5)
1	$ 50,000	$ 8,000		$ 58,000
2	58,000	9,280	$ (67,280)	-0-

Solutions

A.28   (Berman Company; find implicit interest rate; construct amortization schedule.)

a. 14.0%.

$$\text{Let } x = \frac{\$8,000}{(1+r)} + \frac{\$8,000}{(1+r)^2} + \frac{\$8,000}{(1+r)^3} + \frac{\$100,000}{(1+r)^3} = \$86,000.$$

If r = 14.0%, then x = $18,573 + $67,497 − $86,000 = $70.

If r = 14.1%, then x = $18,542 + $67,320 − $86,000 = $138.

b.

Year (1)	Carrying Value Start of Year (2)	Interest for Year = (2) × .14 (3)	Payment End of Year (Given) (4)	Amount (Reducing) Increasing Carrying Value = (3) − (4) (5)	Carrying Value End of Year = (2) + (5) (6)
1	$ 86,000	$ 12,040	$ 8,000	$ 4,040	$ 90,040
2	90,040	12,605	8,000	4,605	94,645
3	94,645	13,250*	108,000	(94,750)	(105)
OR 3	94,645	13,355*	108,000	(94,645)	-0-

*Interest would actually be recorded at $13,355 (= $108,000 − $94,645) so that the carrying value of the note reduces to zero at its maturity.

A.29   a. Terms of sale of 2/10, net/30 on a $100 gross invoice price, for example, mean that the interest rate is 2/98 for a 20-day period, because if the discount is not taken, a charge of $2 is levied for the use of $98. The $98 is used for 20 days (= 30 − 10), so the number of compounding periods in a year is 365/20 = 18.25. The expression for the exact rate of interest implied by 2/10, net 30 is $(1 + 2/98)^{(365/20)} - 1 = 1.020408^{18.25} - 1 = 44.59\%$.

b. Table 1 can be used. Use the 2% column and the 18-period row to see that the rate implied by 2/10, net 30 must be at least 42.825% (= 1.42825 − 1).

A.30   (Present value of a perpetuity.)

$30,000 + ($10,000/.01) = $1,030,000.

A.31   Present value of future proceeds = .72845($35,000) + C = $35,000; where C represents the present value of the foregone interest payments. Table 2, 16-period row, 2% column = .72845.

C = $35,000 − $25,495.75 = $9,504.25.

A.32 a. Will: $24,000 + $24,000(3.31213) = $103,488.72 (Preferred).

Dower Option: $300,000/3 = $100,000.

b. Will: $24,000 + $24,000(3.03735) = $96,896.40.

Dower Option: $300,000/3 = $100,000 (Preferred).

A.33 Present value of deposit = $3.00.

Present value of $3.00, recorded 20 periods, have discounted at .50% per period = $3.00 x .90506 = $2.72.

Loss of $.28 (= $3.00 − $2.72) in foregone interest vs. Loss of $1.20 in price.

Net advantage of returnables is $.92.

A.34 $1.00(1.00 + .92456 + .85480 + .79031 + .73069) = $1.00 x 4.30036 = $4.30.

$4.30 − $3.50 = $.80.

A.35 $600/12 = $50 saved per month. $2,000/$50 = 40.0.

Present value of annuity of $1 discounted at 1% for 50 periods = 39.19612.

The present value of the annuity is $40 when the annuity lasts between 51 and 52 periods. Oberweis Dairy will recoup its investment in a bit more than four years.

A.36 a. $ 3,000,000 x 7.46944 = $ 22,408,320.

b. $ 3,000,000 x 7.36578 = $ 22,097,340
    500,000 x 1.69005 =   845,025
                             $ 22,942,365

c. $ 2,000,000 x 7.36578 = $ 14,731,560
   1,000,000 x 2.40183 =   2,401,830
     500,000 x 1.69005 =   845,025
                             $ 17,978,415

d. $17,978,410 x .20   = $ 3,595,682.

Solutions

A.37 (Friendly Loan Company; find implicit interest rate; truth-in lending laws reduce the type of deception suggested by this problem.)

The effective interest rate is 19.86% and must be found by trial and error. The time line for this problem is:

```
            +$6,000  -$2,000  -$2,000  -$2,000  -$2,000  -$2,000
End of        |        |        |        |        |        |
Year          0        1        2        3        4        5
```

which is equivalent, at least in terms of the implied interest rate, to:

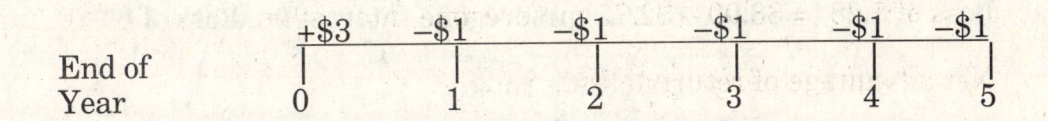

```
            +$3      -$1      -$1      -$1      -$1      -$1
End of       |        |        |        |        |        |
Year         0        1        2        3        4        5
```

Scanning Table 4, 5-period column, one finds the factor 2.99061, which is approximately 3.00, in the 20% column, so one can easily see that the implied interest rate is about 20% per year.

A.38 (Black & Decker Company; derive net present value/cash flows for decision to dispose of asset.)

$40,698. The $100,000 is gone and an economic loss of $50,000 was suffered because of the bad purchase. The issue now is do we want to swap a larger current tax loss and smaller future depreciation charges for no tax loss now and larger future depreciation charges.

The new machine will lead to depreciation charges lower by $10,000 per year than the "old" machine and, hence, income taxes larger by $4,000. The present value of the larger taxes is $4,000 × 3.60478 (Table 4, 12%, 5 periods). Let S denote the proceeds from selling the old machine. The new current "outlay" to acquire the new machine is $50,000 − S − .40($100,000 − S) or $10,000 − .60S, so that for the new machine to be worthwhile:

$$\$10,000 - .60S < -\$14,419$$

OR

$$.6S > \$24,419$$

OR

$$S > \$40,698.$$

A.39 (Lynch Company/Bages Company; computation of present value of cash flows; untaxed acquisition, no change in tax basis of assets.)

a. $440,000 = $390,000 + $50,000 = $700,000 − $260,000.

b. $3,745,966 = $440,000 × 8.51356; see Table 4, 20-period column, 10% row.

A.40 (Lynch Company/Bages Company; computation of present value of cash flows; taxable acquisition, changing tax basis of assets.)

$4,258,199. If the merger is taxable, then the value of the firm V satisfies:

(1)
$$V = 8.51356 \times [\$700{,}000 - .40(\$700{,}000 - V/20)]$$
$$V = \$5{,}959{,}492 - \$2{,}383{,}797 + .17027V, \text{ or}$$
$$.83972V = \$3{,}575{,}695, \text{ so}$$
$$V = \$4{,}258{,}199.$$

To understand (1), observe that:

V = Value of firm

$V/20$ = New depreciation charge

$\$700{,}000 - V/20$ = New taxable income

$.40(\$700{,}000 - V/20)$ = New income tax payable, so

$\$700{,}000 - .40(\$700{,}000 - V/20)$ = New aftertax cash flow to be capitalized at 10% for 20 years using present value factor 8.51356.

A.41 (Valuation of intangibles with perpetuity formulas.)

a. $50 million = $4 million/.08.

b. Increase.

c. $66 2/3 million = $4 million/(.08 − .02).

d. Increase.

e. Decrease.

A.42 (Ragazze; analysis of benefits of acquisition of long-term assets.)

a. $270,831.

Year Dec. 31	Cash Inflows		Cash Outflows		Total (1) + (2) − (3) − (4)	Present Values at 12%	
	Operating Receipts (1)	Salvage (2)	Maintenance (3)	Test Runs (4)	(5)	Factor (6)	Cash Flow (7)
0				$20,000	$(20,000)	0.89286	$(17,857)
1					70,000	0.79719	55,804
2	$130,000		$60,000		70,000	0.71178	49,825
3	130,000		60,000		70,000	0.63552	44,486
4	130,000		60,000		70,000	0.56743	39,720
5	130,000		60,000		30,000	0.50663	15,199
6	130,000		100,000		30,000	0.45235	13,570
7	130,000		100,000		30,000	0.40388	12,116
8	130,000		100,000		160,000	0.36061	57,968
9	130,000	$30,000					$270,831

(7) = (5) × (6).

b. $78,868 = $250,000/3.16987.

A.43 (Gulf Coast Manufacturing; choosing between investment alternatives.)

Basic Data Repeated from Problem	Lexus	Mercedes-Benz		Present Value Computations		
			Factor	Source [B]	Lexus	Mercedes-Benz
Initial Cost at the Start of 2008	$60,000	$45,000	1.00000	T[2, 3, 10]	$ 60,000	$ 45,000
Initial Cost at the Start of 2011		48,000	0.75131	T[2, 3, 10]		36,063
Trade-in Value						
End of 2010		23,000	0.75131	T[2, 3, 10]		(17,280)
End of 2013 [Note A]	16,000	24,500	0.56447	T[2, 6, 10]	(9,032)	(13,830)
Estimated Annual Cash Operating Costs, Except Major Servicing	4,000	4,500	4.35526	T[4, 6, 10]	17,421	19,599
Estimated Cash Cost of Major Servicing						
End of 2011	6,500		0.68301	T[2, 4, 10]	4,440	
End of 2009 and End of 2012		2,500	0.82645	T[2, 2, 10]		2,066
			0.62092	T[2, 5, 10]		1,552
Sum of Present Values of All Costs					$72,829	$73,170

Note A:
At this time, Lexus is 6 years old; second Mercedes-Benz is 3 years old.

[B]T[i,j,r] means Table i (= Table 2 or Table 4) from the back of the book, row j, interest rate r.

a. Strategy L, buying one Lexus has lower present value of costs, but the difference is so small that we'd encourage the CEO to go with his whim, whatever it may be. Also, the relatively new theory of real options will likely prefer Strategy M because it gives the owner more choices at the end of the third year.

b. Depreciation plays no role, so long as we ignore income taxes. Only cash flows matter.

A.44 (Wal-Mart Stores; perpetuity growth model derivation of results in Chapter 6.)

a. Reproduce Exhibit 6.22 for Problem A.43.
Growth Rate for Terminal Value: 10.0%

End of Year [1]	Cash Flow [2]	Factor to Discount to End of 2008 [3]	Origin of Factor [4]	Present Value at End of 2008 14 = [2] × [3] [5]
2009	$ 5,386	0.89286	Table (2, 1, 12%)	$ 4,809
2010	5,923	0.79719	Table (2, 2, 12%)	4,722
2011	6,515	0.71178	Table (2, 3, 12%)	4,637
2012	7,166	0.63552	Table (2, 4, 12%)	4,554
2013	7,884	0.56743	Table (2, 5, 12%)	4,474
After 2013	433,620 Note A	0.56743	Table (2, 5, 12%)	246,048
Total Present Value at the End of 2008.................				$ 269,244

Note A: ($7,884 × 1.10)/(.12 − .10) = $433,620.
Numerator is the amount of the first collection, at the end of 2014.
Denominator is r − g: the discount rate minus the growth rate.
The result of the operation is the present value at the end of 2013 of the perpetuity with growth, whose first cash flow is at the end of 2014 in the amount equal to 2013's amount growing for one year at 10%.
This amount is not a single cash flow, but a single present value at the end of 2013 equivalent to a perpetuity with growth, starting at the end of 2014.

A.44 continued.

b. Change Growth Rate.
Growth Rate for Terminal Value: 9.0%

End of Year [1]	Cash Flow [2]	Factor to Discount to End of 2008 [3]	Origin of Factor [4]	Present Value at End of 2008 14 = [2] x [3] [5]
2009	$ 5,386	0.89286	Table (2, 1, 12%)	$ 4,809
2010	5,923	0.79719	Table (2, 2, 12%)	4,722
2011	6,515	0.71178	Table (2, 3, 12%)	4,637
2012	7,166	0.63552	Table (2, 4, 12%)	4,554
2013	7,894	0.56743	Table (2, 5, 12%)	4,474
After 2013	286,815 Note A	0.56743	Table (2, 5, 12%)	162,747
	Total Present Value at the End of 2008.................			$ 185,943

Note A: ($7,894 x 1.09)/(.12 − .09) = $286,815.

c. Change Growth Rate.
Growth Rate for Terminal Value: 5.0%

End of Year [1]	Cash Flow [2]	Factor to Discount to End of 2008 [3]	Origin of Factor [4]	Present Value at End of 2008 14 = [2] x [3] [5]
2009	$ 5,386	0.89286	Table (2, 1, 12%)	$ 4,809
2010	5,923	0.79719	Table (2, 2, 12%)	4,722
2011	6,515	0.71178	Table (2, 3, 12%)	4,637
2012	7,166	0.63552	Table (2, 4, 12%)	4,554
2013	7,884	0.56743	Table (2, 5, 12%)	4,474
After 2013	118,260 Note A	0.56743	Table (2, 5, 12%)	67,104
	Total Present Value at the End of 2008.................			$ 90,300

Note A: ($7,884 x 1.05)/(.12 − .05) = $118,260.

A.44 continued.

    d. **Comment.** In models such as this, the total valuation comes largely from the terminal value. The terminal value changes more than proportionately to change in the growth rate. See that if we cut the growth rate expected for the long term in half from 10% to 5%, the terminal value drops by over 72%. So much of the valuation resides in the terminal value, and so much of the terminal value depends on the growth rate assumed, and the time period for that growth rate starts so far in the future that the analyst needs to be particularly cautious. The perpetuity with growth model is easy to use, but analysts will be better served to make non-uniform estimates, such as 10% growth for five years, then 8% for the next five, and growth at some macro-economic rate after that.

A.45   (Fast Growth Start-Up Company; valuation involving perpetuity growth model assumptions. (Amounts in Millions)

We find the answer with trial and error, starting with 5 years of fast growth.

Growth Rate for Early Years of Fast Growth:	25%
Growth Rate for Steady State, Terminal Value:	4%
Discount Rate:	15%
Number of Years of Fast Growth:	5

End of Year	Free Cash Flow	Discount Factors from Table 2	Present Value End of Year 0
0	$ 100	1.00000	$ 100.0
1	125	0.86957	108.7
2	156	0.75614	118.1
3	195	0.65752	128.4
4	244	0.57175	139.6
5	305	0.49718	151.7
Terminal Value 5	2,885	0.49718	1,434.5

$305 x 1.04/(.15 − .04)

    Total Valuation...................................... $ 2,181.1

A.45 continued.

Growth Rate for Early Years of Fast Growth: 25%
Growth Rate for Steady State, Terminal Value: 4%
Discount Rate: 15%
Number of Years of Fast Growth: 6

End of Year	Free Cash Flow	Discount Factors from Table 2	Present Value End of Year 0
0	$ 100	1.00000	$ 100.0
1	125	0.86957	108.7
2	156	0.75614	118.1
3	195	0.65752	128.4
4	244	0.57175	139.6
5	305	0.49718	151.7
6	381	0.43233	164.9
Terminal Value 6	3,607	0.43233	1,559.2

$381 x 1.04/(.15 − .04)

Total Valuation...................................... $ 2,470.7

Growth Rate for Early Years of Fast Growth: 25%
Growth Rate for Steady State, Terminal Value: 4%
Discount Rate: 15%
Number of Years of Fast Growth: 7

End of Year	Free Cash Flow	Discount Factors from Table 2	Present Value End of Year 0
0	$ 100	1.00000	$ 100.0
1	125	0.86957	108.7
2	156	0.75614	118.1
3	195	0.65752	128.4
4	244	0.57175	139.6
5	305	0.49718	151.7
6	381	0.43233	164.9
7	477	0.37594	179.3
Terminal Value 7	4,508	0.37594	1,694.8

$477 x 1.04/(.15 − .04)

Total Valuation...................................... $ 2,785.6

We see that assuming a bit more than 6 years of fast growth, followed by the steady state justifies a market valuation (the so-called market cap) of $2.5 billion.

This page is intentionally left blank

This page is intentionally left blank

This page is intentionally left blank

This page is intentionally left blank

This page is intentionally left blank

This page is intentionally left blank

This page is intentionally left blank

This page is intentionally left blank